**Terrorism,
Afghanistan,
and America's
NEW WAY
OF WAR**

Norman Friedman

Terrorism, Afghanistan, and America's NEW WAY OF WAR

Naval Institute Press

Annapolis, Maryland

Naval Institute Press
291 Wood Road
Annapolis, MD 21402

Library of Congress Cataloging-in-Publication Data

Friedman, Norman, 1946–
    Terrorism, Afghanistan, and America's new way of war / Norman Friedman.
    p. cm.
    Includes bibliographical references and index.
    ISBN 1-59114-290-3 (alk. paper)
    1. War on Terrorism, 2001– 2. September 11 Terrorist Attacks, 2001. 3. United States—Foreign relations—1989– 4. United States—Military policy. I. Title.
    HV6432.F746 2003
    958.104'6—dc21

                                                            2003000256

Printed in the United States of America on acid-free paper ∞

10 09 08 07 06 05 04 03   9 8 7 6 5 4 3 2
First printing

Contents

Acknowledgments

For considerable help with this book, I am extremely grateful to Kernan Chaisson of DMS/Forecast International, to Dr. Thomas Hone, to David C. Isby, and to David Steigman. All read and commented on various drafts. All were extremely helpful. David Isby shared his considerable personal knowledge of Afghanistan and of major Afghan personalities, gained in the course of many visits, some of them during the Soviet-Afghan War. I am also grateful to those who invited me to speak on the war and on the changes in the American way of war, and in so doing offered or inspired valuable insights. I am, of course, entirely responsible for the opinions and facts presented here.

I could not have written this book without the enthusiastic and loving support provided by my wife, Rhea. She also read much of the original manuscript. In so doing, she raised some important issues, which I hope the book addresses, and made some vital editorial suggestions, which the book embodies.

**Terrorism,
Afghanistan,
and America's
NEW WAY
OF WAR**

1

The Attacks

The air-traffic controllers were astonished. First one, then two, then ultimately four large airliners were entirely off course, and their pilots were not answering repeated calls. It soon was obvious what was happening: all four had been hijacked. One and then a second airliner, both from Boston, crashed directly into the two towers of the World Trade Center in New York, their jet fuel starting immense and uncontrollable fires. Initially radio commentators ascribed the first crash to a tragic navigational error, caused perhaps by some problem in the airplane's computer. When the second airliner crashed into the other tower, it became horribly clear that the crashes were planned attacks. A third airliner, from Dulles Airport near Washington, D.C., also badly off its planned course, hit the Pentagon.[1] In each case, the airliner was bound for the West Coast and hit a target not too long after takeoff, when it was heavily laden with the fuel which caused much of the damage.

Aboard a fourth airliner, from Newark, United Flight 93, hijackers offered passengers a chance to use cell phones and air phones to contact their loved ones before being killed. Those who did so found out about the three previous crashes, and at least some of them decided to act. They seized control of their airplane, preventing a fourth attack—apparently on the White House or Capitol Building—but the hijackers managed to put the airplane into a fatal dive. All aboard were killed.

Within less than two hours, then, the United States had been hit, on its own soil, three times. Initially it appeared that as many as six thousand Americans had died, including those on board the airliners; later the estimate was cut to a still-horrific three thousand. The two towers of the World Trade Center, which had survived a 1993 bombing, collapsed in less than two hours. Huge flames and columns of smoke made it impossible for helicopters to rescue anyone who reached the roof. Those above the floors where the aircraft hit died; they either were burned alive or had to jump to escape the fires. Remarkably, many of those in lower floors made it out of the buildings, helped by heroic firemen and policemen—many of whom died as the buildings fell. Even after the collapses, a column of smoke and dirt hung for days over lower Manhattan, reminding everyone of the crime.

The fires from the World Trade Center trapped thousands in lower Manhattan. The Coast Guard Auxiliary managed to round up small boats to evacuate many of them, either to New Jersey or midtown Manhattan. The New York City government blocked cars from the bridges and tunnels leading from Manhattan, for fear that terrorists would car-bomb them and thus create further damage. Many New Yorkers found themselves walking home, often several miles, from work.

For days after the attacks, no one was sure how many had escaped the World Trade Center. Friends and relatives put up thousands of Xeroxed sheets with photographs, names, and descriptions, asking for information on those still missing. In a very few lucky cases, survivors of the 1993 attacks, seeing one airplane strike the other tower, had immediately started down. Others had unfortunately heeded security announcements that they should avoid panic and stay where they were. No one had imagined that these huge structures could be brought down. Afterward, the Xeroxed sheets acted as a reminder, ensuring that no one could forget the human cost of the attacks.

Mayor Rudolph Giuliani of New York made a particular difference. His calming presence, both on the streets and in constant broadcasts, including press conferences, helped restore the confidence of badly shaken New Yorkers. Many in the city saw 11 September as only the beginning of a sustained terror campaign. Numerous false alarms, such as one leading to the evacuation of the Empire State Building, did not help. It probably did help considerably that measures taken immediately after the attacks, such as the creation of checkpoints at the bridges and tunnels leading into Manhattan, seemed to reduce the likelihood of other kinds of attacks.

The Pentagon was luckier than the World Trade Center. Apparently hampered by numerous obstructions, the pilot attempting to crash into the building hit somewhat short, bouncing into the base of the building rather than into an upper floor. Fortunately, too, the airplane hit a section of the building which had just been renovated and which was, therefore, largely unoccupied. It was also significantly better fireproofed than unrenovated parts of the building. Even so, 184 personnel were killed. The Navy's command center, on the fourth floor, was destroyed and all its occupants killed.

As an office building in a major city, the Pentagon was not protected by antiaircraft weapons, nor was it fortified. Even so, some in the Muslim world touted the attack as a triumph over the greatest fortress in the world, the central symbol of U.S. military power. For a time, there was speculation that the Pentagon had been struck as a target of opportunity, the pilot having failed to find the White House or Capitol, but it now seems that it was the intended target. The pilot of the third airliner circled several times near the Pentagon to lose altitude before he struck; presumably he would have maneuvered elsewhere had the White House been his assigned target.

After the three targets were hit, it appeared that more was still to come. Rumors abounded. For example, it was reported, incorrectly, that the State Department had been hit by a massive truck bomb. Surely other hijackers were aboard other aircraft, with other targets in mind. Given the narrowly averted fourth attack and the possibility that more were on the way, the Federal Aviation Administration quickly ordered all U.S. air space closed down, for the first time in American history.[2] Aircraft were ordered to land at the nearest airport, where they would be held until the situation was clarified. Airliners en route from abroad were turned away, many landing in Canada. The borders were closed, both to keep out additional attackers and, if possible, to catch any fleeing ones.

There was certainly anecdotal evidence that more had been planned. Some passengers leaving grounded airliners apparently left box-cutters at their seats; similar weapons had been used to seize control of the crashed aircraft. There were many reports of Arabic-looking passengers fleeing as passengers left the aircraft. At this stage there was no means of detaining them, so there was no way of knowing how many other hijacking teams were in place.

The damage inflicted was on the scale one might expect from a small nuclear bomb. Indeed, one might see the three successful attacks as strategic in character. Whoever had mounted them had made cruise missiles out of innocent civilian aircraft, murdering not only those on the ground but also the crews and passengers.

In the hours after the attack, it seemed entirely possible that the government itself would be the next target. During the cold war, a major if not often publicly discussed issue was continuity of government: how to ensure that some sort of government would survive a nuclear attack. This was more than an academic question. If an attacker imagined that he could destroy the entire U.S. government at one blow, then he could preclude any sort of retaliatory attack, since such an attack could only be authorized by the president. Making it clear that continuity of government was assured was necessary, therefore, to underpin the U.S. ability to deter a potential nuclear attacker.

This question now returned. At the moment of the attack, President George W. Bush was out of Washington, visiting a school in Florida. It appeared that the first airliner hitting the World Trade Center was a random tragedy, perhaps the result of a pilot's heart attack. When the second airliner hit the center, Bush realized that the country was under attack; later he said that his reaction was that "they had declared war on us, and I made up my mind at that moment that we were going to war."[3] Almost immediately he appeared on national television to say that "terrorism against this nation will not stand." Bush soon left for Washington aboard Air Force One.

Meanwhile, Vice President Dick Cheney was in his office in the West Wing of the White House. When American Airlines Flight 77 turned toward the White House, the Secret Service rushed him into the bunker below, where he was soon joined by other officials, including Transportation Secretary Norman Y. Mineta. It was from the bunker that Mineta ordered all airliners flying over the United States grounded.

With the president in the air, the White House received a threat to Air Force One. The threat was credible because the airplane's code name, "Angel," was used; later it seemed that a staffer had added the code word to describe a phoned message. Vice President Cheney and National Security Advisor Condoleeza Rice both urged President Bush not to risk returning directly to Washington. Given the attacks already carried out, it was apparent that the terrorists hoped to decapitate the U.S. government. Bush agreed, and Air Force One turned to land at Barksdale Air Force Base in Louisiana. Meanwhile, other elements of cold war continuity of government plans were carried out. For example, congressional leaders were evacuated from Washington. Later, Vice President Cheney would be kept at a secret and secure location specifically to foil any successful decapitation of the U.S. government simply by hitting Washington, D.C. Cold war plans to set up a shadow government, which would operate in the event Washington itself was destroyed, were revived.

At Barksdale, President Bush met reporters and then appeared on television. Then Air Force One took him to Offutt Air Force Base in Nebraska, headquarters of the U.S. Strategic Command, from which he could conduct a secure closed-circuit meeting with his National Security Council

(NSC), whose members sat in the bunker under the White House. He had already told Secretary of Defense Donald H. Rumsfeld that those responsible would have to be punished. Probably only the CIA could offer any quick options at this point.

President Bush returned to Washington the next evening, 12 September. That Friday, the fourteenth, he spoke at the National Cathedral, promising war against the terrorists. Then he flew to visit Ground Zero in New York and met with the families of some of the World Trade Center victims.

The sadistic character of the attacks, which became more and more obvious as evidence emerged (particularly about the one failed attack, the airplane that crashed in Pennsylvania), infuriated Americans. Surely, telling the passengers that they were about to die was a particularly inhuman touch. There had been other cases of sadistic hijackings, the murderers smirking as they killed passengers one by one, but in all previous cases, it seemed, the hijackers had had some policy objective in mind. They wanted to trade their passengers for something—for the release of prisoners, for example. Thus the usual advice to victims of a hijacking had always been to be passive, to go along with the hijackers' commands. But the 11 September hijackers were simply murderers, and cooperation merely led to death on a much larger scale.

Looking back, it might seem that those who had planned the attacks wanted to induce a violent U.S. response, that that was in large part the attackers' objective. At the time, however, it was thought that the attackers had sought to damage the United States, particularly the U.S. economy. For example, the Stock Market, already in decline, fell dramatically after the 11 September attacks. The U.S. travel business almost collapsed, in part because major corporations decided that it was safest to forbid travel by their key executives. A major element in post–11 September U.S. national policy, then, was to restore confidence that the government could indeed protect the population. Efforts included a new emphasis on homeland security in national policy. On the theory that they were an essential element of the U.S. national transportation system, the airlines were offered help to offset their loss of business.

Considerable planning had gone into the attacks. At least four separate hijackings, mounted from three widely separated airports, had been coordinated. In this the attackers had been very lucky. Had the aircraft been subject to lengthy takeoff delays, one attack might have been carried out before the other aircraft had even become airborne. U.S. air traffic could have been shut down at that point, aborting further attacks. At the least, passengers on the other flights might have become aware of what a hijacking was likely to mean.

The attacks demonstrated what many had sensed, that the U.S. domestic airline industry just did not take security very seriously. Boston and Newark Airports, from which three of the attacking aircraft had come, turned out to be particularly porous, with hundreds of missing identification cards in circulation.

There was speculation, moreover, that the World Trade Center attack had been particularly carefully planned—with engineering factors in mind. Months later analysts would argue that the floors the aircraft had hit had fallen within a narrow critical band. That is, had the airplanes hit higher up they would probably have destroyed only the upper parts of the buildings. Had they hit much lower down, presumably the buildings would also have survived, as insufficient structural damage would have been done. New York had already experienced an airplane crash into a major skyscraper: in 1945 an Army Air Force B-25 bomber, far smaller than the jetliners of 2001, had hit the Empire State Building, fortunately causing only limited damage. With this experience in mind, the designer of the World Trade Center had planned against a jet airliner hitting the buildings. What he apparently had not taken into account was the heat a jet's fuel might generate. The two keys to the buildings' destruction were the intense heat generated by tons of burning jet fuel, which had weakened the buildings' structure, and the cumulative effect of the weight of the upper floors as they collapsed, once heat had weakened the structure.

It now seems that the extent of the disaster was possibly accidental. The pilots had relatively little choice in where they struck. They probably tried to hit about the midpoint of the visible sections of the towers, given that surrounding buildings covered much of the towers' lower parts.[4] Although the towers were set well away from neighboring buildings, it seems unlikely that inexperienced pilots (who had seized control from the legitimate ones) could have adjusted altitude quickly enough to have made use of the opening between buildings. The perpetrator, Osama bin Laden, apparently expected little more than that the upper parts of the towers would be destroyed—leaving a gruesome monument to his attack.

The immediate reaction to the attacks was a series of efforts to control air and other traffic within the United States. The internal security effort was designated Operation Noble Eagle. For a time aircraft carriers were stationed off the East and West Coasts, their aircraft covering major cities. The

Air National Guard was mobilized. Airborne radar control aircraft (AWACs) were deployed to track airliners, and fighters were dispatched to escort those that were off course. It was announced that airliners which appeared to have been hijacked for follow-on suicide bombings could be shot down, subject to careful consultation. Passengers on all flights into Reagan National Airport, which is close to downtown Washington, were told that any attempt to stand during a flight (an action which would precede a hijacking) would result in the airplane being routed away from Reagan and the standee arrested.[5] That actually happened in at least one case.

In a wider sense, homeland defense became a major new theme in U.S. military planning. The Marines already had units designed to deal with chemical and other terrorist attacks, and they were quickly assembled into a fourth Marine Expeditionary Brigade (the others were intended for power projection abroad).[6] The Marines' ability to assemble disparate units quickly into an effective task force considerably impressed Defense Department officials interested in creating a more flexible U.S. military.

Prior to 11 September, U.S. military planning had generally concentrated on assembling American resources for deployment abroad. In the global system of joint-service CinCs (commanders in chief), the main responsibility of the North American CinC was to train forces. Now he had a combatant or defensive role. The cold war mission of the North American Air Defense Command (NORAD) suddenly became relevant again, because an enemy had indeed carried out air attacks on U.S. soil. Although not directly connected to the terrorist threat, the issue of national defense against ballistic missiles automatically became more important. U.S. defense against such weapons depended largely on deterrence, on a potential enemy's fear that the United States would destroy him in retaliation for any attack on U.S. soil. However, someone—perhaps a hostile government—had not been deterred at all. What would happen when clearly hostile governments, such as those of Iraq and North Korea, gained possession of nuclear-armed ballistic missiles? Would they, too, be undeterred? Increased emphasis on active defense of the United States was a nearly inevitable corollary of the growing interest in defense against terrorist threats.

The Coast Guard pointed out that the millions of freight containers pouring into U.S. ports were a potential danger. A forty-foot container could easily accommodate even a very crude nuclear bomb, or a chemical or biological weapon. Containers were already widely used to smuggle drugs and even people, so the Coast Guard and the U.S. Customs Service were inspecting them. There was already a program in place to examine "vessels of interest" from particular suspicious places or registered to particularly suspicious firms or countries. However, existing resources ran to only about 2 percent of the containers arriving each year. In the aftermath of 11 September, both the Coast Guard and the Customs Service received considerably more money. It would take longer to build up the necessary capabilities.

Television footage, particularly of the destruction of the World Trade Center, was quickly sent around the world. Americans were surprised by the variety of reactions. In many places, such as Europe, there was heartfelt sympathy and horror. Britain accounted for the largest number of foreigners working in the financial firms in the World Trade Center, just as Americans have a major presence in London financial operations; at first it seemed that as many as six hundred Britons had died (the figure was later cut to about seventy). Prime Minister Tony Blair proclaimed that, in view of the attacks, "we are all [now] Americans." Allied European governments expressed some nervousness about what response the U.S. government had in mind, but generally they were very supportive. Even some hostile governments were supportive. Fidel Castro, for example, expressed his horror at the attacks.

The United States soon invoked Article 5 of the NATO Treaty, under which an attack on one signatory is "an attack on all." The formal announcement came on 3 October, the U.S. government providing its allies with proof of bin Laden's involvement in the attacks. The most visible example of immediate NATO involvement was that NATO airborne radar aircraft were dispatched to the United States. Given the limited number of AWACS in U.S. service, and the need to forward-deploy many of them, this NATO deployment was of considerable value.[7] Later NATO and other allies would contribute more directly to the campaign against the terrorists.

Reactions elsewhere were mixed. In many places, particularly in the Muslim world, many were glad that at last the American colossus had been humbled.[8] In many Muslim countries usually described as moderate, government and elite opinion was sympathetic to the United States, but popular opinion, encouraged to hostility because now it appeared that someone had stood up to that hostile giant, was far less so.[9] Palestinian leader Yassir Arafat offered a blood donation to help those hurt in the attacks (a decade earlier, he had aligned with Iraq during the Gulf War, and being on the losing side had gained him nothing), but reporters saw Palestinians dancing in the streets. T-shirts showing the destruction of the World Trade Center enjoyed brisk sales. In many places where the most popular adjective for the United States was "arrogant," such as China, it seemed that someone had finally succeeded in hurting the colossus which so many habitually blamed for their problems.

No one immediately took credit for the attacks (only much later did videotapes of Osama bin Laden boasting about the attacks emerge).[10] From the first, it seems to have been assumed that whatever entity was involved was somehow connected to the Middle East, by far the most passionate venue of conflict between the United States and local powers. All that was really clear was that the 11 September attacks had been acts of terrorism, extensions of familiar kinds of assaults such as air piracy. Even so, it seems to have been obvious from the first that Osama bin Laden and Al Qaeda were by far the most likely culprits. The CIA reportedly had concluded as much by the evening of 11 September.[11]

One bizarre paradox was that, even though it was soon clear that a Muslim organization had employed Arabs to conduct the attack, polls showed that few in the Muslim world could believe that their co-religionists had carried out so horrible an attack. Surely, a popular rumor went, the Israelis had attacked the buildings in order to put the blame on the Muslims. For example, many apparently imagined that none of the thousands of Jews who supposedly worked in the buildings had come to work that day.[12]

For their part, Americans were uncomfortably aware of reports that fundamentalist Muslims across the Hudson River in New Jersey had been told to aim telescopes at the World Trade Center on that fatal morning, as something was about to happen. A story circulated that a Muslim student in a New York school, scolded by his teacher, had pointed out the window at the Trade Center, saying it would not be there the next day. Such stories would raise questions about how much U.S. intelligence agencies should have known about the 11 September plot.

All of that would come later. In his first post–11 September speech President Bush in effect declared war on terrorism, calling for all governments to outlaw it and to attack its sources. The United States would lead a global crusade. The word "crusade" was later changed to avoid offending Arab sentiment (the previous crusade had, after all, been an unabashed assault against Islam), but the idea that 11 September was part of a wider movement which had to be destroyed has animated later U.S. policy. The president did waver between an assault on all terrorist movements and an assault against movements with global reach, which were the only ones capable of attacking the United States directly, but the concept of a global war against terrorism survived. Governments which considered themselves victims of local terrorism assumed, sometimes incorrectly, that the president's words equated to direct support, often against their neighbors. Cases in point were India, which faced Pakistani-based terrorists in Kashmir as well as home-grown ones working for the Tamil Tigers, and Israel, which faced terrorists across the Lebanese border and in areas controlled by the PLO. In Kashmir and in the PLO areas, the U.S. government was hardly likely to want to take sides.

President Bush appeared before Congress on 14 September. Soon after, Congress voted nearly unanimously (420 to 1) to authorize him to use "all necessary and appropriate force" to destroy those who had attacked the country. It was noticeable, however, that he never asked for a formal declaration of war against those who had attacked. Various reasons for this were suggested. There may have been a feeling that the target, though quite real, was too diffuse to define in classic fashion. To be too specific might be to omit important bases of terrorist operations or important abetters of anti-American attacks. For example, some within the administration argued that the United States should take this opportunity to deal not only with bin Laden and Al Qaeda but also with the Iraqis, clearly a current problem. Conversely, leaving the situation ambiguous might allow the president to negotiate with governments which had helped terrorists but wanted to join the American side. It has also been suggested that the government feared that all insurance claims for the heavy damages inflicted on 11 September would have been rejected under war risk clauses, hence that the country would have suffered much heavier economic damage. As it was, in 2002 insurers were refusing to include terrorist clauses in their coverage. In November 2002, President Bush signed a bill offering government risk insurance against further terrorist attacks, specifically to help industries such as construction recover.

A nervous U.S. public and its government waited for more attacks. None came, but not long after 11 September an envelope, which turned out to be filled with anthrax spores, was delivered to the office of a tabloid newspaper in Florida. Other envelopes went to key congressional offices and to CBS News—and, apparently, to the White House and the State Department. Crudely printed notes suggested that the anthrax was part of the assault on the United States. The attacks peaked and then stopped, but for months traces of anthrax plagued the U.S. postal system. Apparently some envelopes filled with anthrax spores had leaked or even burst open in the sorting equipment. Several people died, including an elderly lady who had probably been infected by leaked spores. That the attack did not last long suggested that whoever had mounted it had possessed a limited quantity of material rather than a laboratory capable of producing as much as was wanted. Only much later did the FBI suggest that the attack had been mounted by a U.S. citizen, probably someone previously connected with the Army's biological weapons program.[13] In their view, the motive was more likely to publicize the threat of biological attack than to augment the 11 September assault, but months later no suspect had been arrested. As it was, anthrax was a relatively weak weapon. The disease was not particularly contagious, for example, nor was it very lethal (several victims survived after massive antibiotic treatment). That much worse agents were well known suggested that the anthrax campaign was a kind of warning.

Some in the United States recalled a history of terrorist attacks mounted in or from the Middle East. They argued that impotent or even nonexistent U.S. responses had only emboldened those mounting them. The first spectacular attack of this sort was probably the destruction of the Marine barracks in Beirut by a truck bomb driven by a suicide attacker in 1983. Although the U.S. government was apparently well aware of which Syrian-backed radical group was behind the attack, it made no attempt to strike back, perhaps for fear of upsetting a fragile peace process in Lebanon. Naval bombardment of Lebanon apparently had little impact on the terrorists. Larger policy had trumped military necessity—and any real interest in punishing those who had killed Americans. The later U.S. air strike on the Bekaa Valley in Lebanon, where the terrorists were based, achieved little. One telling point was that its timing had been ruined by a requirement that it be coordinated with the State Department, presumably to allow the latter to make sure that dependents were safe from any backlash. Coordination had been considered so important that the strike had been fatally delayed, from dawn (when the sun would have shone into the eyes of antiaircraft gunners) to midday, when the terrorists could see clearly enough to down an attacking U.S. aircraft, whose bombardier/navigator was later paraded through local streets. Coordination also made leaks to alert the likely targets virtually inevitable. For that matter, despite having declared several times that Syria was sponsoring terrorism, the U.S. government generally avoided attacking its government and even befriended it as a coalition partner during the 1991 Gulf War.

Terrorism was already of considerable interest by 1980, because by that time the Soviets were providing support for a variety of radical groups, most of them in Europe, which were trying to destabilize U.S. allies and oust U.S. troops. They hijacked airliners, they kidnapped prominent Europeans (and, in some cases, Americans), and they blew up Americans on or near their military bases. Soviet support included finances and weapons and false documents, but also sanctuaries. Terrorists could escape their Western pursuers by fleeing behind the iron curtain. There they could coordinate their operations without fear of local police. This pattern, of using a sanctuary to support operations outside, would also characterize the Muslim terrorists responsible for 11 September and similar outrages in the West. That the sanctuary and the support it provided were vital was indicated by the drastic way in which terrorism declined after the collapse of the Soviet empire in between 1989 and 1991. It was not that all terrorists in the West were somehow Soviet employees, or that all radicals in the West lost interest in their cause as the Soviet Union collapsed. Many of them remained to join anti-globalization movements and even, in 1991, to resume violent operations. However, the simple loss of resources had profound effects.

At any rate, the U.S. response to European and Arab terrorism was for the various intelligence agencies and the FBI to create the joint Counter-Terrorism Center in 1986. In the context of the cold war, however, terrorism seemed far less important than more conventional kinds of military threats. The Counter-Terrorism Center may have become a dumping ground for intelligence professionals deemed unsuitable for more important jobs. It received its greatest prominence during the 1980s, when it turned out that one of its personnel, Jonathan Pollard, was an Israeli spy. Having been dropped by mainstream naval intelligence as unsuitable (but not fireable), he was given what was clearly a marginal position. There, he used his new position mainly to obtain a wide range of documents his handlers wanted. The case illustrates the low estate of counterterrorism within the U.S. intelligence community in the 1980s and 1990s. Moreover, the mere existence of a joint task force appears not to have solved the problem of numerous competing agencies, which could not freely share all the data they obtained. This problem would be cited as a major reason for the lack of warning before 11 September.

The Arab terrorism of the 1970s and early 1980s was largely, though by no means entirely, secular, much of it intended to advance various groups attacking Israel. That fact may have blinded the U.S. government to any terrorist potential inherent in Islamic fundamentalism. Thus there was no apparent resistance to the Pakistani practice of funneling U.S. support for Afghan resistance to fundamentalist groups, some of which turned out to have little use for the United States. There also appears to have been scant sensitivity to the threat such fundamentalists posed to friendly Arab governments, such as that of Egypt. For example, the U.S. government seems not to have appreciated the extent to which the 1981 assassination of President Anwar Sadat of Egypt was a fundamentalist operation. It is also possible that, after the fall of the shah of Iran in 1979 (to fundamentalists), some within the U.S. government decided that the wave of fundamentalism might well engulf the moderate governments and, therefore, it would be foolhardy not to build bridges to possible fundamentalist leaders. The most prominent of these was the blind sheikh Omar Abdel-Rahman, the spiritual leader of a fundamentalist movement. As a major figure in the fundamentalist resistance movement in Afghanistan, he received a visa (despite being on a watch list intended to keep him and similar subversives out of the United States) and political asylum from the Egyptian government. These accommodations seem not to have made him particularly friendly; the sheikh was implicated in the 1993 World Trade Center bombing.

Through the 1990s, the U.S. government position was that in many countries fundamentalists were a legitimate and repressed opposition. The solution to their problems would be to welcome them into democratic politics, not exclude them. That fundamentalists might well destroy any secular state which allowed them into its politics seems not to have been accepted. Thus the United States did not support the Algerian government when it touched off a civil war in 1992 by rejecting election returns which might have brought a fundamentalist party into power. The war was remarkably brutal; often the whole populations of villages which resisted the rebels were murdered. Within a few years a French mass-circulation magazine was asking whether the rebels were trying to export their movement into France itself. In Egypt, fundamentalist revolt against the government may have peaked in 1997 with the mass murder of Western tourists at Luxor, in effect a direct attack against the key Egyptian tourist industry. By that time, within much of the Muslim world, fundamentalism and anti-Westernism seemed to be the coming trend. U.S. official unwillingness to resist, on the grounds that any reaction would be illegitimate interference in local politics, was seen as weakness. Moderate Muslims, the natural friends of the West, were dismayed and lost ground.

Moreover, fundamentalist attacks on the United States were not officially recognized as such. Bin Laden's first attack against the United States may have been two December 1992 hotel bombings in Aden, Yemen, which killed Austrian tourists and narrowly missed U.S. troops en route to Somalia. He was also credited with attacks against U.S. troops in Somalia the following year. The United States withdrew after eighteen Americans died. Anti-Americans later claimed that the main lesson they drew from this was that the United States would not stand and take casualties—even that eighteen was a magic number, indicating what was needed to force American withdrawal. The reality was that Americans had not gone into Somalia for military reasons. They had gone in to help feed starving Somalis, and they saw little point in shedding blood in a humanitarian operation. If the Somalis did not want to be fed, so be it. There was talk at the time of making Somalia a United Nations colony, on the theory that its government had virtually disappeared, but that never happened. This more complex side of the Somali story did not make it into the imaginations of those attacking the United States.

In 1993 militant Islamic fundamentalists tried and failed to destroy the World Trade Center in New York using a truck bomb placed in a garage under one of the buildings. Their explosives proved not powerful enough, and only a few people died in the blast. Considerable attention was concentrated on the subsequent trial, which convicted those involved (including a blind Egyptian-born cleric, about whom the Egyptian government had warned the U.S. government).[14] Virtually none was concentrated on the external network of terrorist organizations, some of them state-sponsored, which had helped make the attack possible. A short time later, a plot to blow up the United Nations and the bridges and tunnels leading into and out of Manhattan was broken up. It turned out that the explosives and false identification had come through the Sudanese mission to the United Nations—through the agency of a fundamentalist government.[15]

In each case, U.S. retaliation was limited to police and legal action against those directly responsible. The government made no serious attempt to strike those abroad who had instigated the 1993 attack or its failed successor.

In June 1996, an explosive-laden tank truck destroyed a U.S.-occupied barracks, the Khobar Towers, in Saudi Arabia, killing nineteen U.S. airmen. Little was apparently done to press Saudi authorities to identify the culprits. Those they caught, they executed without allowing the FBI to question them. Later the incident was considered significant because it involved Saudi fundamentalists like those engaged in later assaults. It also demonstrated that the fundamentalists had a safe haven in Saudi Arabia. The Saudis themselves blamed the Iranians, in effect denying any possible involvement by Osama bin Laden, who U.S. investigators felt was responsible. Bin Laden had already been involved in a 1995 bombing of a Saudi National Guard base in Riyadh.

On 14 October 1996, bin Laden declared war on the United States as well as on Britain and on Israel. On 23 February 1998, citing his authority as a Muslim scholar, fighter, and holy man, he issued a ruling, a fatwa, stating that it was the duty of all Muslims to kill Americans anywhere in the world; they would be justified in claiming a reward by plundering their possessions. Bin Laden published the fatwa under the name of a new World Islamic Front for Jihad against the Jews and the Crusaders, the latter a reference to infidels (British and U.S. troops) invading holy Muslim territory (i.e., occupying bases in Saudi Arabia and in the Gulf). When U.S. embassies in Nairobi and in Dar-es-Salaam, both in Africa, were destroyed by massive truck bombs in August 1998, Osama was the obvious culprit. After 301 people were killed and 5,000 injured, the U.S. government declared bin Laden and his Al Qaeda terrorist organization the "number one" enemies of the United States.[16] Retaliation took the form of Tomahawk cruise missile attacks on terrorist training camps in Afghanistan and on a pharmaceutical plant in the Sudan.

The lesson for the terrorists was apparently that the Americans might well do something, but that it would probably be ineffectual. Later American accounts claimed that the terrorist camp had been the known site of a major meeting. The missile strike had been timed to kill the top leadership of Al Qaeda, which, the Clinton administration claimed, it had missed by only a few hours. The pharmaceutical plant was attacked because it was identified as a center for producing precursor chemicals for nerve gas, and because it was supposedly part of the industrial-financial empire supporting Al Qaeda. Later it developed that evidence for the second conclusion was flimsy at best. Critics charged that the attacks had been mounted specifically because President Bill Clinton hoped that they would distract attention from his ongoing domestic legal problems, which were then escalating (he failed). The attacks seemed to mirror the plot of a current movie, *Wag the Dog,* in which a president, under fire because of his sexual misdeeds, orchestrates a fake war against nonexistent Albanian rebels in order to distract the U.S. media.[17]

The Sudanese attack may have been the result of undue initiative on the part of a new CIA center intended to combat the spread of weapons of mass destruction. Given the president's urgent need for targets to strike in retaliation, any agency which could identify them would gain valuable bureaucratic kudos. In such an atmosphere, a CIA cell might feel encouraged to deduce too much from limited intelligence. That has, after all, happened many times before, in many countries. The same cell which identified the pharmaceutical plant as a target apparently also misidentified the Chinese Embassy in Belgrade (as the Yugoslav arms export agency) about a year later. In both cases, the cell involved may well have imagined that its tentative identification would be subject to extensive review—a review which was never undertaken.

After 11 September it was reported that the original Joint Staff plan for the 1998 strike in Afghanistan had entailed an attack by B-2 bombers, to be followed by two Special Forces battalions on the ground, with Tomahawks to follow up.[18] That would have been a very different attack. Because the manned B-2s could have responded to changes in the situation, at least in theory they would have had a better chance of killing or wounding many more of the terrorists. Special Forces would not only have killed more of them, they would have seized many of their papers, making possible follow-up attacks on other elements of Al Qaeda. The Tomahawks, fired at preset targets, would have been the least flexible of the three attacking elements, hence best suited to a follow-up after most of the damage had been done.

This attack was, however, risky. The Special Forces in particular might well have suffered casualties. Reportedly President Clinton personally vetoed any such attack. If that is what happened, it would have confirmed the widespread perception that the U.S. government was unwilling to take real risks in the war against terrorists. It would take only symbolic steps.

Clinton administration officials offered a different explanation. They admitted that the cruise missile attack was unlikely to be effective but pointed out that intelligence was poor; it was by no means clear that bin Laden was present in the terrorist camp. The Special Forces helicopters might have had to fly as much as nine hundred miles, and they feared losses without hitting bin Laden at all. Yet there was intelligence indicating that bin Laden planned another attack, and any strike might throw him off balance. At the least, it would have demonstrated that Afghanistan was not a sanctuary. Later it emerged that bin Laden had left the camp well before the missiles arrived. As it happened, the attack was delayed so that missiles could be launched after sundown and so that the attack could be coordinated with that on the plant in the Sudan—and that delay may have been enough to save bin Laden. Secretary of Defense William S. Cohen reportedly stated that bin Laden had been tipped off when the State Department evacuated nonessential personnel from Pakistan four days earlier for fear of post-attack riots. If true, this would recall the effects of State Department warnings on the Bekaa Valley raid about fifteen years earlier.

Another possible 1998 initiative was also vetoed. It could be argued that the camp in Afghanistan was a poor target. Its few permanent buildings could easily be rebuilt. Few of those inside would likely be killed by a preset strike. Probably it was not even clear which buildings were worth hitting. On the other hand, it could be argued that the lifeblood of Al Qaeda was the cash disbursed by Osama bin Laden, its chief. If the organization had a center of gravity, it might well be that cash. After 11 September it was reported that the U.S. Treasury Department had long known not only where most of bin Laden's money was, but also how to extract it from the banks— which deposits and which code words were involved. In theory, then, bin Laden and Al Qaeda could have been neutralized by what amounted to a U.S. government bank robbery, an officially sanctioned computer crime. However, the Treasury was unwilling to act for fear of destroying faith in the international banking system.[19] President Clinton was unwilling or unable to focus on terrorism long enough to change the Treasury's mind. It has been reported, however, that in the wake of the 1998 attacks the U.S. government managed to freeze considerable Al Qaeda assets, forcing the organization to shift to other forms of financing.[20]

The net effect of crediting Osama bin Laden personally with the African attacks and then failing to destroy him was disastrous. President Clinton in effect built bin Laden up into a dominant anti-American hero. By personalizing the conflict against him, he ensured that any U.S. failure would contribute enormously to bin Laden's prestige, hence adding to his resources, as potential followers would support him rather than some alternative. For example, bin Laden seems to have benefited enormously from the wide distribution of videos showing the aftermath of the raids, as proof both of his importance and of the Americans' utter impotence against him.[21] Much the same can be said of Saddam Hussein: continued personal American enmity turned him into a symbol of anti-Americanism, and his survival only seemed to demonstrate American impotence.

President Clinton did sign a "finding" targeting Osama bin Laden personally, and the CIA negotiated with the Pakistanis to track and assassinate him. This operation was aborted when the Pakistani government fell in the 1999 coup which brought General Pervez Musharraf to power. Even after the coup, the CIA apparently supported a Pakistani cell which tried to locate and track bin Laden. On the basis of this effort, Clinton administration officials later maintained that they had done their best to deal with Osama's threat. Their critics pointed out that they had set requirements (for timeliness and accuracy) so high that it was very unlikely that Osama would ever be killed.[22] Apparently, once the Pakistan government aborted the assassination squad, the administration opted for a Tomahawk strike. To carry out such an attack required not merely that Osama be located at any one time, but that his movements for the next six hours or more be predicted in detail, which was never even remotely possible. The training camp meeting had probably come closer to this ideal than any other, and it seems that in that case the timing of the Tomahawk strikes was set by other considerations.

There was a parallel diplomatic initiative. The United States had quietly supported the Taliban as a force for stability and perhaps reconstruction in Afghanistan, but it had not formally recognized them. There was, to be sure, considerable U.S. disgust at Taliban policies, such as the virtual enslavement of women and draconian application of Islamic law, but generally governments accept that they cannot have much impact on the internal policies of other governments. However, in 1997–98 the Taliban were not yet the de facto government of Afghanistan. Shifts in State Department leadership helped bring Taliban human rights abuses to the fore. Late in 1997 the United States formally declared itself neutral in the ongoing Afghan civil war. For his part, in the wake of the August 1998 U.S. attacks, Mullah Omar, head of the Taliban, announced that bin Laden was an honored guest. This was later largely taken as the beginning of a bargaining process in which the Taliban expected support and recognition in return for handing over Osama bin Laden.

In February 1999 U.S. Deputy Secretary of State Strobe Talbott met Taliban representatives in Islamabad. He showed them proof that Osama bin Laden and Al Qaeda had been responsible for the African embassy attacks and officially asked the Taliban to hand bin Laden over for trial. If they did so, he said, they would receive economic rewards. They would also be held responsible for any further Al Qaeda attacks. The hope was to bind the Taliban to U.S. security interests, a typical diplomatic approach to the problem bin Laden presented. It seems not to have been imagined that by this time bin Laden was integral to the Taliban regime.

Talks were inconclusive. On 6 July 1999, President Clinton froze all Taliban assets in the United States and suspended all commerce. Responding to U.S. and Russian pressure, on 12 October 1999 the UN Security Council ordered additional sanctions, including the grounding of the Afghan national airline, Ariana, pending the extradition of bin Laden (Resolution 1267).

Meanwhile, attempts were being made to reach a compromise settlement of the ongoing Afghan civil war under the aegis of the "6+2 Group," that is, the six neighboring countries plus the United States and Russia. Of the countries involved, only one, Pakistan, fully supported the Taliban. By August 1999 it was clear that no settlement was possible. Probably in parallel with the July 1999 proclamation, President Clinton approved covert CIA aid to the Northern Alliance force fighting the Taliban, which explains the CIA presence in Afghanistan prior to 11 September.[23]

Attacks on the U.S. presence abroad continued. In October 2000, the USS *Cole,* a destroyer entering the port of Aden in Yemen on the Arabian peninsula, was attacked by two men in a boat crammed with a powerful explosive charge. Both were killed when they triggered their charge. The ship was badly damaged; seventeen sailors were killed. The Yemeni government was less than enthusiastic in its support of the American investigation. Aden itself was considered a hotbed of fundamentalist, anti-American sentiment. Al Qaeda was blamed, and it took credit. In fact, the situation was more complex, in that the attack was actually carried out by a radical Yemeni group with ties to both Al Qaeda and the Iraqis, the latter surviving from the period during which South Yemen was a Soviet-oriented state. However, reports credited an Al Qaeda officer as operational leader of the cell which carried out the attack. He was apparently also setting up a bomb attack on the U.S. Embassy in New Dehli.[24]

In none of these cases did the U.S. government react particularly violently or effectively. One reading of this history, then, would be that terrorists could count on the Americans to take their blows without hitting back, so that terrorism could be counted a relatively safe option. If their purpose was to publicize their prowess in a largely anti-American Muslim world, that might well be sufficient, and it might lead to frequent further acts. Most terrorist organizations are interested mainly in publicizing their causes by what some call "the propaganda of the deed," but they are keenly aware that there are limits beyond which they will be hunted down. However, if a terrorist was really interested in instigating a war between, say, the United States and the Muslim world, then U.S. unwillingness to act would require him to make ever more destructive attacks until U.S. policy changed. It now seems that Osama bin Laden had the latter view, and that

U.S. intelligence either never really understood his character or his motivation, or at the least was unable to convey that information to either President Clinton or, until 11 September, his successor.

There were exceptions to U.S. quietism. In 1986, when Libyan government terrorists killed U.S. troops at a disco in Berlin, the American response was swift. Navy and Air Force bombers struck Libya. This time, with no State Department personnel at risk, the attack was not leaked. Those who doubted U.S. resolve could, however, point at rules of engagement which precluded attacks on most of the targets in Tripoli (due to intermittent cloud cover). The attack might be seen as more symbolic than effective. On the other hand, by demonstrating that Libya had no effective air defense at all, the U.S. strike showed that later strikes could be mounted at will. American policy makers observed that Colonel Qadaffi mounted no more terrorist attacks in Europe. Later, however, it was claimed that the destruction of Pan Am Flight 103, in 1988, had been the colonel's revenge.

Also, the United States fought when Saddam Hussein invaded Kuwait in 1990. The immediate effect of the coalition attack was to eject the Iraqis from Kuwait. However, the victory was more ambiguous as time passed. Presumably the expectation had been that, having lost the war, Saddam would soon have to leave office. As it turned out, Saddam retained his position. He soon began to advertise the outcome of the war as a kind of victory, on the theory that military victory against the strongest power on Earth would have been impossible, whereas survival surely flouted the Americans. It looked like the United States was unwilling to destroy its enemies. The U.S. postvictory strategy included a tough embargo intended to convince Saddam to surrender his weapons of mass destruction. By the mid-1990s Saddam was advertising the embargo as an assault, not on him, but on the innocent population of Iraq. It was by no means clear to Arabs— or, for that matter, to other Muslims—that, unchecked, Saddam would have been a deadly threat. After all, by the 1990s it seemed the Iraqis were no longer likely to attack other Arab states, whereas they did continue to threaten the common enemy (Israel) and Saddam confined himself to attacking Kurds and Shias within Iraq. Muslims often saw the embargo, then, as an attack by the West on the population of a Muslim country, an attack that fit well with a wider sense of long-term victimhood at the hands of the West.

Moreover, the character of the U.S. triumph, its very speed and the widespread use of stand-off weapons, convinced some that the United States was willing to fight only when it could avoid casualties. Some in the

U.S. defense establishment speculated that no future Saddam would choose to fight a Western-style ("symmetric") war, and that future wars would be shaped to attack the inherent weaknesses, rather than the strengths, of American military technology. Such attacks were characterized as "asymmetric." These thinkers remembered Vietnam. The victory in Kuwait had been popular, they said, largely because it cost so little in American blood. Perhaps the United States was unwilling to chance casualties in the future. Overall, it appeared that the pattern was one of half-hearted American action.

U.S. policy was shaped by the perception that bin Laden and his Al Qaeda were a subnational terrorist organization, not an integral element of a foreign government (Taliban Afghanistan). The Taliban might like and protect bin Laden, but governments are different from murderous terrorists. That was a natural view. Governments view other governments as part of the same species, and they do not like to make the destruction of sovereign governments their policy. Surely a combination of rewards and threats could induce the Taliban to behave more rationally, perhaps even to eject Osama. In fact, by the late 1990s Al Qaeda had bought the Taliban.[25] It is only fair, however, to recall that before the two had fused, at least some within the Taliban had shown enmity to Osama and his Arabs, and that some of the Arabs themselves expected to be ejected from Afghanistan.[26] The August 1998 missile raids probably ended this possibility.

This understanding of the situation in Afghanistan, which played to preconceptions within the U.S. government, would seem to have been a serious failure of intelligence, which shaped early U.S. strategy in the war eventually fought in Afghanistan.

A relatively benign view of the Taliban would have been welcome because there was serious U.S. interest in Afghanistan. The country itself has only very limited resources, but it lies between the newly developed oil fields of Central Asia and the sea. At least up to 1998, several American companies sought Taliban approval for oil and gas pipelines from Turkmenistan to the Arabian Sea through Afghanistan.[27] Later it was alleged that such crass commercial interests had blinded the U.S. government to the realities of obscenely harsh Taliban rule and to the strong connection between the Taliban and Osama. Whatever the perceived reality, by 2001 the United States was the main donor of food aid to Afghanistan, a point which may have been obscured by the multilateral character of the aid. U.S. payments for the suppression of the poppy crop were probably the main source of Taliban cash income.

Not surprisingly, there were also threats. Whether or not the Taliban allowed construction of a pipeline, they were certainly a threat to the Central Asian governments in which very large oil reserves had been found. Those reserves were likely to become very important in future. For example, for years American administrations have been uncomfortably aware that the Saudi state is fundamentally unstable, and becoming more so as the royal family concedes more power to its clerics. With the end of the cold war, an alternative to Saudi oil suddenly opened in the form of large fields in Russia and in the old Central Asian Soviet republics. By the spring of 2002, Russia was actually producing more oil than Saudi Arabia.[28]

By the mid-1990s Islamic insurrection, supported by the Taliban, threatened the governments of two former Soviet republics, Tajikistan and Uzbekistan. Russian troops fought in Tajikistan. Both governments asked for U.S. advisers to train their police forces; they arrived in 1997 and in 1998, respectively. Ultimately the Uzbeks formally allied with the United States. Reportedly, Central Command began studies of how these countries could be protected from the Taliban in the event, which seemed likely, of Taliban victory throughout Afghanistan.

In retrospect, the Taliban and their allies were the single most pressing threat to the United States at the end of the Clinton administration, though that was not nearly so obvious at the time. The great foreign policy debate, which carried over to the new Bush administration, was how to deal with governments who were both unfriendly to the United States and gaining possession of weapons of mass destruction and long-range ballistic missiles—countries such as Iran, Iraq, and North Korea. How hostile would China ultimately be? Would Indian-Pakistani hostility boil over into nuclear war? Probably more immediate than any of these questions were political-economic relations with the European Union and relations with Russia, which still possessed (and continues to possess) vast numbers of nuclear warheads. Such problems grossly overshadowed terrorism, because they had the potential to involve the United States in major military or economic warfare. Thus, whatever contingency plans the Clinton administration had to deal with Osama and Al Qaeda were, rightly, almost certainly low on its list of priorities, and they were similarly low on the incoming administration's list.[29]

A planned Bush administration policy review under Dr. Zalmi Kahlilzal of the National Security Council, who was later U.S. envoy to post-Taliban Afghanistan, was apparently never completed, having been set aside while a review of policy toward Iran was conducted. The new Bush administration considered Iran a much more pressing issue; Afghanistan could be set aside. Afghanistan was never placed on the list of state sponsors of terrorism.

The CIA was active in Afghanistan well before September 2001, but mainly or entirely to track Al Qaeda.[30] After the war began, many on the Left claimed that planning had been quick because the U.S. government was already getting ready to attack the country, but that is a misreading of the prewar U.S. mind-set, which persisted after 11 September.[31] One proof of this mind-set was the nature of early U.S. strategy, which envisaged leaving the Taliban in power once they had handed Osama and Al Qaeda personnel over to the Americans.

In the wake of the 11 September attacks, the U.S. government followed a dual policy. On the one hand, it announced that it would hunt down and punish those responsible for the outrages. On the other, it would increase security measures at home to preclude any repetition of the attack. The latter was initially easier than the former, since it was soon clear that very lax security measures for domestic travel had made the hijackers' task relatively easy. For example, several hijackers had bought one-way fares with cash, triggering airlines' profiling systems. Even so, they had been allowed on board the aircraft they seized. Even their weapons, commercial box cutters, had been detected—but allowed on board.

It was, of course, more important to track down the perpetrators. The government adopted a policy under which it could secretly arrest and detain noncitizens. As much as eleven months after the attacks, it was not clear how many had been detained (the usual figure given was about a thousand, most of whom were released) or whether any would ultimately be charged as conspirators. Presumably the hope was, and is, that further conspirators would reveal themselves. They might try, for example, to contact their friends, unaware, due to secrecy, that their cohorts had been arrested. Secrecy might also make it possible to convince conspirators' associates, still free, that they had talked, and thus might cause them to reveal themselves by bolting or trying to silence their former comrades.

It is not clear to what extent such measures were successful. Airport security cameras had captured the hijackers' faces, and existing security measures ensured that their identities (or, at least, cover identities) would also be known. It was much more difficult to trace their relationships and their support networks. Because this task is still ongoing, it is not yet clear how successful it has been. Only one man, already in custody on 11 September, has been charged publicly with membership in the conspiracy.

Much of the evidence was inevitably from communications intercepts. To the extent that the government admitted its capabilities (by stating what evidence it had), it would lose them, as those still active realized which forms of communication were no longer secure. That had already happened in some important cases. For example, in arguing for conviction of some of those involved in the 1998 embassy bombings, the U.S. government revealed that its case was based on intercepted cell phone conversations. That in turn implied an ability, previously probably unknown, to sort through the hundreds of thousands of such conversations ongoing at any one time (by using computers seeking key words, for example). Much later, references to intercepted satellite telephone messages apparently caused Osama bin Laden to abandon his satellite phone in favor of intermittent communication carried out by messengers at Internet cafés in Pakistan—a form of communication far more difficult to intercept or, for that matter, to interpret.

The government thus faced a problem. Its solution was to propose closed military tribunals, which would be able to limit dissemination of evidence. This idea brought protests, the argument being that to deny the accused constitutional rights would be to destroy the essence of the United States, that is, to promote exactly what the hijackers had tried to do. By mid-March 2002 the government had retreated to the point of announcing that any tribunals would hew to the usual civilian standards of proof and, most important, that the accused could bring in civilian lawyers, who could of course reveal just what evidence the government had revealed in trials.

The government also feared that some attorneys might act as conduits between those in custody and networks still more or less intact. It claimed that in some earlier terrorist cases, such as those involving the 1993 World Trade Center bombing, defense attorneys had done just that, making it possible for terrorists in prison to plan and even order further attacks. It therefore demanded and received the right to monitor attorney-client conversations in terrorist cases, a step which many abhorred.

Most Americans were deeply shocked by the attacks. The virtually universal assumption was that some extremist Muslims were to blame. That was not a new idea. For example, when the federal building in Oklahoma City was destroyed, suspicion initially fell on Muslims, and one man was arrested at an airport and detained for hours. Only eventually did it become clear that domestic, not foreign, terrorists were to blame. The United States has a large Muslim, mainly immigrant, population. The hijackers, and indeed the 1993 World Trade Center bombers, were drawn from among immigrants and long-term visitors. To what extent would their crimes cause hysteria against other Muslims? Who could tell which Muslims were guilty, and which were entirely loyal?

In the days just after the attacks, stories abounded. In some places Muslims were attacked, even killed. Other groups suffered. For example, Sikhs were confused with Muslims because they wear turbans and go unshaven. At least one Sikh was killed. Even so, months after the attacks the situation was far better than it had been in the wake of another surprise attack, by the Japanese against Pearl Harbor in December 1941. In 1942 Japanese Americans, most of them noncitizens (due to racist quirks of U.S. law), living on the West Coast were swept up into detention camps, even though there was no evidence of their treasonable activity. Presumably one important difference after 11 September was that the United States was consciously a much more diverse country than it had been sixty years earlier. Too, it had to maintain good relations with Muslim governments, whereas in 1941 it was at war with Japan.

President Bush thus had an enormous responsibility. He was probably aware from the first that the odds were that the attack had been mounted by Muslim terrorists, a suspicion that would have been cemented when the identities of the hijackers became known. He was also aware that any U.S. attempt to punish those responsible would require the cooperation, at least the acquiescence, of Muslim governments. For that matter, the United States was ever more dependent on imported oil. Even though the United States does not import most of its oil from the Middle East, any major disruption in Middle Eastern oil supplies would push up the price of oil and thus might trigger a depression in the West. Bush, therefore, had to convince Americans that even though some Muslims had executed the worst domestic attack in U.S. history, it was vital that Americans not attack Muslims in their midst.

The government was already aware of most of the terrorist groups in the Middle East. Osama bin Laden's Al Qaeda had long figured in its lists, for its combination of ruthlessness, extended reach, and sophistication. It had already been blamed for the 1998 attacks on embassies in Africa. As an indication of how seriously Al Qaeda was taken, in June 2001 a secret study examined the consequences of biological warfare conducted by a terrorist group. The scenario envisaged a group of terrorists strewing material through a suburban shopping mall. The group involved was Al Qaeda.

Even so, it was not certain that Al Qaeda had arranged the 11 September attacks. There was some speculation that Iraq, locked in an apparently endless confrontation with the United States, had mounted the attacks. Iraq had been involved in the 1993 attack on the World Trade Center, and it had supplied terrorists with false papers (some obtained when the Iraqis looted Kuwait). The Iraqi intelligence service had tried to kill President Bush's father after the latter had left office. President Bush therefore refused to name Al Qaeda in his initial speech rallying the country. He did emphasize that whoever was to blame, Americans should not consider the Muslims in their midst the enemy, nor should they consider the Muslim world inherently hostile. Again and again, government spokesmen emphasized this theme. Many newspapers published brief accounts of Islam intended to show that it was not an inherently hostile religion. A few observed, however, that in parts of the Muslim world, religious virtue had been made almost synonymous with hatred for the West. Much of this thinking could be traced back to the Wahhabi sect which runs Saudi Arabia. However, hatred of the West was also strong in nominally secular Arab states, such as Iraq, Libya, and Syria, so it was by no means clear that only a few hard-line sects were involved in the terrorism.

By 13 September bin Laden was a prime suspect. On the seventeenth he was named the perpetrator. President Bush said that he was wanted "dead or alive."[32] By this time Osama was living in Afghanistan, under the protection of the Afghan government. President Bush asked the Afghan regime to hand him over. Pakistan was the chief backer of the Taliban regime running Afghanistan, and Pakistani officers were sent there to demand that Osama be turned over to a U.S. court. Meanwhile, planning began for the war which would have to be fought in the event that the Afghans refused. U.S. forces were ordered deployed to the east. Unlike his predecessor, President Bush was not at all disposed to avoid punishing this kind of terrorism.

The administration's envoys spread around the world, attempting to convince heads of state to join in whatever measures it decided to take. Several, such as President Jiang of China, clearly sought to slow down any U.S. action, arguing that to be legitimate it would have to be based on irrefutable evidence. Within the United States, critics of the diplomatic offensive argued that it was no more than a repetition of the coalition-building which President Bush's father had pursued on the eve of the Gulf War. This time it was surely a waste of time; better to act at once. Others pointed out that Afghanistan is land-locked and access would have to be through or over other countries' territory. If those countries refused access, war in Afghanistan would become impossible until they had been dealt with.

It was, therefore, important that on 19 September the military ruler of Pakistan, General Musharraf, joined the United States in opposing Osama and, ultimately, the Taliban. Given the ties between Pashtuns in western Pakistan and the Taliban, Pakistan would not join actively in a war, but on the other hand, as the main backer of the Taliban, Pakistan could offer extensive intelligence support in a war. On 24 September Russian president Vladimir Putin offered not only his support but also assistance in gaining the support of the former Soviet Central Asian republics bordering Afghanistan on the north. Some of these republics were already supporting Northern Alliance groups fighting the Taliban. On 1 October British prime minister Tony Blair announced that he found the U.S. evidence of Osama's sponsorship of the 11 September attacks "incontrovertible." The next day NATO announced that the United States had provided "clear and compelling proof" of Osama's involvement and, therefore, NATO forces would join any American operation. That same day Uzbekistan, which bordered Afghanistan, agreed to allow U.S. forces to use its territory to support the Northern Alliance, and a thousand U.S. troops were dispatched there to protect any bases involved.

The United Nations Security Council had already adopted (on 29 September) a U.S.-sponsored resolution obliging members to attack terrorists and to cooperate in a campaign against them. Although it had little force, the resolution in effect legitimized any attack the United States might mount against the Taliban. The resolution was important because in effect it undercut the argument that one man's terrorist is another man's freedom fighter; it set an objective standard for states to meet.

Many governments were, of course, less than enthusiastic. Thus on 26 September the Iranians announced that they would not join the U.S. campaign. That was hardly a surprise, given the enmity between the two countries. However, it was clear that Iran would not assist the Taliban, and later it became clear that Iran would in fact provide the United States with limited assistance.

The rulers of Afghanistan, the Taliban, refused to hand over Osama on the Americans' say-so. They demanded evidence. Unfortunately, the evidence was apparently communications intercepts and, perhaps, tracked financial data. Not only was the administration unwilling to compromise its most valuable sources of intelligence, which might provide warnings of further attacks, but it was by no means clear that the sort of complex deductions involved would have satisfied the Taliban. There was much talk of tribal standards of honor, of how the Taliban could not lightly turn over a guest to foreign justice. Thus on 21 September the Taliban formally rejected the demand that Osama be turned over to the Americans, although as late as 27 September the Pakistanis were still trying to change their minds. Ultimately the U.S. government concluded that the Taliban request for better evidence was no more than a stall. Indeed, there was growing evidence that Osama was de facto ruler of Afghanistan.

By late September arrangements had been made. By the thirtieth, more than three hundred aircraft, two dozen warships, and twenty-eight thousand military personnel had been concentrated in the Indian Ocean and the Red Sea, within striking range of Afghanistan. Initially, President Bush wanted to call the undertaking Operation Infinite Justice; several Muslim governments objected, stating that only Allah could provide true justice. The attack on Afghanistan therefore became Operation Enduring Freedom.

To understand how and why the war in Afghanistan was fought, it is necessary to go back to the origins of the terror unleashed on 11 September. Other important factors were the ethnic and other divisions on the ground in Afghanistan, which were both potential opportunities for the United States and likely problems, and an evolving U.S. style of warfare, which made the Afghan War radically different from previous U.S. conflicts. All of these themes will be developed in the account that follows.

For the time being, by the end of September it seemed that the Al Qaeda attack had peaked. Further plots, for example, to blow up U.S. embassies in Paris and in Rome, had been thwarted. There were, to be sure, isolated incidents. For example, soon after international airline flights to the United States were resumed, Richard Reid, a British convert to Islam, tried to destroy an American Airlines aircraft over the Atlantic by detonating explosives in his shoes. A computer disk later recovered in Kabul suggested that previously he had acted as an Al Qaeda scout. Reid failed because fellow passengers and the aircrew were alert enough to subdue him—and because he was not, apparently, really sure of what he was doing. One might see his attack as an attempt by the Al Qaeda leadership to destroy not only the airliner but also a potentially embarrassing witness to their operation. In April 2002, a man flew a light plane into a skyscraper in Milan. A previously unknown Islamic group claimed credit, but others suggested that they were trying to convert an accident into proof that the terrorists were still effective.[33] On the other hand, when an Egyptian (with ties to Egyptian Jihad) killed two people at the El Al counter at Los Angeles International Airport on 4 July 2002, the FBI refused to classify the incident as terrorism. The Israelis, however, demanded that it be placed in that category. Which was it? Was the Egyptian acting alone, or was he acting on orders? Some of his relatives said that he had been very distressed in the few days before he acted. Descriptions of suicide attackers tend to emphasize how calm they were before finally acting. Thus the Egyptian's state of mind suggests powerful coercion by some external organization, perhaps one with access to relatives back in Egypt—a terrorist act.

The Egyptian's attack falls into a widening category of acts which on the surface appear to be individual but which may be connected to wider organizations such as Al Qaeda. At least in the past, governmental agencies have been reluctant to make the connection, because it would have enormous foreign policy implications. For example, in 1999 a copilot put an Egypt Air airliner into a fatal dive into the Atlantic. Among those on board were numerous Egyptian officers returning from training in the United States. Was it murder at the behest of, say, Egyptian Jihad, or was it insanity on the copilot's part? In the past few years the consensus seems to have shifted toward terrorist-ordered murder, particularly considering who some of the passengers were.

2

Warning and Decision

 In the wake of 11 September, there naturally was considerable public interest in whether the U.S. government had ignored some warning. The terrorist attack was widely compared to Pearl Harbor, and for decades after that earlier surprise attack, the question of who had known what was widely argued. Probably the dominant view is that taken in 1962 by Roberta Wohlstetter, in her *Pearl Harbor: Warning and Decision;* signals which might, in retrospect, have been considered clear warnings had been buried in intelligence noise. An eerie parallel to the Pearl Harbor story became clear by mid-2002; prior to 11 September the United States apparently could not exploit all of the information it had collected (and was collecting) due to a lack of translators. In 1941, apparently low-grade Japanese code messages were often left for later translation for exactly that reason. It later turned out that one message assigned specific designations to different parts of the Pearl Harbor area, so that each message indicated just where in the harbor each ship was. Such a system would have been pointless unless the readers, in Japan, planned to attack the harbor and needed to know how to make detailed plans. Thus this "bomb plot" message (assigning the designations) was later seen as a clear indication of a Japanese intent to attack the fleet in harbor.

The Pearl Harbor investigations showed that much had been lost because those gathering and interpreting intelligence failed to cooperate. Better cooperation might well not have helped, but there was no point in risking another attack. Ultimately the U.S. response was to create the Central Intelligence Agency and the National Security Agency, each of which attempts to centralize important kinds of intelligence gathering. Similarly, analysis of the 11 September failure shows dismal levels of cooperation within the federal government. The Bush administration's response, like that of earlier administrations to the lessons of Pearl Harbor, was to bring agencies together in hopes of improving coordination. In November 2002 a new Cabinet-level Department of Homeland Security was created. It would encompass all or most of the Immigration and Naturalization Service (INS), the Border Patrol, the Secret Service, probably the Customs Service, and the new Transportation Safety Agency, whose main role is to ensure the security of airline travel. It is unlikely that the FBI and the CIA will be forced to divest any of their organizations to the new one, but some effort will certainly be made to improve cooperation between the two. There has been talk, however, of creating a new domestic intelligence agency.

We now know that Al Qaeda message traffic was being intercepted well before September 2001, because Al Qaeda had been a known and respected threat for some years. Although not all of the traffic could be interpreted, the trend in volume was monitored. Increased message traffic was picked up beginning in December 2000. Such "traffic analysis" indicated that some sort of operation was in the works in the late summer of 2001, but it could not indicate what the operation was. Possibly responding to disinformation by the terrorists, U.S. analysts focused on likely foreign targets, particularly in Europe and the Middle East. The main clue pointing to the United States was that late in 1998 U.S. intelligence reported that Osama bin Laden planned to attack Washington or New York in retaliation for the strikes against his headquarters earlier in the year.[1] Later it became clear that Al Qaeda had tried unsuccessfully to attack millennium celebrations in Seattle and in Los Angeles. These abortive attacks might easily have been considered the organization's attempted retaliation for the 1998 strikes.

Bin Laden was apparently well aware of the risks of electronic communication, and he probably used human couriers to set up the operation itself. There is much evidence, too, that the 11 September operation was run on an ad hoc basis by Mohammed Atta, so that there was little or no specific evidence prior to that date. However, Osama could not avoid all communication. To the extent that his main goal was prestige, he had to alert his followers that something impressive was about to happen; otherwise someone else might take credit. That alone would be sufficient to explain the monitored traffic. In one intercepted message, Osama himself told his mother that he would be dropping out of sight for a time because of an operation. A 10 September message from a senior Al Qaeda official, Abu Zubayda (who had commanded the *Cole* attack), revealed during the 2002 congressional investigation, stated, "Tomorrow is zero hour." It was translated on 12 September.[2] According to another message, "The match starts tomorrow."[3] None of this of course pointed to the precise character of the operation.

There certainly was abundant evidence of Al Qaeda interest in attacking U.S. civil aircraft, to the extent that the *New York Post* printed the headline "Bush Knew" over an article describing a 6 August 2001 briefing which mentioned a heightened threat. Apparently this was an FBI briefing the president had specifically requested, given rising indications of Al Qaeda activity, but it presented very little new information.[4] Later the president and his advisors very properly answered that the threat, as represented in the intelligence briefing, concerned conventional hijackings, not the conversion of airliners into huge cruise missiles. After all, many Al Qaeda operatives were in prison, and in the past terrorists had often mounted conventional hijackings to secure their release. One possibility considered at the time was that the objective would be the release of Sheik Omar Abdel-Rahman, who had been convicted of plotting the 1993 World Trade Center bombing.

Other evidence, which did not reach senior decision makers, was more specific. In July, Kenneth Williams, an FBI agent in Phoenix, noticed that several men linked to Al Qaeda were attending flight schools in the United States. Others were taking courses involving airport operations and security. The agent thought that Al Qaeda or some other terrorist network might be involved, and he asked for a check of other flight schools for Arab or potential terrorist students. He speculated that an Al Qaeda operative might hijack an airplane and fly it into a building. The memo was sidelined—ironically because available FBI manpower was being concentrated on the heightened terrorist threat indicated by increased Al Qaeda message traffic.[5] At the Phoenix office, terrorism was a low priority, because Phoenix was a major entry point for drugs. Williams himself, who was an expert in terrorism, was assigned to other duties. When the memo surfaced in May 2002, it was taken as evidence that the FBI badly needed reform, that the bureau was unable and unwilling to cooperate with any other federal agency. Another piece of evidence was provided when the FBI arrested Zacarias Moussaoui, later indicted as the "twentieth hijacker," on immigration charges in Minnesota on 16 August. He had enrolled in a commercial flight school but had shown no interest in landings or takeoffs.[6] After he was arrested, local FBI agents assumed he was involved in some kind of terrorism. It turned out that the French had long suspected him of involvement with Al Qaeda and other fundamentalists. The FBI did not put together this new information with the July memo.

An FBI warning of an increased terrorist threat to U.S. civil aviation triggered a routine FAA advisory. There had been so many such warnings in the past that this one caused little or no action. It is not clear whether the FBI had sufficient evidence to take this warning more seriously, but reportedly the bureau's practice of never sharing raw intelligence with the FAA made it impossible for the latter to do so. U.S. airlines had already successfully resisted proposals for better security, made after the loss of TWA Flight 800 (to an accidental explosion, rather than to hostile action) in 1996. Without some emergency FAA directive, they were unlikely to do anything extraordinary.

On 21 May 2002, an FBI lawyer in Minneapolis, Colleen Rowley, wrote a letter to FBI director Robert S. Mueller III charging that the agency's lax attitudes were to blame. "We could have gotten lucky and uncovered one or more of the terrorists," she stated, referring specifically to Moussaoui, who was caught in Minneapolis. For example, it took the FBI headquarters three weeks to decide to arrest Moussaoui, after local agents were called by his flight school.[7] They had to call the CIA for information about his foreign contacts, and FBI headquarters questioned the value of such information.[8]

The actual plot, involving airliners used like bombs, was unprecedented in practice. However, there were indications of past Al Qaeda interest in this sort of attack. In 1994 Algerian fundamentalists hijacked a French airliner with the stated intention of flying it into the Eiffel Tower or some other major French building. Their plot failed because the French pilot refused to carry it out. It was later suggested that the lesson learned by the fundamentalists was that they needed their own pilots among the hijackers. In 1995 a fundamentalist caught in the Philippines, Abdul Murad, said that he had planned to hijack an airliner and crash it into CIA headquarters in Langley, Virginia. That was hardly a clear, specific warning of 11 September.

In 1999 the Congressional Research Service compiled a report on the terrorist threat, which included a reference to hijacked airliners being flown into buildings. However, those who saw the classified report observed that this was one among several possible threats listed on one page, and that the report listed dozens or hundreds of possibilities. That, too, did not amount to a disregarded specific warning.

For their part, the FBI and the CIA could point to numerous thwarted Al Qaeda plots, including several operations in the Philippines (a projected assassination of Pope John Paul II in 1994, plans to bomb a dozen U.S. trans-Pacific aircraft in 1995, and plans to assassinate President Clinton in 1995), plans for simultaneous bombings of the U.S. and Israeli Embassies in Manila and other Asian capitals late in 1994, planned bombings of aircraft operating from Amsterdam (1999), a planned assassination of

President Clinton in Pakistan in 1999, and planned millennium bombings of tourist spots in Jordan, in Seattle, and of Los Angeles International Airport.[9] Critics of the federal agencies argued that virtually all the successes had come out of work done by cooperating foreign intelligence organizations and claimed that neither the FBI nor the CIA had made any serious attempt to infiltrate Al Qaeda or any other radical Muslim organization.

Critics asked how the hijackers, some of them on watch lists, had managed to enter the country and to remain in the United States after their visas had expired. Computers at some key ports of entry, which should have made it possible to check visitors against watch lists, were notoriously unreliable. It did not help that there were so many ways to transliterate Arabic names, and that computers usually were not set up to look for similar, but not identical, spellings of any one name on a watch list. For example, in mid-2002 *USA Today* reported that there were at least forty-one ways to spell the name of Colonel Qadaffi, the Libyan dictator.

Some of the hijackers took advantage of that unreliability. It seemed that the INS had little interest in covering U.S. borders. For example, there was no follow-up when tourist visas expired or any effort to see whether those on student visas actually attended their schools. It emerged that the main criterion for issuing visas, other than examination of a watch list, was whether the applicant was likely to become a burden on the United States: did he have enough cash to live as a tourist or was he planning to work illegally? The emphasis was on making it easier, not more difficult, to come to the United States. For example, in Saudi Arabia the State Department set up Visa Express, a system under which travel agencies pass on written applications. Only a small fraction of applicants are ever interviewed. In light of 11 September, considering that most of the terrorists were Saudis, the existence of such a system is shocking.[10] However, before 11 September the United States relied heavily on foreigners visiting it: for their cash as tourists and students, for example. The main concern of those who wished for better border control was fear that foreigners would enter the country to compete for low-paying jobs. Thus the usual story told to attack poor border control described someone from a very poor country who burned his passport upon arrival, claimed that he was a political refugee, and hoped to make a living driving a cab. There was little reason to imagine that someone that desperate to make a living in the United States would arrive planning to commit terrorist acts. Similarly, the official who interviewed Mohammed Atta when the latter applied for a loan (probably to buy a crop duster to spread poison) was interested mainly in easing his adjustment to

American life. Anti-American comments he is said to have made did not set off alarms, because the mind-set, if it was defensive at all, was directed toward protecting Americans from competition by illegal immigrants willing to work for lower wages. The entire American immigrant experience was of foreigners who would do almost anything to get into the promised land, not of enemies trying to slip by a vigilant border patrol. The eleventh of September showed that open borders had the potential for a very different kind of harm. But the vast majority of visitors are still interested either in tourism or in joining in American prosperity, and the country still benefits hugely from their efforts. It is not, moreover, obvious that shutting down most immigration would stop all attackers. In May 2002, the Coast Guard was alerted that a freighter from the Middle East was carrying a large Al Qaeda team and its weapons for an attack on Los Angeles. The freighter was not found, but clearly it represented an infiltration tactic that no reform of the immigration system would have stopped.

Before 11 September, Washington was awash in rumors and warnings of terrorist plots, few of which were (or could have been) taken seriously. After 11 September, virtually all such warnings suddenly seemed much more credible. For the administration, it must have seemed far better to take warnings, however unconfirmed, seriously than to risk a second surprise. From time to time the administration announced vaguely that the country should be on a heightened state of alert, but it was never clear just what that meant. Possibly the alerts were based on simple traffic analysis, the theory being that a rising level of Al Qaeda communications, or perhaps the movement of money, presaged an operation. At least some of the alerts were based on statements by captured Al Qaeda leaders. It is not clear to what extent they represented empty boasts—which have, after all, been made before.

As of early 2003 it seemed inevitable that Osama bin Laden would strike again, if only to prove to his followers that he was still alive and operating. It was not clear to what extent U.S. forces in Afghanistan had dislocated his operation, reducing his followers, for example, to concentrate on simply staying alive. Nor was it clear whether bin Laden's rivals for domination of the world anti-American movement would mount spectacular operations of their own to attract his followers. Attacks have certainly continued, credit being taken (if at all) by a bewildering series of entities. Examples during the fall of 2002 include the firebombing of a nightclub in Bali, the suicide bombing of an Israeli-owned hotel in Kenya, and an attempt to shoot down an Israeli airliner taking off from Kenya. A November 2002 tape, which may or may not have been made by bin Laden, praised a whole series of such attacks and promised many more.

There was some speculation that the destruction of the Afghan base had seriously dislocated Al Qaeda—but not Muslim fundamentalist terrorists in general. Thus in mid-2001, U.S. intelligence agencies warned that there were plenty of other anti-American organizations operating. As if to make this point, terrorists placed a remote-controlled bomb on board a truck in Karachi, then detonated it outside the U.S. consulate, killing eleven people. It can certainly be argued that bin Laden in decline has a real need to prove that he is a more effective terrorist than his many rivals, and that this need may well propel him to try more spectacularly destructive acts. Conversely, rival terrorists may want to prove their own superiority. None of this is particularly comforting.

The warning issue may have had a more significant dimension. Americans had been subject to terrorism for about thirty years before 11 September 2001. It had been treated as a law enforcement issue; sites of terrorist attacks were crime scenes. Evidence was collected with the object of bringing the criminals involved to justice. Some kinds of information were not collected or disseminated because they could not have been used in court or because they were not really needed to secure a conviction. Conversely, prosecutors felt free to use considerable sensitive information in court in order to secure convictions.

The eleventh of September may have been a painful case in point. In May 2001, the FBI seized Zacarias Moussaoui on visa charges. He had spent eight thousand dollars on flying lessons; his instructors were struck by his lack of interest in landings and takeoffs. The French police knew him as an Islamic radical. The agents questioning Moussaoui wanted to examine his computer; in the past, computers had often held operational details of terrorist plots. However, there was apparently no probable cause—a legal point—which would have justified a search of Moussaoui's computer. FBI headquarters barred any such search—a search which might well have uncovered evidence pointing to the 11 September plot. The underlying logic was that there was no point in collecting evidence which could never be used in court, because the purpose of every arrest was to place the subject behind bars. In a wartime situation, however, the logic of police action is often simply to gain intelligence information. Trials and convictions would have been the least of the outcomes desired. For its part, the FBI could say that it had consulted the CIA and the National Security Agency about Moussaoui but that neither had pressed it for access to the computer.

Most important, there was a tendency to avoid seeing individual terrorist acts as connected parts of a larger war. For example, the murder of an Israeli American extremist, Rabbi Meir Kahane, was treated as an individual crime. Later it seemed that it had been plotted by the Egyptian Muslim Brotherhood, which was closely associated with Al Qaeda. The murderer, El Sayyid Nossair, had numerous documents about bomb making, and some of the documents even hinted at the 1993 World Trade Center bombing. Because they were not obviously connected with the Kahane attack, however, they were not translated at the time, and they came to light only after the 1993 bombing. A massacre at the Empire State Building was played down as an independent act of insanity, probably partly because the New York City government had a strong interest in avoiding the impression that the city's tourist attractions were terrorist targets.

If terrorists are criminals, then they ought to enjoy constitutional safeguards, and the issue ought to be whether they can be (or should be) convicted for their crimes. However, if they are soldiers in an anonymous but hostile army, then they should be taken into custody as a preventive measure. There is no point in trying them (soldiers are generally not held accountable for the crimes of their governments), but also no point in releasing them to take up arms again. The situation would have been clarified had the congressional vote in September 2001 been a formal declaration of war, but the United States has not declared war formally since 1941.

The case of supposed "dirty" bomber José Padilla illustrates the problem. He is an American citizen, but it appears that he is also an Al Qaeda soldier. In the latter capacity he is an enemy soldier. Were the United States formally at war, he would clearly also be a traitor, but that is probably not true in a formal legal sense. That is, in law there is no preventive detention, because it is impossible to say that an individual will surely commit a given crime. In war, however, soldiers are captured all the time for preventative detention, because the mere fact that they are soldiers implies that they will commit hostile acts if released. Which is Padilla? How can an Al Qaeda soldier be identified if he wears no uniform? How close is the joint resolution adopted after 11 September to a declaration of war, and against whom?

Congressional investigators were startled at how often the same names and the same documents cropped up as they reviewed a record going back to 1986, the first year that literature from Al Qaeda's predecessor organization, Al Maktab al Khadimat (the Office of Services), appeared in the United States. At the time, it was concerned mainly with supporting the anti-Soviet resistance in Afghanistan (the organization was based in Peshawar, the Pakistani logistics base for such support). Looking back to the 1980s suddenly made sense, because after 11 September it was clear that the operations really were not disconnected; they were attacks made as part of the same protracted war. That war became explicit when bin Laden issued his 1998 fatwa, but obviously it had been going on for some time. Looking back may, however, be confusing. There is a welter of radical Muslim organizations, all of which probably find attacks against Americans attractive. They naturally cooperate from time to time, but that does not mean that any one leader, such as bin Laden, has firm command at all times.

For example, exactly who was behind the 1993 World Trade Center bombing? Ramzi Yousef, who apparently planned the attack, used a passport provided by the Iraqis. Was he working for them? On the other hand, the Arabs who actually executed the attack were closely connected to Omar Abdel-Rahman, a blind refugee Egyptian fundamentalist mullah closely associated with Egyptian fundamentalists—and with Al Qaeda. One interpretation is that, in effect, the Iraqis subcontracted with Al Qaeda for the attack, Al Qaeda providing the disposable foot soldiers (who were caught in the aftermath). Another would be that Yousef was at the same time an Al Qaeda officer and an Iraqi intelligence asset. The Iraqi connection might mean that the Trade Center attack had been instigated by Iraq as revenge for the successful U.S. Gulf War campaign two years earlier.[11] Osama bin Laden himself was named as an unindicted co-conspirator in the World Trade Center bombing, but that meant very little to the U.S. government. Some of those investigating the 2001 intelligence failure pointed back to 1993, when the only U.S. response to the bombing was an investigation and some arrests. There was no interest in probing more deeply, or in attacking the foreign instigators of the plot. More important, there was no sense that the 1993 attack had been an act of war rather than a crime, deserving serious military retaliation.

After all, it must have seemed absurd to credit a subnational organization like Al Qaeda with the ambition to destroy the United States; terrorists just did not have such lofty goals. They were criminals, and it was best to treat them that way instead of further inflating their egos. Wars are for national governments, not for a few rich individuals and their fanatical friends, aren't they?

To make matters more complicated, when Ramzi Yousef was arrested in 1995 in the Philippines, Khalid Sheikh Mohammed, possibly a relative, was indicted as a co-conspirator (he was not caught). Now in U.S. custody, he apparently planned the 11 September attacks as a senior Al Qaeda officer. Does his connection to Ramzi Yousef mean that Al Qaeda was responsible for the 1993 attack, and that the 2001 attack was a way of redeeming failure the previous time?[12]

By 2000, the CIA was monitoring Al Qaeda and similar organizations. It found that fundamentalists planned a meeting in Malaysia. It now appears that the meeting was called after the failure of planned millennium attacks in Seattle and Los Angeles and the assembled terrorists decided then on the 11 September attacks. None of this was, of course, known at the time.

The CIA discovered the identities of those attending the Malaysian meeting. They included Khalid al-Midhar and Nawaq Alhazmi, both of whom would be 11 September hijackers (they also provided logistics support for the entire hijacking). The CIA passed al-Midhar's name and passport number to the FBI, but he managed to enter the United States anyway. However, it did not tell the FBI or immigration officials that al-Midhar had been linked to a suspect in the *Cole* bombing and hence to Al Qaeda. Nor did the CIA pass Nawaq Alhazmi's name to the FBI, nor, apparently, did it pass on the information that he had entered the United States on 15 January 2000. Both men took flight lessons near San Diego. Finally, in mid-August 2001, the CIA placed both men under suspicion and alerted the FBI and immigration officials, but the FBI could not find them.

There was, then, a real possibility that some of the 11 September hijackers could have been caught. It is not clear whether the arrests of a few plotters would have disrupted the plot. Much depends on how long the operation had been in preparation. After 11 September there were reports of mysterious Arabs who took long airline trips and even managed to get into cockpits by dressing in pilots' uniforms. Undoubtedly they were casing the airline system, but equally clearly they did not fly the particular flights later hijacked. Actual choices may have been made only a very short time before the attacks.

There is also some question as to whether all of the hijackers were aware of the plot, or whether some of them thought they were engaging in more conventional hijackings. Bin Laden himself was taped in an Afghan cave boasting about the operation and implying that some of those involved did not realize, until the end, that this was a "martyrdom operation."

By November 2001 it looked as though there had been three distinct groups of hijackers.[13] Mohammed Atta was in command. While in line for takeoff at Logan International Airport on board American Airlines Flight 11, he used his cell phone to tell Marwan al-Shehhi, on board United

Airlines Flight 175, that the plot was on. It is not clear how he communicated with the two other leaders on board aircraft at Newark and at Dulles, although cell phones would have sufficed. The four leaders chose the dates for the attack and actually flew the airplanes into their targets. Also on board were three men responsible for logistic support, for example, renting apartments and distributing cash for expenses. Finally, there were twelve "soldiers" responsible for seizing and maintaining control of the airplanes. Presumably Moussaoui would have been a pilot; one member of the support team substituted for him. One apparent distinction between the leaders and support staff and the soldiers is that the former were fairly ascetic in their habits, whereas the soldiers were happy to indulge in pornography and liquor.

It now appears that a key Hamburg terrorist cell led by Mohammed Atta was radicalized and recruited into Al Qaeda as a group in about 1997 by a German citizen, Muhammad Haydar Zammar, a charismatic mullah of Syrian descent who preached in the Hamburg mosque they attended. Similar mullahs were working other mosques in the West, producing recruits like Briton Richard Reid, who tried to bring down an airliner using explosives hidden in his shoes. American José Padilla, accused of planning to explode a "dirty" (radiological) bomb, was also a Westerner who converted to Islam and was radicalized by a mullah. The great advantage of recruiting in the West was that recruits like Atta already had legitimate backgrounds and thus were unlikely to attract the interest of authorities. They had not been planted in the West as moles.

The Atta group was receptive to Zammar's message because it was already somewhat anti-Western. However, without him it would probably have continued to live reasonably peacefully in Germany, perhaps mouthing but not acting on its sentiments. Thus Zammar was probably the key figure in the plot. He apparently convinced the Hamburg group to offer themselves to Al Qaeda in 1998 or early 1999.

The Hamburg cell included Atta, Shehhi, and Ziad Jarrah, all of whom were 11 September pilots. Others in the cell were Ramzi Binalshibh, Said Bahaji, and Zakariya Essabar, all of whom fled Germany shortly before 11 September. That Binalshibh had failed four times to get a U.S. visa suggests that he was already well known to U.S. authorities. Not to be left out of the plot, he was important in its logistics.

It was probably a Kuwaiti, Khalid Sheikh Mohammed, working directly for Osama bin Laden, who devised the plan to attack the World Trade Center and the Pentagon. Presumably he was aware of other such plans developed earlier, such as Murad's. There is, however, some possibility that the Hamburg cell conceived the plan and Khalid approved it and passed it up the line to bin Laden. If it was Khalid's plan, then one might speculate that other cells were being ordered to hijack other airplanes; if it was Atta's, then most likely only his cell was involved and the plot was limited to the four airplanes. Anecdotal evidence of other nervous Arabs and of box cutters found on other aircraft suggests that there were other cells and other plots, and thus that Khalid was the planner. Bin Laden's own tapes suggest that at the least he reviewed the plan; most likely he or an associate brought together the necessary resources. Those resources included the Saudi "muscle" needed to seize the airplanes. Bin Laden may also have proposed additional personnel. Perhaps, for example, he decided to add a fourth airplane. The fourth pilot, Hani Hanjour, who failed to hit the White House, had been living in the United States since 1996 and was not connected to the Hamburg cell. He may have been a late replacement for Zacarias Moussaoui, a much more senior terrorist and also not a member of the Hamburg cell.[14]

By late 2000, the planners and support personnel were in the United States. The "soldiers," all from Saudi Arabia, began to arrive early in 2001. There is evidence that they had all spent about a year in Al Qaeda training camps; some had told their parents they were going on jihad to Chechnya. All had come from poor villages and had little or no knowledge of English or of the West; they needed the logistics men to fit into American society. Presumably, Al Qaeda considered it too dangerous to try to insert them into American Arab society. Nor were they necessarily anxious to be martyrs. For example, they carried prayers exhorting them to be strong in prison.[15] By way of contrast, Atta carried (and left behind) papers making it clear that he expected to die.

It seems, then, that in this case, and in other cases, Al Qaeda works by supporting chosen plans generated by more or less independent terrorist cells, rather than by ordering operations on a top-down basis. That would explain why so many proposals for terrorist acts fell into U.S. hands in Afghanistan. With them were captured a few senior Al Qaeda officers who proved all too willing to describe (or at least to boast about) other plots. Since they generally could not name those proposing the attacks, these officers in effect helped bin Laden by their testimony. They showed just how determined Al Qaeda was, and they helped dissipate their enemy's resources. Just how many of the described plots were real was never clear. Examples included attacks against such New York landmarks as the Statue of

Liberty and the Brooklyn Bridge, a scuba attack against warships visiting New York, attacks on airliners using smuggled antiaircraft missiles, the use of hijacked oil tanker trucks, and a plot to destroy high-rise apartment buildings by smuggling explosives into rented apartments. Again, the sheer number of disparate warnings, often issued with the note that the source was unconfirmed, negated them. No one could take them seriously, and no one could decide on which ones to act.

On the other hand, careful collation of statements by various detainees (and the use of other intelligence information) appears to have foiled a plot to explode a radiological (dirty) bomb in a U.S. city. First there were directionless warnings that Al Qaeda was interested in just such a weapon; a few months later there were two arrests.

The 11 September hijackers were well aware that any electronic communications could be monitored; they met face-to-face in Las Vegas for final decisions and instructions. Intercepted communications gave no indication of just what the hijackers planned to do. The only real clue that there was an organization in place was a series of money transfers from known Al Qaeda sources, and those transfers were not identified until after the hijackings. Without detailed knowledge of the Al Qaeda financial support system, it is impossible to know whether other teams were in place prior to 11 September; conversely, the lack of statements about such teams suggests that the U.S. government has not identified the elements of that system. Thus, knowledge of fund transfers from the Middle East would not have provided any advance warning or identification of potential enemy agents operating on U.S. soil.

In the end, then, there were indicators pointing to 11 September, but they were by no means so unambiguous that they could easily have been deciphered. The sheer extent of Al Qaeda ambitions, and its practice of selecting from among many operations proposed by lower-level terrorists, made (and makes) prediction of future actions very difficult. Arrests and financial attacks may well preclude attacks, but it will probably always be difficult to be sure of just what plots have been prevented. At least some of the past reported successes against Al Qaeda, therefore, may well refer to abortive proposals rather than to plots close to fruition; others were more obviously realistic.

None of this means it is pointless to deal with Al Qaeda, only that the most profitable targets are probably the sources of money and the central command rather than the deployed terrorist cells, which may well live independently of Al Qaeda itself.

3

The Sword of the Dispossessed

Osama bin Laden is part of a much larger movement, the latest of a long series of attempts to solve a basic Muslim problem. Islam teaches that Mohammed, its prophet, was the last legitimate prophet, after men like Moses and Jesus. As the ultimate version of the great monotheistic religions, surely it will ultimately supersede the two earlier ones, Judaism and Christianity, as well as all pagan religions. The divinely inspired Koran provides guidance in all spheres of life. If, then, Islam is the perfect religion and the perfect guide to conduct, why is the Islamic part of the world so far behind the Western one? What has gone wrong, and how can it be set right? After all, until about 1400, the Muslim world was far advanced over its Western rival in its science and culture. For example, it was the Muslim world, not the West, which was largely responsible for preserving and extending the fruits of Roman and Greek civilization after the collapse of the Roman Empire. At a time when the Christian West was quite bigoted, Islam embraced a very wide variety of opinions, many of which would now be condemned as heresy by a much narrower Islamic clergy.[1]

The Muslim world was also very successful militarily. For example, Muslims in the Middle East, led by their great general, Saladin, reversed the one medieval Western assault on Muslim territory when they ejected the Crusaders from Palestine. They could also claim that even that Western success had been due not to the rising power of the West but to a debilitating thirty-year war between Shia and Sunni Muslims. Later, although they were being pushed out of Spain, Muslims controlled most of the Mediterranean and expanded into Eastern Europe. In 1453 a Turkish Muslim army seized Constantinople, capital of the Eastern Roman Empire, and the last vestige of what had been an extensive Western presence in the Middle East. Perhaps the high point of Muslim power in Europe was the Turkish siege of Vienna in 1683.

From then on, the fortunes of the Muslim world reversed. After the Turkish army was repulsed, it never returned, and Muslim power was clearly on the retreat. By this time Muslim power in Asia was also under attack, Europeans having struck and seized, or at least subjugated, numerous Muslim states around the Indian Ocean. In 1798 the French conquered Egypt, long a center of Muslim power. By the middle of the nineteenth century, Turkey, the center of the Muslim world, was being described as the "sick man of Europe," ripe for dismemberment. Often it seemed to survive mainly because the European powers feared the power vacuum its destruction would bring, not because of any inherent strength. By World War I, European powers ruled tens of millions of Muslims, to the point that a German attempt to promote a Muslim rising was a rational way to attack the British Empire.[2]

The Turkish ruler, the caliph, was nominally the spiritual ruler of all the world's Sunni Muslims (his spiritual authority did not extend to the Shias, most of whom lived in Iran). That did little good in World War I, when Muslim troops fought alongside Westerners to help destroy the Turkish empire.[3] Thus, the Turkish defeat in World War I underlined the failure of Islam. Turkish revival after the war, under Kemal Ataturk, was consciously anti-religious. In effect, Ataturk said that Islam itself was the problem. He abolished the caliphate outright.

Abolition effectively completed the decentralization of Islam. In the absence of a caliph, individual clerics can issue their own religious decrees (fatwas) based on their understanding of Islamic law and tradition. A Muslim decides whether he respects an individual mullah sufficiently to obey his fatwa. Conversely, a leader such as Osama can generally find a sympathetic cleric who can be relied upon to issue the right fatwas. Because such rulings are personal, they can be contradicted by other fatwas, but they cannot be canceled by governments. Thus the Iranian fatwa against author Salman Rushdie could be denounced, ultimately, by the Iranian government, but it could not be canceled. To the extent that terrorists relied on fatwas to gain popular support, then, there was no particular cleric who could be pressured to reverse the problem. Saudi Arabia illustrates the problem. For many years the senior cleric in the country, Abdel Aziz bin Baz, preached allegiance to the king and willingness to abide a foreign presence. He was widely respected for his scholarship. Although he was supported by the Saudi government, there was apparently little or no feeling that he was merely a government mouthpiece. After he died, there was no replacement of similar stature. Suddenly pronouncements, such as fatwas, produced by clerics posed real threats to the Saudi state despite pro-government fatwas produced by officially supported clerics.

From the 1930s on, a new generation of Arab nationalists asked whether Ataturk was right, whether by going secular they could revive the fortunes of their countries. The humiliation of Arab defeat at the hands of the Israelis in 1948 seemed to justify their case; the existing rulers, legitimized by Islamic tradition, were proving failures like the caliph. Examples of the new wave of secularism include Nasser's Egypt, Assad's Syria, and Saddam's Iraq. However, the new secular rulers did no better than the old Islamic ones: the Israelis proved that their attempts at modernization had failed, as they defeated large and expensive Arab armies time and again.

What had gone wrong and what could be done to revive the superiority of the past? This question has given rise to popular conspiracy theories throughout the Middle East and, more generally, to a culture of victimization within Islam.[4] The sense of victimization means more than resentment at past disasters; it also shapes the response to recent events. For example, the United States intervened in Bosnia to save Muslims from destruction. We might imagine that Muslims outside Bosnia would react positively. The gloss put on the intervention, however, has often been that this was yet another attempt to colonize the Muslim world, a direct continuation of the Western colonization of 1948 (i.e., the creation of the state of Israel). Much the same applies to Kosovo. Similarly, Osama bin Laden justified attacks on Americans in Somalia, who were there to feed a starving population, on the ground that the United States was using that mission as a cover to establish dominance in Somalia and Yemen. Given a culture of victimization, any apparent assault on any Muslim country can be and is presented as an extension of the Crusades.

In addition to the secular approach, there have been two Islamic approaches to the question of failure. One was to blame the backward society of many Muslim states. Islam would succeed, it was said, if the society was modernized, a development by no means inconsistent with Islam itself. For example, nothing in Islam required tribal vendettas. Those following this path may be called Islamists. The current Iranian government is a case in point. The other path, typified by Osama, is fundamentalism, an attempt to return to a golden age of piety—and, often, to an earlier way of life described in the Koran. Although both fundamentalists and Islamists claim absolute devotion to the same religion, their views are radically opposed. In particular, they generally differ as to the relation between the House of Islam and the non-Islamic world. An Islamist accepts that the two can live in peace; he is concerned with the future of the House of Islam itself. A fundamentalist will often reject this view, arguing that there can be no real peace in the world as long as Islam does not extend over the whole Earth. Thus there is a constant state of war, or at least a kind of cold war, between the House of Islam and unbelievers. In the context of a perceived state of war, jihad, struggle, which is an explicit duty of all Muslims, becomes a duty actually to fight the unbelievers. Others might argue that jihad is more properly the inner struggle for piety.

The supposed bin Laden tape released in November 2002 gives as a precondition for ceasing terrorist activities that the United States convert to Islam. To a fundamentalist, such a declaration is no more than a statement of the inherent hostility between Islam and the West. To an Islamist, it is a declaration of war which the United States may well consider a rationale for wiping out Muslims—a suicidal gesture, where no such gesture is needed or warranted.

As for the failure of the Turks, many Muslims regarded the Turkish caliphs as illegitimate because they were not of the tribe of the prophet; the Turks had ruled by right of conquest. It might be argued, therefore, that the disasters culminating in World War I did not prove the secularizers' case but the case of those who argued that a lack of proper piety was the problem.

Many in the West tend to lump Islamists and fundamentalists together as radical Muslims; some writers describe all of them as fundamentalists.[5] Neither group is particularly willing to accept other religious groups as equals, and it is sometimes argued that Islam is unique in this intolerance. That is hardly the case: all the universal religions advertise themselves as exclusive routes to truth. Most make it, at least in theory, a religious duty to proselytize and, if possible, coerce others to conversion. All have gone through periods during which the governments backing them have tried to stamp out all alternatives. All have hard-core adherents, including clerics, who preach intolerance. It takes a fully secular state to force those advocating mutually opposed religions to live in peace with each other. Even now it is clear that not all Westerners regard such a state as a preferred situation.

Many Muslims, then, must be furious that their system is not working. They can read about a glorious past but they experience a squalid present. It is against human nature for them to look to themselves and to the sorts of societies they have built for answers. It is infinitely more attractive to look at a foreign enemy as the cause of present misfortune.

The ongoing humiliation represented by the state of Israel is a case in point. In Arab countries the universal explanation for Israeli success against Arab armies is that Israel had a decisively strong backer, the United States. For example, for years Arab apologists spread the fantasy that the Israeli victory of 1967, which created the current occupied territories, was due to U.S. air power, mainly from the Sixth Fleet. The reality, that the Israelis had won by themselves in the face of Egyptian numerical superiority, was too painful to admit. Arab attempts to expel the United States from its relationship with Israel are all based on the idea that, without American backing, the Israelis would soon be defeated. That Israel succeeds in war because it has a modern, well-educated army capable of sophisticated tactics, whereas the antiquated Arab societies cannot create (or risk creating) anything similar, is not acceptable. The initial Egyptian success in October 1973 apparently helped overcome Egyptian humiliation to the point that the Egyptian government could make peace with Israel, but the general sense that Israel symbolizes Western assaults on Islam appears not to have receded.

In fact, the existence of Israel has been extremely useful to the failed governments of the Middle East. Partly because governments are so corrupt, they are unsuccessful economically: people are hungry, and they are angry. As long as they can claim that Israel lies between them and success (e.g., economic success), governments can deflect popular criticism. Americans who began to read the Middle Eastern press (in translation) after 11 September were surprised to discover the depth of hatred expressed against the United States and Israel, particularly in supposedly moderate states such as Egypt and Saudi Arabia. Arab governments allied with the United States clearly feel secure in the expectation that their American partners will listen to them rather than to the extremist press they tolerate. The press, however, breeds powerful anti-Americanism, which a demagogue can exploit. Bin Laden apparently hopes to turn the existing anti-Americanism of the Arab world into direct pressure to destroy Arab governments by associating those governments as closely as possible with the United States.

To mobilize the Muslim population, bin Laden offers a familiar vision of a golden age. Muslims are taught that Mohammed conquered much of the world after having started as a cowherd. His message, his piety, are credited with his great victories. The history of Islam since Mohammed, like that of other religions (and, for that matter, revolutionary movements) can be read as one of bureaucratization and the loss of ideals. As many Muslims are taught their history, for the first forty years the Islamic world was unified under a single caliph descended from Mohammed's family. Then it split, due, one might say, to personal ambition, the fourth caliph being murdered by his rivals. That created the two main Muslim sects, the Shia and the Sunni. Further fragmentation can be ascribed to personal and local ambitions, which created numerous separate Muslim kingdoms and states. A Muslim furious at his humiliation might well imagine that unity would help solve the problem. Just how that unification could be achieved, however, might present serious problems to the rest of the world—as it just has.

The ideas of unification and a return to a golden age are by no means limited to Muslims. For example, one justification for the European Union is that it is a return to a unity broken by the death of Charlemagne, to a time before nation-states began to destroy each other, culminating in two disastrous World Wars. As for the golden age of piety, students of the Old Testament have long remarked that it tells history as a series of rewards for kings showing good religious behavior and disastrous punishments for those who violate the laws of God. The Koran is a product of the same tradition.

The victory of Afghan resistance fighters over the Soviet Union could be presented as a graphic illustration of the idea that Allah crowns piety with success on Earth. The Soviets in Afghanistan could be presented as the latest in a series of Western invaders. To Americans, the Soviets were anything but representative of American culture, but to outsiders, all Westernized infidels might seem virtually identical. Naturally, men like Osama forgot the extent to which the success of the Afghan resistance was due to Western support, not only with materiel like Stinger missiles but also with training and even with reconnaissance satellite data. Sanctuary in Pakistan, ultimately guaranteed by U.S. power, was another important factor. Moreover, the Soviets were not really defeated, in the sense that casualties were inflicted on so one-sided a scale that they had no option but to leave. Rather, as in Vietnam, they saw little point in continuing an expensive war in a place of little or no intrinsic value. Also as in Vietnam, in reaching the point at which war was no longer attractive, they inflicted horrific casualties on their enemies. Even after the Soviets left, their proxy government survived for several years. The Taliban, who eventually won power over most of the country, seem to have attributed their success to their own piety, but support by the Pakistani government was much more significant.

Victory in Afghanistan must have been a heady experience for those, like Osama bin Laden, who had fought there. Finally Muslims had humbled a Western power. Those who had seen the light (in our terms, had been radicalized) had a new trade: guerrilla warfare. In the decades after Afghanistan, they had plenty of opportunities to follow that trade in defense of Islam.

Osama's declared goal of bringing back the golden age by uniting all of the House of Islam under a single pious (read: fundamentalist) government can be read in two complementary ways. One is that Osama is a modest, pious man determined to correct the disastrous course of Muslim history and usher in a golden age. Thus he is widely admired in the Muslim world as an ascetic who has turned his back on worldly wealth. However, he can also be seen as a classic adventurer who hopes to create and rule a Muslim empire. To become emperor of a new pan-Muslim empire would surely be worth some temporary material sacrifice. Osama himself may well be unable to distinguish between his own drive for power and the pietistic rationale of uniting the Muslim world.

The great obstacle to Osama's ambitions is not the United States but the many existing Muslim states. Their governments have their own ambitions and their own desires for survival. They are not in any hurry to dissolve themselves in the name of Muslim unity. One necessary step on the way to empire, therefore, is to prove to the populations of those states that they can and should be overthrown as traitors to the larger cause. Osama needs some way to incite large numbers of Muslims throughout the Muslim world to revolt on his behalf. He apparently saw the West, and particularly the United States, as an effective means to that end.

There is already considerable support for radical religious movements within the Muslim world, at least partly due to the sheer stress of modernization. People rush from farms or even from a nomadic existence to cities in hopes of bettering themselves. They soon discover that life is less than golden in the cities and that survival requires them to change their way of life. Religion, which was the dominant force in their past, is an attractive way of anchoring themselves in what they perceive as urban chaos. Too, the city is far less controlled than the countryside, and it offers numerous attractions. Those coming from an austere religious tradition see the city as inherently grossly immoral and gravitate even more to what seem to them solid truths of the past. Religion can also help overcome the newcomer's sense of inferiority; he may be naive in the ways of the city, but he is superior because of his moral (religious) strength.

Stress seems to be universal when countries industrialize and urbanize. Such modernization often leads to violence against the apparently faceless forces pushing it. For example, in the anti-clerical West of the late nineteenth and early twentieth centuries, anarchism and left-wing revolutionary forces grew and carried out numerous terrorist acts (such as bombings of banks and investment houses). In a more religiously oriented Muslim world, the natural refuge is the mosque, and the imam becomes the focus of those who feel disoriented. Much the same might be said of some radical religious movements in Latin America. In much of the Muslim world, stress has been alleviated by heavy earnings from oil exports. However, whenever those earnings fall, for example because the market price of oil falls, societies feel considerable stress and fundamentalist revolt can be the consequence. Algeria is a case in point.[6] In recent years Saudi Arabia has suffered serious economic problems, although it has not yet encountered anything like the Algerian problem.

The cry for a return to religious power has another important aspect. Most Third World governments are either single-party dictatorships or absolute monarchies. In both cases, key jobs are often awarded on the basis of political loyalty or kinship (which often mean the same thing) rather than competence. As a consequence, many well-qualified individuals either find no jobs at all or find themselves doing the real work while someone with the right contacts receives the appropriate pay. Having learned their trades in a West more committed to merit, they become bitter. In a Muslim country, this rage takes on a religious flavor. Having been raised in a religious context, victims equate justice and morality with their religion; Islam has a large social-justice component. Surely a return to religious law (sharia) will wipe out the corruption and favoritism they see around them in a social and political system created by men.

These considerations probably explain why so many Western-educated technocrats in places like Iran opted for an Islamic state. Eventually many discovered that the mullahs were no more inherently honest than the royals or the party functionaries, but by that time it was too late.

Governments beholden to political loyalists generally find it better to spend their money on their supporters than on the mass of the population. In many countries religious institutions took over the educational and welfare functions which Western governments generally perform. Algeria and Egypt, both of whose governments have fought bloody wars against fundamentalists, are examples. In both countries fundamentalists gained considerable popular following by providing the sorts of social services, such as elementary education and local health care, which the corrupt governments would not stoop to provide. With education, of course, came indoctrination—a lesson understood by many revolutionary movements of the twentieth century. To some extent both governments radicalized their clergy by trying to suppress rising Islamic movements based on power derived from social action.

Muslim kings would seem to be particularly vulnerable to religious opposition, because their legitimacy is based on a Muslim version of the old "divine right" theory once common in the West. The king or emir is seen as Allah's representative on Earth; his power is derived from that connection. Obedience to the king is an extension of the obedience to Allah demanded of every true Muslim. Conversely, if the king is clearly in violation of Allah's will, then he is automatically illegitimate, and indeed it may be the religious duty of Muslims to destroy him. In theory, a secular state would not be subject to similar religious criticism. However, multiparty states have not arisen or survived in most of the Muslim world. Those who overthrew absolute monarchies tended to create dictatorships.

This stress is particularly obvious in Saudi Arabia, an avowedly fundamentalist state whose constitution is literally the Koran. Those opposing the current royal family argue that its members are corrupt hypocrites, violating almost every tenet of Koranic law in private and while out of the country, while imposing it rigorously in public. The Saudi elite thus finds itself in a very uncomfortable position, and it tends to expand the privileges of the Muslim clergy in hopes that they will point popular opinion toward less dangerous enemies. Western observers increasingly suspect that this type of blackmail was paid on too lavish a scale, and that too many young Saudis, some of them wealthy, agree with their mullahs. Osama himself, and many of the 11 September hijackers, can be characterized in this way.

Since the West is both the model and the driving force toward urbanization and industrialization, naturally it is demonized. However, the West is attacked for another reason as well. The imams and their conservative followers are painfully aware that the West offers strong attractions. To immunize Muslims against them, the attraction offered by the West must be negated; the West must be turned into the enemy of all good Muslims.

Thus the Western presence in the Muslim world is entirely unacceptable. The United States is of course the leading edge of that devastating Western culture. Mullahs who backed Osama, for example, preached that the American military presence in Saudi Arabia was part of a larger plot to colonize the Muslim world. Similarly, American assistance to Muslims fighting for their lives in Bosnia and Kosovo became hidden colonization.

The Taliban, the group which sheltered (and was ultimately dominated by) Osama in Afghanistan, emerged from madrassahs, religious schools in Pakistan. Their curriculum was created at Deoband in India, at a school founded after the British crushed the Sepoy Mutiny—a rising by Muslim rulers and by their Muslim (and Hindu) troops—in India in 1858. The stated purpose of the new curriculum was to shield Muslims from the obvious attractions of the West; thus a madrassah education automatically imposed a strong anti-Western bias. The curriculum concentrates heavily on the Koran and often provides very little secular content, so that graduates may have little idea of the character of the Western society they are being taught to reject.

Osama himself came out of the Saudi Wahhabi tradition, which is also anti-Western and preaches a return to piety as a reaction to corruption. For example, when the Saudis (Wahhabis) conquered Mecca in the 1920s, they destroyed the tombs of Mohammed's mother and of his senior followers, on the ground that they detracted from the appropriate emphasis on Mohammed alone, that they represented a retreat from piety. The Wahhabi sect, which originated in the late eighteenth century, justified a jihad against the ruling the Ottoman Turks (which locals considered a foreign movement) who had conquered the Arabian peninsula.[7]

Wahhabism acquired a political coloration in the 1950s and 1960s, when the Saudi government faced challenges from secular nationalist Arab regimes, from Nasser's Egypt and then from Iraq. The Saudi counter to secular nationalism was a religion-based society; Saudi Arabia is unique in the world in using the Koran as its constitution. Conversely, the secular nationalists considered Islamists their mortal enemies. In the Egyptian case, the main Islamic opposition was the Muslim Brotherhood. One of that group's members, imprisoned as part of an unsuccessful attempt to assassinate Nasser, was Sayyid Qutb, the founder of modern political fundamentalism. The Saudis accepted large numbers of exiled fundamentalists, who naturally received employment as imams and religious educators. The latter role was particularly important in a country so oriented toward religion. The exiles in turn tended to politicize Wahhabism. It was their politicized version which the Saudi government exported from the early 1970s on, in what amounted to a counterattack against the forces threatening the kingdom: atheism, Communism, and secular pan-Arabism. Particularly after the Iranian revolution in 1979, the Saudis also saw the export of religious teaching as a way to win a fight for overall hegemony within the Muslim world, their main rivals now being the Iranians. The Saudi government of the time seems not to have appreciated the extent to which its own foundations were being eroded by the change in religious teaching.[8]

In the fight for hegemony within the Islamic world, the Saudis' main weapon has been funding for religious education. After 11 September, Westerners discovered to their surprise that most mosques in their countries were Saudi-funded and used Saudi—which means Wahhabi—textbooks, preaching doctrines that seemed to emphasize hostility toward Christians and Jews.

The dictatorships and absolute monarchies of the Muslim world rigidly control their presses. That complicated the task Osama bin Laden faced, since he could not expect any success he achieved within the Muslim world to be reported there. Events in the West, particularly the United States, are more often reported than many potentially embarrassing local ones. Thus, often those seeking to affect events in the Muslim world see events in the West as the best means of making the necessary impression on their own populations. The fatwa against Salman Rushdie is a case in point. After the Iranian revolution Iran and Saudi Arabia competed for the allegiance of millions of Muslims. The argument was over which was the more pious. The Iranians apparently arranged the fatwa against Salman Rushdie, which made considerable news in the West, specifically to buttress their religious claims within the Muslim world. They made sure that the fatwa was first demanded not somewhere in the Muslim world but in the Muslim community of Bradford, England. Western protests against the fatwa merely proved, to many Muslims, that their enemies particularly disliked the Iranian mullahs, hence legitimized the mullahs.[9] Thus, any hope bin Laden entertained, in 2001, of creating an earthquake in the Muslim world would depend on what he could accomplish in the West.

Osama benefits from another consequence of rigid control of the press. Probably few believe what they read. Rumors have far greater power than they would have in a country with a freer and hence more credible press. Traditional beliefs tend to be more credible, because the controlled press tends not to challenge them. This situation, however, is being challenged by advent of a satellite television news network, Al-Jazeera, based in Qatar. Americans often describe Al-Jazeera as violently anti-American like the rest of the Muslim press; it has been, they say, far too willing to run Osama's videotapes. But Al-Jazeera has also been willing to force its viewers to accept realities which the officially controlled press avoids. For example, some of its viewers are furious that it shows the state of Israel on its maps, and that it in its discussion programs Israel's right to exist is sometimes accepted. As a product of its region, Al-Jazeera had better accept the anti-American context of much Arab opinion if it wants any viewers at all; but by opening up public discussion, it promotes a degree of realism which may, over decades, help change the region.

Bin Laden also faces a problem. Throughout much of the Arab world, the public is aware that it is powerless. People can vent in public at sanctioned demonstrations, but they know that their chants will have little or no effect on events, which will probably not be reported honestly in any case. But to realize his empire, bin Laden needs large numbers of willing soldiers. How can he inspire them to act? Governments, after all, wield enormous power. Relatively few individuals have the taste for revolution.

By September 2001 bin Laden had been fighting, or financing conflict, for about fifteen years, beginning with support for Afghans fighting the Soviets. The youngest surviving son of a wealthy Saudi building contractor, he had been inspired, he later said, by the war in Afghanistan to put his considerable fortune at the service of Islamic fighters. At his college, King Abdul-Aziz University in Jeddah, Osama was deeply influenced by Dr. Abdullah Azzam, the Palestinian who founded the Hamas terrorist organization. Azzam was famous for his motto, "Jihad and the rifle alone: no negotiations, no conferences, and no dialogues." He published a pamphlet arguing that it was every Muslim's personal duty to defend any territory that had ever been Muslim, which meant not only ejecting the Israelis from the Middle East but even retaking Andalusia, the old Muslim kingdom in southern Spain.[10]

Azzam spread his message throughout the Muslim world, often by videotapes; he was apparently a very charismatic speaker. His goal was a pan-Islamic government, but the war in Afghanistan offered a more immediate opportunity. In 1982–84 he founded the "Afghan bureau," Maktab al Khidmat lil-mujahidin al-Arab (MaK), to support Afghan fighters against the Soviets. Bin Laden became his disciple as well as his main financier and fundraiser. Enthusiastic but probably also naïve, bin Laden reportedly has traveled only to Syria, Sudan, Afghanistan, Pakistan, and the gulf states; he may well have little or no understanding of the West.

In the 1980s the Saudi government was eager to support the war against the Soviets. Fortunately, another of Osama's mentors was Prince Turki al-Faisal, the Saudi intelligence chief. As MaK fund-raiser, bin Laden worked with the Saudi government, with the Pakistani Inter-Services Intelligence (ISI) organization, with the Egyptian government, and with the Muslim Brotherhood fundamentalist network. He also recruited many Arab fighters for the Afghan War. At this stage Osama apparently had no larger political outlook; he was interested mainly in helping the Afghans. He contributed to all the resistance fighters but apparently favored two of the more conservative ones, Gulbuddin Hekmatyar and Rabb al-Rasoul Sayyaf. Hekmatyar was the favored instrument of the Pakistani ISI; Sayyaf had formed a Wahhabi party (that is, he favored the Saudi version of Islam) and, therefore, received considerable direct Saudi aid.

Bin Laden's actual participation in the Afghan War appears to have been limited. He was widely reported to have provided money and to have provided (and possibly operated) heavy construction equipment in support of the rebels. He built a fortified camp at Jaji, which was besieged by a small Soviet force for about a week in April 1987. Bin Laden's force withdrew after about a dozen of the initial fifty Arabs had been killed. This defeat was converted, at least in the Arab press, into a victory, on the theory that never before had the Afghan Arabs held their ground for any length of time. It may have been bin Laden's sole experience of combat, and he often embellished it afterward.[11]

Bin Laden probably first tasted power at this time. He seems not to have been a very charismatic leader, but it was far more important that he provided necessary cash and probably also construction equipment to enlarge and fortify caves which the warriors could use as refuges.

About 1985 or 1987, in connection with his Afghan work, bin Laden met Ayman al-Zawahiri, an Egyptian often described as the brains of the Al Qaeda organization.[12] Al-Zawahiri apparently inspired him with the idea of a pan-Islamic empire, presumably seeing in Osama the source of funds he needed. As a fundamentalist Muslim, bin Laden was well aware of the golden age of unified Islam. He probably began to see himself as a likely future caliph—the spiritual and temporal ruler of that unified realm—even though he was not of the tribe of the prophet, which is a traditional requirement to be caliph. Many experts on terrorism attribute to al-Zawahiri the insight that it would be impossible to overthrow Muslim governments without first attacking their source of support, the United States. Hence the 1998 fatwa against Americans, issued by Osama but likely inspired by al-Zawahiri. In the late 1980s bin Laden created what amounted to a foundation to finance such fighters—and, soon, Islamic terrorists—called Al Qaeda, "the base." Given the goal supplied by al-Zawahiri, bin Laden made his "Afghan Arabs" the fighting core of Al Qaeda, which was formed about 1988–89.[13]

One consequence of al-Zawahiri's importance to bin Laden and his organization is that later many Egyptians joined Al Qaeda, reportedly to the discomfort of the Saudis who were the original core of the organization—and who had fought in Afghanistan. Another measure of al-Zawahiri's power over bin Laden was that his own lieutenant, Mohamed Atef, became both an Al Qaeda military commander and bin Laden's personal security chief. He was also bin Laden's brother-in-law. When Atef was killed in Afghanistan, he was succeeded by another Egyptian, Sayf al-Adl, a former Egyptian Special Forces colonel.[14] According to the 1998 U.S. indictment of bin Laden, Al Qaeda merged with Egyptian Jihad. However, given the dominant role of the Egyptians, it might better be said that the Egyptians took over Al Qaeda, seeing in it the resources they needed to win their war against the Egyptian government.[15]

The Afghan resistance, particularly the element with whom the Afghan Arabs fought, was tied closely to the Pakistani army and its ISI intelligence arm. Its personal patron was General Zia ul-Haq, who had established an Islamic dictatorship in Pakistan in 1977. General Zia died in a 1988 aircraft bombing, and Pakistan held new elections, which gave Benazir Bhutto the premiership. The Islamists considered her an enemy. Among bin Laden's first projects was an attempt to unseat her.[16]

Osama returned to Saudi Arabia in 1989 after the Soviet withdrawal from Afghanistan and claimed that he helped the Saudi government create its first jihad group to oppose the Communist-oriented South Yemeni government, in what the Saudis probably hoped would be a replay of the Afghan operation.[17] Soon the Iraqis invaded Kuwait. The Saudis welcomed U.S. and other foreign troops to help defend them against a further Iraqi attack. Bin Laden later claimed that he was profoundly angered by the Saudi decision to welcome U.S. and other foreign troops to fight the Gulf War and then enforce the peace terms. He argued that Saudi Arabia was a particularly sensitive place because it contained two of the holiest sites in Islam, Mecca and Medina, the objectives of Muslim pilgrims. Non-Muslims were never permitted in those cities. Osama took this stricture further. He saw the foreign incursion as the first time since the beginning of Islam that foreign troops had been permitted in Arabia, a direct contravention of Mohammed's dying declaration that there should be no religion but Islam in Arabia. As an alternative to foreign troops, Osama claimed that he had proposed raising a force of Muslim volunteers similar to that which had won in Afghanistan. The Saudis apparently regarded the offer as ludicrous.[18] As for Osama's larger claim, non-Muslims had been working in Saudi Arabia for years, and limited numbers of U.S. troops had been stationed in the kingdom since the mid-1940s at bases such as Dharan.

Osama may have been naive, but it is more likely that he was looking for a rationale to overthrow the Saudi government. His rather large ego may have been offended when he was not lionized upon his return from Afghanistan; surely he had been the conquering hero.[19] Moreover, unlike most of the Saudi elite, he could claim to have followed through on his religious principles, living a virtuous and modest life rather than the typical dissipated one. Again, he was likely infuriated that the Saudi establishment did not practice what it preached, that his form of religious virtue brought no real rewards.

While pressing his case against the Saudi royal house, bin Laden recognized the power of religious education as a way of building a following. He spent much of his own money supporting madrassahs, and thus gained the support of many mullahs who described him as a pious man. At least in theory, those educated at schools he backed came to associate him with the movement to revive Islam.

Osama announced that the Saudi royal house was illegitimate and should be replaced. The Saudi government raided his compound near Jedda, and he decided to leave the country. He obtained permission to go to Pakistan but went instead to Afghanistan, which was in a state of civil war. Rather than remain, he went to the Sudan, which had a fundamentalist government. Once there, he managed to extract most of his fortune from Saudi Arabia, before its government froze his assets. In the Sudan, Osama apparently sought favor with the country's rulers by investing in local businesses. It is by no means clear that he was particularly successful, since by 1994 he seems to have been badly short of cash.[20] In 1994 the Saudis stripped him of his citizenship. That same year, there was an attempt to assassinate him.[21]

There were plenty of wars in which the fundamentalist Muslims bin Laden recruited could fight. Even before the Soviet state formally disintegrated, Muslims were fighting Christians in Nagorno-Karabakh in the southern Soviet Union. Later, Muslims fought in what had been Soviet Central Asia, in places like Uzbekistan. They were reacting in part to another humiliation, the overthrow of the Central Asian Emirates by the Czarists in the mid-nineteenth century, when the Russian Empire was on the march toward Afghanistan and even India beyond it. There were other post-Soviet battlefields, too, in places like Chechnya.

When the Soviet threat which had helped hold it together dissipated, Yugoslavia began to disintegrate. Soon Orthodox Christians were "ethnically cleansing" Muslims in Bosnia. Would the Muslim powers stand by and see their brothers destroyed? Was the real problem that the Bosnian Muslims were not orthodox enough?

Further east there was a Muslim insurgency in Sinkiang, which had once been called Chinese Turkestan. Muslims were also fighting in the Philippines, where they were a minority, for control of some of the southern islands. These islands had once been part of a Muslim empire embracing what is now Indonesia and Malaysia. The old dispute between Thailand and Malaysia, centering on Muslim provinces incorporated into Buddhist Thailand (and on Buddhist provinces incorporated into Muslim Malaysia) generated its own insurgents.

If indeed Allah was smiling on the pious, these wars could be seen as the opening for Al Qaeda and like-minded organizations to create the long-desired unitary fundamentalist state.

The fundamentalist Sudanese government held an Islamic People's Congress in 1995, during which bin Laden met with leaders of groups from Pakistan, Algeria, Tunisia, and Palestine (Islamic Jihad and Hamas). At about the same time, he reportedly sought a tactical alliance with Hezbollah, meeting its security chief, Imad Mughniyeh. The alliance was tactical because the two groups were opposed, Hezbollah being a Shia organization backed by Iran and Al Qaeda a Sunni organization. Al Qaeda personnel went to southern Lebanon to learn from Hezbollah how to destroy large buildings. When the Khobar Towers were bombed in 1996 and the two African embassies were bombed in 1998, investigators initially thought they were dealing with a Hezbollah operation. Al Qaeda, however, has been blamed for both attacks, which suggests that Al Qaeda had convinced Hezbollah to train its personnel.[22]

By 1996, there was evidence linking bin Laden to the 1993 bombing of the World Trade Center. Early that year, the CIA set up a special bin Laden unit.

In May 1996, in hopes of improving its position with the United States, the Sudanese government ejected bin Laden and al-Zawahiri. By this time both France and the United States were pressing the Sudanese to arrest bin Laden. When they finally did, the Sudanese offered him to the United States, but the U.S. government demurred, claiming that it had no grounds on which to try and imprison him. President Clinton later said that this choice was the worst mistake of his administration. It can be traced in large part to the then-current U.S. perception that the problem was state-sponsored terrorism, the implication being that without a state behind him, no terrorist could do much damage. Thus the Sudanese decision to eject bin

Laden, already identified by the State Department as a major financier of terrorism, seemed at the time to have been a triumph rather than the fumble it turned out to be.[23] At least two other later possibilities were not followed up.

The U.S. government failed to convince the Saudis to take bin Laden. Instead, he was permitted to fly to Afghanistan, where he rejoined the Taliban. He formed a unit of Arab fundamentalists, the 055 Brigade, which ultimately became a kind of praetorian guard for the Taliban regime. He also continued to plot against the United States. The flight from the Sudan may have been costly, because the business ventures had not really been very successful and the Sudanese government failed to pay its debts to bin Laden.[24]

For the moment, however, the Taliban were far from pleased with bin Laden, and his flight to Afghanistan was probably a considerable embarrassment to him. He tried to present it as equivalent to Mohammad's hegira (flight) from Mecca to Medina, presaging his ultimate victory eight years later.[25] To gain support in the Muslim world, he gave spectacular press conferences in Afghanistan—without gaining any permission from the ruling Taliban. A Pakistani journalist recalled a May 1998 conference as "total theater." For example, bin Laden surrounded himself with armed bodyguards who turned out, on examination, to be, in effect, hired Afghan extras (as the journalist learned, because he and they spoke the same Pashto language). Even the drama of being smuggled into Afghanistan and then driven around for five hours was a fraud, as the journalist realized that the site of the interview was very close to the border. The ruling Taliban learned of the press conference only from a BBC broadcast. Their leader, Mullah Omar, apparently asked how bin Laden could hold a press conference without his permission: "There is only one ruler. Is it me or Osama?"

Yet by this time bin Laden's Afghan Arabs were more and more important to the Taliban in their fight against the other Afghan factions. There are also reports that bin Laden had personally advised Mullah Omar on how to centralize his government. It is not, then, entirely clear whether Omar thought that he could dispense with bin Laden and his Afghan Arabs. On the other hand, the record of pre-Soviet Afghan governments, such as that of Mohammed Daoud, suggests that rulers thought they could dispose of supporters who had previously thought themselves crucial—and that sometimes they were destroyed instead.

For bin Laden, the key question was always how to mobilize support within the Muslim world. He found that few in the Middle East really cared about U.S. troops in Saudi Arabia. He therefore added a far more emotive goal: evicting the United States and Israel from the Middle East. Since that was already a popular rallying cry, he could be assured that many would cheer any success he enjoyed.

Bin Laden's next problem was the crucial one. He needed active adherents. One way to get them was to prove to the many who dislike or hate the United States that he was the most effective enemy of this country. He was probably most appreciative when the Clinton administration named him the number one terrorist after the attacks on the U.S. embassies in Africa in 1998. By this time he had already procured a fatwa to the effect that it was lawful, even virtuous, for Muslims to kill Americans anywhere in the world. The failed, even farcical, American missile attack on Afghanistan in 1998 could be interpreted as proof both of U.S. weakness and of Allah's favor to Osama, since he survived.

The embassy attack did not attract enough Muslims to bin Laden's cause, and, moreover, it did not do nearly enough to dramatize the conflict between the United States (or the West) and the Muslim world. Bin Laden sought a war in which the support of, say, the Saudis for the Americans would clearly amount to treason against Islam, hence to delegitimization. That in turn would justify revolt under his banner.

To this end Osama designed attacks sadistic enough to inspire a violent enough counterattack to prove his point. This was quite different from both the usual terrorist attack and from the American interpretation of the attacks. Terrorists typically try to publicize their cause to attract adherents. They are aware, however, that if they go beyond a limit, they will attract a counterstrike too devastating to survive. For example, governments which may otherwise offer them sanctuary will feel compelled to give them up. Bin Laden's 11 September attacks clearly went well beyond any acceptable level of violence, but they made sense if they were *intended* to excite American reaction.

Americans assumed that bin Laden (or whoever had ordered the attacks) was interested mainly in doing the maximum amount of harm. For example, the World Trade Center attacks could be read as economic warfare on the theory that business confidence would not long survive mass deaths in the financial sector. It seemed that the anthrax attack must have similar origin, that it was attractive as a means to sow panic. Many wrote or spoke of the vulnerabilities inherent in a modern, open, computer-oriented society. When would bin Laden's hackers destroy the Internet?

Undoubtedly those proposing various attacks against the United States are aware of our vulnerabilities. Yet Osama, as paymaster and selector of initiatives, must know that his resources, particularly his human resources, are limited. He depends on moles in Western societies. All are potentially vulnerable to the attractions of those societies, so of necessity all have limited reliable lifetimes. Many may be detected or otherwise foiled. Each operation must make bin Laden's point, both to the enemy (the United States) and to the Muslim audience. Although a subtle attack like a raid on the Internet might well disturb Americans, it would have little or no impact in the relatively unsophisticated Middle East. There, the dramatic image of two burning, collapsing buildings in the center of the enemy's territory was what counted. It would seem to follow that bin Laden is likely to expend his limited resources on those attacks which both enrage Americans and are most visible in the Muslim world: spectacular bombings of well-known places, preferably killing large numbers of American civilians. He is less likely to expend energy on subtler attacks such as biological ones or computer assaults. Because Osama's followers are unlikely to share his detailed objectives, they probably do not feel similar restraints. That is why biological-weapons laboratories were found in Afghanistan; some of the Taliban said that they had become interested in this form of attack only after reading (on the Internet) that the U.S. government found it frightening.

Bin Laden's expectations of the outcome of 11 September apparently proved incorrect. His attacks did inspire many to dance in the streets of the Muslim world, but they were not willing to chance insurrection. Dictatorships and absolute monarchies are well aware of the dangers of runaway public opinion, and their police tend to be very effective.

Bin Laden did finally get the violent American reaction he sought. However, once the United States began to strike back, it became obvious that backing bin Laden could be dangerous. Perhaps piety alone was not enough to deflect bombs and shells. The crowds in the streets dissipated. Sales of t-shirts celebrating bin Laden fell off dramatically. Moreover, it was soon clear that, thanks largely to its ability to project power by sea, the United States did not rely on bin Laden's target regimes to help it suppress him. The Saudis could easily affirm that no Americans had jumped off from their soil to fight in Afghanistan.

Accepting 11 September as a catalytic attack carries a chilling implication. After the attack, the U.S. government adopted a very careful attitude, blaming only the terrorists and specifically avoiding placing any blame on Muslims as a whole. From bin Laden's perspective, it refused to take the bait he offered. Bin Laden may feel that his bait was not attractive enough, that is, that his attack was not outrageous enough to snap U.S. patience and bring on the sort of apocalyptic war he imagines he wants. His experience of the world outside Saudi Arabia and Afghanistan being limited, he probably had little idea just how effective a U.S. attack against Afghanistan might be. After all, the Soviets had tried for a decade and yet failed to defeat the Afghan resistance.

Bin Laden probably feels that an even more outrageous attack is needed to catalyze the desired all-out war. Whether he or his friends can carry out such an attack remains, of course, to be seen. It is natural for our own security organizations, which failed to predict the 11 September attacks, to characterize them as brilliantly sophisticated; otherwise, they look even worse. But for all their horrific impact, the attacks were not so very difficult to carry out, given the poor pre-attack state of domestic air security. The attackers did need some fairly basic knowledge of aircraft, but it seems that they felt insecure. Computer flight simulators, which can be bought for a few dollars, probably would have taught them most of what they needed; why go to flight schools? Someone had to know that airliners are tracked over most U.S. airspace using transponders, and that these devices can be turned off from the cockpit, but even that is not particularly sophisticated knowledge. The hijackers did enjoy a considerable measure of luck in that all of their airplanes took off within a few minutes of each other. Had the usual delays been at work, one of the attacks might have occurred before the other airliners even took off. All U.S. airliners might then have been grounded after the first attack, sparing the other targets and the other passengers. As it was, the airliners nearly stalled out on their final tight turns into their targets. There may, then, have been sophisticated planning involving networks of sleeper agents, but the entire gruesome attack may also have been the work of a very few agents. Does bin Laden have hundreds or thousands of followers who want the chance to die, or does he have only a few dozen fanatics? Surely the odds are that there are few with the necessary skills.

The other side of the equation is that bin Laden's immediate objective is to get the United States to kill very large numbers of Muslims. It would be well worth pointing out to the Muslim world that bin Laden is not so much an enemy of the United States as a potential mass murderer (indirect, to be sure) of those he claims to champion.[26] In his view, of course, mass deaths are entirely acceptable as a means of achieving salvation, but the likely dead may have different views.

The attack on the United States is a particularly vicious example of a catalytic tactic which may be more widespread, and older, than we imagine. By definition, a catalyst advances a chemical reaction but is not itself affected or exhausted. Thus bin Laden likely imagines that he can bring about a massive racial war which will not destroy him personally but will create the conditions he seeks for gaining further power. This is not a new idea.[27]

Bin Laden is probably intelligent enough to doubt that destroying the World Trade Center would destroy the United States. He may just have been clever enough to guess that, once terrible crimes had been committed, the United States would feel compelled to strike back. Many American commentators have quoted Japanese admiral Isoroku Yamamoto, after Pearl Harbor, to the effect that the Japanese attack had awakened a sleeping giant. They have seen in the current mobilization proof of bin Laden's miscalculation. However, it is possible that bin Laden counted on exactly this reaction to his horrific crime, and indeed that the measured U.S. response disappointed him.

Just how important was or is Osama bin Laden? His money certainly made it possible for a variety of fundamentalist terrorists to realize plans which otherwise would have been unaffordable, such as the 11 September spectacular. There is some question as to just how inspirational he is versus how badly various terrorists wanted to flatter him enough to finance them. It is also quite possible that as a relatively unimportant figure in the 1980s, he gained real prominence only after President Clinton named him the world's number one terrorist after the 1998 attacks in Africa.

In effect, bin Laden's Al Qaeda is a holding company for numerous local movements, providing support for members carrying out an Islamic terrorist offensive against the West and anyone else bin Laden and his associates deem anti-Islamic. Thus Osama and Al Qaeda are mortal enemies to many Muslim governments, including that of Saudi Arabia; he deems them "takfir," anathema, because they are inherently illegitimate. Bin Laden's direct threat to the Saudi state led the Saudis to make several attempts to deal with him. In 1999 it asked the Taliban to turn him over, dead or alive (preferably dead). The Taliban professed themselves furious, ejected the two Saudi envoys, and closed the Saudi consulate in Kabul.[28] The Saudis still considered Osama a major threat. At about the same time, the CIA was reportedly contracting with a Pakistani hit team to kill bin Laden.

For its clients, Al Qaeda was not merely a source of support; it was a way of focusing effort. Support would be forthcoming for specific initiatives deemed worthy of it. That is why so many videotapes describing proposed terrorist attacks were found in Afghanistan. Although it has links with numerous Islamic revolutionary groups, Al Qaeda is apparently closest to Al-Gama'a al-Islamiya and Islamic Jihad in Egypt and to Harakat ul-Ansar (HUA) in Kashmir. Bin Laden's closest advisor, al-Zawahiri, is an Egyptian, and HUA is the Pakistani-backed fundamentalist terrorist organization active in Kashmir.

Al Qaeda is active around the world. As an indication of the sweep of Al Qaeda interests, in March 2002 a Russian newspaper, *Komsomolskaya Pravda,* published some details of satellite (Iridium) phone calls credited to bin Laden's number prior to 11 September. The 1,100 calls listed added up to 2,200 minutes of air time, which suggests that most of them were short, perhaps coded. The greatest number (238) were to the United Kingdom, the second greatest to Yemen (221), which bin Laden may have used as an intermediate communications center. A tenth were to Iran. Other calls were to Azerbaijan, Pakistan, Saudi Arabia, Sudan, and Egypt, probably in that order of frequency. None, at least on this telephone, was to the United States, which would make sense, since bin Laden would have suspected that any direct communication with the terrorist cells in the United States might have revealed them. Too, he was probably using other communications channels, such as e-mail. The Iridium phone, for which several years of service had been paid, was not used at all after 11 September; its number was revealed by an Indian newspaper early in March 2002.

Al Qaeda was designed as a decentralized organization, which made it difficult to attack in conventional military terms. Like a legitimate transnational company, it had, in effect, no central office, no physical place the destruction of which would eliminate it, although it has been damaged badly by the loss of sanctuary in Afghanistan. However, like all other activities, it needed cash to operate. Exactly how much is not clear, but cash needs clearly rise if the organization has to fight or actively protect its operatives, as in the aftermath of the Afghan disaster. Bin Laden began with a personal fortune inherited from his father, a very successful building contractor.[29]

Al Qaeda obtained its financial nourishment in four ways. One was legitimate commerce. Bin Laden apparently had business talent, and he created or subsumed companies in fields as disparate as pharmaceuticals and shipping. His legitimate companies could, in turn, be used to support his terrorism. For example, ships owned by his companies could transport materiel. In December 2001, the Royal Navy detained the merchant ship *Nisha,* possibly owned by a bin Laden company, which was thought to be

carrying "weapons of mass destruction," presumably chemical or biological, to be used against Britain.[30] Although the ship was ultimately released
after a search, the suspicion remained that as many as twenty of bin
Laden's ships would be used to attack the West. As in much of the commercial world, it was difficult to be sure of just which ships bin Laden controlled through a network of holding companies.

Second, bin Laden could convince like-minded Muslims to contribute
to the cause. For example, he matches sources of support, particularly in
Saudi Arabia and the Persian Gulf states, with those, such as "sleepers,"
needing money to carry out operations. After 11 September the U.S. government attacked terrorist finance on the theory that it was the one identi-
fiable part of the enemy machine. In so doing they tried to close down numerous purportedly charitable Muslim foundations in the West. Some had
begun as relief foundations to help the vast numbers of refugees created by
wars in places like Afghanistan and the former Yugoslavia. The line between relief and the support of "freedom fighters"–cum-terrorists was
never entirely clear.

Third, Al Qaeda itself constituted a real threat to many governments in
the Muslim world. To the extent that bin Laden attracted respect among
Muslims, he could achieve results by declaring any particular Muslim government illicit or anti-Islamic. Many Muslim governments feel relatively
weak, so the threat was real. Note, however, that the degree to which it was
credible depended on just how much prestige bin Laden could amass. His
successes against the West thus generated further influence and capital;
conversely, a major failure might radically reduce the threat he posed. As
long as he enjoyed prestige, he and his associates could exact what
amounted to tribute or blackmail: a government which paid enough would
not be attacked. This was not a new idea; the various Palestinian organizations had financed themselves for years in just this way, the Saudis being
among the major payers.

Also, Al Qaeda became involved in the civil war in Sierra Leone, apparently primarily to obtain diamonds.[31] Money could be raised by trading
them, or they could be used to launder money. Diamonds are, after all, the
classic portable form of wealth. In this Al Qaeda copied other terrorists. For
example, it has been reported that Hezbollah and other groups transferred
home millions of dollars obtained by selling Congolese diamonds. Al Qaeda
also depended heavily on the other great convertible commodity, gold.[32]

To further complicate any attempt at tracing back money to bin Laden,
he could ask some Muslim charity in the West to support one of his

terrorists, for example, with a no-show job on the promise that he would help it later.

Reportedly bin Laden's financial structure is modeled on that of the Bank of Commerce and Credit International (BCCI), founded by Pakistanis and largely paid for by the rulers of the United Arab Emirates. BCCI was used by the CIA to move money to Afghan freedom fighters, but it also harbored terrorist funds and laundered drug money. It collapsed in 1991.[33]

The idea that terrorism is the route to a new unified Islamic world ruled by a new caliph is not new and will not die with bin Laden. For example, another fundamentalist terrorist organization, Abu Sayyaf, headed by a Filipino, Khadaffy Janjalani, is trying to create a Muslim empire beginning in Malaysia, the Philippines, and Indonesia. It has not done nearly as well as Al Qaeda, however, because it has not yet found a failed state to hijack. But if bin Laden does not survive the trek out of Afghanistan, it or some equivalent, may be the next beneficiary of his backers.

4

The Afghan Base

Afghanistan has been a battleground for centuries. During the nineteenth and early twentieth centuries, for example, it was the venue of the "Great Game," the struggle between czarist Russia and Britain for dominance in Central Asia and thus for access to India and, to a lesser extent, to China. The British tried and failed to take the country over, suffering badly in the process. The 1979 Soviet invasion was seen, probably incorrectly, in the West as another move in a more modern version of the game, the ultimate Soviet goal being direct access to the Persian Gulf and its vital oil. Probably the greatest single error all the powers involved in Afghanistan made was to imagine it as an entirely unified country with a government which could deliver its entire population and area. The reality seems often to have been more local or tribal.

The country is split along ethnic and linguistic lines, each group extending across the border into one or more neighboring states. However, ethnic groups overlap; only in the Pashtun south is the country mono-ethnic. In other areas the country can be described more as geographically split.[1] There are also important personal and political divisions within the ethno-linguistic groups. Overall, there is a real national identity, which makes Afghanistan different from, say, the former Yugoslavia. No group in Afghanistan seems to advocate separation to join its brethren across the border (although some do advocate absorbing areas across the border into a greater Afghanistan). National identity helps explain why Afghans have resisted foreign invasion, as in several celebrated Anglo-Afghan wars, the last in 1919, and as in the Soviet invasion and occupation from 1979 onward. In turn, the two twentieth-century wars helped strengthen a sense of Afghan nationhood.[2]

For centuries Afghanistan was part of the Persian (that is, Iranian) Empire. Afghans tend to define their state in opposition to Iran. Resistance to

Iran ties neatly with the Sunni form of Islam practiced in most of Afghanistan, which is opposed to the Shia form dominant in Iran.

Probably the most important ethnic groups are the Pashtuns (Pathans) in the south, many of whom live in northern Pakistan; the Hazaras (ethnically Mongol Shias) in the West; and the Uzbeks, Turkmen, and Tajiks in the north, each of which is allied to those in the relevant former Soviet republic: Uzbekistan, Turkmenistan, Tajikistan—the former republics of Soviet Central Asia. Hatred between members of different groups is an important factor in Afghan politics and warfare. For example, at times Sunni Pashtuns have massacred Shia Hazaras, whom they despise. However, not all splits are along ethnic lines, as at times Sunnis from different groups have united against the Shi'ite Hazaras.

Within an ethnic group, individual loyalty is generally to the tribe, not even to the entire ethnic group. The tribes certainly share an identity, but they are also independent of one another. To the extent that national governments have existed, they have been coalitions among tribes. Too, tribal loyalties and feuds are extremely important. The Soviets, for example, discovered that the key factions within the Afghan Communist Party had ethnic rather than ideological roots.[3] Any attempt to bring the entire country under a unified administration would encounter such problems.

This sort of division is common. In theory, those creating nation-states in Europe avoided the problem by drawing boundaries congruent with ethnic ones, but in reality many European boundaries cross ethnic lines, with serious consequences, such as the disasters of post-Tito Yugoslavia. Notoriously, in many places in the Third World colonial governments drew boundaries across tribal homelands, so that those boundaries in no way corresponded to ethnic or tribal feelings or loyalties. Often those thrown together from different tribes fight each other; tribal or ethnic warfare has been particularly prominent in Africa. In the case of Afghanistan, there was no colonial master. Instead, the boundaries were set by the outer limits of British, Russian, Persian (Iranian), and to some extent Chinese expansion through ethnic homelands.

Given this divided ethnicity, events in Afghanistan automatically resonate across its borders. Anyone who can unite Afghanistan, for example, will have claims on the areas occupied by their ethnic relatives across the border, the most important case probably being "greater Pashtunistan." At the very least, Afghanistan can become a sanctuary for disaffected members of those groups. Conversely, each of Afghanistan's neighbors automatically has an intense interest in who governs the country and in how that government operates.

The Pashtuns are the largest ethnic group, about 40 percent of the population in 2001, and have been dominant since the formation of the Afghan state in the eighteenth century. The Pashtuns (the "hill tribes" to British writers of the past) are one of the largest and most cohesive tribal groups in the world. In their culture, political legitimacy derives from a great council (*loya jirga*). The main code of conduct is the largely unwritten Pustunwali (which often contradicts Islamic Sharia law). Major concerns are honor, revenge, and the requirement to show hospitality to those seeking it. The Taliban cited the latter as a reason for resisting U.S. demands to turn Osama over. The United States sponsored a *loya jirga* as a way of building a legitimate post-Taliban Afghan government. The main drawback to this approach is that the *loya jirga* is a specifically Pashtun concept, possibly not applicable to the other tribes. The sense of honor (which precludes "turning the other cheek" when insulted) may cause major problems in cases in which American aircraft mistakenly attacked Afghan civilians. Much of the resistance to the Soviets was reportedly due to the sense that their plan to nationalize Afghan land amounted to theft, which Afghans were honor-bound to avenge at any cost.

In Pashtun legend, Pashtuns are descended from Afghana, a grandson of the biblical King Saul. He had three children, Sharkbun (from whom the Abdalis are descended), Kharshbun (from whom the Yusufzais are descended), and a daughter, Zohah (from whom the Ghilzais are descended). Each tribe comprises numerous subtribes. The line through the daughter automatically makes the Ghilzais (about 4.4 million) less suitable for national leadership. The first Afghan king was an Abdali, Durr-i-Durran (the Pearl of Pearls). His tribe was renamed the Durrani after him. Durranis ruled Afghanistan from 1826 through 1978; the last king, Zahir Shah, is a Durrani. In 2001, there were about three million Durranis in Afghanistan. Hamid Karzai, the current president, is a Durrani, of the Populazi subtribe. The Ghilzai, however, dominated the Democratic Republic of Afghanistan—as well as the Mujeheddin resistance to the Communists. Najibullah, the last Communist ruler, was a Ghilzai. Reportedly the Ghilzai have largely been detribalized.

More Pashtuns live across the border in Pakistan than in Afghanistan, and the desire for a unitary Pashtun state is an important theme in Afghan politics. Yet it is also true that there is a sense of Afghan nationhood, and that Pashtuns in Afghanistan do differentiate themselves from their cousins across the border. The border, the Durand Line, was drawn by the British government of India in 1893, after the Second Anglo-Afghan War (1878–80).[4] It cut off most of the Pashtuns, the British motive apparently being to tame Afghanistan by first civilizing those Pashtuns who were now under their rule. By 1901 the attempt had been abandoned, and the Pashtuns in India granted considerable autonomy. They were still considered dangerous. All of those movies about the British in India and the "northwest frontier" are really about the Pashtuns.

This situation continued when India was partitioned and the tribal lands were incorporated in Pakistan. Afghans do not regard the line as legitimate. For example, Afghanistan voted against Pakistani membership in the United Nations on the ground that Pakistan was illegally occupying Afghan territory.[5] Conversely, the Pakistan government tried to convince the Taliban, which it supported, to accept the Durand Line. Despite their considerable dependence on the Pakistanis, the Taliban refused, because to have accepted would have marked them in many Afghan eyes as tools of a foreign power. To further complicate matters, the treaty setting up the Durand Line expired in 1993.

From a Pakistani perspective, Pashtun nationalism was always a threat. Pakistan has other restive minority groups, such as the Baluchis and Sinds. In 1971 one of those groups, the Bengalis, managed to secede and turn East Pakistan into a separate country, Bangladesh. That made the Pakistanis more determined to control their other minorities. For example, Pakistan and Iran cooperated in a war against Baluchis on their mutual border. Any major victory by the Pashtuns would naturally encourage separatism. The formation of a Pashtun state (greater Pashtunistan) or the rise of a dominant Afghan nationalism would probably destroy Pakistan.

Historically, Punjabis have dominated the Pakistani state and its army, so Pashtuns have a sense of grievance. Pashtuns see their legitimate border as the Indus River, and some demand all of Baluchistan and even the port of Karachi. Pakistani state authority is already weak among the Pashtun population of the country's northwest frontier tribal territories. In the early 1970s the Afghan king actually discussed formation of "greater Pashtunistan." The situation is reminiscent of that of the Kurds, except that the Pakistanis could see a solution. Pashtun domination of Afghanistan had to be based on something other than some form of Pashtun nationalism. Thus a Pashtun-dominated state based on fundamentalist Islam certainly met Pakistani security requirements. Reportedly the Pakistanis deliberately backed Islamists in the war against the Soviets for precisely this reason.[6] Much of the civil war which engulfed Afghanistan after 1992, when the old Soviet-installed regime was toppled, was a war of Pashtuns against other major ethnic groups (particularly Tajiks, Uzbeks, and Hazaras).

After the Pashtuns, the next largest ethnic group is the Tajiks, accounting for about a quarter of the Afghan population (about 6 million) in 2001. Most live in settled communities and are detribalized.[7] Ethnically they are Iranians, but they are also Sunni Muslims. About four million live across the border in Tajikistan. Others live in Uzbekistan, Kyrgyzstan, and in western China. Tajiks formed the core of the wartime Northern Alliance army.

The Hazaras, the main Shia Muslim group in the country, accounted for about 18 percent of the population in 2001. Pashtuns see them as agents of Iranian culture and influence and, therefore, tended to massacre them under the Taliban regime.[8] However, they do not live in areas contiguous with Iran, and in practice the Iranians have not supported them. The two massive Buddha statues destroyed by the Taliban were in Bamiyan, a center of the Hazara population. Their destruction was probably in large part a direct attack on the Hazaras, who regarded the statues as part of their cultural heritage. Taliban massacres made the Hazaras within the Northern Alliance particularly anxious to take Kabul when the U.S. government tried to slow the operation.

Uzbeks, most of whom are detribalized, accounted for about 6 percent of the Afghan population in 2001. They were the largest Turkic ethnic group in the country. Most live across the border in Uzbekistan; the majority of those in Afghanistan escaped across the old Soviet border before World War II. Their main center is Mazar-i-Sharif. Their National Islamic Front (Junbashi Mili-yi Islami), led during the war by Gen. Abdul Rashid Dostum, was one of the three main components of the Northern Alliance.

Finally, Turkmen accounted for about 3 percent of the Afghan population in 2001.

Although the modern Afghan state, which began to coalesce in the late nineteenth century, was dominated by Pashtuns, it represented a loose agreement among the major ethnic groups.[9] That agreement was destroyed in 1973, when Prince Mohammed Daoud, the king's cousin and former prime minister, overthrew the monarchy in a bloodless coup and seized power. His goal was to create a modern unitary state, which meant, among other things, suppressing ethnic autonomy. It also meant suppressing local customs—which was bitterly resented. In this effort, Daoud enlisted the country's Communist Party, and thus gained Soviet support.[10]

Afghan revolts against this government began not with the Soviet invasion but with Daoud's attempt to change the country. Indeed, the Soviets brought in advisors and then troops specifically to support Daoud against Islamic rebels. Daoud himself was killed in a 27 April 1978 putsch by Communist army and air force officers. His replacements proved ineffective against an increasingly national rebellion.[11] The following year the Soviets invaded and overthrew the current Afghan ruler because they considered him ineffectual, and they feared that his collapse would lead to an Islamic insurgency which might spread back into the Soviet Union.

From a Pakistani perspective, Daoud himself was a threat, because he was likely to press them on Pashtunistan. Islamists, who had begun to form their own organization in Kabul, fled to Peshawar, Pakistan. In these men and their nascent organization the Pakistanis saw a way of countering Daoud's nationalist message on Pashtunistan. They selected Gulbuddin Hekmatyar and his Hezb-e-Islami (Islamic Party) as their favored instrument.[12]

Pakistani preference for Hekmatyar survived the military coup which brought an Islamist, Gen. Zia ul-Haq, into power in 1977. Like many Islamists, General Zia described his new regime as an antidote to the corruption of the earlier democratic (and secular) government. He went so far as to hang the last elected premier, Zulfiqar Ali Bhutto (the father of Benazir Bhutto, who later became premier). Zia adopted a national strategy of Islamization to couple Pakistan to other Muslim states and thus to counterbalance growing Indian strength. He also hoped that Islamization would attract secular India's Muslim population and so make it more difficult for India to unify against Pakistan.

By 1977 the Pakistanis were already worried about events in Afghanistan. From their point of view, the 1978 coup against Daoud, which put a Communist-oriented regime in place, was a disaster. The Soviet invasion a year later, which generated such headlines outside Central Asia, was probably seen more as an escalation of a very serious existing problem than as something entirely new.[13] There was a real fear that, having occupied Afghanistan, the Soviets would move south through Baluchistan, which bordered that country, to the Indian Ocean, their historic objective.[14] The escalation in Afghanistan, however, was also an opportunity, because it greatly widened an ongoing revolt against the Communist government.[15]

General Zia's overall antidote to the Soviet presence across the border was to support a specifically Islamic or fundamentalist resistance. To sustain that resistance, he sponsored madrassahs, which promoted a particularly harsh and intolerant form of Islam, in the border region.[16] General Zia's Islamic orientation led him to favor these schools in a larger sense. For example, even though they provided little secular education, in the army and in the Pakistani civil service their certificates were taken as equivalent to diplomas issued by secular schools.[17] A quarter-century later the World Bank maintained that the poor education provided by the madrassahs was a major brake on Pakistani development. Yet in a very poor country, conventional education suffered badly, as the government lacked the money to sustain it. That left the madrassahs, many of them paid for by international religious charities. The World Bank estimated that in 2002, 15 to 20 percent of the madrassahs were still offering what amounted to military training.[18]

Throughout, by supporting Islamists rather than Afghan nationalists, the Pakistanis seem to have hoped to place in power a post-Communist regime which would endorse the Durand Line. No purely national resistance would have been able to do so. It is not clear to what extent, if at all, the CIA realized how Pakistani national concerns colored the ISI's decisions. For example, the official reason for Pakistani involvement in Afghanistan was always a desire for defensive, or strategic, depth in the ongoing fight against India, not for control of a potential Pashtun nationalist or separatist threat. Pakistani views were crucial because Pakistan was the only sanctuary from which operations could be mounted against the Communist regime.

It was not altogether clear that a viable nationalist alternative existed. The Afghan government under Daoud had not permitted political parties. Thus no one could claim legitimacy on the basis of past electoral success or of some known national following. Only the Islamists, who had competed with Communists in their attempts to seize power, had the necessary organization. At the outbreak of war the only two effective organizations were Gulbuddin Hekmatyar's mainly Pashtun Hezb-e-Islami and Burhanuddin Rabbani's mainly Tajik Jamiat-e-Islam; Pakistan supported Hekmatyar. Through the war, they were the dominant resistance parties, and they received the bulk of support.[19] Afterward, Hekmatyar and Rabbani were, in effect, the main rivals for power. An attempt to raise a nationalist resistance based on a Pashtun-style *loya jirga* based in Peshawar, Pakistan, came to nothing. In traditional fashion, it would have honored Islamists, but it would not have given them the sort of political leadership they (and the Pakistanis and Saudis) wanted. The *loya jirga* found it impossible to gain Pakistani support.[20] Similarly, the other main initial source of funds, Saudi Arabia, saw little point in supporting anything but an Islamic resistance.[21]

The Pakistanis clearly favored Hekmatyar as a resistance leader. Critics later charged that Hekmatyar seemed far more interested in massacring his opponents than in fighting the Soviets.[22] He was described as a Leninist, in the sense that he was dictatorial and cared only to gain power. Probably this tendency was pronounced only after about 1987. Hekmatyar's concentration on gaining power, however, would have been entirely consistent with an Islamist program one of whose objectives was to take over Afghanistan, not merely eject the Soviets. Hekmatyar's forces conducted only one major offensive, and that one entirely unsuccessful, at Jalalabad in 1989. Even that operation was apparently carried out only at the demands of the Pakistanis, and it may have been intended largely to legitimize Hekmatyar as a resistance leader.

The Pakistanis provided weapons to other leaders, but reportedly favored Hekmatyar. By merely arming all the contending factions, however, they ensured a postwar struggle for power. [23] Hekmatyar's underfunded rival, Ahmed Shah Mahsood, carried out two very successful offensives and apparently created a modern Afghan army.[24]

With the Soviet invasion, and later with the presidency of Ronald Reagan, the U.S. government was interested in the war in Afghanistan. It was willing to supply money and weapons, but it had no real control over events. Since the U.S. government had no desire to become involved publicly, it was glad to have the ISI act as a conduit to the rebels. The CIA officers responsible for supporting the war in Afghanistan stayed in Pakistan, and ISI chose whom to support.

From a Pakistani perspective, aside from the considerable resources it provided, the U.S. alliance was invaluable because it deterred the Soviets from practicing hot pursuit. Pakistan became a sanctuary for many of the anti-Soviet rebels. They did, however, operate covertly inside Pakistan, using the KGB-type Afghan intelligence service as a proxy.[25]

Other countries bordering Afghanistan also became involved in the ongoing war. The Soviet invasion of Afghanistan coincided with the Iranian revolution. To the extent that resistance in Afghanistan was Islamic, it automatically merited Iranian support—and it helped keep the Soviets away from a sensitive border. China has a short border with Afghanistan. By 1979 it felt threatened by the Soviets, and the Chinese government saw support for Afghan rebels as a way of weakening the Soviets. China became a conduit for weapons to support the Afghan resistance. But there was a price to pay. In Sinkiang, Chinese Turkestan, there is a large Muslim population which has often sought autonomy or even independence; the Afghan struggle tended to encourage these rebels.

The Soviet Union was already entrenched on the northern Afghan border, in largely Muslim republics: Kazakhstan, Turkmenistan, and Uzbekistan. The northern Afghans had brothers across the borders. Many of them already resented Soviet rule, and many were interested in a return to Islam as a way of venting anti-Soviet feelings. A fundamentalist success in Afghanistan might well cause risings across the border, which was one reason the Soviets were so determined not to be driven from Afghanistan. Conversely, no one fighting within northern Afghanistan would enjoy cross-border refuge.

The Soviets discovered that many of the Afghan leaders could be rented, though not bought. Entire tribal groups would accept and sign contracts of good behavior for limited periods. An Uzbek, Gen. Abdul Rashid Dostum, became a particularly important ally. Thus, quite aside from any military success, the Soviets could pacify portions of the country, concentrating on others they considered more vital.

Too, given tribal and ethnic loyalties, the Afghan resistance to the Soviets could never be unified. Ironically, that was one reason the Soviets were unable to crush it; it had no obvious center. Instead, different local leaders fought their own wars, backed by the Western powers, which funneled assistance largely through Pakistan. Often they fought each other. Several attempts to form a unified opposition front or a provisional government failed.[26]

The war in Afghanistan tore up the country's political system. Before 1973 Afghanistan had a traditional society in which tribal chiefs and religious men ruled. Loyalty was local. The chiefs of particular tribes in particular areas in turn could meet in a *loya jirga* to determine national policy. Social cohesion was ensured by links of precedence. Tribes might fight each other, but only on a limited scale. Daoud's unitary state was to have been built by smashing this sort of decentralized society. Part of that attack was necessarily to destroy the prestige of local religious leaders. The tribal chiefs naturally resisted the attacks, but in a wartime situation leadership was exercised not by leaders chosen in traditional ways, that is, based on past practice, but by those who proved their capability in battle. In this sense Afghanistan was being turned into a modern society in which success in action generally outweighs advantages such as family history. Moreover, those who proved themselves in battle saw no reason for their writ to be limited to their traditional tribal areas or to their home grounds. As a consequence, they found it difficult or impossible to agree on a national government.[27]

As it became clear that the Soviets could not easily defeat the Afghans, it became fashionable among wealthy young Arabs to go to Afghanistan to fight for Islam. The situation has been likened to that in Europe at the time of the Spanish Civil War. Idealists and the disaffected found a cause they could embrace. Many of them were radicalized as a result. The difference was that those who fought in Afghanistan won. Many of them interpreted that victory as a success for Allah, a boost to Islamist visions of causality. In addition, Afghanistan is a very poor country, and the relatively wealthy Arabs found that their money offered them enormous advantages. Those who survived had, in a British term often applied to World War II, a "good war." Clearly fighting for Allah brought deserved benefits. As for those who died, the war was holy, so they would go to a graphically understood version of paradise. It was even said that some of the Arabs deliberately sought death in combat in the expectation of a happy afterlife.

When they evacuated Afghanistan in 1989, the Soviets left behind the Najibullah government, which had been their puppet in place in Kabul. Factional infighting probably helped prolong its life. It was somewhat more successful than the Soviets had been in suppressing rebels, and it lasted three years before being overthrown. Presumably for it the key disaster was the end of the Soviet Union at the end of 1991, and thus the end of military supplies and other assistance.[28] By this time the United States had largely disengaged from Afghanistan, and American ties with the ISI were eroded by its support for the Iraqis during the Gulf War of 1991.[29] In November 1991, the Russians convened a peace conference, but the three Pashtun parties were not invited because they had refused to attend previous meetings.

The Kabul government itself could not survive without a link to the north, which was protected by militias it paid, including Gen. Abdul Rashid Dostum's Uzbeks. When the Soviets stopped their funding, that government had to cut its costs. One way to do so was to squeeze Dostum, who was accused of padding the ranks of his troops. He defected in February 1992, dooming the government. The last Communist ruler, Najibullah, agreed to a UN-sponsored plan for a multiparty interim government. On 19 March he announced that he would resign. That day a resistance alliance seized Mazar-i-Sharif, blocking the road from Kabul to Russia. Ahmed Shah Mahsood became the spokesman for the victorious alliance of the north, although by this time many of his forces were actually those which had served the previous regime, Dostum's being the main example.[30] For their part, the Pashtuns feared that the northerners would keep them out of power. Mahsood moved before the Pashtuns could agree to act. His and Dostum's forces entered Kabul on 25 April.

Hekmatyar was still the favored Pakistani agent, and he still had reason to hope that he could take over the country. His force began rocket attacks on Kabul. As leader of the largest northern party, Rabbani became head of the provisional government, taking office in June 1992. His defense minister was Mahsood, Rabbani's chief supporter and the most successful guerrilla military leader. This government was to have given way to an elected government that October, but instead Rabbani was elected by an assembly dominated by his supporters. He was to have been replaced at the end of an eighteen-month term, but he survived as de jure chief of state, the man whose government the United Nations and most other governments recognized until 2001. Hekmatyar considered his own appointment as prime minister meaningless, and he continued to fight for supremacy.

The split between an alliance of non-Pashtuns from the north and the Pashtuns of the south would continue through the post-Soviet era and would mark the U.S.-led war in Afghanistan. The Northern Alliance which took Kabul was the direct successor to the army which kept Rabbani in power. The Pashtuns of the south, ultimately led by the Taliban, opposed them. Because the Pashtuns were not monolithic, some tribes rejected the Taliban and ultimately supported the anti-Taliban coalition in the war. Even so, the tribal fault lines defined the way the 2001 war would be fought.

For both Rabbani and Hekmatyar, Kabul was the prize in this post-Soviet civil war. The city, which had survived the war against the Soviets, was largely destroyed. Rabbani and Mahsood managed to stave Hekmatyar off, despite shifts such as a January 1994 reversal by Dostum in favor of Hekmatyar.

Outside Kabul, the country fell under the control of regional commanders or warlords.[31] Each set up what amounted to a local government. Each needed a substantial army to maintain power, but the funding which had been so plentiful during the anti-Soviet war was gone. Thus each paid for his army by taxing and by extorting tolls on roads passing through. Because each was at war, he needed large resources, so taxation amounted to extortion. Armies bred the sort of arrogant misbehavior which the population inevitably resented. That was hardly conducive to rebuilding the badly damaged country. It became easy to argue that what the country needed was a strong national government.

Hekmatyar was still the ISI's favored instrument, but by 1994 it was clear that he could not win the civil war. The ISI itself was still linked to the memory of General Zia, the dead dictator. The government of Benazir Bhutto cast about for an alternative and found one in a new Taliban organization backed by the main Pakistani Islamic party. Bhutto advertised them as preferable to Hekmatyar because they were less corrupt. Because ISI continued to back Hekmatyar, for about a year and a half Pakistan was backing two competitors for power in Afghanistan. The ISI finally dropped Hekmatyar when the Taliban defeated him in 1995. He then retreated to Iran, but he continued to nurse hopes of taking over the country. With the Taliban gone in 2001, Hekmatyar returned, this time to fight against the interim Karzai government and its American and other foreign supporters. That was why, in May 2002, the CIA tried (but failed) to kill him using an armed Predator unmanned air vehicle (UAV).

The early description of the Taliban as honest, if conservative, became common in the Western media; they seemed preferable to the corrupt warlords they fought. The U.S. government initially supported the Taliban at President Bhutto's suggestion; she told the U.S. ambassador that she controlled them. Americans supporting the Taliban typically described them as similar to the conservative Muslim rulers of Saudi Arabia, hence congenial to the United States.[32] Americans might not find their internal social policies altogether attractive, but they could be construed as well-adapted, even popular, in a conservative Muslim country.

The Taliban presented themselves as disinterested religious scholars disgusted with the lawlessness in the country. They graduated from madrassahs in Pakistan directly into a combat role. They made a typical fundamentalist promise: because they followed the rule of Allah, they would clean up the rampant corruption and even intimidation casually practiced by the warlords competing for power in Afghanistan. Their precise origins are unclear; the Taliban described themselves as a group of former resistance fighters who came together out of disgust for the extortions of warlords near Kandahar.[33] In their first operation, their leader, Mullah Omar, supposedly killed a soldier raping a women. In October 1994 a Taliban force "rescued" a trade convoy en route from Quetta in Pakistan to Kandahar. Western reporters were surprised that unseasoned religious students could defeat what they imagined were battle-hardened Afghan armies.[34]

By March 1995 the Taliban controlled about a third of Afghanistan, and Hekmatyar was in retreat. Mahsood, however, drove them from the approaches to Kabul. Yet in September 1996, the Taliban took Kabul. There they killed Najibullah, the last of the Soviet heads of state, who had taken refuge in a United Nations compound. In a May 1997 coup, Taliban troops took Mazar-i-Sharif, forcing Dostum to flee abroad. Probably the key to the coup was that one of Dostum's subordinates went over to the Taliban. This success, however, did not last long. The Taliban suffered badly when those in Mazar-i-Sharif revolted, and Mahsood managed to push them back almost to Kabul.[35] Dostum was back in Mazar-i-Sharif in November 1997, but he was finally ejected in August 1998 in what the Taliban hoped would be a final offensive. By the fall, the Taliban controlled about 90 percent of the country, and Mahsood was the only real barrier to their final victory.

They never quite succeeded. Worse, from their point of view, was the February 2000 escape of a famous Herati commander, Ismail Khan, from Kandahar, where he had been held since 1997. He inspired an attempt to revive resistance in the form of a Northern Alliance sponsored largely by the Iranians. The Northern Alliance troops who entered Kabul in 2001, for example, wore Iranian fatigues. Iran opposed the Taliban, who persecuted the Shia minority inside Afghanistan. Moreover, Iran represented a radically different approach to Muslim government: it was an Islamist (modernizing) state, whereas Taliban Afghanistan was a fundamentalist and profoundly reactionary one. India also backed the Northern Alliance on the theory that the Taliban were an extension of Pakistani power and that a Taliban triumph might translate into more pressure on Kashmir. Conversely, anything that drew off Pakistani resources would reduce the threat the Indians felt.

The Northern Alliance included Mahsood and also Dostum, who had returned to northern Afghanistan in 1999. They made some gains, but not decisive ones, so that by 2001 the Alliance controlled less than a third of the country. By this time it was receiving Russian support, because the Taliban were involved in Islamic rebellions in the former Soviet Central Asian republics and in the ongoing war in Chechnya.[36]

From the beginning, the key Taliban advantage was substantial Pakistani financial backing. All of their rivals had to squeeze the local economy merely to keep their armies intact. With external backing, the Taliban could maintain an army without extortion, and they could bribe much of the way to power without risking the loss of that army. Merely eliminating extortion would make them popular, or at least acceptable. Anyone outside Afghanistan would credit the well-financed Taliban with bringing stability and honest government. In fact, it did not really matter what program they had in mind.

In 2000 the Pakistanis were still backing the Taliban. In July 2000 the Pakistani government announced open military support for them, which helped materially in their fall offensive. However, this support did not prove decisive.[37] It no longer seemed that the Taliban could win the Afghan civil war. By 2001 President Pervez Musharraf was tiring of them; the ISI began to seek alternatives. With their efficient intelligence service, the Taliban discovered the candidates and killed most of them. Even so, Musharraf told the Taliban that unless they could win the Afghan civil war by late 2001 he would stop supporting them.

The Taliban badly needed reliable troops. They also had to destroy Ahmed Shah Mahsood, their only real enemy. Al Qaeda offered solutions to both problems. Osama's Arabs (the "Afghan Arabs") could be counted upon to fight. Soon they formed the 055 Brigade, the only effective unit in the Taliban army. The Afghan Arabs were also the only Taliban formation capable of night fighting.

As for Mahsood, on 7 September two Afghan Arabs posing as journalists were allowed to interview him. They asked to take his picture, but their camera was a suicide bomb. Mahsood was mortally injured, and he died two days later. Later it was widely suggested that the murder and the 11 September attacks were connected. The murder seemed to ensure the safety of the Afghan power base, from which operations against the West could now be mounted. As it was, the Northern Alliance did not disintegrate, and within weeks it, rather than the Taliban, would be in Kabul. For the time being, however, the assassination showed just how vital Al Qaeda support was for the Taliban rulers.

Much of the Taliban claim of peace and stability had to do with eliminating extortionate tolls exacted on roads passing through warlord-controlled territory. For a country without any seacoast, road traffic was absolutely crucial. Afghanistan has a long tradition of smuggling goods through Pakistan, and a powerful Pakistani transport mafia evolved. It had a very strong interest in eliminating the warlords and their extortion, and in return it helped finance the Taliban. Truckers were among those most vociferous in their praise of the peace the Taliban had brought to southern Afghanistan.[38]

The Taliban's promises of stability together with considerable bribery secured them power, particularly in the southern city of Kandahar. Kabul was more problematic. Despite its devastation during the long wars, it was much more cosmopolitan, hence, more alien to fundamentalists. The city's cosmopolitanism probably inspired the Taliban to be particularly strict in their attempts to enforce religious law.

Given their fundamentalist beliefs, the Taliban presumably assumed that true (enforced) piety would automatically solve their country's devastating problems. They certainly enjoyed no postwar American support; the Americans disengaged once the Soviets withdrew. Their view seemed to be that merely ejecting the Soviets would solve the country's problems. In fact, the war had horribly damaged the country, both in material and in human terms. Too much basic infrastructure had been destroyed. Much of the potential grazing area of the country was ruined by land mines liberally strewn through it by the Soviets. It was sometimes said that Afghanistan was the most-mined country on Earth. The means of storing the wheat typically grown in Afghanistan were largely gone. The only really profitable cash crop, it soon developed, was the poppy. Afghanistan and northern Pakistan had been major heroin sources even before the war against the Soviets;[39] now Afghanistan became a major source of heroin for Europe. Later the Taliban regime would receive a large subsidy from the United States to block poppy cultivation and exports. For a time that subsidy would be its main source of revenue.

Given more than a decade of war, too many Afghans had grown up in refugee camps in Pakistan, learning few skills. Just as important, they had little idea of the sort of relatively relaxed society Afghanistan had supported before the war against the Soviets. Another barrier to reconstruction was a devastating brain drain. Many Afghans fled when the Soviets invaded, but some, particularly educated people, found jobs in Kabul. Others hoped to return to a post-Soviet Afghanistan. The civil war made that impossible, and it caused a further exodus, which is likely to impede any post-Taliban reconstruction. The old professional and intellectual class would probably have formed the main constituency for a secular or moderate Islamic post-Taliban state.

The Taliban version of Islam, particularly its treatment of women, soon became notorious in the West. The Taliban boasted that they had eliminated the widespread rape practiced while the country was anarchic. They did so largely by confining women indoors, banning them not only from any profession but even from any sort of education. Popular entertainment was banned. Television was illegal, and television repairmen became criminals. Most Afghans, particularly in cities, practiced a relatively relaxed form of Islam, and they did not take kindly to the newcomers' extreme edicts. That the population at large was less than enthusiastic was soon evident; the Taliban had to maintain a massive religious police force, run by the Ministry of Virtue and Vice, and to carry out frequent public executions.

To retain power, the Taliban needed a Praetorian Guard. Osama's Afghan Arabs provided it. Like other such units, they were rewarded with special treatment. For example, they seem to have enjoyed the pick of Afghan women, a point emphasized later by their enemies. The foreigners got the best houses and the best goods. After all, they were the bulwark behind which the Taliban could enforce the piety needed to make Allah look kindly upon them. Those Afghans who objected to the special treatment were often imprisoned or killed.

To a Saudi like Osama bin Laden, this was a familiar situation. In Saudi Arabia itself, special religious police were needed to enforce the edicts of the Koran. One way to read the situation would be to say that the all-corrupting influence of the West necessitates stern measures to keep piety alive.

Osama and most of the Arabs could not even speak Afghan languages. Thus by 2000 it was clear to most Afghans that in defeating the Soviets they had replaced one foreign occupier with another. This was particularly true in northern and western Afghanistan. The south and east were friendlier to the Taliban because of ethnic ties. The Arabs shielding the Taliban might be foreigners, but the rulers were clearly part of the local Pashtun population.

The Taliban were led by Mullah Omar, who claimed divine inspiration. He was described variously as a key figure, the only one who could hold together the disparate factions within the movement, and as a deeply ignorant man who had come to power by happenstance. In September 2001 it was estimated that about 10 percent of Taliban authorities were uncompromising followers; another 30 percent accepted his interpretation of Sharia but argued for a more lenient approach; and the rest were opportunists. Differing interpretations of Mullah Omar's importance affected any estimate as to whether his death or disappearance would destroy his regime.

To the outside world, the Taliban regime was an abomination. With the population starving in the worst drought in thirty years, and dependent on United Nations food assistance, the regime concentrated on vital questions like the proper length of a man's beard. As the Taliban's situation worsened, its obsession with piety deepened. To Mullah Omar, the drought was evidence not of some natural force but of divine displeasure. Greater piety might reverse it. Islam, for example, prohibits graven images, yet among Afghanistan's cultural treasures was a pair of huge Buddhist statues. The Taliban destroyed them. When many foreigners, including some of the major Islamic leaders outside the country, protested, they pointed out that the world had done little to feed starving Afghans. Why respect the world's views regarding the statues? Probably it was at least as important that senior Wahhabi clerics in Saudi Arabia strongly supported the destruction of the idols.

Given Pakistan's initial sponsorship of the Taliban, it was no surprise that the country recognized the Taliban regime as legitimate. Similarly, given the fundamentalist character of the Taliban, and the fact that they derived from Saudi-sponsored madrassahs, it was natural for Saudi Arabia to recognize the Taliban and to seek close ties with them. The only other state to recognize the Taliban regime was the United Arab Emirates (UAE), a close ally of Saudi Arabia.

Quite aside from military support, bin Laden provided the Taliban with much of the cash they needed in order to survive. The Taliban thus valued bin Laden highly, and it seems unlikely that they could ever have handed him over to the West or even, for that matter, dealt with him in Afghanistan. For example, at one point the Saudis asked that bin Laden be handed over, and a Saudi diplomat said that it would be particularly convenient if he were handed over dead. The Taliban cleric to whom he was speaking called for a pail of ice water, saying that he had to pour it over his head to assuage his fury at so unspeakable a suggestion.

After 11 September, the Taliban made a variety of excuses as they refused to hand bin Laden over. He was a guest, and the tribal law of hospitality forbade expulsion. He was under house arrest, his access to a satellite telephone cut off. For a time he was reportedly defense minister in the Taliban government, perhaps the only description which hinted at his central importance to the regime.

Afghanistan became a center of bin Laden's pan-Islamic movement. Virtually all the countries bordering the country were affected. As the Soviets had feared, as they withdrew the fundamentalist virus crossed the border into what had been Soviet Central Asia, the republics of Kazakhstan, Kyrgyzstan, Tajikistan, Turkmenistan, and Uzbekistan. All were Muslim territory conquered by the czars during the nineteenth century, and revolts in all had been suppressed by about 1924, when the Stalin drew the borders of the republics. Russian control was an emotive issue because the region contains the ancient Muslim capitals of Bukhara and Samarkand, famous for their medieval learning and their influence throughout the Muslim world. The Russians tried to enforce control by Russification—by moving in ethnic Russians to tip the ethnic balance—and by industrialization, which would break up the old nomadic way of life. Afghanistan became involved because some of those in Central Asia hoped that it would help them resist Soviet conquest.[40] One consequence of Russification was the presence of large Russian ethnic populations which the post-Soviet Russian government felt bound to defend against Islamic revolts. As in many other places, the fact that borders were drawn for imperial purposes caused problems.[41] There was also intense resentment of Soviet-era crimes, such as forced land resettlement and horrific damage to the environment (and, by extension, to the population), at least in Uzbekistan, in the interest of increasing cotton production. A Soviet attempt to reduce the problem by creating an official form of Islam failed miserably. As in Eastern Europe, religion became a major rallying crew against an oppressive regime. In this case, it was Islam.

The Soviet army force which attacked Afghanistan in 1979 consisted mainly of Central Asian troops, and the experience of fighting Muslim guerrillas probably radicalized many of them. Some of them were able to desert and thus to reach madrassahs in Pakistan. Late in the war, leading madrassahs began to reserve places for Central Asians, who learned the concept of jihad as war.

For the decade following the end of the Soviet Union, Russian troops often found themselves fighting in the "near abroad," in Central Asian republics whose governments were trying to resist fundamentalist incursions. A revolutionary fundamentalist movement intent on creating an Islamic state extending over former Soviet Central Asia was formed by a former Afghan commander, Juma Namangani, and a mullah, Tohir Abdukhaililovich Yuldashev.[42] It fought a bloody civil war in Tajikistan against local authorities and their Russian allies between 1992 and 1997. The war ended in a cease-fire which split the movement between those interested in a political settlement and those who continued to demand an Islamic state. A hundred thousand Tajiks crossed the border into Afghanistan. Conversely, the Russians fighting in Tajikistan considered Afghans the problem, and they often shelled Afghanistan and even crossed into it. The settlement of the civil war left a guerrilla base in Tajikistan, and a government unable to eject it.

In Uzbekistan, separated from Tajikistan by weak Kyrgyzstan, President Islam Karimov was well aware of the threat of fundamentalism. He continued Soviet-era policies intended to destroy any sort of militant Islam, but many argued that he was actually radicalizing the population. For example, Muslim clerics were regarded as deadly enemies; men were sometimes jailed simply for attending services.[43] That was not to suggest that the government lacked enemies. For example, several December 1997 murders were attributed to the militants. A reporter in Tashkent found many Uzbeks who regarded President Karimov as the main bulwark against the fundamentalists, one they greatly appreciated.[44]

With the Tajik civil war over, Tajikistan offered no refuge to Uzbeks who wanted to fight their government. Taliban Afghanistan, however, did. In 1998 Namangani and Yuldashev formed the Islamic Movement of Uzbekistan (IMU). The Uzbek government blamed the IMU for a February 1999 attempt to kill President Karimov using a car bomb. For their part, the IMU tried to intimidate the Kyrgyz government to allow it free passage from its semisanctuary in Tajikistan. The Tajiks managed to push the IMU into Afghanistan, although it continued cross-border operations.

The Taliban welcomed the IMU and allowed it a base at Mazar-i-Sharif. They supported continued IMU attacks against Uzbekistan, across the border. These attacks also helped it, because its main enemy, Ahmed Shah Mahsood, was an Uzbek dependent on supplies funneled through Uzbekistan. IMU operations in Mahsood's rear were credited with his September 2000 defeats.

This history helps explain why the governments of the former Soviet republics supported Northern Alliance armies, and later the U.S.-led coalition, in fighting the Taliban.

In the east, Al Qaeda (or the Taliban) supported a growing Islamic insurgency in Sinkiang, Chinese Turkestan. The Chinese tried to buy off the Afghans by selling them army weapons, but to little avail. In the west, the Sunni Al Qaeda supported insurgency in Iran, despite the Iranian state's Islamic orientation. In effect Iran represented a national form of Islam, whereas Al Qaeda sought a universal Islamic empire. The Iranians became major Northern Alliance supporters. In the south, despite their need for Pakistani support, the Taliban linked with Pashtuns across the Pakistani border and supported the fundamentalist opposition to the Pakistani state. Further afield, Osama clearly hoped to take over Saudi Arabia.

Meanwhile, the Pakistanis became more dependent on the Taliban. When they took power, Pakistan was already engaged in a lengthy struggle with India over Kashmir, a province bordering the Punjab in the north, which itself borders Afghanistan. The issue in Kashmir was clearly religious. The majority of Kashmiris are Muslims. Ali Jinnah, founder of Pakistan, expected the province to become part of his country; Pakistan, after all, is an acronym in which the *k* stands for Kashmir. However, when British

India was partitioned in 1947, the new secular Indian state was awarded control of Muslim Kashmir because the Hindu ruler of the state chose that way. A Pakistani attempt to conquer Kashmir soon after independence failed, as did war in 1965. The example of Islamic resistance to the Soviets suggested another alternative. The Pakistani ISI began to promote an Islamic guerrilla movement whose aim was to eject the Indians from Kashmir. By 2001 this movement, operating largely in the Punjab and in Kashmir itself, had largely been defeated. Its connection with the Pakistan Army was being dramatized by army artillery support for groups penetrating the border. It seemed likely that the Indians would strike back directly at Pakistani territory.

The guerrilla movement in Kashmir was run by fundamentalists. Its personnel were often recruited from the same tribes who provided the Taliban. Once Pakistan depended on such paramilitary forces for victory in Kashmir and upon the same groups for influence in its rear area in Afghanistan, its government was effectively tied to them. More and more it seemed that the road to success in Kashmir lay through Afghanistan, as that was where the necessary terrorists could be recruited and trained—and could find refuge from the Indians. To the extent that the fight in Kashmir was carried on by the Taliban, Kashmir became a refuge for Taliban and Al Qaeda fleeing Afghanistan, as the U.S. government charged in June 2002.

Moreover, Pakistan tied itself to Saudi Arabia and the Persian Gulf states. They financed part of its military budget in return for a pledge of Pakistani armed support in the event of some local threat. That pledge could not be completely fulfilled in 1990–91 because India seemed to be threatening Pakistan at the time.

Pakistan is an avowedly Muslim state, and that religious difference justified partition from India. Initially the motive was apparently secular; the feeling among Pakistani leaders was that Muslims could not advance within a largely Hindu India due to the tyranny of that majority. As in any other Muslim state, there was and is tension between a more or less secular modernizing elite and a conservative majority tending toward a fundamentalist view of Islam. Periodically the Pakistan military has overthrown the secular Pakistani government on the ground that the politicians are corrupt; this is much the justification fundamentalists have used in their own attacks on secular governments of largely Muslim countries. Fundamentalist parties became natural allies to the military in its coup attempts. In return, when it could, the Army favored the fundamentalists.

In the fall of 2002, after war had begun in Afghanistan, President Pervez Musharraf decided that the fundamentalists had gone much too far. He imprisoned many of them, and in effect he demanded that the country turn toward Islamism—that it modernize its society. He publicly rejected jihad as holy war and argued that jihad could and should mean a struggle to make Pakistan an Islamic showcase. Many commentators pointed out that no other Muslim government leader had had the courage to make any such declaration. Musharraf's declaration makes the distinction between Islamists and fundamentalists particularly clear.

Since the 1940s the United States has periodically been allied to Pakistan. Those seeking a more secular path may have looked to the United States as a force for modernization. They were badly disappointed in the 1990s. By that time Pakistan was developing its own nuclear bomb, reportedly using Chinese plans, to balance an existing Indian nuclear capability. U.S. policy opposed any form of nuclear proliferation, and it did not make any distinction between a country reacting to someone else's bomb and a country introducing nuclear weapons to its own region. A law was passed blocking U.S. military aid to any country developing nuclear weapons, and the U.S. government announced that Pakistan fell into that category. New aircraft were not delivered; U.S. warships on loan had to be returned. Many Pakistanis were furious. Given that India, their sworn enemy, already had the bomb (having tested one in 1974), surely this was no more than rank hypocrisy. It did not help that there was dark talk in the United States of fears that Pakistan's would be a "Muslim bomb," available to Arab countries facing Israel. Given widespread reports that Israel already had a substantial nuclear arsenal, fundamentalists could easily point at American opposition to a Pakistani bomb as no more than favoritism directed at enemies of Islam.

The Pakistani military, then, had its own reasons to dislike the United States. They had taken considerable risks during the war in Afghanistan and could rightly claim a major share in the cold war victory there. Yet as soon as the war ended, they had been abandoned. Their one plausible attempt to develop an equalizer against massed Indian forces had been opposed, to the point where the best means of delivery, the U.S.–made F-16 fighter-bomber, had been embargoed. The U.S. government was clearly leaning heavily toward India, which it saw as a future ally against China—a major Pakistani arms supplier. A strong anti-Americanism, then, could be added to growing fundamentalist presence in the Pakistan military.

5

The Terrorist International and Its Predecessor

 President Bush declared war against terrorism, arguing that it was a universal evil against which all civilized people could unite.

It has been argued that by definition no such war is winnable, that there will always be some degree of terrorism in the world. A universal war against terrorism, then, is like the war against drugs or the war against crime. Success can be real, but only if it is defined as keeping the threat below some threshold. For example, in New York City in the 1980s there were as many as twenty-four hundred murders each year. The administration of Mayor Giuliani was credited with a major victory because it cut the rate to fewer than six hundred per year. People were still being murdered, but the city felt vastly safer.

Meeting with his war cabinet, President Bush developed a criterion for victory in the war. His advisers quickly rejected any goal of eliminating terrorism altogether. Instead, the NSC proposed as a war aim "eliminating terrorism as a threat to our way of life." The president pressed for broader language, extending "our way of life" to "all nations who love freedom."[1] In a December 2001 interview, he defined victory as reaching the point at which "we can sleep safely, knowing that America won't be under attack by people who don't fear us and/or our coalition. That we can rout terror wherever it exists."[2] That is, the president was seeking what amounted to a deterrent against terrorists, comparable in concept to the deterrent which protects the country against other governments. Any future bin Laden, contemplating an attack on the United States, would have to reckon with his own destruction. At least in the president's mind, this was more than a fight against any particular terrorist group, despite much talk in the Muslim world to the effect that it was no more than camouflage for an assault on Islam.

Many writers on terrorism have pointed out that conventional warfare, which no one is willing to ban, often involves apparently indiscriminate attacks against civilians. Are all governments really terrorists, seeking to maintain a kind of monopoly on power? The vital distinction is that governments that order military action accept responsibility and can be attacked in retaliation. They have fixed locations and stated policies. Whatever a government does can be traced back to it. Someone has to take responsibility. The government involved may face military action; it may literally be destroyed. It can, then, be deterred. A government also faces a kind of internal deterrence, in that some degree of popular acquiescence is generally needed for it to take aggressive action. State sponsorship of terrorism is a way of avoiding responsibility, of limiting the victim's ability to deter action. A truly nonstate actor, like Al Qaeda, cannot, in theory, be deterred because it has no easily located headquarters. Without the possibility of deterrence there is not, in theory, anything which can limit its action. Such actors are anathema to governments simply because they cannot be controlled, at least not by the usual tools governments have. Nor are terrorists generally responsible to those they claim to represent, because they often operate on a criminal or extortionist basis. Thus they are not controllable within the international system. If there is a general argument against allowing terrorism to survive, it is simply that the survival of terrorists of any stripe is ultimately a threat to all organized governments.

During the cold war, it was often suggested that the true terrorists were the state intelligence organizations which sponsored nominally independent operators, and thus that terrorism could be controlled to some extent by deterrence. This approach was typified when U.S. forces attacked Libya in 1986 after the Libyans ordered the bombing of a disco in West Berlin (frequented by U.S. military personnel). Conversely, when the United States did not attack those responsible for the bombing of the Beirut barracks in 1982, it could be argued that deterrence had not even been attempted. The issue in bin Laden's case has always been whether he is actually the tool of some particular government, which could be pressed to destroy or abandon him. It no longer seems that this is the case, although bin Laden benefited enormously from his control over the Taliban government in Afghanistan.

Thus, in order to provide the desired degree of deterrence for future security, the war on terrorism demands several things. First, there must be sufficient intelligence to identify the source of any terrorist attack. That seems to have been available in the case of 11 September. Second, there must be a way of finding and destroying the particular group responsible. Again, much has been done since 11 September to destroy bin Laden and

Al Qaeda, although surely more will have to be done. Third, this type of capability must be well advertised and robust. Simply destroying bin Laden and Al Qaeda is likely to spread a sense of deterrence, and thus it becomes a necessary first, but not last, step.

Improving U.S. homeland defense is also an important step. At the very least, it raises the bar for anyone trying to carry out a major terrorist attack. That in turn makes it much more likely that such an attack will be detectable, because more terrorist resources will have to be brought into play.

No anti-terrorist defense can be anything close to perfect. Israel's horrific experience with suicide bombers proves as much. However, a real effort can pay major dividends, at the least convincing terrorists that they might as well avoid the United States because it is no longer a soft target.

For the United States, there is a particular interest in dealing with Osama bin Laden and his organization: Osama declared that it was lawful and just to kill Americans—not everyone in Europe, say, but Americans—and his organization is carrying out that policy. A government's first duty is to deal with those who would kill its citizens. That is why they pay their taxes and obey their laws. On the other hand, bin Laden is a threat to many others as well, who will be quite happy to see him dead. Terrorism in general is a threat to governments and to world order, but usually dealing with it is essentially a police issue. Osama was different because he had seized control of a government, with all the resources that entailed. Perhaps it would be better to think of the current problem as an attack by a government which, having only very limited resources at home, chose a covert kind of military action to spread itself. The tentacles outside Afghanistan probably will not wither completely after the Taliban are destroyed and Osama is dead, but they will enjoy far less financial support. That in turn may well be crippling.

It is important, however, to remember that, in much of the world, one side's terrorists are the other side's freedom fighters, perhaps the only hope of overcoming very long material odds. That is not to suggest some kind of moral equivalence between organized governments wielding armed force and self-appointed terrorist chiefs, but rather to point out that it is unlikely that all governments in the world will ever unite to deal with all terrorists. Probably every government in the world has, at one time or another, sponsored irregular forces to impose pressure on its enemies. When irregulars limit themselves to attacking enemy troops, they are guerrillas, and are seen as more or less legitimate. However, they often find themselves attacking civilians who may seem to sympathize with the enemy, either to reduce that support or to demoralize their enemies.

To that argument some will inevitably reply that some struggles (which ones vary with the observer) are more important than an abstraction like the international system. In this sense the United States is taking a stand in condemning all terrorism. It is arguing that the system of independent and responsible states is the best overall hope humanity has for a better future. That system is admittedly flawed. In the past, the U.S. position was not only that the state system was the only acceptable one, but that the U.S. government had no business trying to change the political character of any foreign state, no matter how repugnant that might be.

Meanwhile, most governments do not accept that sponsoring terrorism necessarily endangers them. As a case in point, for years, since the time of partition in 1947, Pakistan and India have feuded over Kashmir, an overwhelmingly Muslim principality ruled by a Hindu prince who decided to join India rather than Muslim Pakistan. For the Indian government, Kashmir became a symbol of the secular pluralistic quality of the country (which, incidentally, has one of the largest Muslim communities in the world). For Pakistanis, the recovery of Kashmir became a matter of national identity and honor. After fighting and losing several wars over Kashmir, for Pakistan, guerrilla warfare and terrorism became attractive weapons. Any Pakistani government renouncing those weapons would find itself very unpopular. Given the scale of the terror inside Kashmir, any Indian government surrendering to the terrorists would also find itself hounded from office. At least in this situation, and in many others, it can be argued that prohibiting terrorism is a way of enforcing the status quo. If you won the last round, you do not want to fight another, so terrorism is an unalloyed evil. If you are dissatisfied, then at the very least terrorism becomes attractive. Very few countries in the modern world have entirely renounced terrorism and its cousin, guerrilla warfare.

None of this is to suggest that terrorism usually succeeds. Typically it is intended to exhaust a society into accepting terms as a condition for peace. In some very important cases, as in Europe in the 1970s, terrorists sufficiently enraged those around them that police work became very effective, and movements were wiped out almost completely. The important distinction is between local terrorist movements with limited objectives and what President Bush called movements with global reach—the ones the United States wants to destroy. It is very difficult to get widespread agreement on which movement is local and which is not. For example, is Hamas a terrorist organization, or is it the sword of the nascent Palestinian state? If you are Israeli, the answer is very clear, but if you are an Arab sympathizer with the Palestinians, U.S. action against Hamas is not an attempt to gain justice, it is armed support for an enemy state.

Often enough a government withdraws or concedes because, finally, the price exacted in continued assaults does not seem worthwhile. In the fall of 2001, for example, Peter Mandelson, a British politician and former minister for Northern Ireland, predicted that Britain would abandon that province due to what amounted to war-weariness in the face of continued terrorism. He felt that those on the British mainland would be less and less willing to bear that burden. Mandelson in turn was attacked for encouraging the terrorists. One key point was that, in Mandelson's mind, few on the British mainland regard Northern Ireland as integral to their country. It might be rather different if a few terrorists staged a campaign to separate, say, Manchester from England. Too, Mandelson clearly feels that the Irish Republican Army (IRA) has a finite agenda. Giving in to their brand of terrorism will not necessarily lead to further demands (although that is by no means obvious).

One effect of 11 September was to demonstrate to the remnants of failed terrorist movements that they could still succeed. In March 2002, Italian left-wing terrorists claimed credit for having shot an economist working on new labor laws, which many on the Left hated and feared. The terrorists described themselves as successors to the failed Red Brigade movement of the 1970s, saying that 11 September proved that even without massive technological backup, terrorists could severely damage a modern society. This incident suggests just how interconnected terrorism may be, in terms of mutual encouragement if not material assistance.

When President Bush declared war on world terrorism, he in effect argued that the world's terrorist organizations are linked. He then had to step back and limit the war to terrorists "with global reach," which in effect means Al Qaeda and its close relatives. There was some talk that this pullback was due entirely to a desire to form a coalition at any cost; many coalition members sponsored local terrorist groups, such as Hamas. On the other hand, terrorists and governments which sponsor terrorism do tend to help each other, often despite considerable ideological differences. The terrorist international, if there is one, is a coalition, not an alliance, each member looking for advantages in its own fight.

At the very least, those trained in terrorist tactics by one organization had skills which could be employed only by other terrorists. Control of those within a terrorist organization was not always very rigid. For example, in 2001, IRA (or allied) operatives were reported helping to train Colombian FARC guerrillas. It was by no means clear whether this collaboration represented IRA policy, or whether it was free-lancing that the IRA command was unlikely to condemn.[3]

Those who were already victims of local terrorist groups declared that no war against terror could be complete without draining the terrorist swamp entirely. Any major terrorist group which survived could, the theory ran, become a refuge for surviving personnel and thus the basis for a new kind of international attack. It might not matter that the group in question began with a local focus. Thus the Israelis expected their American allies finally to declare that Hamas and similar organizations should be outlawed, and that the states, such as Syria and Iran, which back them should be punished severely. Similarly, the Indian government expected severe American sanctions to be levied on Pakistan, which backed terrorists or guerrillas fighting Indian rule in Kashmir.

For governments which have backed terrorist organizations, they are probably very much a double-edged sword. Those who have learned to overthrow neighboring governments can come home to overthrow the sponsor government.[4] They may begin as secret arms of intelligence organizations, but they gradually become more independent—at which point they can become embarrassing.[5] At one time the Pakistani government saw the ISI and its protégés as a valuable weapon to gain strategic depth (in Afghanistan) or to liberate disputed territory (in Kashmir). However, by 2001 the ISI and its terrorist friends were widely described as potential enemies of the Pakistani regime.

In his 2002 State of the Union address, President Bush named three states as members of an "axis of evil" bent on exporting terrorism: Iran, Iraq, and North Korea.

Iran is an interesting case in point. In theory, the Iranian mullahs long ago decided to use terrorist groups to export their brand of Shia Islamism. One of their major instruments is Hezbollah in Lebanon, which was responsible for bombings in Lebanon in the 1980s, including those of the Marine barracks and of the U.S. Embassy. The Israeli seizure of the small freighter *Karine A*, carrying fifty tons of arms, proved that the Iranians were providing Yassir Arafat's militia with arms. Given such actions, in 2002 Iran headed the State Department's list of state sponsors of terrorism. Teheran even hosted a June 2002 terrorist conference.[6]

On the other hand, the Iranians have limited their operations. Their support of terrorists in the Persian Gulf, in Central Asia, in Africa, and in Turkey has been declining. They condemned the 11 September attacks on the United States, and, while rejecting the U.S. war against the Taliban, they offered passage to any U.S. airmen who might be shot down in Afghanistan. To balance that, they apparently allowed Al Qaeda personnel passage to and from Afghanistan, although those personnel were warned not to stay in Iran. Is the Iranian cup half empty or half full? To what extent is the cooling Iranian support of most terrorists a consequence of a widely felt desire for closer relations with the United States?

Moreover, there is a split within Iran. Its fundamentalist mullahs run its military and its security service. They obviously hate the United States and the West, and they support Arab terrorists. On the other hand, Iran has an elected pro-reform government. The sheer size of the majorities that government receives in elections suggest that the mullahs' days are numbered—if Western action does not drive the public into their hands. By the spring of 2002 there was evidence that many Iranians were seeking some sort of connection with the United States, and even that the "axis of evil" speech was driving them away from the clerics. Whether that would ultimately lead to some sort of democratic Islamic state, the most desirable outcome, was by no means certain. The conservative mullahs still control the security forces, and it appears that, unhindered, they will make common cause with other enemies of the West. Despite their enmity for the Sunni Taliban, the mullahs did not hand Al Qaeda operatives infiltrating Iran over to Western captors. Reportedly the survivors of the Afghan disaster had to promise not to try to destabilize the Iranian state, and they were hustled out of Iran as quickly as possible.

There have also been reports of collaboration between Hezbollah and the Sunni Al Qaeda, despite what would normally be mortal enmity between the two. Hezbollah in particular has expertise in demolition which, presumably, would be useful to Al Qaeda. Some saw Hezbollah's typical operational style in the attack on the Khobar Towers barracks in Saudi Arabia in 1995 (the Saudis blamed the Iranians, not local dissidents, for that attack). Continued Hezbollah operations, often against Israel, help explain Iranian inclusion in President Bush's "axis of evil."

As for Iraq, clearly Saddam Hussein wanted to hobble any American attempt to overthrow him, but equally clearly he preferred not to sponsor groups which may ultimately become too independent. Since the Gulf War Saddam sought revenge against the United States for his humiliation in Kuwait. His intelligence service plotted against, for example, former president George H. W. Bush (his headquarters were attacked by Tomahawks in retaliation). Saddam also seemed to renege on his promise, which helped end the Gulf War (and thus which at least in theory saved him from destruction), to abandon his programs for nuclear and biological/chemical weapons. Having ejected UN weapons inspectors in 1988, and apparently having revived the programs they were suppressing, he in effect gave the U.S. government the justification to attack him in March 2003.

Saddam apparently liked to keep the Israeli pot boiling, both to tie down a potential enemy and to gain support elsewhere in the Arab world. In 2002 he seemed to have concluded that the United States could not mount a decisive attack against him as long as the Israeli-Palestinian dispute remains unresolved. Thus he supported Palestinian terrorist groups, and he advertised compensation for the families of Palestinian suicide bombers. In the past, Iraq has certainly used terrorist means (such as murders) to deal with its enemies abroad, but only under the tight control of its national intelligence service. Indeed, one argument that Iraq was tied directly to the first World Trade Center bombing was that its architect, Ramzi Yousef, was using false Iraqi documents, which would only be provided to an Iraqi intelligence officer. Later Iraq apparently welcomed Al Qaeda terrorists in its war against its own Kurdish minority. Does that tie Iraq to 11 September?

The answer is probably no; any tie between Saddam and Al Qaeda is likely to be a temporary one of convenience. The Iraqis may well have provided low-level assistance to Al Qaeda operatives. If, as some have suggested, Ramzi Yousef was *at the same time* both an important figure in Al Qaeda and an Iraqi intelligence officer, then the 1993 World Trade Center bombing really would tie the two together. However, Al Qaeda envisages the destruction of the (secular) Iraqi state. In theory, movements like Al Qaeda do not mix easily with either secular governments (like Iraq's) or with national Islamist governments (like Iran's). However, it is likely that such governments are glad to exploit Al Qaeda strength, on the theory that ultimately they can deal with the Al Qaeda movement. The question is whether such association makes it essential to deal with such states. For example, there were persistent reports that, during the summer of 2000, Mohammed Atta, who apparently led the 11 September hijackers, met in Prague with a senior Iraqi intelligence officer. Did that imply Iraqi involvement in the plot, or were the Iraqis happy to help at a low level, on the theory that "the enemy of my enemy is my [temporary] friend?" If the assistance was not particularly vital, it can be argued that Iraq cannot be blamed for 11 September. On the other hand, if the Iraqis are willing to help Al Qaeda when required, then there must be a real fear that such help may include providing the terrorists with weapons they now lack, such as poison gas or even an atomic bomb.

To the Iraqis, Osama bin Laden was presumably valued, if at all, as a lever to eject the Americans from the Gulf. With the Americans gone, Iraq could win a war of conquest (a theme perhaps repeating Saddam's hopes during the Iran-Iraq War). To bin Laden, the Iraqis were a way of gaining material support needed for his revolution, which in turn would sweep them away. Presumably both sides see immediate value in damaging their common enemy, the West.

The U.S. government was probably far more concerned with the threat the Iraqis would pose to the Gulf states once they completed their programs to produce weapons of mass destruction. By 2002 it seemed clear that the containment effort of the 1990s had failed to stop the Iraqi programs. A U.S. attack to disarm Iraq was seen as preemptive.[7]

In the past, for example in his attack on Iran in 1980, Saddam Hussein showed a willingness to attack first and think afterwards. If indeed his intelligence service finds terrorists a useful means of attacking his enemies, then Iraq may well have provided terrorists with support and refuge. In this way Iraq performed some of the functions which during the Cold War were performed by the Soviet Union and its client states. Eliminating Saddam's Iraq may depress terrorism just as the fall of the Soviet Union did. The attack would also deter other potential state sponsors of anti–U.S. terrorism.

North Korea is yet further removed from the current terrorist war. However, it has enthusiastically embraced terrorism (or special attacks) in the past, having gone so far as to deploy special forces specifically to assassinate the South Korean President and, successfully, to have killed most of a South Korean cabinet. North Korea is also the main source of missiles to rogue states such as Libya and Syria. Such missiles, particularly if they are combined with chemical or nuclear warheads, might be a decisive way of deterring the United States from dealing with such states. Conversely, deterring or even eliminating the supplier of such weapons would be a way of indirectly warning rogue states that they could not expect to support terrorism and survive.

Many who heard the President's speech felt that two more states should have been named: Saudi Arabia and China.

If there is any swamp in which Al Qaeda terrorists seem to breed, it must be Saudi Arabia.[8] The Saudi Wahhabi form of Islam is the ideology underpinning Al Qaeda and the Taliban. The rulers of the Saudi state base their legitimacy on their perceived Islamic piety. The perception of Saudi royal legitimacy in turn depends on the officially-supported Wahhabi clergy. Yet it is painfully clear that the Saudi elite, headed by the royal family, do not adhere to the strict law either behind closed doors or when they are abroad. Given the officially supported Wahhabi version of Islam, this contradiction is potentially explosive. The Saudi solution has been ever-increasing support of Wahhabi clerics, in hopes that they would deflect any popular discontent away from the royal system. Saudi royal rule is backed by a large secret police apparatus. The clerics are backed by religious police.

The Saudi situation has another aspect as well. When the Saudi kingdom was founded, it was a remote desert place to which a very austere religion, the Wahhabi form of Islam, was presumably well suited. Trade with outsiders was limited and relatively insignificant. For many years, however, the situation within Saudi Arabia has been dominated by oil sales—to the non-Muslim West. Probably few Saudis live in anything approximating the desert environment of the past. The strictures of the Wahhabi faith are probably ill-suited to this situation. The contradiction between the way they live and what they have been taught as religious truth is probably very disconcerting, and it may add to the effectiveness of fire-and-brimstone mullahs. For their part, increasingly radicalized mullahs may see little point in moderating their popular message for fear of destroying the state—and the economy—which feeds them.

This situation may be inherently unstable. At the very least, the best way to deflect attention from the sins of the royals is to attack the West and Israel as its local client. Thus the average Saudi is often told that personal salvation lies in jihad against the West. That is one reason so many Saudis turned up in Afghanistan, and later in Al Qaeda—and also why many rich Saudis were happy to give Al Qaeda money. Whether such donations were sincere, or were in effect blackmail (to convince the clerics to attack some other hypocrite) may be irrelevant. What is clear is that much of the Al Qaeda problem can be traced to Saudi society, though not directly to the Saudi state. Since 11 September, the U.S. government has often thanked the Saudi government for its help against the terrorists, but U.S. news media have often reported obstructionism.

The reality, that it has endangered itself by financing dangerous clerics, makes the Saudi government very uncomfortable. It cannot admit that extreme forms of Islam are themselves unacceptable, because it justifies its existence by its strict adherence to Wahhabi Islam. One consequence is the bizarre spectacle of senior Saudi ministers blaming Zionists (i.e., Israelis) for terrorist acts for which Al Qaeda has already taken responsibility. However, it also appears that the Saudis recognize that they are in difficulties and that their society has to modernize in order to survive. For example, their public offer to broker an Arab-Israeli peace on the basis of UN resolutions was unrealistic (the Israelis would have lost much of their territory), but it did indicate a willingness to accept the existence of Israel, which for Saudis is a radical step.

For the present, the United States cannot afford to abandon Saudi Arabia, because the kingdom contributes so much of the world's oil. Although the United States itself is little dependent on Saudi oil, that is irrelevant, because the world oil market is so interconnected. Any major cut in production by one supplier will raise the price for all users. As the boycotts after the 1973 Middle East War demonstrated, sharp price increases can easily plunge the entire West into recession or even depression.

Heavy U.S. investment has created air bases and command centers in Saudi Arabia that would be difficult to duplicate. On the other hand, the Saudis were notably reluctant to allow use of their territory for the assault against Afghanistan. When war with Iraq came in March 2003 the Saudis did not permit any use of their air bases, although they may have permitted U.S. use of command facilities (as in the Afghan War). Saudi strictures were not crippling, mainly because Kuwait welcomed coalition forces.

Nor is it clear whether Saudi oil has the significance it previously had. That may be particularly the case as oil from South Russia and the former Soviet Central Asian republics comes on line. Indeed the U.S. government may sense the opening of a window of opportunity for dealing with the Saudi swamp—at the least, for applying the pressure for the Saudis to deal with their own society.

Then there is China, recognized by many Americans as a long-term threat, but currently an ally in the war against terror. Like North Korea, China exports missiles and the technology to make them. At least in the past, China espoused a national strategy of attacking any hegemonic power. Once that explained assaults against the Soviets, but now the United States is the only superpower, hence the only threat to China.

China has its own Islamic terrorist/guerrilla problem in Sinkiang. Some reports suggest that the Chinese offered the Taliban army weapons in return for restraining those guerrillas. Too, for many years China has supported Pakistan as a counter to India, which it sees as a long-term threat. That makes it very likely that China assisted the Taliban if the latter were in turn supporting Islamic terrorists in Kashmir—as is virtually certain. Does that make China part of the swamp? Probably not on anything like the scale of the axis members and Saudi Arabia, but it does provide ammunition for those in Washington who regard China as the next major threat to the United States, and who feel that China can be dealt with as part of the war against terror.

There are of course other states which have, willy-nilly, acted as refuges for Al Qaeda and bin Laden, particularly Somalia and the Sudan. The argument has been made that any failed state, like Somalia, becomes a potential base for Al Qaeda. That is not entirely obvious. In an entirely lawless state, wealthy foreigners like the Al Qaeda Arabs become potential targets. They may be able to set up a microstate under their own control, but that takes substantial effort which cannot go into terrorism. In many semilawless places, like Yemen, which have been suggested as post-Afghan bases for Al Qaeda, there are indeed tribes which might welcome bin Laden and his followers, but those tribes have local enemies who would be quite happy to plunder their guests. The Taliban in Afghanistan were a different proposition, because in their case the state had been hijacked altogether by the terrorists—to the extent that the war against Afghanistan could be seen not as a war against terrorism but as a war against a well-defined national government. Moreover, from Al Qaeda's point of view it was probably essential that the Taliban state they hijacked was a going concern, capable of precluding local attacks against Al Qaeda itself.

Before bin Laden created Al Qaeda, there were numerous local terrorist organizations working in the Muslim world. They were interested in solving local problems, for example, destroying Israel or converting Egypt into a fundamentalist state. Bin Laden's achievement was to form links with numerous local organizations, so that they could be coordinated to conduct local attacks in support of his broader vision of Islamic empire, with himself as ruler. To the extent that Osama and his immediate associates are the coordinating mechanism, his destruction would also end the coordinated global threat offered by the local groups.

Once U.S. forces struck in Afghanistan, the situation was further complicated in that Al Qaeda forces driven from that country had to seek refuge elsewhere. To what extent could they rely on earlier interterrorist bonds? For example, Islamic terrorists of the Abu Sayyaf organization, which Osama helped establish, are currently fighting in the Philippines. There they have carved out a small territory, a potential sanctuary in which Al Qaeda can regroup. The Philippines has already been a staging ground for Islamic terrorists; for example, some years ago it was the Philippine police who seized Ramzi Yousef with a computer full of plans to attack American targets such as trans-Pacific airliners. More recently, it has been reported that Osama himself sent his youngest son to the Philippines to keep him out of reach of U.S. attackers. As the Afghan War wound down, U.S. Special Forces were sent to the Philippines to train local troops, and thus to help deal with the terrorist enclave there.

Is the terrorist international a new phenomenon, or have we seen something similar before? If we have, we can have a better idea of where it is likely to go and of how to combat it. The industrialization of the nineteenth century saw the sort of dislocation which bred widespread discontent. A variety of revolutionary movements—Communist, Socialist, anarchist—grew up in different countries. Some envisaged a new worldwide workers' state (like Osama's new caliphate), others were more interested in solving problems within their own countries. This was much more than intellectual ferment. The radicals attacked. They murdered prominent citizens in hopes of destabilizing governments. They actually took over the city of Paris (as the Paris Commune) in the aftermath of French defeat by Prussia in 1871. After the commune was crushed, radicals survived in cells throughout Europe and the United States. Periodically they attacked symbols of society such as bourgeois cafés and even the New York Stock Exchange. The intellectual descendants of the turn-of-the-century radicals are the current antiglobalists.

Each group always hoped that by its example it could excite a larger revolution which would create the sort of ideal society it sought, which in theory would assuage the widespread pain of society. Thus the communards hoped that they would become the center of a new kind of France. Their defeat did not convince their adherents that they were wrong, merely that the force wielded by society was still too strong to address. In 1914 they hoped that the outbreak of war would cause all workers to understand that they owed loyalty to each other rather than to their governments; surely they would rise to create the workers' paradise. The stress of war, it seemed, might break the state, just as in 1871 the stress of war had nearly destroyed the French state and ushered in the Paris Commune. In reality workers turned out to be nationalists, and the pan-national dream remained just that. The Soviets adopted its rhetoric, but only to advance their national ends.

Yet this brief history presages what we are now seeing in the Muslim world. The Taliban emirate in Afghanistan might be likened to the Paris

Commune, and the decentralized world of late-nineteenth-century radicals to its aftermath. What is essential to keep in mind is that radicals of various stripes found a degree of common cause; they held international conferences, and groups in one country would generally offer refuge to those forced to flee others. Moreover, the movement as such had no head who could be killed, merely a common set of ideas. Many governments found the prospect of a world revolutionary movement terrifying. They contributed to their problems by overreacting, sometimes turning peaceful strikers into revolutionaries by attacking them as such. By the early years of the twentieth century, it must have seemed that the existing world order was shaky, and that it might disintegrate altogether under the pressure of a shadowy revolutionary-terrorist movement. As it turned out, time largely solved the problem. It was not that the revolutionaries died out or were caught. Most of them survived. However, as the immediate pain of industrialization receded, and indeed as workers found a practical voice in unions, the power of the terrorists declined. At least as important, the revolutionary movement kept fragmenting in a self-destructive way. The fragmentation was not really ideological, although ideological differences were often cited to explain why one group splintered from another. Rather, the movement threw up too many leaders who decided that they wanted their own loyal groups. That is likely the fate of any Muslim terrorist movement: the promised leadership of the whole Muslim world (or even of the whole world) is too attractive to surrender to any other madman.

Another interesting parallel is in governmental support of terrorism for political ends. The czarist government of Russia, for instance, was faced with serious internal revolutionary problems posed by a variety of groups, ranging from Communists and Socialists to anarchists. At the same time, it supported its pan-Slavist ambitions partly by financing terrorists in parts of the Austrian Empire. One such terrorist precipitated World War 1 and, indirectly, the triumph of the Russian revolutionaries, by shooting the Archduke Franz Ferdinand in 1914. The moral is that terrorism is dangerous. Americans who associate the rise of Osama bin Laden and his brand of jihad with U.S. sponsorship of Afghan guerrillas during the Soviet occupation of that country may see World War I as a kind of unintended blowback.

Some analysts of terrorism have argued that its decentralized character precludes any effective counter-attack.[9] They argue that the U.S. military, for example, is a highly centralized organization designed to attack other centralized organizations. That may be simplistic, and the history of coun-

terterrorism suggests a U.S. strategy. Is there anything the loosely connected terrorist cells share, any center which can be attacked? One answer
might be information—not so much information about their mutual enemy (which is easy to gather) as information allowing them to distinguish
ally from enemy. In recent years U.S. defense analysts have been more and
more interested in the effect of attacking an enemy's information as a way
of crippling him. The cells survive because they are largely invisible to the
authorities hunting them. How do they recognize each other? How can a
cell member be sure that when he approaches a potential ally, he is not
committing suicide? In a large organization, there is some central registry,
at least of accredited friends. For example, imagine two U.S. military
planners. How does each know the other is legitimate? Uniforms and even
offices are not enough, because the one can be stolen and the other, often,
illicitly occupied. The key guarantee of legitimacy is the myriad checks
which the surrounding organization routinely carries out. The system fails
from time to time, but usually the bureaucracy protects it. A heavily decentralized terrorist international lacks any such protective bureaucracy. It is,
therefore, inherently vulnerable to attacks which begin with deception—
with the destruction of the limited information each cell has about who its
friends really are. That is the same reason that "stings" can be so effective in
the fight against crime.[10]

Standard police work, including infiltration, makes the cells' information critically important, because it is their key to survival. Infiltration is
of course also important to the cells' opponent, because it can provide
early warning. For example, when the World Trade Center was bombed in
1993, the attack came as a surprise. It was suggested at the time that U.S.
police forces, as well as the FBI, had been rendered powerless by restrictions on political work imposed at the time of the Watergate scandal in
1973–74. Infiltration of Muslim extremist groups was undertaken after
1993, but bin Laden was able to overcome it by establishing separate cells
dedicated to the particular plot that was carried out on 11 September.
However, it is also likely that Osama's reasonable distrust of groups already
operating in the United States drastically reduced the number of cells that
he could maintain and thus the scale of any attack he could mount. Now
that considerable Al Qaeda documentation has fallen into American
hands, he or his successors probably cannot be sure of which cells or lines
of support remain unknown to his enemies, and this uncertainty in itself
may have a useful deterrent effect.

The Czarists, much concerned with a terrorist threat, instinctively understood the value of deception. They set up false anti-Czarist organizations in hopes that those prone to radical activity would join and thus be neutralized. Often such tactics worked, but there were some major problems. For example, it paid to run a false-front organization: organizers might work to convert mildly anti-Czarist intellectuals to active revolutionaries worthy of government scrutiny. Those who survived became real revolutionaries, and they helped destroy the czarist government. On the other hand, the mere knowledge that some apparently legitimately anti-Czarist organizations were police fronts must have worried other revolutionaries, who always had to fear betrayal. Incidentally, such fears contributed to the paranoid style of Soviet politics, which for decades was conducted by those who had lived under exactly such attacks. For example, in his communications with the North Korean government before the outbreak of war in Korea in 1950, Stalin always used his revolutionary pseudonym, Filippov, rather than his name (and Stalin itself was a pseudonym). He was acting like a hunted conspirator rather than as the head of state of a superpower. Similarly, virtually all key decisions were communicated by telephone rather than being written down—although exactly what malevolent police organization might have seized written records was surely no longer clear.

In addition, setting up active anti-Czarist organizations carried the danger that some of the double agents involved might operate on their own initiative. The most celebrated case was that of Yevno Azef, "Comrade Valentine," who enlisted as a police agent and eventually headed the Terror Brigade.[11] In this capacity he routinely reported planned operations to his case officer, and the police quashed them. Comrade Valentine was Jewish, and he learned that Prime Minister Stolypin had proposed anti-Jewish pogroms specifically as a way of diverting Russian public opinion from very real grievances. Valentine therefore organized the assassination of the czar's uncle, Grand Duke Sergei (who was governor of Moscow) and forgot to inform his case officer. He left Russia soon afterward, supposedly aided in his escape by his existing official contacts. There is some speculation that he had personal ambitions and intended to play the radicals off against the state to support his own rise, but ultimately the radicals decided that he was in fact a police informer. Although they condemned him to death, he survived to die in his own bed a few months after the revolution broke out.

Later, the Czarists' successors, the Communists, were more successful. After the revolution, they were confronted with numerous survivors of the

Czarist regime, who could reasonably hope to exploit public unhappiness with their government. They could not hope to send agents to hunt down all such potential enemies, particularly as the governments with which they had taken refuge might well protect them. Instead, they established the Trust, a fraudulent counterrevolutionary organization. It sent emissaries to the Czarist groups. The Trust seemed by far the most successful opponent of the new Communist regime, hence the one worth supporting. It therefore collected not only the money which might finance counterrevolution but also the best of the surviving Czarists. Once it seemed to have attracted all that could be expected, the Trust was shut down and most of those who had gone to Russia to help it were shot, including the celebrated Sidney Reilley, "ace of spies." Then the Soviets took the next step: they announced that the Trust had been their fraud. In turn, this announcement had to make any counterrevolutionaries who had not been caught wonder whether any successor movement was legitimate. This tactic, establishing a fraudulent organization in order to attract and destroy potential opponents, was repeated in several guises after World War II. Its victims included Western intelligence organizations.

The idea of the Trust is suggestive. When the African embassies were bombed in 1998, the U.S. government announced that Osama bin Laden and Al Qaeda were responsible; it even called bin Laden the "most wanted man" or the "worst terrorist." While such titles may be grossly negative in the West, for someone like bin Laden they are valuable endorsements, useful for attracting both money and followers. An alternative strategy would have been to announce that, after much snooping, the U.S. intelligence agencies had found that some other terrorist (call him Abu X) had been responsible and that Osama was illegitimately taking credit. U.S. intelligence was after Abu X, and surely it would soon destroy him; but for the time being he, not that poseur Osama, was the man to destroy.

The Abu X movement would be the U.S. equivalent of the Trust. It would suck in the money and the men Osama might otherwise field. The next step, of course, would be to use the men to mount a spectacularly unsuccessful attack, killing as many of them as possible, and then (if possible) maintain the fraud. It is not clear whether any such tactic was proposed at the time. Presumably it would have been rejected on the grounds that the U.S. security system lacks the necessary skills and is far too leaky to make it work. On the other hand, even the knowledge that the United States was assembling a false-front organization might well make it more difficult for Osama to recruit his force, or to maintain it. It might become possible, for example, to spread a rumor that Osama himself was the false-front operative. Recent statements about help given by various senior Al Qaeda operatives, such as Abu Zubeidah, may be a step in this direction.

This sort of operation was not limited to the Czarists. In England, for example, it now seems that the famous Guy Fawkes gunpowder plot was designed by the government of the day mainly to expose Catholics who might have caused it trouble; and during the late nineteenth century it appears that the government concocted a plot (to blow up Queen Victoria) specifically to discredit and destroy the Irish Fenian movement.[12]

The Czarists also tried to use black (i.e., covert) propaganda (i.e., convert) to split the population from the revolutionists. For such propaganda to work, it has to be rooted either in reality or in widely accepted notions among the target population (Czarists used anti-Semitism, a very popular theme in Russia, which made their canards credible; many of the radicals were Jewish). A parallel objective in the current war would be to split the mass of Muslims away from organizations such as Osama's. It can reasonably be argued that Osama's goal is a war which might destroy most of the world's Muslims. Thus it might not be too far a stretch to claim that Osama is or was part of a secret organization the goal of which is to destroy Islam while appearing to help it. As for Osama's nominal goal of creating a single Islamic empire, it might be suggested that his real goal is to use that unity to destroy Islam once and for all. A black propagandist might spread the word that the jihadis were mortal enemies of true Muslims, hence should be shunned and, ideally, killed. Of course, much would depend on just how credible the propaganda was.

Perhaps the greatest problem the Czarist police had was that the revolutionaries enjoyed sanctuaries beyond the Russian border. Some governments were happy to extradite them back to Russia, but others regarded the rather repressive Czarist state as somewhat illegitimate and refused to punish anyone for crimes not committed on their soil. The British in particular had a long tradition of sheltering revolutionaries as long as those individuals kept the peace in Britain. Moreover, given their liberal traditions, the British found the Czarist autocracy particularly odious and thus sympathized with the revolutionaries. That is why, for example, the Reading Room of the British Museum still displays the library cards issued to Karl Marx, Leon Trotsky, and Vladimir Lenin, all definitely enemies of the Czarist and other continental states. For that matter, the United States also served as a sanctuary, protecting various revolutionaries, including those opposed to the British. Switzerland, too, was a sanctuary. The Czarist reaction to the British sanctuary was to attempt to provoke acts of terror on British soil, thus ending the sanctuary. That is, an agent provocateur could, hopefully, cause a revolutionary enjoying sanctuary to act in such a way as to end it. Joseph Conrad's novel *The Secret Agent* describes just this tactic.

These examples suggest just how far removed from conventional warfare counterterrorism can be. Yet the conventional warfare end of the war matters. The terrorist international of pre-1914 Europe lacked power because it had no national government backing it. Everywhere it was at the mercy of local authorities. Its sanctuaries could easily reverse policy, as indeed they later did. The situation changed radically with the Russian Revolution, because the new Soviet state backed what had been one of many terrorist splinter groups, the Communists, and provided Communist subversives abroad with a real sanctuary and with real support. The understanding of what that could mean led several governments to try to crush the Communists in 1918–20. Afghanistan was of course nothing like Russia, but the absence of a sanctuary is significant now. To the extent that Osama and his friends realize how valuable sanctuary can be, it seems likely that they will sooner rather than later try to take over another country or countries.

Until very recently, various European governments allowed Muslim terrorists to operate freely on their soil on condition that they commit no acts of terror there. The situation changed only when it became clear that no such promises were likely to be honored. Examples include France, which long allowed terrorists what amounted to free passage across its territory. Germany has acted as a sanctuary in much the pre-1917 British mode. In their case there is a special circumstance. The Germans have avoided any semblance of a police apparatus comparable to that created by the Nazis; hence, fundamentalists are able to operate particularly freely. Germany was apparently the primary base area for the terrorist group which carried out the 11 September hijackings. Its leader, Mohammed Atta, secured residency by registering at a technical university in Hamburg. From the terrorists' perspective, residence in Western Europe was particularly attractive because passengers arriving from there were less likely to be scrutinized than those coming from the Middle East. With the advent of the European Union, there are no cross-border controls within most of Western Europe. Too, throughout Western Europe there are large Muslim populations in which to hide, and in which to seek support through radicalization in some mosques.

As for the information end of the war, an open society may find it uncomfortable to support deception as a means of warfare. In 2002 the Defense Department tried to set up an Office of Strategic Information (OSI), nominally to tell the U.S. side of the antiterrorist story to the Muslim world but also as a way of centralizing any disinformation effort. The disinformation effort should have been secret, but soon it was leaked to the U.S. news media, apparently by those running existing public information offices, who resented what looked like competition. Given the important role deception played in World War II, and in the cold war, it would seem most important to use in this war.

In February 2003 U.S. and Pakistani forces made a major contribution to any possible war of deception by capturing Khalid Sheikh Mohammad, alleged planner of the 11 September atrocities and number three officer in Al Qaeda. Khalid was widely described as the man through whom all major plots had to be cleared, and the man to whom every operative of the dispersed organization reported. He was, in effect, the institutional memory of Al Qaeda. Naturally, the emphasis among commentators was on how (or whether) his brain could be unlocked. However, the simple fact that probably Khalid alone knew everyone in Al Qaeda may be far more significant. After all, without a central office it has no archives. That must seem an advantage in that archives can be captured and exploited. Yet archives exist because organizations need records in order to operate, not because they feel they have some sort of duty to future historians. What happens when such records do not exist, or are not accessible? Al Qaeda is probably organized into cells which try to avoid contact with each other, for the sake of security. They do, however, apparently need support provided by the larger organization. How do they know that an emissary from the central office is genuine? Khalid was probably the answer because he knew everyone. His role became much more important after the U.S.–led attack on Afghanistan destroyed many others who could have assured cells of their bona fides. Without Khalid, the cells are no longer nearly as safe as they were. They are vulnerable to stings. Merely understanding their vulnerability (which will be evident as Khalid's computer is exploited) will tend to dampen their enthusiasm, because the one constant in cellular organizations is a tendency to paranoia.

6

A New Kind of War

While Osama bin Laden was forming his terror international, the U.S. military was struggling to develop a new kind of war, described alternately as the Revolution in Military Affairs (RMA) and Network-Centric Warfare. The new concepts were attractive for two different reasons. One was the rise of information-handling technology. It seemed inevitable that a new kind of technology would make for a new kind of warfare. In the past, American productivity had shaped American tactics: the American way of war, in World War II and in Korea and Vietnam, was to bury the enemy in firepower, to substitute firepower and mechanized (i.e., mass-production) mobility for personnel. If the U.S. economy was moving away from producing masses of things and moving toward processing masses of information, perhaps U.S. strategy should change to suit that evolution.

At the same time, the U.S. services were caught in a squeeze. Anyone attending seminars on the future of U.S. defense in the 1990s came across the "train wreck." The projected defense budget was static; perhaps it might rise a few percent a year. Unfortunately, if the services' hardware programs were projected ahead, on this basis they were unaffordable. It was unlikely that, in the aftermath of the cold war, the budget could rise enough to pay for the full range of new programs demanded under various defense reviews. The problem was twofold. First, although the Soviets had been eliminated as a threat, the United States faced credible threats in many parts of the world. Indeed, the threats might be more difficult in a post–cold war world, because they could arise nearly simultaneously. During the cold war, it could have been assumed that the Soviets would decide which threats to mount, and that they would mount only a limited range at any one time. Now the attackers would probably be independent, so several different threats might be posed more or less simultaneously. Thus it seemed that the number of separate U.S. units or commands around the world could not readily be reduced.

In addition, system costs were rising. Cold war forces had been procured on the basis that if war came they would be used intensively, but only for a limited time. Thus the U.S. Army might need five hundred attack helicopters, but if the big war lasted only a month, it would need only five hundred helicopter-months' worth of spare parts. Initial experiences of post–cold war conflict, in places like the Persian Gulf and Bosnia, showed that although relatively small forces might be engaged, they would have to operate at high intensity for protracted periods of time. For example, a mere fifty helicopters operating for ten months would use up the stock of spares intended for five hundred under cold war conditions. That is why, for example, the U.S. Army found it difficult to operate many Apache helicopters after the Gulf War, until stocks of spare parts had been rebuilt, and why helicopter operations in Bosnia proved so expensive in material terms. This expense was entirely apart from any desire to buy more sophisticated successors to existing systems.

Weapons expenditure rose unexpectedly, because the basis for predicting it changed. Again, cold war analysts wanted enough weapons to fight a short, hot war against well-defined targets. During the post–cold war the United States found itself fighting frequently and unexpectedly. Although only limited numbers of weapons might be used on any one occasion, repeated use could be costly. For example, between 1991 and 1999, about a thousand Tomahawk cruise missiles, a third or a quarter of the planned war reserve, were fired, and new missiles were not being made quickly enough to make up for that level of usage.

Several strategists proposed a new way of fighting, based on the most efficient possible use of information. Imagine, they said, that remote sensors could create an accurate picture of the battle space. This picture could be disseminated to numerous tactical units, providing each with a usable portrait of the situation well beyond the horizon defined by its own on-board sensors. Given such a picture, each tactical unit could make effective use of long-range but very accurate weapons; it could dominate a space well beyond that defined by its horizon. Instead of the usual practice of concentrating shooters against a single target, the shooters could be dispersed, making it difficult for an enemy either to predict their target or to destroy them preemptively. The shooters in turn would share (in effect) not only details but also knowledge of the battle space. Shooters could, moreover, be coordinated so that the effects of hitting particular targets could be orchestrated, to mutually reinforce each other.

If relatively few weapons were available, it would be essential that their effects be observed, so that only targets not destroyed earlier be reattacked. Indeed, it would be best if damage assessment was so quick that weapons already in the air could be reassigned. It was a short step from this requirement to a desire to deal with pop-up and relocatable targets as they appeared, by reassigning weapons.

Keys to such operation were remote sensing; precision navigation (so a missile sent to a location indicated by a sensor would hit its target); high-quality communications, initially to distribute the tactical picture and to coordinate the shooters; and some means of hitting targets based entirely on locations indicated on the distributed map of the battle space. Ideally there also had to be some means of feedback in the form of assignable sensors talking back to whoever commanded the battle. It turned out that all were at hand. The information needed to develop a wide-area tactical picture could be assembled using a combination of reconnaissance satellites, reconnaissance aircraft, UAVs, and local devices such as unattended ground sensors. Powerful computers could assemble all of this data into meaningful tactical information. Other satellites offered high-capacity communications. Widely distributed but powerful computers could make sense of the information received from the satellite systems. As for precision, the new Global Positioning Satellite (GPS) system made it possible to direct a weapon to a planned location, whatever the range from which the weapon were fired.

It appeared that an RMA was at hand. The concept of such revolutions had been publicized by the Soviets; after 1945 they felt that the combination of nuclear weapons, jet aircraft, and missiles had drastically changed warfare. Late in the 1970s they announced that computers (which they called cybernetics) would have a similar impact; indeed, their attempt to build a massive Soviet computer industry to keep pace with the Western military helped destroy the Soviet state. By the mid-1990s it looked as though the projected revolution was at hand. Its prophet, Andrew Marshall of the Defense Department's Office of Net Assessment, cautioned that such a revolution meant the combination of new technology with new tactics. Tanks, for example, were not in themselves revolutionary. The combination of tanks with blitzkrieg tactics, which defeated France in 1940, was. Indeed, the case of France offered a cautionary example. French tanks were actually superior to those of the Germans, and they were more numerous. The

Germans, however, understood how to use their tanks in ways the French had not imagined. One hallmark of the tank-led revolution in military operations was that the Germans equipped their tanks with radios so they could operate more rapidly in a coordinated way. In the 1990s the United States unquestionably led the world in computers, but those machines still supported what could be described as a largely pre-computer style military establishment. Marshall asked how that establishment could transform itself to fully exploit the new power of the computers.

The computer-led revolution could be described in various ways. One of its main proponents, Vice Adm. Arthur Cebrowski, called it Network-Centric Warfare, on the theory that the netting of tactical information and of shooters was its key aspect.[1] He pointed out that if all the shooters shared the same tactical picture and the same objectives, they could act independently ("self-synchronously") to gain those objectives. Ironically, although the admiral described the concept as revolutionary, in fact it mirrored evolving naval practice using ship-to-ship data links (Admiral Cebrowski was a naval aviator).

Another reason to call the new kind of war network-centric was that to implement it, the center of gravity of defense spending would have to shift from combatant (shooter) force structure (in the navy, platforms; in the army, units) to sensors and command/control. Any network-centric force would have fewer bullets to fire, but on the other hand, it would be able to fire them far more precisely. Conversely, a force attempting to use the new concepts without being very plentifully supplied with sensors and communications might well find itself in difficulties.

Admiral Cebrowski pointed out that this change required deep understanding of just how a war should be fought. In the past, it had been assumed that one side would win simply by destroying the other's forces or industrial assets. That could have been done either with massed conventional forces or with nuclear weapons. It could not have been done with small numbers of highly precise weapons, at least with conventional ones. What, then, could the new kind of military force do? What should it do?

One answer was that combat was generally about finding and attacking the center of gravity of the enemy force. Once that center was destroyed, the enemy would collapse. Surely the idea was particularly applicable to a new world of precision warfare. The Joint Chiefs of Staff approved a document, Joint Vision 2010, outlining the new concepts, including the attempt to decide a war by attacking the enemy's center of gravity without having to fight through his massed forces.

The new idea was attractive because it dealt with the post–cold war problems, chief among them unpredictability. The cold war had presented only a few important combat scenarios. For example, a U.S. Army officer could spend his entire career studying the problem of Soviet attack through the Fulda Gap in Germany, or of a North Korean attack on South Korea across the Demilitarized Zone. Now U.S. forces found themselves responding to numerous crises as they arose, rather than being placed, early in a crisis, to defuse it. Placement late in a crisis required that U.S. forces be made much more mobile. The more mobile the force, the less it could carry with it. No matter how many missiles were made, only so many could move to a distant theater quickly enough, so the ones which got there had to be effective. For that matter, the longer the range at which the forces which arrived could fight, the wider the area they could affect. Since the forces arriving would have to be compact, they could not take much with them in the way of sensors or, for that matter, logistics backup. Joint Vision 2010 included phrases such as "precision engagement" and even "precision logistics," for a system which provided just what was needed when it was needed.

Joint Vision 2010 was always briefed in a very abstract way, using graphics showing floors and columns and ceilings but no concrete examples of concepts such as the center of gravity. Those supporting the idea pointed to historical examples. For example, the Mongol horde which overran so much of Europe was exactly the sort of lightweight force the new way of war envisaged. The Mongols won by concentrating on the center of gravity of the opposing force, its leader and his immediate associates. Once they had been killed, the European army disintegrated. Unfortunately, modern armies and modern states are generally designed with exactly such threats in mind. A dictatorship such as Iraq might collapse at the death of its ruler, but even then the enemy army might fight on, particularly if animated by nationalism or some other ideology.

To many, Joint Vision 2010 was little more than a new version of the old idea of strategic bombing. Before World War II, U.S. air theorists had argued that strikes against key enemy targets could destroy an enemy's military power, even before anyone had to fight through his territory. Although World War II experience suggested otherwise, they responded that strategic air power had failed in that war only because it was still imprecise. Had it been focused well enough, it would have won. The postwar emphasis on nuclear weapons seemed to reflect the victory of air power advocates, although experience in Vietnam was less than encouraging for them.

The air power enthusiasts argued that their weapon had failed in Vietnam largely through misapplication and through the clumsiness of existing non-nuclear weapons.

Even so, they faced a serious problem. Was there always a center of gravity suitable for attack? If not, all the precision weapons in the world would not achieve the sort of quick victory the enthusiasts envisaged. Skeptics could point to a paucity of obvious centers of gravity in modern societies. It is not even a matter of how industrialized they are. What, for example, is the center of gravity of the United States? In a primitive country like Afghanistan, it is much more difficult to identify a targetable center of gravity. It may be that virtually no country has anything like a center of gravity, the destruction of which will bring enormous advantages.

Even without a center of gravity, the new kind of warfare envisaged a scarcity of weapons, none of which would have particularly devastating effects. For these weapons to cause the desired consequences, they would have to be delivered according to some sort of plan which focused on their particular effects on the enemy's system, rather than on simpler measures of destruction. That in turn suggested that attack planning would have to be far more sophisticated than in the past, and that it would depend heavily on intelligence not merely about the enemy's order of battle, but about the structure of his political and military systems. Even then it would not be at all certain that the desired outcome could be assured.

Was there any alternative? By the time Joint Vision 2010 was being advertised, many in the U.S. military were familiar with a theory which had been advanced by Col. John Boyd, USAF (ret). Boyd's perception was that all military operations could be described in terms of an "OODA Loop," the sequence of Observation, Orientation (understanding what has been observed), Decision, and Action. Combat could be seen as the interaction of the two sides' loops. Boyd's view of the French defeat in 1940 was that the French decision cycle had been far slower than that of the Germans. Many accounts of the campaign report the continual surprise with which the French General Staff greeted reports of German attacks; it seemed the Germans were everywhere and that the staff could not design an effective counterblow, despite overall French numerical superiority and the technical superiority of French tanks. The puzzle, of how a superior French army was defeated so very quickly and, moreover, of why it surrendered while still largely intact, had led some scholars to believe that the French generals were traitors who hated the Republic more than they hated the Germans. Boyd's view was very different. If the French decision cycle lagged the

Germans' badly enough, the French would indeed find themselves more and more surprised. They would collapse in what amounted to a nervous breakdown. Boyd's ideas proved persuasive, and many American officers learned about the OODA cycle.

Perhaps, then, the new kind of war could be decisive because, given better overall information, those running it could indeed outfox their enemies, springing surprise after surprise. Very long-range precision fire would help, since the enemy would be unable to guess its targets. The ability to concentrate fire rather than troops on the ground might also make it far easier to deceive the enemy.

The French example suggests another interpretation. Those fighting any war vary radically in their morale and in their willingness to take casualties. Veteran troops are usually described as battle-hardened, but they can also be described as war-weary; Frederick the Great once said that he hated veteran troops because they knew what was coming. Once troops are at war, they may continue fighting at least partly to avenge dead comrades and relatives, but when the war is over, they remember how brutal it was and often find it difficult to fight again. How much did French memories of World War I, which was certainly horrific, affect the impact of the German assault?

The new style of warfare carries further implications. For example, information is never perfect. Small units armed with long-range weapons may mistakenly attack each other. To avoid that, they have to be dispersed. Advocates of network-centric warfare often say that, given a netted tactical picture, a few can do the work formerly done by many: a brigade can cover the same area as, say, a division. They only rarely add that the brigade (in very dispersed form) must *replace* the division altogether because a denser force distribution is self-defeating. Similarly, the new style of warfare may demand that aircraft operate in smaller numbers and in more dispersed fashion. In the past, they massed to hit fixed targets, and one achievement of the Gulf War was simply to coordinate hordes of aircraft via computer-generated air tasking orders. If, however, most of the targets the aircraft hit are transient or pop-up ones, and if aircraft often have to be redirected in flight, then such mass coordination creates serious problems. Redirecting any one airplane causes changes in the flight plans of many others; this ripple effect can and probably will upset the entire air plan.

Thus it can be argued that the new style of warfare may be peculiarly well adapted to the post–cold war situation in which the United States finds itself, in which there is never time to deploy very large units and small U.S. units in forward areas must fight very effectively. Even if there is time to fly massed units to a distant theater, there is unlikely to be time to set up the supporting infrastructure they need: their spare parts and maintenance equipment and their weaponry.

The new kind of war, moreover, is strike warfare: a commander finds and destroys particular targets. That is certainly the rule in some kinds of warfare. For example, in air defense, what counts is shooting down enemy aircraft. However, in some cases occupation of an area is as important, and that requires numbers in place. Occupation can, it is true, be made more efficient by netting if it is made reactive: if the remote sensor grid picks up an intruder, units under net control can intercept it. As a case in point, at one time police forces operated largely by foot patrol: an individual policeman walked his beat, dealing with problems, often before they became crimes. Foot patrolmen were expensive, though, and police cruisers were substituted. The connection between police and neighborhood deteriorated, often noticeably. The most extreme departure from the old technique of occupation was the SWAT tactic practiced by the Los Angeles Police Department. Because the area they had to cover was so huge, they relied on reports and descended, often by helicopter, on the scenes of crimes. They counted on sheer speed and good communications to reach scenes quickly enough to catch the criminals. This technique completely broke any connection with the various communities making up the city, and it may have been responsible in part for horrors such as the riots in Los Angeles. In other words, a strike technique really was not equivalent to some earlier forms of warfare.

It is usually said that on land fire must be combined with movement by some force which occupies ground. For example, an enemy force which finds itself under fire can dodge and hide. However, that same fire can force it into the arms of a blocking ground force. The combination may be devastating. Conversely, an enemy force can disperse to limit the effect of precision fire. However, dispersion makes it vulnerable to a concentrated ground unit. The effect of such units is to force the enemy to concentrate and, therefore, to present long-range weapons with lucrative targets. Thus, although the new style of war was conceived specifically to eliminate the need for massed forces, it may be ineffective on land without some ground units. It is possible to trade off the size and weight of those units against the firepower they can generate or call down from outside. Such a trade-off can make the ground unit much lighter.

Moreover, widely dispersed firepower-heavy units cannot be expected to hold ground (or, for that matter, to do peacekeeping). Thus, in at least some warfare areas the new kind of war could not work on its own. It would be most effective in combination with more conventional forces. Indeed, the combination of the two might be much more effective than either by itself. Should the United States, then, retain conventional forces while developing the new revolutionary ones?

The train wreck loomed. Some time early in the twenty-first century the United States would find itself unable to afford anything more than a mediocre version of conventional forces. Although in total those forces would dwarf those of any other country, in fact they would be distributed around the world. What would count would be locally available U.S. forces, and they might not seem quite so impressive. After all, it took about six months to assemble the massive force deemed necessary to eject Saddam from Kuwait. A decade later much of that force had been demobilized. Although most of the hardware remained, its operators were gone. If Saddam chose to fight again, he would inevitably face a much smaller U.S. force.

During the 2000 presidential campaign, George W. Bush announced that he would solve the defense problem not by adding much to the budget but by modernizing the military. Moreover, within a more or less fixed budget he would assemble a national missile defense. This combination was not accidental. Bush well understood that any U.S. national power depended on the strength of the economy, and that defense spending generally weakens the economy. Moreover, he had pledged not to raise taxes, but to cut them, as an economic stimulus, while avoiding deficit spending, so there would not be much more money for the military in any case.

By 2000, national missile defense was a contentious issue. Several states hostile toward the United States, including Iran and North Korea, had very active long-range missile programs. After the 1996 Taiwan Straits crisis, a Chinese general pointedly asked whether the United States would willingly trade Los Angeles for Taipei (in Taiwan) in a future crisis. In the past, the United States had relied on nuclear deterrence to protect its citizens from Soviet nuclear-armed missiles, but the Chinese statement suggested that some potentially hostile governments did not believe the United States would ever use nuclear weapons in war. The only alternative might be some form of missile defense. It could be argued, moreover, that countries would buy long-range missiles if their governments imagined that the threat of those missiles could deter the United States from defending its friends and its interests in their areas of the world. As a result, much depended on just how seriously the foreign missile threat should be taken.

The CIA was skeptical, but a high-level official panel headed by Donald Rumsfeld argued that the missile threat was imminent.

National missile defense, even on a small scale, would be very expensive. Its cost would have to come out of a fixed defense budget, which was already too small to pay for the existing force structure. Bush was convinced that the answer was to redesign the defense establishment, in line with the new kind of warfare. When he became president, he met with Andrew Marshall. Donald Rumsfeld was made secretary of defense with a mandate for "transformation," which many read as the new kind of war. Admiral Cebrowski became head of a transformation office.

It is difficult to say just how much had been accomplished by September 2001. Joint Vision 2010 and its derivative, Joint Vision 2020, were apparently too abstract to be widely appreciated. The ideas of the new kind of warfare spread very slowly through the defense establishment. The services resisted the sort of cuts in force structure which would have been needed to pay for the new systems; clearly their leaders did not believe that the new kind of war would work as advertised. That was perfectly reasonable. Not all projected revolutions in war succeed. In business, failed ideas have limited consequences, such as the collapse of the dot-coms (which had, incidentally, been hailed as models for the new kind of organization needed to fight the new kind of battle). In war, bad ideas are literally fatal.

On the other hand, much of the technology needed for the new kind of warfare was already going ahead; the only question was how soon it would reach production and how much of it would be bought. The United States fought three wars in the 1990s, in the Persian Gulf, in Bosnia, and in Kosovo. After each, the role of air power, using new remote sensors and new guided weapons, was intensely debated. To the extent that proponents of the "revolution in military affairs" were selling a new kind of strategic air power, these debates were really about the new kind of war. Those on the ground tended not to press for their own version of the new kind of war, because the technology they would need was still some years away. By the late 1990s the U.S. Army knew that it could connect its vehicles and even its soldiers by data link, and that it could provide most or all with some means of seeing beyond the horizon using remote sensors. However, actually setting up the digital net involved was extremely difficult—and expensive—and as of 2001 it was a small-scale experimental effort, on the brigade level at most, rather than the sort of operational effort understood by the airmen and by the navy (which had first introduced netting about forty years before).

That having been said, the three wars of the 1990s demonstrated the promised connection between remote sensing and high-precision weaponry. The great requirement was for someone using a remote sensor, or even seeing a target on the ground, to be able to call in a weapon: for precise direct fire to be replaced by remote fire. Beginning with the Vietnam War, bombs could be guided by laser, so that a designator on the ground could be used for this purpose. However, laser-guided bombs could not be directed to targets unless some laser could be pointed at them, either from the air or from the ground. A tactical picture based on remote sensing could be used to plan attacks, but generally it could not be used for their execution. During the Gulf War, the sole effective exception was the Tomahawk cruise missile, which could accurately fly to a predesignated address rather than to a geographical feature a pilot could recognize. Because Tomahawks were scarce and expensive, and because the targeting process was complex, these weapons were directed only at particularly important targets. Too, the Tomahawks required detailed mapping data for guidance.[2] The Defense Mapping Agency had barely enough time, in the six months between the invasion of Kuwait and the outbreak of war, to provide the necessary digital maps. What if war had broken out more suddenly?

There was, to be sure, an emerging alternative. The United States was deploying the Global Positioning Satellite system. Using it, anyone on or above the surface of the earth could quickly establish his position in three dimensions, as long as four satellites were in view and their signals could be received. When the Gulf War broke out the GPS system was still incomplete. No U.S. weapon used GPS for guidance, but there was already considerable interest in doing so. Because GPS receivers were inherently inexpensive, the system offered the possibility that an inexpensive weapon could be fired to a predetermined address anywhere in the world. No emergency mapping effort would be needed, although it was certainly true that someone had to be sure that the address to which the weapon was sent was the correct one.

Thus the Gulf War was fought largely by the sort of force developed during the cold war, using cold war tactics. Air attacks, for example, were directed almost exclusively at predesignated targets, initially on the basis of a fixed air plan. Although the weapons were not nuclear, the thinking was reminiscent of earlier strategic bombing plans. There was little expectation of hitting any single decisive target; rather, the goal was to disable Iraqi industry, to tear down Iraqi command and control systems, and to isolate the battlefield in Kuwait. To do that numerous targets had to be hit, some of them on a massive scale.

The ground force employed against Iraq was massive. Indeed, a major explanation for the long pause between the Iraqi invasion of Kuwait and the coalition reaction was that so much time was needed simply to assemble a force of overwhelming strength. In this war the new network of GPS satellites was significant mainly because they made it possible for the coalition ground force to attack out of an apparently trackless desert.

There were some important innovations leading to the future, however. National sensors, mainly on board satellites, were used to prosecute the war, and their outputs were used to help evaluate weapons effects so that targets could be reattacked as necessary. One important issue was the dissemination of satellite data, particularly of images. Satellites dumped their data down to specialized centers in the United States, and personnel at those centers decided what to send to forward users. In several cases forward commanders found it impossible to change satellite reconnaissance priorities, not because of technical limitations but because the agencies controlling the satellites refused their requests.

There was also an innovation in controlling close air support, which normally involves forward air controllers on the ground working with the troops being supported. Under some circumstances, in the past, light aircraft were used, marking their targets with white phosphorus rockets. However, it seemed unlikely that such aircraft could survive over a modern battlefield. Yet a forward air controller in an airplane would have important advantages. He could spot moving tactical targets over a wider area. Too, he could deal with moving tactical targets even if there were no friendly troops on the ground. The U.S. Marines developed a new technique, the Forward Air Controller–Airborne (FAC-A), occupying the back seat on board an F/A-18D fighter. The new concept was so successful that the other services adopted it. In the Afghan War, Navy F-14s would often act as strike controllers.

In the aftermath of the Gulf War success, the great question was whether the whole force deployed had been needed. The ground phase of the war was so short that, to some, it appeared unnecessary. Surely the shattering air attacks had panicked the Iraqis so badly that their army had cut and run—at least in the view of the U.S. Air Force. Others pointed out that the U.S. Army had succeeded not because the Iraqis had given up but simply because it was so much more competent, and so much better equipped, than they. The Iraqis had certainly found the protracted air war discouraging, but it had not been enough. The immediate issue was future budget priorities: who would win the battle of Washington? As it turned out, no one service did. As budgets gradually tightened, all would feel roughly equal pain. From a strategic point of view, the judgment was that air power was effective, but not so effective that ground forces could be neglected. The new kind of strike-oriented warfare was still nascent.

The great question at the end of the war was how much the large ground force assembled in the Persian Gulf had contributed to the rout of the Iraqis. It was unlikely that the United States and her allies could easily reassemble a Gulf War–style force in the event that Saddam struck again. Saddam came to claim victory on the basis that, whatever the allies had done in 1991, they could never do again. Since the 1991 attack had failed to dislodge him, nothing else could. On the other hand, several times in the 1990s Saddam retreated in the face of air and missile attacks, which suggests that he took their potential quite seriously.

Saddam's repeated claims of victory, and his stubborn resistance to the disarmament agreement which had ended the war, raised the question of just what would it have taken to win the war in a more decisive way.

The sheer mass of the forces used in 1991 made extensive basing, hence extensive coalition agreements, vital. It gave Saudi Arabia a veto on U.S. operations. Without large bases, it would not really have mattered whether the United States had twice as many aircraft and twice as many troops; most of them could not have gotten to Kuwait or to Iraq in the first place. Quite possibly the United States would have been limited to the strike aircraft on board the aircraft carriers (ultimately, six of them) in the Red Sea and in the Gulf, and to the Marines on board the amphibious ships in the Gulf—who, in the event, did not have to land over heavily mined beaches. The force need in March 2003 was in fact far smaller than in 1991. On the other hand, its weapons were far more precise.

Not only must the United States win with very limited forces, it must build up and fight very quickly because it often faces several potential conflicts more or less simultaneously. In the case of the Gulf, the United States very fortunately was confronted by only a single crisis. The only other sensitive area, the Korean border, was quiet, although the North Koreans did make gestures which convinced the South Koreans to limit the number of troops they could deploy to the gulf. However, during the run-up to war against Iraq in 2002–3, the United States also faced a potential crisis in Korea.

The Gulf War established a pattern. Aircraft were by far the most efficient means of delivering weapons against distant ground targets. Because, inevitably, they would be relatively scarce in a forward area, it would be vital to ensure their freedom of operation. Thus the first priority had to be to destroy enemy air defenses. Before the Gulf War, it was assumed that no country's air defense system could be knocked out for the duration. An initial blow might make the first attacks easier, but surely there would be reserves of equipment and personnel, and throughout the war special defense suppression missions would be needed. Moreover, elaborate planning would be needed to keep an enemy from detecting the intended strike targets and intercepting the strike aircraft. The perceived need to keep the enemy guessing made it vital to develop an elaborate coordinated air strike plan, embodied in the Air Task Order (ATO). The sheer complexity of the ATO in turn ensured that it could not be rewritten very quickly to deal with fast-changing targets (the cycle was generally seventy-two hours). In particular, the ATO was unlikely to be effective against pop-up or moving targets. Unfortunately, the war demonstrated that many of the most important targets might not be fixed, hence might not be attackable on the basis of a fixed ATO. For example, the coalition was never able to destroy the mobile launchers from which the Iraqis fired their Scud missiles. Late in the war, simply by moving aircraft around cities on about a twenty-four-hour cycle, the Iraqis could ensure their safety. Ironically, in the Persian Gulf it turned out to be entirely practical to neutralize the bulk of Iraqi air defenses in the first night or two.

Once air defenses had been neutralized, a period of bombing would ensue. That would be followed by a third phase, a ground war. Since U.S. air war technology was so good, there was apparently fairly general agreement that the air war would carry few costs for the United States. Whatever deterrent a prospective Third World opponent could develop would have to be associated with the ground phase following the air war. That was certainly Saddam's view. He promised the "mother of all battles" if American and allied forces entered Iraqi territory. Surely tens of thousands of U.S. and allied troops would die. As it happened, few did; some figures suggest that Iraq was safer, from a combat point of view, than many contemporary American cities.

In the mid-1990s, NATO, including U.S. forces, tried to stop an ongoing war in Bosnia involving the Bosnian government and separatist Bosnian Croats and Serbs. Experience in this war helped modify the tactics and concepts used in and derived from the Gulf War. NATO first began to plan air operations in response to a 1992 UN Security Council directive to use "all measures necessary" to end hunger and atrocities in Bosnia-Herzegovina. NATO leaders were reluctant to act, for fear that they would be dragged into a costly and unwinnable war. By the spring of 1993 NATO was conducting military operations, but they were largely limited to enforcement of a no-fly zone over Bosnia set up in April by the UN and to air-dropping relief supplies, the Serbs having closed off many airports and roads. U.S. space surveillance systems were being used.[3] To avoid ground fire, the relief transports often had to drop their loads from high altitude. With GPS now generally available, they were able to do so without sacrificing much accuracy.

In July 1993 the UN authorized NATO to provide close air support strikes to stop threats to civilians or to UN peacekeepers—should they be requested. NATO air arms began to practice for this mission. For their part, the Serbs practiced tracking the NATO aircraft with the radars they would use to control air defense missiles. By August 1993 NATO air operations over Bosnia-Herzegovina were considered the largest ongoing military air operation over southern Europe since World War II.[4] About two hundred combat and support aircraft were involved, and about ninety-three hundred sorties had been flown since April, including about fifteen hundred simulated close air support missions since July. As yet, no weapons had been dropped. The no-fly zone stopped military operations by all sides in the ongoing war, but the threat of close air support apparently had little effect. The Serbs may not have believed that fellow Europeans would ever fight them to save Muslims; their general, Radovan Mladic, later boasted that he understood the West better than it understood himself.

Despite the presence of some troops on the ground, the main armed force available to NATO was always its air arm. The enemy, the Serbian army and its Bosnian Serb auxiliary, was well aware of the vulnerability of a fixed air defense system. They relied on mobile radars, switching them off whenever an antiradar attack seemed imminent. Given large numbers of NATO aircraft capable of attacking the radars, the tactic tended to preserve the radars but it also kept them from dealing with NATO aircraft. For its part, NATO created a medium-altitude sanctuary (above ten thousand feet) for its tactical aircraft. The altitude limit was set by hand-held missiles which could not be disabled by NATO defense-suppression tactics.

There was no question of striking at a wide array of fixed targets, because the Serbians in Bosnia had no valued infrastructure. For the first time, it was clear that virtually all the important targets were movable. Weather made it difficult to find or hit many of them. The United States deployed UAVs (Predators and Gnat-750s), which often spotted key targets. They could fly under the weather, and they could penetrate the many valleys. To some extent UAVs answered the Gulf War complaint that photo satellite service was not fully available to forward commanders It turned out that navy maritime patrol aircraft (P-3Cs), with their long endurance and their large crews, could often provide extremely useful intelligence. The use of these large aircraft would be repeated in Kosovo and then in Afghanistan.

Airborne radar aircraft, both the air force AWACS (E-3) and the navy's Hawkeye (E-2C), were used to control friendly aircraft and to detect enemy attempts to interfere with U.S. and allied air operations. These aircraft in effect neutralized the Serbian air force. Even when there was no air opposition, a radar aircraft helped keep track of developing allied air attacks. However, the air war in Bosnia and later in Kosovo was generally directed from a single combined air operations center (CAOC) in Aviano, Italy. In the JSTARS (E-8A) radar aircraft, which had first been used in the Persian Gulf, the Army and the Air Force had a means of detecting moving ground traffic. At least in theory, JSTARS could detect enemy armor as it concentrated well beyond a force's horizon, to deliver a counterattack. Once detected, the armored mass could be attacked from the air or, in future, by missiles carrying antitank bomblets.

Like Afghanistan, Yugoslavia is extremely mountainous. The classic technique of air control, in which a controller on the ground radios to an airplane nearby, often was impossible, as mountains cut the line of sight. The immediate solution was to provide an airborne command post high enough to communicate directly with both the controller and the strike airplane, in this case an EC-130 ABCCC (air borne command, control, and communications aircraft). The EC-130E also linked strike aircraft back to the NATO air CAOC in Aviano.[5] These aircraft had been in service for some years, but Bosnia was probably their first major operation.

Thus far the concept was not far removed from classic close air support, which is tied to a ground force in place. However, ultimately the point of NATO air power might well be (and in fact was) to coerce the Serbs, preferably without engaging a NATO ground force. How could targets be spotted then? Narrow valleys could hide them from satellites. Airplanes would be affected by weather. The new UAVs, however, could fly into valleys, and they could fly under weather. They could radio back what they saw, either directly or via satellites.

Air planners usually distinguished between fixed targets, which were the subject of massive air plans, and the pop-up targets associated with an on-going ground battle, and which were engaged using forward air controllers. In Bosnia, however, some of the most important targets, which would have to be struck by tactical aircraft, were mobile or at least movable. The UAVs could spot them. They would have to act, in effect, as forward air controllers. A new type of attack tactic was invented: real time in the cockpit, or RTIC.

In this concept, the CAOC receives whatever intelligence data (such as UAV) video it needs to decide to order a strike; it acts as a kind of remote forward controller. It combines those data with existing images of the area to be attacked. The combination is fused and sent to the selected strike aircraft via a data link. The airplane's computer displays the images involved on the airplane's display screens; another screen displays the usual nine-line targeting message used by close air support controllers. Typically a pilot receives a general image of the area into which to fly, taken from existing files, then an orienting image, then the image produced by the UAV. The data link can also carry commands directly to the airplane's mission computer, directing the airplane onto the necessary heading or even focusing its sensors as needed. By 1996 RTIC was a reality, and F-16s assigned to close air support were being fitted with a suitable data link, the improved data modem.[6]

The implications of RTIC were revolutionary; it was a step toward network-centric warfare. The various remote sensors, such as those on board a UAV, offered the CAOC a view of the entire battle space. On the basis of that tactical picture, it could allocate resources and strike targets. That was a radical departure from the past, when the only way to attack moving or pop-up targets was to pre-allocate a strike airplane to a particular area and then assign it to a controller. That combination was adequate as long as there were numerous strike aircraft and, preferably, limited numbers of targets and controllers. However, the RTIC-CAOC combination was far better suited to a situation like that in Afghanistan, in which relatively few strike aircraft were available at any one time yet targets might be scattered over a very wide area. Indeed, RTIC, with its ability to direct aircraft to targets only after they were airborne, was ill adapted to the kind of massed air planning employed during the Gulf War; redirecting too many aircraft would cause serious problems. Redirecting a very small number, however, would likely be quite effective.

The standoff between NATO aircraft and Bosnian Serb air defenses continued through most of 1994. On the ground, the UN mounted a Protection

Force (UNPROFOR) intended to protect Bosnian civilians, most of them Muslims, against "ethnic cleansing," largely by Bosnian Serbs supported by the Serbian Army. It was expected that UNPROFOR would deter but not confront militarily attempts at ethnic cleansing. In several heartbreaking and utterly embarrassing episodes, most notably at Srebrenica, the Serbs called its bluff: it was unable to protect areas it had declared safe havens.

The Serbians pushed harder. In November 1994 they used an airfield in Serb-held Croatia to attack the safe areas guaranteed by the United Nations, and NATO was authorized to strike both the airfield and its missile defenses. It conducted the first large-scale coordinated multinational strikes in its history. A second major raid responded to a perceived Serbian missile threat against NATO aircraft patrolling the country.[7] These operations mirrored earlier U.S. and NATO practice. Probably the main lesson the Serbs learned was that fixed missile sites could be and would be destroyed. The war on the ground continued, at times in an uneasy standoff between UNPROFOR and the Bosnian Serb Army. Negotiations for a settlement also continued on a sporadic basis. To some extent, NATO air power came to be a deterrent against Serbian attacks on safe areas, particularly on Sarajevo, the capital of Bosnia-Herzegovina. The UN tried to negotiate a safe zone around the city from which attacks would not be tolerated, and it demanded free access to the city for food and other relief supplies.

On August 1995, while preliminary negotiations for a settlement were proceeding, the market at Sarajevo was hit by heavy mortar fire, apparently by a Serbian unit; twenty-eight people were killed. Protecting Sarajevo, a declared safe area, from such an atrocity had become more and more important to the UN commanders because the Serbs had violated other sanctuaries in the past. Thus this action triggered a heavy NATO air attack coordinated with British and French artillery bombardments.[8] The initial phase was intended to destroy all fixed and truck-mounted Serbian air defenses in eastern Bosnia. Targets included command-and-control sites. This phase was successful, in that no radar-guided missiles were fired at the NATO strike aircraft, although a few small man-portable missiles were. The next objective was Serbian military capability on the ground, beginning with ammunition dumps and including repair and storage depots. Then effort shifted to the Serbian guns around Sarajevo. Although the NATO effort was concentrated around Sarajevo, it could clearly shift to other Serbian centers within Bosnia. Overall, the concept was to cripple ongoing Serbian operations while making it clear to the Serbs that their longer-term military strength was being destroyed.[9] Thus, at least in theory, the Serbs could choose between an immediate settlement and a significantly worse situation later. By 21 September the Serbs had withdrawn their heavy weapons from the area around Sarajevo and the bombing had stopped. The Serbs acceded to the proffered peace conditions (the Dayton accords), and UNPROFOR gave way to the NATO IFOR (Implementation Force) backed by a powerful NATO air component.

It was not immediately clear what had caused the Serbs to give up. Besides air attack, they had been badly punished by artillery bombardments. Moreover, they were under military pressure by both the Bosnian Muslims and the Bosnian Croats then allied with them. It may have become clear to the Serbs that, if the war went any further, they would lose to their local enemies—in part because they, not the others, would be suffering UN-approved attacks.

The August-September NATO strikes were similar in concept to those conducted during the Gulf War. They were carefully planned, and they generally were not directed against pop-up or movable targets. The Serbs had a valuable fixed military infrastructure, the destruction of which opened them up to their enemies, including both the Bosnians they had attacked and the better-equipped Bosnian Croats, who also wanted some of the same territory. On the other hand, the strikes involved an important new precision weapon, the GPS-guided Tomahawk missile. GPS guidance was significant for future operations because it did not require a massive pre-attack effort to map the area of operations and because a GPS-guided Tomahawk launched from the sea did not have to spend time over mapped territory to locate itself.[10]

On a political level, the attacks on Muslims within Europe probably contributed to the later growth of fundamentalism. The assaults were widely reported throughout the Muslim world as a holocaust. Muslim heads of state met to declare that there would be real consequences unless the West did something to stop the slaughter—then apparently did nothing themselves. However, fundamentalists did see Bosnia as an opportunity to prove themselves. Although many Muslim Bosnians had little use for them or for their rigid form of Islam, they managed to ingratiate themselves with the postwar Bosnian government, to the point that the government supported charities which later turned out to be conduits for Al Qaeda. The Iranians felt compelled to compete with the Sunni Arabs, so their activists, too, gravitated to Bosnia. The U.S. government covertly supported the Bosnians, flying in arms (or, at the least, tolerating arms shipments from Muslim states).

In this it contravened European attempts to impose peace through an arms embargo on all sides. It could be argued, however, that the embargo was so porous that the shipments merely helped the Bosnians survive until the situation became so outrageous that NATO intervened.

In 1999 a similar war broke out in Kosovo, a province of Yugoslavia under at least nominal Serbian control. From a U.S. or NATO point of view, the point of the war, Operation Allied Force, was to stop Serbian genocide and ethnic cleansing. The Serbian leader, Slobodan Milosevich, had already tried to destroy the Muslim population of Bosnia-Herzegovina, using mainly Serbian ethnics living in Bosnia. One argument for intervention in Kosovo was that further assaults on Muslims—further attempts to impose what Muslims often saw as a holocaust—would cause horrific international problems. Western Europe could not really afford to demonstrate that it was a classic Christian entity attacking Islam. There were, of course, exceptions. Both Greece and Russia felt close affinity for the Serbs, and the Greek population in particular demonstrated hostility to the NATO war effort. The Russians presented the NATO operation as bare-faced aggression against a fellow Slav state.

This time there was no U.S. or NATO ground force in place. Even those NATO governments which supported the war shrank from the large losses they assumed a ground struggle would cause. Very little effort had been made to convince Western populations that Kosovo was worth bleeding for. After considerable discussion, NATO agreed to intervene in the war under U.S. leadership. The NATO governments, including that of the United States, were willing to support an air campaign, but they were much less willing to commit ground troops. The initial expectation was that air power would be so effective that the Serbs would collapse within forty-eight hours. That did not happen; NATO ended up bombing for seventy-eight days. Some advocates of the initial air war plan later argued that it had been crippled by NATO officers who exercised veto power over U.S. strikes.

Probably the gross miscalculation was political. The NATO approach was that Milosevich had personally chosen the repugnant policy of attacking Muslim Kosovars. However, there is much anecdotal evidence that many Serbs liked the policy and that Milosevich had, in effect, mobilized Serbian nationalism. Serbia, moreover, has a culture of victimization, and Milosevich had made it his theme. His political career began on the field in Kosovo on which the fourteenth-century Serbian state was defeated by the Muslim Ottomans. His cry was, "Never again." Later it was clear that few

Serbs had any real desire to control Kosovo but that most regarded repression of the Kosovars as a perfectly reasonable policy. Under these circumstances it was by no means clear that Milosevich could easily be separated from either his corrupt backers or his generally supportive population.

For the strategists, given the prohibition on ground operations, the question was whether—and how—air power by itself could eject the Serbians from Kosovo. Initially the NATO governments found that the only targets they could agree to hit were tactical ones, such as Serbian tanks and antiaircraft missiles. The most important tactical targets, the squads which were killing and terrorizing the Kosovars, were essentially invisible from the air and hence not subject to attack.

As in Bosnia, the Serbs used mobility to protect their air defense system. That in turn forced NATO pilots to fly higher. As in the past, individual pilots had to identify their targets before attacking them with their precision weapons. The higher they flew, the more susceptible they became to decoying; the Serbs proved very capable at camouflage and deception. NATO placed no observers on the ground, because the NATO governments were entirely unwilling to risk ground troops of any type. After the war the Serbs displayed numerous decoy tanks and aircraft. It is still not clear just how effective the decoys were. The Serbs withdrew from Kosovo in good order and not under NATO inspection; thus there were no independent assessments of whether the withdrawal included damaged or disabled vehicles and weapons. In any case, one way to read the survival of Serbian forces is that a tactical air offensive would have limited impact unless observers on the ground could identify at least some of the valid targets. Remote sensors could not suffice. Thus a U.S. and NATO policy barring all troops, including special forces, might be blamed for the tactical failure of air attacks.

Aside from decoying, high-flying tactical aircraft were likely to make mistakes. The Serbians were quick to publicize accidental attacks on their civilians in hopes that the NATO public, less than enthusiastic about the war, would not abide them. The Serbs also hoped that, given such stories, their sympathizers, particularly the Russians, would be impelled to intervene on their side. Sometimes it seemed that Serbian propaganda dominated Western coverage of the war.[11]

As tactical bombing produced no visible results, a series of alternatives was tried. One idea was that precision strikes could destroy resources, such as factories, vital to Milosevich's key supporters. In theory they would be interested in stopping the attacks so as to keep their property intact.[12]

Another approach was to attack vital government and ruling-party buildings to convince Milosevich himself that unless he gave up he or his government would be shattered. For example, Tomahawk missiles destroyed the headquarters of the Serbian ruling party. The accidental attack on the Chinese Embassy in Belgrade, mistaken by targeters for the Yugoslav arms export agency, was probably part of this campaign.

Yet another approach was to demonstrate to the populace of Belgrade that Milosevich was incapable of protecting them. For example, the Serbian electric system was attacked, literally to put out the lights in Belgrade. By the end of the war, the Serbian power grid and transportation systems had been badly damaged, and they might have been destroyed altogether by continued bombing.

The political-strategic strikes seem not to have been terribly effective. As in many other instances of air attack, civilians who might not have been enthusiastic government supporters rallied to their leaders in the face of foreign attacks. They seem to have found the very precision of the U.S. and NATO strikes encouraging, since it limited their own physical risk.

Alternatively, there might be some way to force an enemy to move and concentrate tactical forces, creating valid and lucrative targets. A maneuver force on the ground might have this effect.

After seventy-eight days of bombing, it was not clear what else had to be done. Then, rather abruptly, even surprisingly, the Serbs collapsed. Various explanations were offered. It seemed, for example, that Milosevich had imagined that somehow the Russians would come to his rescue. However, on 2 June, Russian envoy Victor Chernomyrdin told him that the Russians were backing NATO, a statement that probably reflected U.S. and European economic and diplomatic pressure. There was some speculation that the Russians promised that they would protect Serbia itself by occupying a sensitive sector of Kosovo.[13] Another possibility is that the Russians wanted to stop the war before NATO troops were engaged, that they feared having to come to the aid of a fellow Slav government. Since Russia shares no border with Serbia, any such aid might have been difficult to provide.

Several former Serbian leaders claimed that they had given up to save Serbia, that had the war continued Serbian cities would have been carpet-bombed into the ground. That explanation was probably self-serving, intended to explain to the Serbians themselves why their leaders had abandoned the war. The carpet-bombing thesis played to a longstanding Serbian sense of victimization. Leaders yielding to overwhelming force yet extracting reasonable conditions (Serbia remained unoccupied) could present themselves as victors of a sort, just as Saddam had done. This theory is implausible because NATO leaders promised again and again that they would not be carpet-bombing Serbian cities. Nor did they have the physical ability to do so.[14]

Overall, advocates of air power argued that continued pressure wore down Milosevich and his supporters, that it had to be clear to all of them that NATO had no reason to relent. They also had to face a possible ground war. None of these explanations is particularly convincing. For example, beginning in 1992 the UN imposed crushing economic sanctions on Serbia, which effectively destroyed its economy without any bombing. Milosevich remained in power, with considerable popular support. Serbians were unhappy with his failure in Bosnia, and they did not like to absorb ethnic Serbian refugees after that failure, but they did not abandon their nationalism. Indeed, this type of punishment apparently strengthened support for Slobodan Milosevich and his policies.

Conversely, for Milosevich, Kosovo was not so much a prize as a means to his end of retaining power in Serbia. Pressing for a Greater Serbia free of Muslims was a popular policy. On the other hand, Serbia has a culture of victimization, so beyond a point Milosevich could actually gain by bowing to clearly overwhelming NATO pressure. Few if any Serbians really wanted Kosovo, except for symbolic reasons (it had been the scene of a famous Serbian defeat in 1348). Thus both sides could be satisfied: Milosevich could retain both his popularity (he thought) and the force which guaranteed his power. NATO could get Kosovo, and in the process it could halt what Muslims considered as an ongoing holocaust.

The one military force which really mattered to Milosevich was probably the paramilitary organization used to enforce ethnic cleansing. The same units maintained his power within Serbia itself. Through most of the war, the paramilitaries operated in small units, essentially immune to air attack because no single bomb could kill many of them. Toward the end of the war, the Kosovo Liberation Army (KLA) began operating against the Serbian paramilitary units. To counter the KLA, the Serbian paramilitaries had to mass, creating lucrative targets for NATO air strikes. In at least one case, a Serbian unit was badly damaged in this way. That in turn was a direct threat to Milosevich: without his paramilitaries, he might lose power back in Serbia, power which he really wanted to retain.

Since the KLA did very little fighting, it was easy to ascribe victory to the bombing campaign, or else to Russian diplomacy. However, another way to view the war would have been to say that bombing became effective only when it was linked to a force on the ground—and that the force in question did not have to be a NATO army. In this view, the KLA functioned as a coalition force, and its presence was crucial. That is, neither NATO air nor the KLA had much chance of winning on its own. The combination offered dramatic advantages, particularly when those on the ground could be supported by very precisely aimed weapons.

Kosovo, then, suggested how a future minor war could be fought. Agility made it unlikely that very massive U.S. ground forces could be brought to bear in a reasonable length of time. In the case of Kosovo, even though such forces were brought into position, it was soon clear that the U.S. government itself had no great interest in placing them in action, for fear of casualties. How, then, to get "boots on the ground," if indeed ground forces were so important? The KLA was the answer: always seek a local coalition partner sufficiently interested in the outcome to fight as needed.

There was, of course, a caveat. Coalition partners are not proxies or mercenaries. They may well be supported by U.S. cash, but they do not answer to U.S. command; they have their own objectives and interests. The KLA understood the goal in Kosovo as the ejection of the Serbs in order to create a new country. The United States and NATO understood the goal as ending ethnic cleansing and restoring the prewar status quo—for Serbs as well as for Kosovars—under NATO protection and control (the overthrow of Milosevich was a somewhat more remote goal). Naturally the goals espoused by the two sides clashed, and naturally there was embarrassment in the United States when NATO forces felt compelled to stand by and allow their coalition partners a more or less free rein.

Nor, for that matter, did all the NATO partners always agree with U.S. military officers, who were nominally in charge. Bombing targets had to be approved by officers from other countries, not least because their governments were providing either aircraft or bases, or both. U.S. advocates of a pure strike or air-power approach later charged that the offensive had been ineffective mainly because of delays in approving targets and endless vetoes of particularly lucrative ones—and also because partners sometimes seemed to undermine security. Again, allies are not proxy forces; their governments have their own agendas.

In a larger sense, a coalition partner has its own objectives, and whatever will encourage it must be tailored to its views and its needs—which may not be well understood at the outset. Nor may they be entirely acceptable to other coalition partners or even to the United States. This issue almost came up in the Gulf War. At that time the United States and Britain pursued a secondary strategy of encouraging ethnic groups to rise against Saddam Hussein. The principal groups involved, which might have become coalition partners, were the Kurds in the north and the Shi'ites in the south, which together constituted a majority of Iraqis. Saddam's government had oppressed both groups, the latter in particular because of ethnic affinities to the Iranians, his great enemies.

Ultimately the ethnic coalition strategy was unacceptable—to other engaged parties. Both the Kurds and the Shi'ites wanted their own states. Had Kurdistan been formed, Kurds in Turkey would probably have revolted, demanding union. Turkey had long suppressed its own form of Kurdish nationalism, and the Turkish government, a vital ally, would have been less than enthusiastic at the formation of Kurdistan out of northern Iraq. A Shi'ite victory in the south might have incited rebellion by Shi'ites on the northern Saudi coast—and probably greater influence for Iran. Given Iranian enmity, this outcome would have been unattractive to both the United States and to Saudi Arabia, the main base for the ground war.

Even so, that a coalition strategy was seriously advanced in Iraq, indeed that attempts were made to foment the necessary rebellions, shows just how attractive the use of local partners can be. As it was, the coalition concept was based on fear that unless Iraq were seriously weakened the war could not be fought. When Iraq turned out be quite weak, neither strategic bombing nor the coalition concept was really needed. The bombing was conducted, but the war ended before any of the ethnic revolts could reach fruition. The coalition strategy was reflected in the postwar imposition of no-fly zones (so that the Iraqi air arm could not suppress possible revolts) and in the creation of a protected zone for Kurds in northern Iraq.

In general, the great advantage of using a local coalition partner was that U.S. forces would generally not be perceived as conquerors; they were merely supporting some locals. That made excellent sense, since generally the U.S. objective would not be to seize or control territory but to displace an unacceptable local government attacking U.S. interests. For example, in both Kosovo and in Bosnia, the U.S. interest was to halt anti-Muslim "ethnic cleansing" for fear that if it continued it would ignite a much larger war (in the case of Kosovo, perhaps a southern European war beginning with Greece and Turkey fighting each other). There must also have been a feeling that, had the slaughter of Muslims continued, the Muslim states would have declared some form of war against the West. Not everyone agreed that such steps were desirable or noble. For example, within Russia the war in

Kosovo was presented almost uniformly as an assault by NATO against a Russian sphere of influence, a revival of the old cold war enmity.

There were other lessons, too. In Bosnia and then in Kosovo UAVs provided dramatic real-time video, which was often used for targeting. The same video could be piped into higher-level headquarters, even into the Pentagon. High-level officials saw what they thought were vital targets, and they ordered strikes without knowing much about other ongoing operations competing with those choices. This sort of intervention had the potential to be disastrous. At the very least, it distracted senior decision makers from the broad issues of the war. Worse, the targets which looked important might be insignificant compared to others, but directions to hit specific targets might preclude attacks on the others. There was no possibility that a decision maker in Washington could be aware of the full range of what was happening in even a small area, in Bosnia or in Kosovo.

The immediate solution was to cut off transmission of UAV video to places like the Pentagon. However, the temptations offered by modern telecommunications remained. Surely a commanding officer far from the scene of the war could now see most of what an officer farther forward could, without distractions such as explosions. Surely, thus undistracted, he could make better command decisions.

Maybe, given video transmissions, a commander no longer had to move to the war zone. That was very important for agility: a commander and his staff would necessarily have a substantial "footprint," and some nearby country would have to be approached to provide space for a headquarters. In peacetime the U.S. Central Command, responsible for Central and Southwest Asia, is headquartered at MacDill Air Force Base in Tampa, Florida. What if it could stay there, undisturbed, through combat? In that case the headquarters could swiftly react to a crisis anywhere in its area of responsibility without being dislocated.

On a more technical level, the great lesson of Kosovo was that munitions worked, but that finding targets and aiming at them was another problem. The UAVs could fly low enough to see the targets, but on the whole that was not enough to attack, because pilots still had to find those targets again in order to attack them. The solution would be a network, in which aircraft and missiles could be directed at target locations revealed by a network of sensors. One key was GPS, because it allowed a sensor to associate a target with a particular address—to which an airplane could deliver a guided bomb. Still a rarity in 1999, GPS-guided bombs were clearly coming. The alternative to GPS would be a laser designator on the ground, wielded by a soldier who could actually see a target. In Yugoslavia, moreover, because pilots had to see the targets they attacked with laser-guided bombs, weather created sanctuaries the enemy could and did exploit.

Because so many of the targets in Kosovo were either mobile or fleeting, it was clearer than in the past that the time delay between seeing a target and hitting it had to be cut. There was some success, reflected in the use of many Tomahawk missiles during the war. On the other hand, NATO forces entirely failed to hit the single most important set of mobile targets, those comprising the Serbian air defense system. Overall, air planning was still characterized by the sort of rigid air tasking order used in the Persian Gulf. Thus attacks on fleeting targets were conducted as deviations from planning rather than as the rule.

One surprise of the war was that, although NATO enjoyed access to several nearby land bases, carrier aircraft turned out to be unusually productive. One reason why was that carriers could move to evade weather which grounded aircraft based ashore. Another was that the carriers could move into position closer to targets. It helped enormously that the small Serbian navy made no attempt to disrupt allied naval operations.

Although operations were conducted on a relatively small scale, those conducting and controlling them were widely dispersed. Thus secure long-haul communications were crucial, as in the Gulf War. Many U.S. commanders, but not all, had access to SIPRNET, a classified equivalent of the Internet, via which they could exchange information and plans. However, secure bandwidth was not always sufficient. Coordination was difficult because allied partners lacked access to the SIPRNET, although there was an equivalent NATO system.

Overall, although the Kosovo air war was fought after the advent of network-centric concepts, those concepts had not yet been absorbed. Thus the bulk of investment still went to shooters, such as strike aircraft, rather than to methods of finding and analyzing small numbers of fleeting targets. This reality was reflected in complaints that there were too few linguists, targeters, and analysts, and too few UAVs and sensor/ELINT aircraft such as EA-6B Prowlers.

At a higher level, command relationships were poorly arranged before the outbreak of war. Responsibilities were not always clearly defined. Each government within NATO, for example, had a veto even over details of targeting. This problem was probably inevitable in a true coalition war without any one dominant partner.

By the end of the 1990s, then, U.S. ideas of how to fight wars in the Third World had moved far beyond those displayed in the Gulf War. Few observers realized as much. The new American style of warfare would be demonstrated in improved form in Afghanistan in 2001. For their part, Americans wondered whether the 11 September attack was a response to American success in the Gulf War and in later years, simply a way of evading conventional U.S. strategy. That seems unlikely because 11 September was not mounted by the Iraqis, that is, by those who had learned from the Gulf War. The Iraqis and other regional powers continued to develop conventional forces, not least because they were concerned much more with countering each other than with dealing with the United States. After all, U.S. intervention is rare compared to threats or attacks by local powers. Thus, to the extent Saddam Hussein rebuilt his forces, they resembled the ones he commanded in 1991, because those forces are designed to deal with, say, the forces wielded by Saudi Arabia and Iran, his two likeliest regional enemies. Designing forces specifically to deal with the United States would be pointless. To the extent that Osama bin Laden is a very distinct entity, the form of the 11 September attacks and the form of Al Qaeda are responses to his own needs and circumstances, rather than to American military capabilities.

7

Coalitions

At the outset, most of the world's governments publicly decried the 11 September attacks and declared their support for the United States. That was not, however, tantamount to offering whatever facilities the United States might need. Nor, at that point, was it clear to any government what cooperation might mean. Only after President George W. Bush announced that Al Qaeda and the terrorists had been responsible, and would have to pay, did the U.S. government begin the scramble to recruit partners. Probably the most remarkable feature of the buildup to war was that so many governments decided to join the U.S.-led coalition. The United States, in fact, fought the Taliban and Al Qaeda at the head of two connected coalitions, one external to Afghanistan and one within it.

Under Article 5 of the NATO Treaty, an attack on any one signatory is taken as an attack on all. The United States invoked this article, and the NATO governments agreed. The British government was particularly enthusiastic, partly because Britons and British firms had been among the leading victims of the World Trade Center attack. The initial British contributions to the war included special forces (SAS units), warships to operate in the Arabian Sea, and aircraft to fly out of Oman. Later the British sent a massive Royal Marine Commando unit to Afghanistan. Overall NATO assistance included the provision of AWACS aircraft which could replace U.S. aircraft operating over the United States, thus releasing aircraft for action near Afghanistan. However, most NATO governments were slow to offer combat troops. Their contingents proved most important for peacekeeping once the new government had been installed in Kabul.

The Russians in particular supported the war against terrorism. In the fall of 2001 Russia was already a fairly friendly foreign power. In the war against terrorism the Russians had several connected motives. One was their desire for support in the ongoing fight in Chechnya, where the rebels were probably associated with bin Laden and the Taliban.[1] Defeat of the Taliban would help sap Chechen resources. A second was their need for security against fundamentalists in areas of Russia bordering former Soviet Central Asia, an area the Russians characterize as the "near abroad." The Russians were already supporting the Northern Alliance against the Taliban on the clear understanding that a full Taliban victory would release fundamentalists determined to overthrow the former Soviet republics, such as Uzbekistan, bordering Afghanistan. Any such movement would then expand farther north, eventually into Russia proper. Given such considerations, the Russians explicitly pressured their former republics, as members of the Commonwealth of Independent States (CIS), to cooperate with the United States. They accepted a U.S. military presence in the near abroad, a step which earlier might have been inconceivable. These steps were also part of a more general attempt by the Russian government to strengthen its connection with the United States, which offered it invaluable economic assistance and markets.

For the United States, Russia was the main access route to the Northern Alliance, the force still fighting the Taliban inside Afghanistan. Once war broke out, Russia helped arm the Northern Alliance, in some cases providing weapons for which the United States paid. There was also a broader issue. As a former oil man, President Bush was probably unusually well aware of the leverage Saudi Arabia could exert on the West, due to its commanding position among oil producers. The Saudi government had (and has) only limited interest in the war against terrorism, because so much of the problem can be traced to its own official ideology of Wahhabi Islam.[2] No real pressure could be brought to bear on the Saudis unless there was a viable alternative to their oil. Russia alone offered that alternative. Moreover, given their need for money, Russian oil producers were unlikely to cooperate in any OPEC attempt to squeeze the world oil supply or to attack the West in retaliation for a war against the Taliban. The Russians in turn saw oil income as a vital support for their economic recovery.

Perhaps more surprising was the Chinese reaction to the war. Normally the Chinese would have complained that any U.S. attempt to deal with the Taliban would be part of a larger strategy of encirclement. But because the Taliban had persisted in supporting Muslim Uighur rebels in Sinkiang despite Chinese attempts to buy them off with weapon sales and advisers, the Chinese willingly supported the war.

The United States sought assistance from Pakistan and Saudi Arabia, both of which might be considered closely involved. It was particularly urgent to secure Pakistani help, since Pakistan offered direct air and ground access to Afghanistan, and since Pakistani military intelligence had unequaled access to that country. Because Pashtuns in northwestern Pakistan considered themselves allied to the Taliban across the border, there was a realistic fear that they would rise in revolt if the Pakistani government backed the Americans.[3] Even so, Pakistani president Musharraf backed the United States, providing both overflight rights and crucial air bases. Given the strong sympathy that northern Pakistani tribes felt for the Taliban, there was no real possibility that Pakistan would allow the construction of a land line of communications from the Indian Ocean into Afghanistan.

Musharraf also offered to seal the border with Afghanistan to prevent Pakistanis from joining the Taliban forces. That was probably impossible, given the feelings of the Pashtun tribes in the north. One of the Pakistani parties was in effect an arm of the Taliban. Its mullahs preached jihad, encouraging young men to go north to fight. By late October, at least two thousand were over the frontier, and another nine thousand were massing. Pro-Taliban Pakistanis, probably including some lower-level ISI operatives, also made sure that some supplies crossed the nominally sealed border.

In retrospect it seems that Musharraf found the war a very useful opportunity. For well over a decade his government had fallen further and further into the hands of fundamentalists. From the outset of his administration in 1999, Musharraf had been determined to reverse course, to stop the fundamentalists from destroying Pakistan itself with their violence, including massacres of Shi'ites by Sunnis. His connection to the West had been damaged. Pakistan was increasingly impoverished. Because the fundamentalists had been invited into Pakistani power by the military, probably only a military man could hope to eject them. Alone of major Muslim chiefs of state, President Musharraf had the courage to take the fundamentalists on. On 12 January 2002 he addressed all Pakistanis on television: "The day of reckoning has come. . . . Do we want Pakistan to become a theocratic state? Do we believe that religious education alone is enough for governance? Or do we want Pakistan to emerge as a progressive and dynamic Islamic welfare state?" Surely Islam meant more than fundamentalism and hatred. Although Musharraf's action helped the U.S. government in its ongoing campaign, it was an act with even greater and deeper implications. Of course, to what extent it succeeded will not be clear for years.

Saudi Arabia housed the best potential base in the region, Prince Sultan Air Base, with its new American-built air operations center. The Saudis denounced the terrorists, but they refused to accept any new American armed presence on their soil. They did allow Americans to operate from the air operations center.[4] It is not clear whether there was any viable alternative, such as a ship. However, in the wake of the war there were reports that the Saudis wanted the Americans out (there were also denials), and it seemed that some alternative operations center would have to be built in one of the Persian Gulf states.

Public declarations were not private ones. They did not necessarily mean that a government would accept, say, blanket overflights, or U.S. basing, or U.S. offensive weapons on its soil. The position often seems to have been that, the less visible the U.S. presence, the more acceptable it was. Because they seem to resemble airliners, tankers and electronic surveillance aircraft (such as P-3s) often seem to be far more welcome than combat aircraft. It may well follow that a division of labor, in which combat aircraft come from mobile U.S. territory (aircraft carriers), but support aircraft are land-based, is practicable. Conversely, as the United States fights wars on that basis, the crucial role of the support aircraft may become more obvious. Whatever internal opposition is mounted against collaboration with the United States may thus be directed against not merely combat aircraft but also against vital support types.

All of this is aside from the fact that any aircraft require special facilities and special stocks of spares. That differentiates countries which already host U.S.-built aircraft, such as Saudi Arabia, from those which do not, in which stocks must be built up before operations begin. The Saudi refusal to allow combat operations from its soil was therefore particularly significant.

The internal coalition partner, the Afghan resistance to the Taliban, would be essential to any U.S. attack, because it would be so difficult to bring large numbers of American troops into action. Troops need both a base from which to operate and a supply line to support them. Any massive supply operation would have to involve movement by sea. Afghanistan is land-locked, and the neighbors bordering both it and the sea are Iran and Pakistan. There was no possibility that Iran would actively support a U.S.-sponsored operation which would leave a U.S. proxy or ally on her border. At best she might be a friendly neutral during combat, particularly if the Iranian government could be convinced that the resulting Afghan state would be friendly or neutral.

Gen. Tommy Franks, who commanded the U.S. Central Command and thus ran the war, was later quoted as calling for a multidivision effort in Afghanistan.[5] However, from a logistical point of view that was impossible, at least in the short term. Conceivably a base could have been built up, over time, in the former Soviet Central Asian republics, particularly in Uzbekistan. But Franks's comment can be read as an attempt to show that military intervention in Afghanistan was impossible.

If U.S. troops could not be brought into action in large numbers, and if ground troops were nonetheless needed, the only solution was to form a coalition with Afghans resisting the Taliban. Even though the Taliban controlled most of Afghanistan on 11 September, they were still fighting several internal enemies, most notably the Northern Alliance. Despite the very serious blow of losing its most charismatic commander, Mahsood, just before 11 September, the Northern Alliance remained coherent and was a potential coalition partner in any fight for Afghanistan. But the Northern Alliance was itself a loose coalition. To some extent its elements represented countries ranged around the northern and western borders of Afghanistan.[6] If it was to act in unified fashion, the governments of those countries, which had wildly varying goals of their own, had to view the Northern Alliance as an acceptable instrument. However, there was no equivalent to the Northern Alliance fighting the Taliban in southern Afghanistan. That area was the closest equivalent to Taliban home country. Aside from any popularity the Taliban might enjoy in the south, it had an excellent intelligence service there. It could act preemptively to destroy likely enemies.[7]

The Taliban were sponsored by—indeed, to a considerable extent were the creation of—the Pakistani government. That government in turn wanted any new Afghan government to include at least some Taliban. On the other hand, the Northern Alliance had been fighting for years. It saw no point in including its deadly enemies in a new coalition. For that matter, to the extent that Americans saw the Taliban as their own enemy, the idea of including them in a postwar government was less than attractive.

The governments of the surrounding states generally did not demand particular policies. What they really wanted was a post-Taliban Afghan government that would not threaten any of them and would be reasonably stable. Post-Taliban Afghanistan would have to be neutral; it could not become, for example, a U.S. client state. Reasonable stability in turn required that such a government balance the interests of the ethnic groups in the country, since recent history had clearly shown that domination by any one ethnic group would lead to revolt by others. That had destabilized even the Communist regime backed by the Soviets.

By way of contrast, the Taliban threatened all neighboring governments, since they regarded both secular and national Islamic states as illegitimate.

Moreover, the regime apparently considered itself duty-bound to stir revolts in bordering states. The Taliban badly needed Pakistan, but there came a point where even the Pakistanis regarded them as a kind of monster moving beyond their control.

To the U.S. government, then, the first step in displacing the Taliban was to create the basis for a credible successor regime. To that end, all interested parties were invited to a meeting in Bonn. Afghanistan has always been a fractious country, with a fragile sense of unity; thus the Bonn meeting went slowly. Ultimately the U.S. government was embarrassed, as the Taliban collapsed so quickly that Northern Alliance troops could seize Kabul well before Bonn had produced any sort of result. For a few days the U.S. government even tried to hold back the Northern Alliance troops in hopes that the successor government could be formed first, but then it had to give way. Coalition partners have their own agendas, after all.

External coalition partners were needed for two distinct reasons. One was operational. The United States had virtually no intelligence sources within Afghanistan, but two potential allies, Saudi Arabia and Pakistan, were deeply engaged there. Both governments pledged cooperation, but each presented problems. Having worked with the Taliban for years, Pakistani intelligence agents might well sympathize with them. They were unlikely to be altogether forthcoming with information, and they might well choose to let key Taliban and Al Qaeda personnel escape. Similarly, the Saudis undoubtedly had strong ties with the Taliban, and it could never be clear whether individual Saudis would feel that it was their religious duty to help them.

The situation was further complicated in that the United States reportedly had few if any intelligence agents capable of speaking the local language or of living in Afghanistan for a prolonged period. Without considerable experience, Americans were likely to find it difficult or impossible to make sense of local politics and of local squabbles.

Also, Afghanistan is land-locked. Allies on the borders could provide access or, at the least, allow overflights. At the most, they might offer bases. The more cooperative allies included the various former Soviet republics around the northern Afghan border, particularly Uzbekistan. A secret agreement was probably reached in mid-September to move U.S. troops into that country, initially to secure air bases which would be used to airlift supplies for the Northern Alliance. Early in October initial elements of the U.S. Tenth Mountain Division arrived in Uzbekistan. The Uzbek government was particularly receptive to U.S. requests because it had been fighting an Islamic revolutionary group tied to the Taliban for the past three years.

Pakistan occupied a particularly important position, because it lay between Afghanistan and the Arabian Sea. To the extent that U.S. logistics is seaborne, any U.S. force would find it far easier to get to the Pakistani coast than to former Soviet Central Asia. This coalition might be compared to Saudi Arabia during the Gulf War: an essential means of gaining access to the battle zone.

There was, however, a significant problem. Pakistan and Saudi Arabia were the strongest outside supporters of the Taliban regime; to a considerable extent it had been placed in power by Pakistani military intelligence. Substantial fractions of the populations of both countries strongly supported the regime and its ideology, and they would not be at all amenable to U.S. attacks on the Taliban. Thus whatever support either Pakistan or Saudi Arabia provided would be limited and low key. It would not extend to anything remotely like Gulf War–type basing for large army and air force units.

Pakistan was a particularly difficult case. During the Soviet war in Afghanistan, it had become a close U.S. ally. However, since the end of the cold war it had suffered a series of humiliating U.S. assaults, such as arms embargoes, based on U.S. nuclear antiproliferation policy. In Pakistani eyes, the United States was manifestly favoring its main enemy, India. For example, India did not suffer when it exploded its first bomb. Yet when Pakistan drained itself to build its own bomb, in what it saw as self-defense, the United States imposed stringent sanctions and stopped delivery of modern military aircraft, which, in Pakistani eyes, were a first line of defense which might stop Indian attackers short of requiring nuclear retaliation. Americans tended to extol the Indian democracy and attack Pakistani governments, whether democratic or dictatorial.

When the United States declared war on terrorism, moreover, the Indian government seized the declaration as a further indication of U.S. favor. After all, for years Pakistani military intelligence had waged a terrorist war against India in Kashmir. Surely it was time to squelch that war, and surely the fighters in Kashmir were closely related to those in Afghanistan.

Yet Pakistan was vital to a war fought in Afghanistan; India was virtually irrelevant. It was time for the U.S. government to mend fences, and the Pakistanis recognized the opportunity. President Musharraf declared himself on the side of the antiterrorist coalition and ordered his intelligence service to help the Americans. Later there would be unofficial American claims that the Pakistanis had been less than wholehearted, even that they had airlifted Pakistani Taliban out of besieged areas of Afghanistan, but the Pakistani aid was still quite valuable.

It did not help that the Indian government itself was both more nationalistic than its predecessors and in some electoral trouble. Shortly after the recent Afghan War ended, terrorists invaded the Indian parliament and killed thirteen members. The Indian government demanded that the Pakistanis hand over the perpetrators and abandon all terrorist activity in Kashmir. There seems to have been some hope that, by rousing Indian nationalism, the governing party could gain in local elections. The situation was reminiscent of 1914, when an outraged Austrian government saw in a terrorist act an opportunity to wipe out its enemy, Serbia, rather than to accept a reasonable response on Serbia's part. This time the Indians talked of nuclear retaliation, and of ending once and for all the problem of Pakistan.

Pakistan benefited from friendship with the United States in that the U.S. government went to particular lengths to cool passions and to resolve the crisis short of war. Yet neither side could agree about Kashmir, and the potential for a serious explosion remained. For the moment, the outcome was that Pakistan abandoned its support for terrorists in Kashmir. The terrorists themselves apparently had different ideas, and they remained active through mid-2002. The Indians refused to accept Pakistani assurances that they were no longer supporting the terrorists, and they continued to threaten large-scale retaliation, which of course could lead to a nuclear war. It did not help that many in both governments and in their corresponding militaries clearly regarded nuclear weapons as little more than unusually powerful explosives.

The Pakistani view was that clear distinctions could be drawn between the Taliban and the Kashmiri separatists, so that it was possible to oppose the one while supporting the other. Yet the terrorists themselves saw no such distinction; they were interested mainly in promoting Islamic statehood. Thus Taliban were run to earth in the homes of Kashmiri separatist terrorists.

From an Al Qaeda perspective, there was a potentially useful connection between Afghanistan and Kashmir. In the spring of 2002 substantial Pakistan Army units were operating on the Afghan border, helping hold down any Taliban or Al Qaeda trying to cross the border back into Afghanistan. Kashmiri terrorist action led to an Indian buildup on the Kashmir border, and that in turn required that most of the Pakistan Army be deployed to face it—and thus be removed from the border with Afghanistan.

Pakistan was closely linked with Saudi Arabia, a longtime ally. Military relations were probably particularly close because the Saudis underwrote part of the Pakistani military and they had presumably been cemented during the anti-Soviet war in Afghanistan, when the Saudis financed rebel forces also supported by Pakistan. Too, the Saudis financed many of the madrassahs in northern Pakistan.

Osama and his henchmen were products of the official Saudi Wahhabi ideology; fifteen of the nineteen 11 September hijackers were Saudis. Much of Al Qaeda's financial support came from individuals in Saudi Arabia, and any attempt to cut off that support would require Saudi help. Before and after the attack, it was clear that the Saudi government was finding itself torn between the Wahhabi clerics it supported (and their Taliban supporters) and its U.S. ally. In August, Prince Turki al-Faisal was dismissed as the head of Saudi intelligence. He had been deeply involved in the Afghan campaign against the Soviets and reportedly had developed ties with Osama bin Laden. On the other hand, he had also gone to Afghanistan to try to convince the Taliban to surrender Osama.

For years Saudi Arabia had been built up as a potential U.S. operating base for the Middle East and Southwest Asia. The U.S. government badly wanted to use the facilities there, particularly the huge Prince Sultan Air Force Base. On the other hand, the Saudis clearly felt that they could not buck wide-scale support for Al Qaeda. Shortly after 11 September they declared that although they supported the U.S. right to retaliate against Afghanistan, they would not provide any sort of basing for troops or aircraft attacking Afghanistan.

That leaves open the question of just how much other support—for example, intelligence—the Saudis provided. Saudi Arabia is a very efficient police state, so in theory its government should be well aware of any local dissident activity. However, to the extent that the dissidents claim that they, rather than the government, are properly pursuing the official ideology, intelligence agencies may be infiltrated or even taken over by the dissidents. At the least, they may not pursue the particular kind of dissident who supported Osama.

Saudi Arabia did allow the U.S. Air Force to use the command facilities at Prince Sultan Air Force Base, even though U.S. military aircraft were not welcome. The average Saudi does not—or at least did not—associate the presence of a few officers with a large-scale military operation. Accounts of the operation have helped close that gap of understanding, and it seems less likely that the air force will be allowed to use the base in future. By late

2001 it was widely reported that the U.S. Air Force was moving all of its assets to other states in the area, such as Oman and Kuwait. For example, the U.S. Air Force was building a new air headquarters in Kuwait. It is not clear to what extent public reports of this type were intended mainly to assuage Saudi public opinion.

Other gulf states, such as Kuwait, Bahrain, and Oman, did welcome U.S. and British aircraft.

There was one other important operational issue. The U.S. government considered it vital to demonstrate that it would be fighting the unpopular Taliban government of Afghanistan, not the Afghan people. In 2001 many Afghans were eating only thanks to a United Nations food program (financed, incidentally, mostly by the United States). Any war in Afghanistan would inevitably disrupt it, at the least because the trucks involved were likely to become targets. No Muslim government could support a war which would starve large numbers of Afghans, partly because the embargo of Iraq was already a very emotive issue in the Muslim world. The U.S. response was to mount an air campaign to drop food packages. This effort seems not to have been very effective, but it had enormous political value in holding the anti-Taliban coalition together. As it was, the war was so quick that more conventional means of food relief were soon in place.

The other external coalition requirement was more political. The U.S. government did not want its operation in Afghanistan portrayed as colonialism. It wanted a long list of other governments in support—if possible, contributing forces, albeit often small ones. In some cases, such as that of the United Kingdom, the military support proved vital. Once the Taliban were ousted, moreover, the coalition partners could help sustain any replacement regime in a way which would counter any claims that the United States had simply annexed Afghanistan, and thus that it deserved much the same treatment the Soviet occupiers had received after 1979.

Moreover, the U.S. government badly wanted to overcome any view in the Muslim world that a war in Afghanistan was somehow an attack on Islam and on Islamic governments. It was, therefore, extremely desirable to enlist various Islamic governments in the larger war against terrorism. Conversely, Islamic rulers could expect U.S. support locally if they supported the war. That probably explains why Yassir Arafat, ruler of the Palestinians and arrayed against a U.S. ally, Israel, was so anxious to announce his support for the United States. He remembered that his support for the Iraqis in 1991 had gained him nothing. Too, like the Indians, the Israelis thought that the universal war against terror meant that the United States would strongly support their own attacks on Palestinian terrorists and their backers.

Again, the requirements of the particular war the United States was about to fight trumped any more universal attack on terrorism. In later speeches President Bush was careful to refer to a fight against terrorists with global reach, meaning organizations with universalist goals, like Al Qaeda, not local ones such as Hamas or Arafat's own Al Fatah or Al-Aqsa Brigade. In this he was reflecting the sensibilities of the Saudi, Jordanian, and Persian Gulf state governments.

Yet it was much more difficult to unravel the connection in many Arab minds between an escalating war in Palestine and the wider American war against terror. Initially the Bush administration tried hard to avoid engagement in the morass of the Israel-Palestine conflict, knowing too well that no earlier administration had enjoyed the slightest success there. The problem was the central position the war held in many Arab minds, a position Arab governments had been happy to reinforce.

Virtually all the Arab governments have two connected and longstanding problems. One is legitimacy. None of the Arab governments is a democracy, and many of the monarchies are of recent foundation, hence not supported by longstanding tradition. The second problem is that none has been particularly successful economically, despite, in many cases, massive amounts of either oil money or foreign aid. The two are connected. In order to stay in power, governments favor their powerful supporters and suppress independent activity, including the sort of economic activity which brings prosperity. All of the local governments therefore need some way of proving their virtue. To the extent that their populations all understand that destroying Israel is a sacred duty, each government can reasonably explain its own failures as necessary consequences of the uncompleted task of destroying Israel.

Moreover, it is very difficult to back away from that position. In 1948 the Arab governments told the Arab inhabitants of Palestine to leave, so that their armies could feel free to destroy the Jews. Once that had been done, the Arabs could return to take the land. That did not, of course, happen. Many of those who did not take that hint were ejected by Israelis who saw them as future enemies. The refugees could not be welcomed into the Arab countries because they would be visible evidence of failure, making for instability. Instead, they were largely kept in miserable refugee camps on the Israeli borders. They were told that at some future time the failure would be redeemed. However, many of them probably understood that redemption could come only through their own efforts; they became radicalized. As that happened, they became more and more dangerous to any Arab government foolish enough to accept them in large numbers, as the Jordanians learned when Palestinians in their country rebelled in 1970. The same problem destroyed Lebanon beginning in 1975.

By 2001, then, many Arab governments had painted themselves into a very dangerous corner. On the one hand, they had to maintain friendly relations with the United States, which was increasingly the source not only of cash but also of arms. On the other, they had to tell their populations that they favored destroying the main U.S. ally in the region, Israel. Moreover, only a continued state of war with Israel was consistent with what they had been telling their people for decades. Yet U.S. policy was to broker some kind of settlement with Israel, which could be guaranteed only if the Arab states totally reversed the only popular policies they had. Worse, any real settlement with Israel would probably entail accepting radicalized Palestinians, the only ones who would feel sold out, into their countries, since a new Palestine itself could not support its current population.

The Israeli-Arab conflict was a constant, but by 11 September it had escalated dangerously. A Palestinian uprising (intifada) against the Israelis had begun some time earlier, and photographs of Israeli troops firing at stone-throwing Arabs had been published throughout the Arab world. It seems in retrospect that the intifada was Yassir Arafat's way of withdrawing from American-brokered negotiations with the Israelis; he feared peace much more than continued war. To other Arabs, the intifada was a stirring attack on a common enemy, and behind the immediate enemy lay the Americans. The visible manifestation of the problem was street demonstrations throughout the Arab world celebrating 11 September.

Even so, the U.S. government considered it essential to make a viable case in the Arab world. Thus, for about three weeks after 11 September its representatives toured the Middle East trying to convince various governments that Osama bin Laden and his Taliban backers were responsible for the attacks. Apparently in some, but not all, cases they could deploy sensitive intelligence to bolster their arguments.

This campaign seems to have had very little impact on most Muslims. A year after the Afghan War, polls show that most Muslim populations reject the war on terror, that generally they regard it as little more than an assault on Islam. It may be argued that the problem is that few Muslim governments feel any need to convince their populations of the rightness of their policies, indeed, that the problem is the result of rigid censorship and information control in most of the Muslim world. Only in a freer atmosphere will a U.S. effort to convince a foreign government equate to an attempt to convince a wider population.

Europe was a different proposition. There the United States sought a combination of intelligence and physical military assistance. The formal call for military assistance came on 3 October, when the United States invoked Article 5 of the NATO Treaty. By that time several countries, including Britain, had already moved forces into the area to help fight the war.

As the 11 September investigations proceeded, it became clear that much of the Al Qaeda network which had prosecuted the attacks had relied on support from cells buried in Western Europe, particularly in Germany. If this network could be destroyed, further Al Qaeda attacks could be aborted. At the least, the problem of U.S. internal security might be reduced to monitoring those coming from Arab countries.

Cooperation varied. The French had long been fighting Algerian fundamentalists. They complained that, in the past, more liberal governments, such as the British, had offered terrorists a haven. Now they were happy to help. The British discovered, to their surprise, that some radical Muslims in their own country were part of Al Qaeda, and they were helpful. Spain, often the destination for Arabs fleeing North Africa, was also very helpful.

It turned out that Germany was the center of European Al Qaeda activity, because German antiterrorist laws were relatively weak. Moreover, liberal German educational laws made it easy for Al Qaeda operatives to gain legitimate residency by registering at German colleges, as the leader of the 11 September hijackers, Mohammed Atta, had. Germans remembered all too well what strong police had accomplished under the Nazis. Homegrown terrorists, such as the Baader-Meinhof gang, had exploited imposed postwar weakness, and as a reaction the German police had grown much more powerful—only to be weakened again as soon as the internal terrorist problem was solved in the 1970s. Al Qaeda and its associates had been careful not to encourage police interest on German soil. Now it seemed the problem was back, and attitudes slowly changed.

Intelligence collaboration in Europe had immediate results. At least two plots, one to attack the U.S. Embassy in Paris and one to attack targets in Belgium, were stopped.[8] By October 2001, President Bush could report that two hundred suspects had been detained abroad. By mid-November, the CIA alone had generated at least 360 arrests from fifty countries (more than 100 each from Europe and the Middle East, 30 from Latin America, and 20 from Africa).[9] The FBI had prompted further arrests. At about the same time, the United States had about eleven hundred suspects in custody (of which only seventy-four remained in custody in mid-2002, the U.S. arrests apparently having proven far less productive than the foreign ones). The wave of arrests was credited with having aborted at least four planned attacks overseas, including the one against the U.S. Embassy in Paris. In some countries, such as Singapore, the CIA was able to alert governments that did not realize that Al Qaeda had created cells on their territory. In most cases, suspects were arrested and questioned abroad. Some of the countries involved, such as Egypt, routinely use torture, and the prospect of being turned over to their police may in itself convince suspects to talk. Reportedly several Middle Eastern governments were particularly helpful.[10]

In all, by mid-October 2001, forty-four countries had provided overflight permission and thirty-three had provided landing rights for U.S. military aircraft. In addition, thirty-six had offered military forces or equipment for raids against the Taliban, and fourteen had accepted U.S. forces on their territory. Special forces were deployed to Afghanistan by the Australians, the Canadians, and the British. The British were the most important coalition military supporters, but many other countries contributed. Their assistance became more important in the maritime phase of the war, when a large multinational force operated in the Arabian Sea. Several countries contributed to the peacekeeping force formed in Afghanistan after the Taliban collapse.

Within the United States, the period of coalition building was derided as an excuse for inaction. Colin Powell was now secretary of state; during the Gulf War he had been chairman of the Joint Chiefs of Staff. To critics, he was merely repeating the strategy of the Gulf War, which had ended, ignominiously, in his failure to press home the successful attack and thus to destroy Saddam Hussein. That failure in turn had been ascribed to limits imposed by the coalition partners, particularly the Saudis. Would they restrain the United States the same way this time? Surely U.S. power would suffice to overthrow the Taliban, so why court foreign governments?

All of the coalition members helped in the war in Afghanistan, yet the critics were right: it turned out that none was essential in the sense that none had the ability to veto U.S. activity. That was a key point. For many foreign governments, it would have been very difficult *not* to exercise a veto. For example, it would have been far more popular, within Pakistan, for the government to have protected the Taliban with a veto, than to have provided essential assistance to unbelievers destroying a Muslim state.

The key, it turned out, was U.S. sea power, which provided bases near Afghanistan in international waters. Given those seagoing bases, the United States could fight the war virtually without help. That removed any country's veto and, paradoxically, encouraged many governments to join the coalition against the Taliban.

8

Objectives

Afghanistan was the obvious initial objective in the war against Al Qaeda. It was the movement's main base, the place from which the assault on the United States had been mounted. To the extent that the Taliban could be identified with Osama bin Laden and his organization, it could be said that the 11 September attack had been carried out by the irregular armed force of the Taliban, and the Taliban thus became a natural target for retaliation. However, the destruction of the Taliban regime in Afghanistan could offer the U.S. government much more.

Generally, the role of Afghanistan in supporting the terrorists was described in terms of camps used to train and indoctrinate Al Qaeda recruits, but the reality went much deeper. Like any other terrorist organization, Al Qaeda is necessarily conspiratorial. The great threat to its existence is always infiltration and deception. Operating in enemy territory, the organization has to expend most of its energy and resources on its own security. Those receiving instructions, for example, must always fear that those they meet are double agents, and communications must always be circumspect because there is a fair chance that they are being intercepted.

By way of contrast, in a secure area business can be conducted openly, without much fear of compromise. That is one reason why the most important members of Al Qaeda had to be brought back to the secure area, Afghanistan, not only for training but also for indoctrination and to receive key instructions. The secure area is also essential for morale. Without it, all members of the organization spend their entire lives under cover in what they see as enemy territory, always waiting for the police to knock on their doors. They are under tremendous strain, and from time to time they break. Trips "home" allow them to recover the necessary strength. (These concepts are familiar to anyone reading the memoirs of, for example, Soviet spies and saboteurs operating under cover in the West.)

For Al Qaeda, moreover, Taliban-ruled Afghanistan could serve as a model of the sort of world they were trying to create. In effect it proved that their struggle had a viable goal. Those selected for suicide ("martyrdom") missions could see what their attacks could achieve. Further, Afghanistan offered the sort of worldly rewards which encouraged Al Qaeda operatives. In Taliban-ruled Afghanistan, for example, the Taliban ensured that Al Qaeda personnel had their pick of local women.

Many of those who went to Afghanistan later recalled personal holy agreements with Osama bin Laden himself, who was particularly convincing in a country where he had enormous power. Without that power, in a more hostile environment, Osama would have had less time in which to indoctrinate his followers, and also a much less convincing story to tell. Other influences might have been effective, whereas in Afghanistan the official ideology faced no competitors.

Al Qaeda did have other operating bases, but they were nothing like as secure as those in Afghanistan, simply because local governments could not be relied upon. By way of contrast, to a considerable extent the Taliban had become an extension of Al Qaeda, so Al Qaeda had become the de facto government of Afghanistan.

Thus the destruction of the Al Qaeda state became the obvious first step in a war against the organization. Once that state was gone, Al Qaeda would be much more vulnerable to classic police and intelligence attacks. In addition, while Al Qaeda could operate from its sanctuary, it could effectively threaten all Muslim governments. Denied sanctuary, it could be attacked by each government it had victimized.

Moreover, destruction of the Taliban regime would offer other governments a deterrent. To the extent that the Taliban regime's protection made bin Laden's attacks possible, it became vital to destroy that regime as a warning to others who might be willing to harbor future bin Ladens. Much has been made of the willingness of suicide attackers to die and, hence, of the impossibility of deterring them. That is certainly true on an individual basis. It also seems to be the case that some aspects of Islam make it easier to convince a potential bomber to accept a suicide mission. But the key to deterrence is those who do the convincing. They and their protectors are the appropriate targets, and the Taliban in particular fill this bill. It is also arguable that the corrosive effect of modern culture will eliminate the fanatic suicide bomber problem within a few decades, so that anything which restrains our enemies now is well worth our while.[1]

Potential supporters of Osama or his ilk will, we hope, now understand that the United States has real teeth and will bite when provoked. That alone was probably worth the price of the war. Yemen was a case in point. The 2000 attack on the USS *Cole* was not orchestrated by the Yemeni government, but it was obvious that the Yemenis were reluctant to allow Americans to interrogate those involved, and it seemed likely that although the lowest-level conspirators would be caught and executed, higher-ups would escape. Since Al Qaeda had probably ordered and carried out the attack on the ship, the Yemeni government was in effect shielding the terrorist organization. It felt safe doing so, because in 2000 there was no chance whatever that the United States would physically punish Yemen for obstructing the investigation. Nor would the United States shield Yemen from any consequences of an attack against Al Qaeda.

Direct U.S. military action in Afghanistan dramatically changed perceptions, so that afterward the Yemenis welcomed U.S. Special Forces and conducted armed raids against supposed Al Qaeda camps in their country. It is not clear just how effective the raids were, but they certainly confirmed the notion that demonstrating U.S. resolve in one country could have positive effects elsewhere in the Muslim world. Earlier events had demonstrated that inaction would merely encourage further attacks.

For that matter, simply demonstrating to the Muslim population at large that the United States could and would fight back would tend to separate really fanatical terrorists from those who might be happy to demonstrate but would prefer not to die as a consequence. This seems to have worked, and probably to have reduced the ranks of those willing to work for or with Al Qaeda and similar organizations.

Al Qaeda extended well beyond Afghanistan. It had cells throughout Europe and the Muslim world. Its money probably came mostly from Saudi Arabia, which was, at least for a time, off limits for U.S. strikes. However, with the secure base gone, the war against Al Qaeda would be largely an intelligence and police operation. Breaking into the secure base area could be extremely valuable, because in this one area Al Qaeda operatives would feel free to maintain records. Whether or not many Al Qaeda troops were killed or captured, the records themselves might well be worth the effort. They would probably reveal the identities of many moles in foreign countries, the location of their bases, and even the character of planned attacks.

For example, it was often said that Al Qaeda was a kind of terrorist holding company. Apparently local cells would develop proposals for attacks, submitting them to Osama for approval and for the necessary support. As a consequence, U.S. troops in Afghanistan found videotapes of proposed attacks. One such tape led to the destruction of an Al Qaeda group in Singapore and to the frustration of its plan to attack U.S. military targets there.

This objective, of seizing key Al Qaeda records, extended beyond any interest in overthrowing the Taliban regime itself. Al Qaeda was not actually identical to the Taliban, in the sense that the foreign terrorist arm had its own sanctuaries, many of them in caves near the Pakistani border. To the extent that the caves seemed very secure, seizing them was likely to reveal key information. Caves were also likely to contain important Al Qaeda resources, the capture of which might weaken the terrorist movement.

Much effort was expended in the hunt for Osama bin Laden himself; initially President Bush said that he was wanted "dead or alive," and Secretary of Defense Donald Rumsfeld famously said that dead was preferable. At the least, capturing or killing bin Laden would make it clear to any successor that his grandiose schemes can and will be brought down. Bin Laden may now claim to look fondly upon the prospect of martyrdom, but the ego involved in staging major operations makes it unlikely that he considered this one suicidal from the start.

As the campaign continued without bagging Osama, the question arose of just how important his destruction would be. Some said that his inspiration would live on. However, bin Laden created Al Qaeda by bringing together (and holding together) a fractious assemblage of terrorist organizations. Quite possibly he was the only one who fully grasped the financial support system he had created. Possibly, too, his leadership skills were crucial. His disappearance might then cause Al Qaeda to break up. Terrorists would certainly remain, and they might not be much deterred, but the terror international might be much less coherent. Splits between terror units might in themselves help break up the problem, as groups denounced each other to gain stature. That was certainly the case with earlier terrorist movements.

A third objective was both more important and much more difficult to attain. The U.S. government sought to improve its standing in the Muslim world. It was painfully aware that its own propaganda had been ineffective. Through the 1990s the United States had often been the chief protector of Muslims in the world. It was U.S. pressure which ended ethnic cleansing in Bosnia and which began the process that ejected the Serbs from Kosovo, sparing many Muslims. Contrary to the suppositions of most Arabs, it was U.S. pressure which often restrained Israelis infuriated by Palestinian terrorism. None of this apparently had much impact on world Muslim opinion. Worse, U.S. actions were often turned against the United States. For example, the effort to stop ethnic cleansing in the former Yugoslavia was often dismissed as a kind of colonialism, an effort to displace a nascent Muslim state.

In theory, success in this objective would drastically reduce the attraction Al Qaeda exercised, and thus might ultimately starve it of resources. Experience suggests, however, that it does not take enormous popularity to keep a small terrorist organization in business.

Even so, American policy was shaped in part by the need to capture "hearts and minds." In September 2001 much of the Afghan population was destitute because several decades of war had destroyed so much of the country's agriculture. A large United Nations operation was feeding many Afghans, but this operation could not continue during a U.S.-led assault. The U.S. response was to replace the UN operation with aerial delivery of food, the U.S. Air Force flying C-17s from Pakistan. Critics suggested that the food was often misdelivered and that the humanitarian drops were ineffective. Even so, the costly effort to deliver food by air reflected an important wartime theme: the United States was at war with the Taliban, not with the people of Afghanistan.

Against all of these objectives, there was one extremely important negative one. Past foreign invaders of Afghanistan had acted to seize what they saw as strategic ground. Afghan nationalism proved potent, and both the British and the Soviets suffered badly when they tried to occupy the country. From the beginning, the U.S. government emphasized that it had no wish to rule Afghanistan; it merely wanted to eject a local government which had attacked the United States. Some U.S. spokesmen went further. For example, early in the war Secretary of Defense Donald Rumsfeld ruled out any attempt at nation building in Afghanistan, saying that the future Afghan government was no business of his.

In fact, the situation was somewhat more complex. Destroying the Taliban regime and then leaving a successor government to its own devices might be nothing more than inviting some similar regime back into power, hence inviting Al Qaeda or some successor back into position. Given the ethnic connections between the unruly tribes of northern Pakistan and the southern Afghans, continuing turmoil in Afghanistan would likely spread across the border. If something like the Taliban or Al Qaeda took control of Pakistan, then that anti-Western entity would also take control of the Pakistani nuclear arsenal, a chilling thought for Americans. Thus the U.S. government did have a direct interest in the future of Afghanistan, but it also had a strong sense of self-restraint.

It helped enormously that many Afghans saw Al Qaeda as a foreign force, just the sort of alien government against which Afghans had revolted in years past. The Al Qaeda Arabs generally did not speak any Afghan language (Osama certainly did not), and they lorded it over the local population. Later, stories would be told of Al Qaeda Arabs simply seizing Afghan women they liked as conquerors' spoils. Afghans who got in their way were usually summarily killed.

There was also another issue. In 2001 Afghanistan was one of the largest world producers of the poppies from which heroin is made; most European addicts used Afghan heroin. In the year before 11 September, much of the income of the Taliban government came from U.S. payments to suppress heroin production. To some extent the famine in Afghanistan could be blamed on farmers who grew poppies (which were profitable) rather than rebuild their ability to grow staples such as wheat. At least in theory, one advantage of Western control of Afghanistan might be to reverse this process—if that proved possible. On the other hand, many of the individual warlords who joined together as the Northern Alliance derived their income from taxes on poppy sales. They would have to be weaned off this form of sustenance.

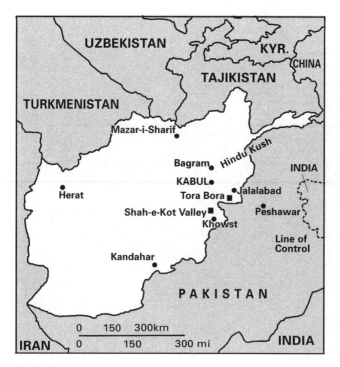

Afghanistan

Smoke and flames covered the southern tip of Manhattan after two airliners hijacked by Al Qaeda terrorists crashed into the two towers of the World Trade Center on 11 September 2001. The U.S. Coast Guard mobilized almost instantly both to patrol the harbor against further attacks and to evacuate thousands stranded at the tip of Manhattan by the attack. U.S. Coast Guard (PA3 Tom Sperduto)

The attack destroyed several buildings housing much of the U.S. financial industry. This is a small part of the damaged area. Given the supposed sophistication of Osama bin Laden, the planner of the attacks, it seemed to some that the assault was intended specifically to destroy the U.S. financial system. If so, it could be seen as the sort of "center of gravity" attack favored by some current strategists. That it failed to have anything like the apparently intended effect brings such strategies into question. U.S. Navy (PHC Eric J. Tilford)

The Pentagon was also hit, but in its case the damage was localized. Here firefighters try to contain the fire. U.S. Air Force (T.Sgt. Jim Varhegyi)

A combination of good luck, a difficult approach, and a very robust building limited damage to the Pentagon to part of one of its five sides. In all, the attack killed 125 people in the building, plus the 58 passengers and 6 crew members of American Airlines Flight 77. As Secretary of Defense Donald S. Rumsfeld vowed, the damage was made good within a year. U.S. Navy (DoD Photographer Sgt. Cedric H. Rudisill)

After the attacks, homeland defense became a major military function. In the past, U.S. strategy has been forward-oriented, on the theory that threatening enemies in their own homelands is a far better way of ensuring the security of the United States. Here the carrier *George Washington* (CVN 73) operates off the East Coast, her fighters providing air defense against further potential hijackings. Carriers were later instrumental in winning the war in Afghanistan. One question for the future must be to what extent direct defense of the U.S. homeland will tie down forces needed to deal with threats farther away. U.S. Navy (PH3 J. Scott Campbell)

Anti-American protesters on 8 October 2001 burning the Stars and Stripes during a rally in Lahore against the U.S.-led military strikes on neighboring Afghanistan. As Pakistan prepared to celebrate fifty-five years as a nation in 2002, analysts warned that Islamic fundamentalism, the military's stranglehold on politics, and growing poverty threatened to turn the country into a "failed state." Agence France Presse

(Facing page)

Americans were surprised by the extent of pro–Al Qaeda demonstrations throughout the Muslim world after the 11 September attack. Violent anti-American demonstrations greeted the onset of war in Afghanistan, despite U.S. attempts to explain that the war was retaliatory. The great question seemed to be, why do they hate us? Was the appropriate response to Al Qaeda an attack on root causes such as widespread poverty? Just how relevant was the apparent rage in the Muslim street? Here members of the Afghan Defense Council brandish toy guns—and a portrait of their hero of the moment, Osama bin Laden—in Lahore, Pakistan, 23 October 2001. Agence France Presse (Arif Ali)

By the fall of 2001, the Northern Alliance had been fighting the Taliban for years. Many of its troops were motivated by a realistic fear that a Taliban victory would presage a massacre of non-Pashtun ethnic groups, members of which formed the Alliance. Here two Northern Alliance soldiers help defend the Salang Heights, about one hundred kilometers north of Kabul, 26 September 2001. Agence France Press (Alexander Nemenov)

In September 2001 a Russian commentator remarked that the United States would find war in Afghanistan difficult because it had no nearby bases. He omitted the floating bases operated by the U.S. Navy, from which about 75 percent of combat sorties over Afghanistan were launched. Here a Navy F/A-18 Hornet launches from the carrier *Kitty Hawk* in the Arabian Sea, 2 November 2001. U.S. Navy (PH3 John E. Woods)

It was a long way from the Arabian Sea to objectives in Afghanistan. Land-based tankers were essential. Here a Royal Air Force VC-10 tanker fuels a pair of F/A-18s of VFA-22, the "Fighting Rednecks," 31 October 2001. Ironically, less than a decade earlier the U.S. Navy had retired its long-range A-6 Intruder attack bombers, the theory being that combat would generally occur in littoral areas, where most of the world's population lives. The few deep targets, it was thought, could be reached by Tomahawk missiles or by very long-range land-based bombers. U.S. Navy (Lt. Steve Lightstone)

The Marine operation in southern Afghanistan, which established Forward Operating Base Rhino, was possible because it could be mounted from a seaborne base, on board amphibious ships, rather than from a land base requiring the consent of a neighboring state. The Marines staged through Pakistan, with Pakistani permission, but it was vital that they did not have to build up a base there. Here, in the Arabian Sea, troop-carrying Marine helicopters, CH-46E Sea Knights, await launch from the major amphibious ship *Bataan;* the dock-landing ship *Whidbey Island* is in the background, 14 December 2001. U.S. Navy (PHC Johnny Bivera)

Initial air attacks focused on fixed military targets, such as these tank revetments outside Kandahar. One effect of the early part of the air campaign was to destroy Taliban air defenses, so that U.S. attack aircraft could operate freely. This photograph of smashed Taliban armor was taken postwar, on 25 January 2002. U.S. Navy (PH1 Ted Banks)

Heavy bombardment may often miss targets, but it has enormous psychological value. It seems in retrospect that B-52 strikes against Taliban positions sufficiently impressed Northern Alliance commanders that they could and should advance. Only heavy bombers could supply a sufficient weight of bombs in a short enough time to achieve the required effect. Here a B-52 of the Air Force's 28th Air Expeditionary Wing takes off from Diego Garcia, an island in the Indian Ocean, on 22 October 2001. Parked in the foreground are other B-52s and B-1B bombers. U.S. Air Force (S.Sgt. Shane Cuomo)

Once the Northern Alliance began to move, coalition aircraft provided its artillery. Air attacks were called in and controlled by Special Forces personnel, including Air Force tactical air controllers. This is Air Force M.Sgt. Bart Decker, an eighteen-year veteran.
Agence France Presse

Not all targets were found by Special Forces on the ground. In many cases reconnaissance aircraft were cued by electronic intelligence aircraft, such as this EP-3E ARIES II of VQ-1 (World Watchers) shown at Manama, Bahrain. U.S. Navy (PH2 [SW] Michael Sandberg)

Afghanistan marked the first combat use of armed UAVs like this RQ-1 Predator (the missiles are Hellfires). After the war, a Hellfire-armed Predator was used in Yemen to kill a major Al Qaeda leader. U.S. Air Force

The Air Force's Rivet Joint (RC-135) electronic reconnaissance aircraft were also key to finding tactical targets in Afghanistan. Electronic reconnaissance offers the widest coverage of any airborne sensor, and is typically used to cue imaging systems such as those aboard UAVs; much clearly depends on whether and how much an enemy uses radios and radars. The mere existence of such sensors encourages an enemy to shut down radios and rely on runners, which in turn drastically slows the enemy's responses in combat. It is possible that victory in Afghanistan was largely due to the sheer pace of the operation, and, conversely, to the slow pace of Taliban and Al Qaeda responses. U.S. Air Force

Plumes of smoke rise from the Taliban-controlled village of Rahesh on the Shomali plain north of Kabul, 9 November 2001, after two U.S. aircraft strikes. Punishing U.S. airstrikes on Taliban positions north of the capital helped Northern Alliance forces break through outer Taliban defenses. In ten tumultuous days, the Taliban lost two-thirds of their territory and saw many of the trappings of government fall into the hands of their enemies. Associated Press (Marco DiLauro)

Ethnolinguistic Groups in Afghanistan

The Marines' view of the situation from Rhino, 30 November 2001. Support from the sea and by air made it possible to maintain a base surrounded by tens of thousands of Taliban (note the sign at lower right). The mere existence of a very powerful Marine force at that base, in turn, made it possible to form a Southern Alliance that fought the Taliban. Associated Press (Jim Hollander)

(Facing page)

There was no Southern Alliance at the outset; the vast majority of the population of southeast Afghanistan were Pashtuns, who felt an ethnic solidarity with the Taliban—and who regarded the Northern Alliance as an attempt by northern tribes to wrest control of the country from the Taliban. It was, therefore, crucial that the U.S. Marines establish a combat force deep in this area, near Kandahar, at what they called Forward Operating Base Rhino. Two Marines of the 15th MEU (Special Operations Capable) sit atop their Light Armored Vehicle (LAV), 11 December 2001. U.S. Marine Corps (Sgt. Joseph R. Chenelly)

The war did not end with the fall of Kandahar, as pockets of Taliban and Al Qaeda troops remained. The hope was that they would concentrate to fight. Here Gen. Tommy Franks, head of Central Command, briefs reporters on the last major attempt to destroy a concentration of enemy troops, Operation Anaconda, in the Shah-e-Kot Valley. The array of flags on the right indicates the presence of coalition forces, usually Special Forces, in the operation. As it turned out, intelligence failures and the unwillingness of the U.S. Army to request a pre-assault bombardment (by the Air Force) made Anaconda far more difficult than it otherwise might have been. Central Command (S.Sgt. Jack Siemieniec, USA)

Operations to find and destroy Taliban and Al Qaeda caches of weapons and explosives continue. They are essential to ensuring the success of the new government in Kabul. Here a Navy SEAL watches the destruction of munitions his team found during a Sensitive Site Exploitation operation—a raid on a suspected arms cache, 12 February 2002. SEALs and other Special Forces from several countries played key roles in the war, to the extent that some wags termed it a "Special Forces Olympics." Only small units, for example, could hunt down some kinds of enemy positions and arms caches. U.S. Navy (PH1 Tim Turner)

(Facing page)

P-3Cs turned out to be extremely useful during operations such as Anaconda. Many aircraft now have long-lens electronic cameras and a wideband data link, via which they can provide troops on the ground with photographs they need, effectively on demand. By way of contrast, large UAVs were controlled centrally, and their images went to an air headquarters because they were intended primarily to find targets for air attack. This VP-1 aircraft was photographed on 22 October 2002. U.S. Navy (PH2 Michael Sandberg)

As coalition forces took Afghanistan, it seemed likely that some Al Qaeda and Taliban would try to escape by sea, via Pakistan. An international naval force patrolled the northern Arabian Sea in hopes of stopping them. The U.S. cruiser *Cowpens* and the Australian frigate *Darwin* are shown in the Indian Ocean, 12 February 2002. This operation was the first since World War II in which Australian officers sometimes had operational control of U.S. warships. U.S. Navy (PH2 [NAC] David C. Mercil)

9

Striking Back

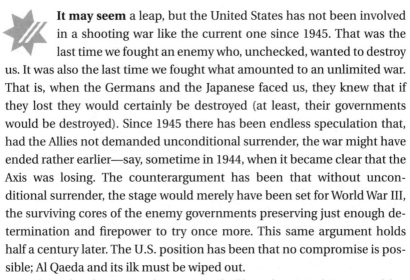**It may seem** a leap, but the United States has not been involved in a shooting war like the current one since 1945. That was the last time we fought an enemy who, unchecked, wanted to destroy us. It was also the last time we fought what amounted to an unlimited war. That is, when the Germans and the Japanese faced us, they knew that if they lost they would certainly be destroyed (at least, their governments would be destroyed). Since 1945 there has been endless speculation that, had the Allies not demanded unconditional surrender, the war might have ended rather earlier—say, sometime in 1944, when it became clear that the Axis was losing. The counterargument has been that without unconditional surrender, the stage would merely have been set for World War III, the surviving cores of the enemy governments preserving just enough determination and firepower to try once more. This same argument holds half a century later. The U.S. position has been that no compromise is possible; Al Qaeda and its ilk must be wiped out.

In the wake of 11 September, many asked how the United States could or would respond. Would it repeat the Gulf War, using bombers and then building up a ground force? Would it simply fire some cruise missiles to show its fury? Unlike the wars the United States fought in the latter half of the twentieth century, this one needed little explanation: two strategic attacks against the United States were all the proof that Americans needed that the enemy was serious. It is interesting, in retrospect, that previous attacks, which caused fewer casualties, did not have anything like the same effect.

President Bush demanded options for action immediately after 11 September. His CIA director, George Tenet, offered much-expanded covert action.[1] The Northern Alliance would be reinvigorated; a six-to-eight-man CIA paramilitary team could be inserted to work with each major Alliance leader. Initially, six such teams were approved. The CIA would receive the broadest and most lethal authority in its history, "exceptional authority" to attack and destroy Al Qaeda wherever it could be found.[2] Chairman of the Joint Chiefs, Gen. Henry H. Shelton, a veteran of the Clinton administration, offered three levels of action: missiles, bombers, and "boots on the ground." To Shelton's apparent relief, the president opted for the largest rather than the quickest option: all three.

The single most remarkable feature of the war the United States and her coalition partners prosecuted was the speed with which it was begun and then fought.[3] That speed in turn was possible largely because the new type of warfare made it possible to fight using very limited forces.

Possibly the single key U.S. decision was to attack the Taliban, rather than try to attack bin Laden or Al Qaeda directly. At the very least, the Taliban state was shielding the man responsible for the mass murder of Americans. Damaging or destroying it would, moreover, tend to deter other states which might be inclined to harbor bin Laden and Al Qaeda.

The Taliban, moreover, had major military weaknesses. Their only really good troops, bin Laden's Arabs, were not very numerous. They had to be divided between front-line service and direct protection of senior members of the Taliban government. Thus the numbers available to stiffen resistance in any one place were likely to be limited. Indeed, the numbers involved anywhere in Afghanistan were small; a few hundred or a thousand effective troops could achieve a great deal. It was also significant that the Taliban had not made any of the experienced Afghan resistance leaders their military leaders; instead, leadership was reserved to clerics with little or no military experience. That was understandable. The Taliban were rebels, and in many modern revolutions (and postrevolutionary governments) political loyalty has trumped military experience when it comes to handing out vital commands. That the Taliban revolution was Islamic rather than, say, socialist, was immaterial; loyalty to the rulers was paramount.

The Gulf War had amply demonstrated that U.S. military technology could overcome the sort of defenses any Third World state could deploy. However, as one Afghan put it, what was the point of firing a million-dollar missile to destroy a tent worth a few thousand? The Afghans themselves had already wiped out most of the buildings in cities like Kabul. Moreover, it was difficult to see why the destruction of modern facilities would distress a ruling Taliban party whose main wish was to transport the country back into a mythical, golden preindustrial age. As for the Taliban army, the Northern Alliance had already learned that it could take considerable fire and hold its ground. How could a few precision weapons affect the outcome? After all, at such a distance, the United States surely could not deploy a mountain of bombs or missiles, so each weapon would have to count heavily.

A Russian writer agreed that the Taliban deserved destruction, but he noted that the United States lacked bases near Afghanistan.[4] To him, that limited the bomb tonnage that could be deployed. The only way to package firepower compactly enough would be to use nuclear weapons—but politically they were out of the question. Given Russian feelings about the Afghans in the previous war, it was understandable that the writer seemed rather to regret the political limits the Americans undoubtedly felt. Another Russian helpfully pointed out that the various Afghan tribes were susceptible to bribery; he recalled contracts various Afghan commanders had signed guaranteeing good conduct for various periods.[5]

A Maritime War

These comments, which were typical, missed some important points, about both U.S. resources and precision weapons. In fact, the United States did possess bases within air range of Afghanistan, in the form of aircraft carriers. That the U.S. Navy offered viable alternatives to air bases should not have been altogether surprising. The 1998 missile strikes had shown that Afghanistan was well within naval missile range. However, this was the first time in history that a government had relied on its fleet to strike a land-locked country more than 350 miles from the sea and separated from the sea by a third state (in this case, Pakistan).

The Afghan War would be very largely a maritime war. Even troops, in the form of Marines, could come from the sea. Tomahawks were fired by submarines and destroyers operating in the Gulf of Oman. Given sufficient refueling, carrier-launched strike aircraft could match Tomahawk range. On the sea the United States could move its bases at will: aircraft carriers and major amphibious ships. At least through early November, the carriers were the only source of tactical air strikes, because the Air Force had few tactical aircraft in the area. Their only local base, Oman, was far from Afghanistan. Late in November the Air Force began using at least one former Soviet air base in Tajikistan.[6]

One irony of the naval air situation was that, some years earlier, the U.S. Navy had deliberately limited strike aircraft range on the theory that it would most likely be operating within a few hundred miles of a beach, in a littoral area, where upward of 80 percent of the world population lives. Thus it was not considered urgent to replace the A-6 Intruder, the longest-range naval strike aircraft. The few targets deeper inland could be engaged by Tomahawk missiles. All of Afghanistan, however, was deep inland. Moreover, a few cruise missiles would not suffice. There were too many potential targets, and in too many cases attacks would have to be made in support of ground troops, the missions changing as a battle unfolded.

Fortunately, the longest-range tactical attack aircraft, the F-14 Tomcat, had by 2001 been modified to deliver precision munitions; it also carried a laser-illumination pod (LANTIRN), which proved extremely valuable during the war. The majority of carrier-borne strike aircraft were shorter-range F/A-18s.

Sea basing does impose limitations. In order to gain mobility, ships carry only limited numbers of aircraft and munitions. Hence the importance of the new generation of precision-guided weapons: accuracy can sometimes make up for limited numbers if the targets in question are relatively small and concentrated. Too, carrier-based strike aircraft have to be tanked in order to strike deep inland. During the war, these aircraft relied heavily on land-based U.S. Air Force and Royal Air Force tankers in Kuwait, Oman, and the UAE.[7] The British made a major contribution to the air war simply by providing tanker support (about 20 percent of all tanking).[8] Since tankers are noncombat aircraft and resemble airliners, no one in Oman or Kuwait decided that the entire operation could be derailed simply by vetoing the presence of the tankers. In any case, the Omanis and Kuwaitis would not have had a full veto, since carrier aircraft could refuel each other (by, for example, the buddy system). As it was, the only carrier-based refueler, the S-3 Viking (a former antisubmarine aircraft used for surveillance), could not deliver fuel at altitudes above seventeen thousand feet. F-14s and F/A-18s had to get down to that altitude to fuel then climb back up—burning up much of the fuel they took aboard in the process. Fortunately for the U.S. Navy, the new F/A-18E/F offer considerable buddy-tanking capability at the same speeds and altitudes used by strike aircraft.

Ultimately, the war would involve three strike aircraft carriers (the *Enterprise, Carl Vinson,* and *Theodore Roosevelt;* the latter relieved *Enterprise* at the end of October). In November, the carrier *John C. Stennis* was sent to the area. Each strike carrier had on board four fighter squadrons (one squadron of F-14s [two on board *Enterprise*] and three squadrons of F/A-18Cs [two on *Enterprise*]), a squadron of four E-2C Hawkeyes, one of four EA-6B Prowler jammers, and one squadron of eight S-3Bs.

There were also two amphibious ready groups built around the 15th and 26th Marine Expeditionary Units and the large-deck amphibious ships *Ba-*

taan and *Pelelieu.* These two units would later be the principal U.S. ground force in southern Afghanistan, and as such would play a crucial role in the war.[9]

The USS *Kitty Hawk,* normally based in Japan, deployed without all of its usual air wing (retaining some strike aircraft). It secretly embarked Army Special Operations helicopters (to transport the 75th Ranger Regiment) to operate over southern Afghanistan (Army helicopters based in Uzbekistan covered the northern part of the country). In Haiti (1994) the U.S. Navy had demonstrated that Army helicopters could operate from a carrier. They had operated from some surface ships in the Persian Gulf as early as 1987. *Kitty Hawk* arrived on 16 October, its role partly to demonstrate that the United States could conduct at least some special operations without using Pakistani bases. It was successful enough that naval planners began to consider providing a floating special forces base on a permanent basis. By the beginning of November *Kitty Hawk* once again had its usual aircraft on board, and it participated in some strikes on Afghanistan before returning to Japan.

In addition to the carriers, the United States had a base at Diego Garcia in the Indian Ocean. By the end of the war it was hosting eight B-1B and ten B-52 bombers. Bombers on Diego Garcia averaged one mission every other day (four B-1 and five B-52 sorties per day). Although B-2s were used early in the war, they could not use Diego Garcia; they flew all the way from the United States, taking on fuel from tankers along the way.[10] From a tactical point of view, the Diego Garcia-based bombers were likely to be less effective than carrier-based aircraft. Each bomber could orbit to deliver its bombs one by one, but once those bombs were gone it had to fly all the way back to Diego Garcia to reload. The larger number of carrier-based aircraft were much closer, and they could maintain a more continuous presence. The new technology of GPS guidance made it possible for one airplane to hit multiple targets during each mission. Reportedly, B-52s were fitted during the war to set GPS coordinates on guided bombs, but this was a manual process subject to error (in one case, a GPS-guided bomb was misaimed, killing three Americans).

Overall, naval aircraft flew about three-quarters of all sorties and dropped about a third of the bombs by number. The Air Force flew about a quarter of combat sorties and dropped about three-quarters of the bomb tonnage, including the 15,000-pound "Daisy Cutter."[11]

At the outset of the war the British had a powerful naval force in the Gulf of Oman for a previously scheduled "Saif Sareea II" exercise. It included the carrier *Illustrious,* with Sea Harriers on board, and the amphibious carrier

Ocean, as well as the Tomahawk-armed submarines *Trafalgar* and *Triumph* and the amphibious ship HMS *Fearless* (which embarked one hundred Royal Marines on 26 October for helicopter transfer to southern Afghanistan (three hundred more followed in the next few days). HMS *Illustrious* remained in the Indian Ocean, off the southern Somali coast, through early 2002. At the end of January the helicopter carrier *Ocean* left Great Britain for the Indian Ocean, where it would replace *Illustrious* and the amphibious ship HMS *Fearless.* British submarines participated in the Tomahawk attacks at the outbreak of war.

The British also contributed aircraft, most importantly Tristar and VC-10 tankers, which could fuel U.S. naval aircraft in flight. But they also provided surveillance aircraft: British AWACS (E-3D), Nimrod R1 electronic surveillance aircraft, and Canberra PR.9 photo reconnaissance aircraft. All apparently operated out of Oman. Australia provided two tankers.

Australia, Bahrain, Canada, France, Germany, Greece, Italy, the Netherlands, and Spain all contributed warships to a coalition force intended mainly to intercept any Taliban or Al Qaeda personnel trying to flee by sea. Canadian Auroras, French Atlantiques, and Spanish and Dutch P-3s provided naval surveillance. The Canadian frigate *Vancouver* formed part of the *Stennis* battle group. The Italian group was centered on the carrier *Giuseppe Garibaldi;* Italy also contributed eight Tornado bombers and some paratroopers to Operation Enduring Freedom. Initially the French offered warships already in or near the Indian Ocean, where France maintains a considerable naval presence. In December 2001, however, a battle group built around the new carrier *Charles de Gaulle* arrived in the Indian Ocean for coalition operations the French Navy called Operation Heracles. Its aircraft participated in Operation Anaconda. The French government was sufficiently impressed with its value that it began to reconsider building a second carrier, a project which had been abandoned for some time. Two German frigates left Germany on 2 January 2002 to begin surveillance of the Somali coast, against the threat that Al Qaeda refugees would establish a base there. The Germans also contributed five fast patrol boats to the Indian Ocean interception operation.

For the first time since 1945, Japan became involved in a distant naval operation, albeit explicitly for support, not combat. A group built around the helicopter-carrying destroyer *Kurama* and the missile destroyers *Sawagiri* and *Kirisame* left Japan on 9 November. Proposals to send more advanced *Kongo*-class destroyers were dropped.[12]

Land Basing

There certainly were efforts to gain land bases. Even though some bordering states, all ex-Soviet, were sympathetic, any bases established on their soil would have to be built up, since spares and maintenance facilities were not already in place. Thus whatever air base facilities they offered could support only a very few aircraft at the outset. Uzbekistan allowed U.S. Army helicopters (UH-60s, AH-64A Apaches, and MH-47 Special Forces Chinooks) to operate from Khanabad, near the border area in which the Northern Alliance was fighting. The United States deployed units of the Tenth Mountain Division to Uzbekistan to protect the aircraft based there; later it was said that Uzbekistan had in effect concluded an alliance with the United States. Tajikistan offered bases, but it was not until November 2001 that the U.S. Air Force began to survey them. Kyrgyzstan, which does not directly border Afghanistan, offered basing for French strike aircraft.[13]

At the outset, the Saudis announced that they supported the Americans but that they would not allow any U.S. combatants on their soil.[14] Thus Saudi Arabia refused to allow U.S. aircraft to use the huge Prince Sultan Air Base. During the Gulf War, the Saudis had welcomed a U.S. command center to Riyadh, but in that war they had been major coalition partners.

Pakistan offered bases, albeit initially on a covert basis, and apparently not for combat aircraft. It only admitted this on 11 October, by which time U.S. aircraft were using bases at Pasni, on the coast about 150 miles west of Karachi, and Jacobabad in Baluchistan. The latter apparently accommodated special operations C-130s. Pakistan Air Force bases at Dalbandin and Samungli were used as advanced airstrips, for fueling and similar operations. These bases made possible the Special Forces assault on 17 October and the Marines' occupation of Forward Operating Base (FOB) Rhino. Helicopters from U.S. amphibious ships began shuttling personnel and equipment into Pasni about 12 October. In addition, Kuwait allowed operations by Air Force F-15Es beginning on 19 October.

Command Arrangements

Compared to those in Kosovo, the forces engaged in Enduring Freedom enjoyed a major advantage in command arrangements. CENTCOM, or Central Command, had a preexisting command structure, which was moved into place to fight the war. No time was lost in deciding who had precedence. Command relationships were clear from the outset, and, moreover, did not have to be built up for this specific operation. The Defense Department saw the war in Afghanistan as the first of a series of quick short wars the United States might face—"come as you are" wars. One of its solutions was to demand that permanent Joint Task Forces be set up, assignable to operations as they were needed. Probably the success of the preexisting CENTCOM command structure helped inspire this idea. By 2001 satellite communication systems were so good that it could be argued that command could effectively be exercised from a great distance. In fact, the U.S. commander, Gen. Tommy Franks, stayed in his Tampa, Florida, command center at MacDill Air Force Base, the home of Central Command. Later it was argued that as a result he missed some important nuances of the Afghan situation.

There was little question but that commanders in Tampa could receive whatever information they wanted—if they knew what they wanted. For example, Pentagon briefers often made a point of how Tampa could and did receive live Predator video from Afghanistan via satellite links. That traffic, however, was one way; it appears that communication back to forward commanders was far slower. Moreover, it is not clear that commanders at the Tampa level really needed micro-details such as what a particular Predator was seeing. They were responsible for larger issues.

Locating headquarters in the United States brought an unanticipated problem: the United States is several time zones from the Persian Gulf, and since one major advantage of keeping the command center in one place was to give it access to resources in the United States, in effect, the center had to keep U.S. time. It could communicate with forces engaged in Afghanistan on a more or less real-time basis, but that communication generally occurred late at night in the gulf. As a consequence, those charged with keeping Tampa up to date found themselves working extraordinarily long hours and becoming much more fatigued than they should have been. Conversely, those in Tampa found it difficult to follow daytime operations in the combat zone on anything like a current basis. Moreover, there were suggestions that Central Command did not always understand local conditions, and that this failing explains the failure at Tora Bora and also the very severe limit applied to the force the Marines built up at Camp Rhino. In both cases, Central Command was apparently preoccupied with limiting American presence on the ground, either due to a concern with Afghan sensibilities or in order to limit American casualties. Presumably a better understanding of what was actually happening in-country would have shown that such concerns were either groundless or should have been discounted.[15]

Central Command is an all-service (joint) organization. Its service component headquarters, such as its air, naval, and ground headquarters, were all located in the Persian Gulf region. Unlike other joint headquarters, however, CENTCOM does not normally have fighting units dedicated to it. No local power would cheerfully accept truly permanent basing. Indeed, a grievance against U.S. basing in Saudi Arabia nominally motivated Osama bin Laden. Local governments, such as that of Kuwait, have allowed some stockpiling of equipment, and they have earmarked bases for U.S. use—at their discretion. Thus units are assigned to CENTCOM for a particular operation, in this case the attack on the Taliban. For example, the U.S. Navy maintains a Fifth Fleet staff in Bahrain, but in practice it commands only limited forces on anything like a permanent base. When war broke out, Fifth Fleet suddenly took charge of several carrier battle groups and also of several amphibious ready groups. The corresponding Army headquarters, in Kuwait, is Third Army.

Since the Gulf War, the U.S. Air Force had built a combined air operations center at Prince Sultan Air Force Base in Saudi Arabia. Although it could have been duplicated elsewhere, the CAOC was extremely valuable for its excellent facilities, including satellite and other communications links. The Saudis initially refused to allow U.S. forces to use it, relenting only late in September (the U.S. government denied the report of refusal). As it was, the air war was run out of the CAOC, which proved absolutely vital, because it was the one place from which the full sweep of the air war could be understood. Thus it was the one place from which aircraft, both for surveillance and for strike, could be maneuvered. Aircraft employment was crucial because the aircraft were both so vital (for attacks) and so few in number (on station at any one time).

The use of the Saudi base was undoubtedly a delicate issue. Those within the kingdom who opposed the war did not understand the deep significance of American use of the Prince Sultan facility. However, its use has now been widely publicized, and it is likely they will be less understanding in future. U.S. air power will probably still need a command center near the battle zone. This requirement, and the likelihood of future vetoes, might justify the long-discussed joint-services command ship, tentatively designated JCC(X). Facilities have been built up in Qatar against the possibility that a Saudi headquarters will not be available again, for example, in case of a war against Iraq.

Precision Air Attack: The New Kind of War

Advocates of the new kind of warfare understood that the point was not whether an expensive weapon destroyed an intrinsically valuable building or other target. It was that the destruction of some particular targets was likely to have a disproportionate effect on an ongoing war. This concept is now called effects-based targeting. For example, all the fanaticism in the world would not make it possible for a Taliban tank crew to keep going when the fuel ran out, or to keep firing without ammunition. Without rations, the same troops would quickly lose their enthusiasm for battle. If deep air strikes could be mounted, and if the appropriate targets could be defined and detected, then precision weapons could be deployed effectively.

The outbreak of war in Afghanistan came a few years after the appearance of a new generation of U.S. precision weapons. In the past U.S. forces had relied mainly on laser-guided bombs. An attacking pilot had to find the target visually, and it had to offer sufficient contrast for a laser tracker to lock onto it. The bomb would then home on the reflected laser light. That was fine for distinctive targets. However, many targets were difficult to see. Those searching photographs and other images could often locate them well enough to measure their positions accurately, but a pilot would be hard-pressed to find them from the air. The new bombs, mainly the joint direct attack munition (JDAM), flew to preset coordinates based on satellite navigation (GPS/INS). First used in Kosovo, JDAM was ideally suited to a war like that in Afghanistan. Another precision weapon, the wind-corrected munitions (bomblet) dispenser (WCMD), first appeared in Afghanistan. Because they involved no visual lock-on, they were usable in bad weather to an extent far beyond laser-guided bombs. On the other hand, they were not as accurate as laser-guided bombs, and they could not be used against moving targets.

Laser-guided bombs and JDAM placed different requirements on forward air controllers. For JDAM, all the controller needed was a set of target coordinates. A hand-held GPS receiver could measure the controller's coordinates, and in theory he could then easily calculate target position. A laptop computer and a modem could transmit the results to an orbiting bomber. The equivalent laser designator was relatively heavy, and probably many of the forward observers could not easily carry it. Apparently there were cases in which an observer with only GPS capability could not direct laser-guided weapons, and the opposite. The best solution would be a bomb combining both methods of guidance, using one or the other. Current plans envisage embedding GPS in laser-guided bombs for just this reason.

Another interesting consequence of the advent of JDAM was that a heavy bomber could, in theory, engage multiple targets using it, whereas the same airplane probably would not be able to use laser-guided weapons. Advocates of JDAMs thus saw them as a way of transforming the U.S. strategic bomber force into a powerful tactical weapon. Moreover, using JDAMs a controller could hit several targets in quick succession. About half the smart bombs dropped in Afghanistan were JDAMs, the others being laser-guided. Most of the JDAMs were dropped by Air Force heavy bombers; most of the laser-guided bombs were delivered by Navy and Marine Corps tactical strike aircraft.

There were, to be sure, some problems, in part because equipment had to be jury-rigged. In theory controllers should have had radios which would transmit GPS coordinates directly into bombers and thus into JDAM bombs. In fact, it seems that pilots or aircrew often had to enter coordinates they received by voice radio, and that they sometimes made mistakes. In one case, during the Al Qaeda prison revolt in Mazar-i-Sharif, a controller called in a JDAM—which exploded fifty feet away, perhaps because the pilot erred in entering coordinates. Fortunately for him, a Northern Alliance tank absorbed most of the blast. In another case, several Americans were killed when a JDAM landed on them, their coordinates having been entered in error. In this case the GPS unit involved had just received a new battery, and its operators forgot that it automatically reset itself to its own position when that was done. Bombs often had to be dropped near friendly troops, and existing ones produced too much blast for comfort. For example, the Air Force credits each bomb with a personnel incapacitation (PI) radius; on this basis friendly troops should be at least 500 meters (about 1,640 feet) from a 2,000-pound bomb. In theory, at 225 meters 10 percent of friendly forces will be incapacitated for at least five minutes. Because blast effects vary as the cube root of distance, the keep-out zone for much smaller bombs is not very much smaller; for a laser-guided 500-pound bomb it is 425 meters.[16] Such distances would seem to make large JDAM bombs unsuitable for anything like close support. On this basis the Air Force has argued in favor of much smaller guided bombs, such as its projected small-diameter bomb. Others reached broadly similar conclusions; for example, the Navy much preferred smaller to larger laser-guided bombs.

Overall, the percentage of guided bombs dropped in Afghanistan was much higher than in any previous war: as of 7 December, of about twelve thousand bombs dropped, sixty-seven hundred, or 56 percent, were "smart." That was practicable because so many of the bombs were so inexpensive. About half the price of all smart bombs was consumed by 93 Tomahawk cruise missiles. By way of comparison, about 35 percent of the twenty-four thousand bombs dropped during the 1999 Kosovo war were smart, and that far exceeded the percentage in the Gulf War (about 10 percent).

As in the Gulf War and later conflicts, precision warfare required remote sensing. In Afghanistan, for the first time, the United States was able to maintain persistent (i.e., twenty-four-hour) airborne surveillance, so that virtually any movement on the ground could be seen and dealt with. Persistent wide-area surveillance would make it impossible for individuals to know whether they were about to be attacked, and presumably imposed substantial pressure. Electronic surveillance would make it difficult for any individual to use a radio or even a cell phone to coordinate action.

The stated objective was to be able to hit a moving target within five minutes of identifying it. It was tacitly accepted that many targets would be visible only for minutes or even tens of seconds. Previous Air Force practice had emphasized attacks on static targets by a large force obeying an air tasking order, as in the Gulf War. Apparently the air tasking order concept was also used in Afghanistan, but only to vector aircraft to their operating areas. Actual targeting was almost always done only after aircraft had arrived on station. Thus navy pilots later said that in something like 80 percent of cases they had not known their targets when they left their carriers.

The various surveillance platforms were linked with each other, or at the least with the CAOC in Saudi Arabia. Given the CAOC, it was possible to use real-time intelligence to fight the battle. In the past, intelligence collection had generally been pre-planned. Predators would be despatched after analysis of what had been collected was completed, when it showed that there was an important target on the ground.

This time intelligence streaming into the CAOC from surveillance aircraft was used instantly to cue other platforms, ultimately including strike aircraft. The widest view was provided by electronic intelligence aircraft such as the EP-3E Aries II and the RC-135 Rivet Joint. Wide-area aircraft, such as JSTARS (E-8), the P-3C, the surveillance version of the S-3, and the unmanned Global Hawk, were distinguished from narrow-view aircraft, the smaller UAVs (I-Gnat and Predator) and the manned U-2. For example, interception of Al Qaeda communications activity by, say, an Air Force Rivet Joint (RC-135) might lead the CAOC to shift a wide-area surveillance airplane (such as a JSTARS) to the indicated area. It in turn would cue a narrow-view aircraft, which in turn would cue a strike aircraft using the RTIC technique developed after the Bosnian war (see chapter 6).

Since the links between control center and airplane are line-of-sight, and they would be blocked by Afghan mountains, the RTIC center was in an airplane flying over Afghanistan.[17] RTIC required a data link connected the control center to the strike airplane. By 2001 it was clear that the standard tri-service Link 16 could do this job, but installation in fighters was proceeding relatively slowly. Link 16 had, after all, been bought as a means of controlling air defense aircraft. As the Afghan War proceeded, the Air Force announced that it would install Link 16 on board its F-15E Strike Eagles, and by late 2001 plans called for quick installation in all U.S. Air Force fighters.

Unmanned air vehicles were often the source of RTIC data. Apparently, coordination between the UAV and the strike airplane often broke down. Big Safari, an Air Force special projects office, offered a twofold solution to this problem. One was a radio link between the UAV operator and the strike pilot. Second, Predator video was linked directly to the aircraft. For example, UAV video was also sent directly to at least one AC-130U gunship, which attacked the Taliban the UAV had detected.

In theory, Predators were intended to both support air attacks and provide imagery to ground forces. During Operation Anaconda, however, they were apparently used mainly to find targets for air strikes. Too, live Predator video was generally piped, not to troops on the ground, but rather to command centers, such as that at Bagram running the Anaconda operation, and Tampa.

The Army read the same facts somewhat differently. It considered UAVs effective but complained that there were too few Predators. With too few UAVs on tap, the Anaconda area of operations was not sufficiently reconnoitered from the air. Landing zones considered safe were actually swept by enemy fire, resulting in the deaths of seven special operations troops. This problem was analogous to one encountered in the Gulf War, when the best surveillance systems, mainly satellites, seemed to operational commanders not to be responding to their needs. One possible Army solution was to activate shorter-range UAVs (Hunters) that had already been bought but had not yet entered service. Hunters had already been used in Bosnia-Herzegovina. Another UAV, Shadow-200, is being bought to support brigades. There was, however, some question as to whether any of the smaller UAVs would have been effective at the high altitudes (eighty-five hundred to ten thousand feet) encountered in Anaconda.

After Anaconda, the P-3, rather than Predator, was described as the Special Forces' favorite surveillance asset, probably because it combines so many sensors in one package and is so responsive to their needs.[18] A P-3 could, for example, carry a SEAL, a Special Forces man, who was well aware of the needs of ground combatants, in a way a Predator operator most likely would not have been. A P-3 also combined wide-area search sensors with more sensitive narrow-area ones, so that some of its sensors could cue others under the direction of the on-board crew. For example, a P-3 could observe enemy vehicles and alert Special Forces on the ground to ambush them. Its thermal camera could detect enemy troops and their hideout caves. The P-3 also has an imaging radar. Conversely, troops could ask directly for the P-3 to look over the next hill, rather than apply for better Predator coverage via, say, the CAOC in distant Saudi Arabia. A P-3 has a wideband tactical common data link which can pass its video directly to troops below (the link was installed to support operations in Bosnia and then in Kosovo in the 1990s). In addition to their surveillance role, P-3s fired small numbers of precision weapons (SLAM-ERs, AGM-84Hs) at Taliban targets.

As in past wars, some important sensing was done from space.[19] One great advantage of space-based sensors is that their targets are rarely aware they are present. The Afghan campaign was, however, the first for which commercial high-resolution imaging satellites were available: the French SPOT and the U.S. Ikonos. Although the U.S. government claimed "shutter control" over Ikonos, it was by no means clear that such action would be constitutional. The government solved the problem by letting an exclusive contract for all Ikonos images of the war zone. One incidental advantage of buying such unclassified images was that they could be shared with coalition partners. As for the SPOT, presumably the French government imposed control in its role as a coalition partner. The consequences of SPOT and Ikonos control included keeping images of U.S. and coalition deployments from the Taliban—and from Western news media. Space-based cameras had important limitations, however. Given their orbits, they spent very little time over Afghanistan. Their images tended not to capture the complexity of the Afghan terrain; lower-flying manned and unmanned aircraft did far better in that capacity.

The surveillance problem may have mirrored a basic strategic problem: exactly what was the object of the war? Was the object to wipe out the Al

Qaeda leadership? In that case, defeating the Taliban was no more than a means to an end, at least for the United States, and it was perfectly legitimate to consider detection of Al Qaeda and Taliban leaders more important than, say, support to an assault by U.S. or Northern Alliance forces. If, however, the liberation of Afghanistan was taken as the war aim, then excess use of sensors to hit the enemy leadership might be considered inefficient or even self-defeating. By its nature and its heritage, the CAOC was more likely to emphasize the strategic goal of destroying the enemy leadership over the tactical needs of deployed ground forces. A platform like the P-3, largely independent of detailed CAOC control, would naturally be more attuned to the needs of the troops below.

Special Forces

A new feature in Afghanistan was acceptance of Special Forces as vital sensors for air attacks.[20] That applied both to liaison with forces such as those of the Northern Alliance and to finding targets well behind enemy lines. Controllers made flexible air operations practical, as aircraft could orbit over Afghanistan until they were assigned to particular controllers. Otherwise they would normally have hit preset targets, with only an option to divert to targets found by, for example, Predator UAVs. The first step in the air offensive, then, was to infiltrate Special Forces into Afghanistan. Air Force enlisted tactical air controllers (ETACs) or combat controllers (CCTs) were integrated with Army Special Forces A-teams.[21] Equipment varied; some used tripod-mounted laser designators, others GPS devices which could transmit the positions of selected targets. Stories later emerged of controllers on horseback, using radios and laptop computers to call in air strikes. Northern Alliance commanders soon came to depend on the controllers for vital fire support. One of them recalled that, when the Taliban fired on his position, a Northern Alliance commander covered him with his own body, on the theory that although a commander could be replaced, the controller was absolutely vital. One report credited the controllers and the air strikes they directed with winning the battle for Kabul in twenty-five days, rather than the six months that planners had envisaged. For example, one controller wiped out a Taliban force of about a thousand by designating its front a "kill box" and calling in a B-52 strike. In this case the bombs were apparently an unguided "stick" three or four hundred meters long. The ground shook, the building on which the controller was perched began to collapse—and fire from the Taliban force ceased. Most of the time, however, controllers used guided bombs, either JDAMs or laser-guided.

Two-man Air Force tactical air control parties (TACPs) accompanied U.S. Army units when they entered intense combat during Operation Anaconda.[22] By that time the army was well aware that the TACPs made aircraft into flying artillery—and that it had no organic artillery of its own. The TACPs are assigned permanently to army units. Normally a battalion (three companies) has six TACPs with it; in this case companies wanted TACPs of their own. In one case, Al Qaeda troops ambushed a company from a ridge line about eight hundred meters away. The controller called in a fighter, which attacked the line and silenced the ambushers.

When President Bush decided to attack Afghanistan, war planning became the responsibility of Gen. Tommy Franks, whose initial reaction was reportedly to demand three Army divisions. Logistics made any such deployment impractical. Franks soon learned that the only troops he could move quickly enough were Special Forces and Marines, together amounting to a fraction of the force he imagined. He was ordered to make do and to rely heavily on U.S. air power and on the only indigenous force fighting the Taliban, the Northern Alliance. The connection to the Northern Alliance thus became vital. It in turn was largely a matter of special or irregular forces, both CIA and Army.

Franks developed two alternative plans. The more modest called for taking a few objectives before winter set in. Then operations would pause, as the Afghans normally do not fight during the winter; they would resume in the spring. The alternative was to keep pushing in hopes of winning before winter.[23]

Initial contacts with the Northern Alliance, and with southerners who might be convinced to turn on the Taliban, were made by the CIA. The agency reportedly reactivated some operatives who had worked in Afghanistan during the war against the Soviets. Personnel of the agency's Special Activities Division were the first Americans to enter Afghanistan, as early as 27 September. The division, a resurrected paramilitary arm, has its own helicopters, airplanes, and UAVs (some of the latter were armed). There was much talk of the agency's failure to develop human assets inside Afghanistan, even of its lack of native speakers, and it is not clear to what extent such claims were camouflage for ongoing operations, such as those by Special Activities. Note that some accounts refer to that CIA unit as the Special Operations Group (SOG); SOG was active in North Vietnam during the Vietnam War.

The division's operatives met Special Forces teams who arrived later. In at least some cases CIA operatives were integrated into twelve-man Special

Forces A-teams. The experience of Team 555 (part of 5th Special Forces), which has been described publicly, was probably typical.[24] Different teams specialize in different areas of the world; Team 555 included speakers of the main Afghan languages. The team was attached to Mohammed Fahim, a Tajik warlord, whom they met in Uzbekistan on 13 October. Fahim was un-impressed by what he saw as desultory U.S. air strikes. It fell to the team to explain that U.S. strikes on preselected targets were designed to weaken the Taliban as a necessary precondition to an advance. Their air controller was soon calling in air strikes directly supporting Fahim's force. It helped that the team included an Arab linguist, who could call the Taliban after an air strike. The Taliban assumed he was Al Qaeda because he spoke Arabic, so they would describe bombing errors, for example, that a bomb had hit five hundred meters to the west. Often the team could call in a strike on the corrected position immediately afterward. The team in turn was able to call on U.S. surveillance aircraft, such as P-3s and unmanned Predators.

Probably far more important was the personal link forged between the team and the warlord, who later became defense minister in the interim Afghan government. It was the A-team, not U.S. bombers, which con-vinced Fahim that the Americans were indeed on his side and would stay the course. He came to value their advice, including tactical advice, and their ability to provide him with the needed fire support. The Taliban were well aware of the importance of the Special Forces, and they offered a bounty of fifty thousand dollars for a team member's death. However, that seemed to have little or no effect, even when Special Forces were staying with Afghans. At least some teams were in place by the end of September 2001, at which point the U.S. government announced their presence, to the Special Forces' disgust.[25] Fortunately, the announcement did not help the Taliban to capture any team members.

Note that the Northern Alliance was a co-belligerent, a coalition partner, and by no means a U.S. proxy. It had existed long before the United States became interested in overthrowing the Taliban. Indeed, initially Northern Alliance leaders were skeptical of U.S. interest in anything beyond killing Osama bin Laden and his friends. That was one reason they were slow to advance. Too, because it was a separate entity, the Northern Alliance, or, rather, its separate members, had distinct policies. For example, the Ira-nian government had backed the Northern Alliance, whereas it was by no means willing to join in the U.S.-backed war.[26]

Special forces also conducted reconnaissance and, apparently, small-scale raids. At the very least, raids in the Taliban rear would force them to divert forces for internal security. More generally, special forces were said to have been given an open "hunting license" against Taliban and Al Qaeda troops, with very relaxed rules of engagement.[27] At the most, Special Forces operations would drastically limit Taliban ability to move forces around inside Afghanistan. The only raid which received any publicity was a large-scale attack by the U.S. Army Delta Force on Mullah Omar's home near Kandahar.[28] It may have been intended partly as a way of gauging enemy combat capability; the lesson was that the Taliban would gladly fight, but however resolute they were, U.S. troops could handle them. As it happened, the raid was conducted near the airstrip at which the Marines would later establish Base Rhino.

Based in Uzbekistan, Army MH-47E Chinooks of the 160th Special Operations Aviation Regiment supported Special Forces beginning on 19 October 2001. During the first three months, the Chinooks flew seventy-two infiltration and eighteen extraction missions. Those numbers presumably refer to raids rather than to support of Northern Alliance forces, since teams attached to the Northern Alliance commanders advanced with them.[29]

Finally, U.S. and allied Special Forces could conduct missions not considered essential by the coalition partner. Chief among them was the hunt for Osama bin Laden and other Al Qaeda leaders, including Mullah Omar. That was certainly the widely reported role of British and Australian SAS troops.[30] Several U.S. allies contributed contingents of their own special forces, beginning with the United Kingdom's SAS (Special Air Service). Australia contributed its own SAS; Canada, Denmark, Germany, Norway, and at least one other country provided special forces of their own.[31] It is not clear to what, if any, extent foreign SAS units contributed to air targeting.

In all, almost two thousand Special Forces troops operated inside Afghanistan; one official called the war "the Olympics of Special Forces."[32]

The Armed Predator and Command Relationships

In addition to its role in liaison with the Afghans, the CIA was also responsible for covert operations. It deployed a major new piece of equipment, an armed version of the Predator UAV, which carried a pair of Hellfire antitank missiles. The agency had been operating Predators over Afghanistan for some time before the war, and one of them had spotted Osama bin Laden, who early in 2001 was already clearly a major enemy. U.S. officials were frustrated that they could film their enemy but not attack him. The CIA therefore sponsored an Air Force effort to arm the Predator, specifically to destroy bin Laden.[33]

Reportedly, however, the agency was frustrated when it tried to use the armed Predator on the first night of the war.[34] An armed Predator spotted a convoy moving down a road; there was an excellent chance, according to the CIA operator, that Mullah Omar, the Taliban head of state, was in one of the vehicles. He was a juicy target, but there was a longstanding U.S. policy against attacking foreign heads of state, stemming from the 1975 revelations of plots against Fidel Castro. Normally a pilot seeing a target of opportunity would decide on the spot whether or not to attack it. However, when UAV video was fed back to a command center, the issue could be bucked anywhere up the line, even back to Central Command headquarters in Florida. In fact, the CIA's rules of engagement apparently required such high-level approval for any attack. The decision was referred not to an operational officer but to the ranking JAG (judge advocate general) officer—to a military lawyer. The JAG vetoed the attack. It was all right to hit the building into which those in the convoy went, but not to attack a vehicle whose only significance was that Mullah Omar was on board.

The story might have been apocryphal, but it was told to emphasize the legalism binding the pre–11 September U.S. military and the dangers inherent in modern telecommunications. According to the rest of the story, Secretary of Defense Rumsfeld was furious at the lack of aggressiveness it showed. Normally no one would have imagined burdening a senior commander with a shoot/no-shoot decision at the level of the Predator. He would have much broader issues to consider. The whole idea of military accountability is that officers take responsibility for their own actions. Moreover, advocates of information-based warfare have generally argued that more information will be made available at lower levels of command so that better decisions can be made at that level. The story illustrated the reverse; it recalled the disaster of piping UAV video into the Pentagon during the wars in Kosovo and Bosnia. It invited too much interference from the highest levels, aside from illuminating the plague of lawyers which seemed to infest U.S. society.

This aspect of network-centric warfare has received little attention. The communications net which provides all shooters with the over-the-horizon information they need has two opposite potentials. One is to decentralize decision making and thus to speed up combat, perhaps decisively. That is the reason the Navy has pressed hard for netted resources. The other possibility is that the most senior officers can see details of tactical operations on a scale previously impossible. They may well become obsessed with those details. That is not a new problem. During the Vietnam War, colonels and generals often observed firefights from their command helicopters. They could not resist interfering, and later it was said that, as a result, they tended to neglect the wider issues of the war.

Considerable attention has gone into filtering information so that low-level commanders do not get confused by the full size of, say, a battlefield ashore. Perhaps it is equally important that higher-level commanders be shielded from the details of local operations.

The UAV/Hellfire combination was used extensively during the war, albeit not always successfully. For example, in May 2002 it was reported that the CIA had tried to use one to assassinate Gulbuddin Hekmatyar, an Afghan warlord opposing the new provisional regime and even offering payment for anyone willing to kill Americans. This time there was apparently no hesitation in firing, but the attack was unsuccessful.

Initial Strikes

The attack on the Taliban began at about 9:00 P.M. (local time) on 7 October 2001, about three weeks after the 11 September attacks. They were mounted by about twenty-five Navy carrier-borne strike aircraft, by fifteen long-range bombers (B-1Bs and B-52s based at Diego Garcia and B-2s from the United States, plus possibly some bombers from Fairford, in the United Kingdom), four missile ships, and two submarines (one British). The ships fired fifty-three Tomahawks, which preceded the bombers. About thirty targets were hit. Precision was such that only twenty-two civilians were inadvertently killed that night. The first day attack, by carrier-based bombers, was conducted on 9 October.

There seems to have been little question in U.S. military minds but that the main resource the United States could deploy in Afghanistan was tactical aircraft armed with the latest precision weapons. Since the war was being fought so far from home, only a few such aircraft were available, and they were too valuable to risk their loss at the hands of the antiquated Afghan defensive system. As in earlier wars, the point of initial air operations was to eliminate the enemy air defense system. Thus the Tomahawk missiles and then air strikes were directed at the Taliban air force and at fixed Soviet-type antiaircraft missiles. One surprise of the campaign was apparently that the hand-held missiles, with which the Afghans themselves had destroyed so many Soviet aircraft in the earlier war, were not in evidence. Presumably many of these missiles had been rendered inoperable by outdated batteries and rocket motors.

For about the first week of the air war, coalition strike aircraft apparently flew high enough to avoid hand-held missiles. At least one commander, on board the carrier *Theodore Roosevelt,* reported that his pilots had been fired upon by such weapons, albeit without effect. However, on 16 October it was reported that a U.S. AC-130U Spectre gunship had attacked Taliban forces near their stronghold of Kandahar. Since a Spectre is effective only in a permissive environment, and since Kandahar would have been specially well defended, this announcement seemed to indicate that the hand-held threat had been discounted and the Taliban air defense entirely neutralized.

A second important initial objective was to destroy the land communications lines the Taliban were using, to force them to resort to radio communications. Both bombing and Special Forces units could participate in such operations. To some extent the Taliban were already relying on radio (including cell phones), because Afghanistan had never had a particularly good telephone system and its rugged geography made wiring difficult. Taliban reliance on radio offered the attackers several advantages. First, radio intercepts could be used to pinpoint Taliban and Al Qaeda leaders. Accounts of the war were replete with claims that bin Laden and his colleagues had been heard (by radio) exhorting their troops. In some cases it appears that what was being heard was taped, and that the leaders sought by the United States were far away when the tapes were broadcast. Even so, location by radio emission was prized. Too, Taliban use of radio opened the possibilities of jamming and also of deception. The importance of radio is made evident by the sheer number of radio intercept platforms (such as the EP-3E Aries II and the RC-135V/W Rivet Joint) deployed to the theater of operations, and also by the frequent wartime references to radio intercepts in the U.S. press.

The Taliban knew that they were being monitored and jammed, and they tried to overcome the problem by using couriers with written notes. That practice in turn badly delayed their responses to attacks, making coordinated responses almost impossible. The emphasis on striking Taliban operational communications was part of the new kind of warfare, which emphasized the importance of the OODA Loop (Boyd cycle) of response to battlefield attacks.

Communications jamming was the responsibility of Navy EA-6B Prowlers (which were not needed for their usual mission of attacking enemy air defenses) and Air Force EC-130H Compass Call aircraft.[35] Because Afghanistan is so mountainous, jamming aircraft often had to go closer to their targets than would otherwise have been necessary (otherwise mountains would have blocked their emissions). They were thus, at least in theory, more vulnerable to antiaircraft fire, and the EC-130Hs in particular received extra self-defenses, such as flares to deal with shoulder-fired missiles.

It is possible that bin Laden and the Arab Taliban leadership were sufficiently aware of the use of radio intercepts, perhaps from experience during the war against the Soviets, to take precautions such as taping messages and playing them only when the speaker was long gone. They may also have noticed that the Russians publicly described the use of electronic intercepts to kill an important fundamentalist leader in Chechnya.[36]

The Taliban did have one defense against the U.S. air offensive. They kept reporting that U.S. aircraft had killed large numbers of civilians in hopes of infuriating enough Muslims and Europeans to force the United States to stop the war. Indeed, they began moving their units into civilian areas so that U.S. air attacks would inevitably kill civilians. Similarly, mosques were sometimes used to shelter military personnel and equipment.[37] Much the same tactics can be discerned in every air war since Vietnam; exaggerating civilian casualties is always attractive, and it is either difficult or impossible for media to decide whether the claims are honest. By late October some left-wing parties in Europe were claiming that the bombing proved that the United States was morally equivalent to the Taliban in that each was more than willing to kill civilians. It was claimed, for example, that U.S. bombs had killed more Afghans than the Taliban had killed Americans on 11 September. The rejoinder, that any Afghan civilians had been killed accidentally, by a force trying to avoid hitting them, whereas Americans had been killed on purpose, seems not to have made much impact on the European Left. Nor did critics notice that many fewer Afghans died in the entire war than had died in the civil war won by the Taliban, at Taliban hands.

European support for the war consequently began to slip, particularly among left-wing parties. Thus Italian foreign minister Renato Ruggiero and former U.K. foreign and defense minister Doug Henderson called publicly for a quick halt to the bombing. The Belgians proposed an EU resolution calling for a global antiterrorist approach to be guided by the United Nations, which would have meant stopping the U.S.-led war. In Germany, some of the Greens in the governing coalition opposed the bombing, but

Chancellor Gerhard Schroeder rejected their position, pointing to polls showing 65 percent of Germans favored military intervention by German forces. Much the same thing happened in France, where some members of the Socialist government debated against support for the U.S. campaign. Most Americans appear to have been unaffected by this effort, and European distaste for the campaign had little or no short-term effect. European governments, moreover, were beginning to realize that, undefeated, Al Qaeda was likely to attack them as well as the Americans, so that they had a very real interest in the outcome of the war.

As was expected, as soon as attacks began there were violent demonstrations throughout the Muslim world. The day after the first bombings, mobs demonstrated in Egypt, Indonesia, Pakistan (several killed), and the West Bank (two killed, more than two hundred injured). The situation in Indonesia was so serious that the Australian government warned its citizens not to venture out of doors there. The next day riots in Pakistan intensified, three being killed. Riots continued, so that on 12 October they occurred in Bangladesh (Dacca), Egypt, Indonesia (Jakarta), Iran (Teheran and Zahedan), Malaysia (Kuala Lumpur), South Africa, Turkey, and, of course, Pakistan (Lahore, Quetta, Peshawar, and Karachi). President Musharraf had to despatch twenty thousand troops and police to deal with three thousand rioters in Karachi. On 14 October rioters tried to penetrate the base at Jacobabad, where twenty U.S. helicopters were stationed; at least eight were killed when the Pakistan Army opened fire. Two Pakistani policemen were killed in Karachi. It seemed that Pakistan itself was becoming unstable. The Saudi and Indonesian governments sought to distance themselves from the United States, particularly after a heavy U.S. bomb killed civilians near Kabul. On 19 October a big demonstration in Indonesia demanded that the bombing cease. As late as 26 October, a reported fifty thousand Pakistanis demonstrated in Karachi to demand that the bombing stop. However, by that time it was clear that the United States was determined, and demonstrations soon petered out. This collapse was taken by some to indicate that the "Arab street" could not sustain opposition to determined U.S. action.[38]

There was, to be sure, an initial sense of disappointment among Americans, because so little happened on the ground between the onset of air attacks early in October and the opening-up of the ground war early in November. Bombing seemed desultory, and without detailed accounts of what was being hit and why, the public began to see it as no more than a demonstration of U.S. displeasure with the Taliban, and an impotent one at that. That the main objective of the bombing was to prepare the ultimate battleground by sapping the Taliban ability to regroup and even to communicate was not obvious, nor indeed could it have been made obvious without disclosing details of planning, which would have been, to say the least, counterproductive. Misunderstanding of the strategy involved is probably to blame for the widespread sense that the United States changed air attack strategy, from the old idea of hitting fixed targets (as espoused by the Air Force) to close air support (as the Army and the Marines have always wanted). The reality is that the initial campaign made the ground campaign feasible, and that the apparent shift had to do with a change in what was happening, and probably not in basic comprehension on the part of the targeters.

Once the air defense had largely been destroyed, U.S. aircraft could operate freely throughout the country. Initially they hit mainly pre-briefed targets, such as fuel dumps and tank repair facilities, the loss of which would damage any Taliban operations. Attacks on land lines were intended to force the Taliban to use radios, whose radiation would reveal the locations of commanders. There were also attacks against known Al Qaeda training camps and headquarters, but they were apparently understood to be symbolic: little damage could be done, and Al Qaeda had long since vacated the camps.

The main targets, however, were the Taliban themselves. Air power was applied in two complementary ways. One was in direct support of the Northern Alliance. The other was largely independent; its object was to cripple Taliban movement. The country was kept under constant surveillance, the air control center quickly cuing attack aircraft and, ultimately, gunships (AC-130s) to deal with any observed Taliban. Aside from inflicting substantial casualties, this kind of operation kept the Taliban on the run, preventing them from regrouping.

There were also strikes on caves thought to be Al Qaeda or Taliban refuges; the Air Force announced that it was using a 5,000-pound earth penetrator (GBU-37), dropped by B-2 bombers, in the hope that those inside would flee rather than risk entombment. This tactic was not particularly successful. On the other hand, in at least one case a GBU-37 penetrated a tunnel system in which ammunition had been stored, igniting explosions and then a fire that lasted four hours.

U.S. strategy evolved in the course of the war. At the outset, air strikes were disconnected from the Northern Alliance operation. The hope was probably that the Taliban themselves would not see the war as unconditional, that they would choose to give up Osama bin Laden and his terror network in order to survive. At this stage the main issue was bin Laden. Despite some U.S. statements to the contrary, handing over bin Laden and his main subordinates would probably have halted U.S. air attacks and might even have ended U.S. aid to the Northern Alliance. At least in theory, the Taliban would have been able to maintain power. This concept would have been in line with classical U.S. foreign policy, which abhors attempts to change the internal politics of other states. It may have seemed to many in Washington that this was exactly how the successful war in Kosovo ended—with Slobodan Milosevich left in power in the one place he prized, Serbia, and with the Kosovars and NATO happy that ethnic cleansing had ended in Kosovo.

Thus initial U.S. attacks were be limited to demonstrate that the United States did not mean to destroy the Taliban altogether. Surely the Taliban would recognize that simply handing over bin Laden would end the attacks.[39] On this model the Taliban would have calculated that they could, honorably, hand over bin Laden in the face of overwhelming force. This basic concept was fatally flawed; by 2001 Osama and his Al Qaeda fighters were integral to the Taliban state.

Nor, it turned out, was there much chance of simply encouraging moderate Taliban to stage a coup against Mullah Omar. Those around him were too tightly bound to him, because they had fought together all the way from Pakistan, beginning in 1994. By 2001, key decisions were all made by Omar and his "Kandahar group," ten of the twenty men closest to him. This group gave Omar the title "commander of the faithful" in April 1996. Reportedly it was Osama who advised the Taliban to make the Kandahar group their secret leadership council (1997); they and Mullah Omar alone decided to join Osama and Al Qaeda in an alliance. However, most of the Pashtuns supporting the Taliban were opportunists who joined only in 1996, after a Taliban victory seemed inevitable. This "moderate Taliban" group included tribal leaders and military leaders from the war against the Soviets, as well as most officials and senior civil servants in Kabul. Ultimately the Taliban expected to centralize power, and the Pashtun tribal chiefs knew that their apparent (and limited) independence was unlikely to last. As traditional nationalists, they opposed giving power to the foreign Arabs brought in by Osama. It was such moderates that Gen. Abdul Haq was seeking out when he was betrayed and caught by the Taliban a few weeks later. None of the moderates would dare to rise against the Taliban, for fear of their secret police (and the Al Qaeda Arabs), but none of them was likely to fight for the Taliban if it became obvious that the tide was turning against them. The key evidence was probably the establishment and survival of a substantial U.S. Marine Corps base in Taliban country, near Kandahar. It is possible that the base was established only after the U.S. military command became aware of the situation in the south, and of the precondition for a local rising.

Bin Laden and his Arab fighters, it emerged, were what kept the Taliban in power in the face of a less and less enthusiastic populace. Osama also quickly emerged as the main source of Taliban financial support, although the Taliban also collected considerable money from Afghan poppy growers. For the Taliban, the Arabs performed much the same function as the Republican Guard had performed for Saddam Hussein; ultimately they protected the Taliban from the bulk of their own army, which might eventually have tired of them. Conversely, the Arabs were likely to fight hard because they were unlikely to survive defeat. Either their former Afghan victims would kill them, or they would be shipped back to their countries of origin, where governments would kill them because they were too dangerous. When mixed Arab and Afghan Taliban forces were imprisoned later, the Afghans often did kill the Arabs as foreign enemies. The Taliban also had some hope that the U.S. attack would unite their disparate population in a patriotic war.

The Strategic Shift in the North

After a few weeks without movement, the United States shifted strategy. The Northern Alliance would be supported directly, to the extent where it would likely defeat the Taliban. The U.S. perception at this stage was that once the thin crust of Arab troops was broken, the Taliban army would collapse. Clearly the average Afghan soldier had little interest in dying for the Taliban and their foreign overlords. In the course of the war, several times non-Arab Taliban troops tried to surrender and the Arabs kept them fighting by killing those they regarded as too weak. The Americans hoped that the Afghan troops might even revolt in the name of the same Afghan nationalism which had proven so potent during the Soviet occupation a decade earlier.

From the point of view of prewar American strategists of the new kind of war, the surprise was that the Taliban army did not collapse as its Arab component was attacked. Air power by itself was powerful but not decisive. In prewar terms, American strategists had argued that an enemy could be forced to surrender if his "center of gravity" were destroyed. It could be argued that the Arab troops were the center of gravity of the Taliban regime, since they were apparently its main prop. Yet merely hitting them did not suffice. What destroyed the Taliban army was the combination of very focused air attacks *and* pressure by the Northern Alliance army.

It turned out that Afghans had little appetite for destroying the ethnic Afghan Taliban and their supporters altogether. In a country wracked by endless tribal warfare, it is unacceptable to pursue victory all the way to killing the losers. After all, they are likely to have relatives who will demand vengeance if all are killed. Victories are all temporary. Those who surrender must be forgiven. There was no sense that, having gathered under the Taliban banner, Afghans had been converted to their ideology. Most were opportunists, joining what seemed to them to be the winning side. Americans did not understand; once the Taliban had been overthrown, that was enough for most Afghans. The foreigners (Arab fighters) were a different story. This attitude actually accelerated the defeat of the Taliban, since most of the Taliban troops were Afghans well aware that they would not be killed if they surrendered. Indeed, the war was replete with incidents of Al Qaeda Arabs killing Afghan Taliban who were trying to surrender.[40] Thus the key coalition partners did not share the American war objective, which was the complete destruction of Al Qaeda and its Afghan friends.

The larger lesson is that coalition warfare without any concentrated U.S. force on the ground, stiffening the coalition partners, is unlikely to be entirely successful, at least from the point of view of U.S. objectives. Thus, if it takes a coalition partner on the ground to make the new kind of warfare effective, then at least some U.S. troops must be on the ground to work with the coalition force. That is certainly consonant with earlier experiences of coalition warfare.

It was soon clear that without visible U.S. support, the Northern Alliance armies would not advance. Their leaders would not have sufficient confidence in the power the United States could exert on their behalf. They could not even see the carefully targeted precision air attacks being carried out well behind the Taliban lines. The Taliban themselves may well have been encouraged by the limited character of the initial attacks. Individual soldiers may not be terribly impressed that, say, a fuel-storage depot or an arms dump is destroyed. Few of them were killed in the precision bombing raids. They had expected something much worse. Many of them had experienced more massive, if worse-directed, attacks by the Soviets more than a decade ago. Northern Alliance commanders had roughly the same military experience. They, too, expected massive barrages. At the outset, the virtues of precision were lost on them. Only after combat had been joined would these commanders come to appreciate just how well precision weapons could be used to support them.

These points contradicted the entire trend of U.S. air attack thinking and technology. At least since Vietnam, the trend in U.S. weapons has been toward greater precision. Initially the argument was that stand-off weapons could drastically reduce the exposure of air crews attacking key targets such as bridges and power stations in North Vietnam: often one or two sorties could be substituted for hundreds, and the bombs could be released further from their targets. Then there was increased attention to precision as a way of making attacks more surgical, on the moral ground that it was important to reduce collateral damage. That is, strikes against military targets can always be justified, but attacks against civilians are barbaric. If stand-off attacks are the modern way of war, then, it is almost as important to spare enemy civilians as to hit the things which prop up the enemy regime or its ability to fight. Most recently the cry has been that increased accuracy makes it reasonable to reduce the explosive power of weapons to a bare minimum, not merely to avoid collateral damage but also to pack bombs into the internal bays of stealthy aircraft.

It is probably true that massive fireworks, in the form of (say) carpet bombing, are not particularly effective—militarily, at least. However, war is as much psychological as material. It may be that in our search for efficiency we have entirely lost sight of the psychological effects of heavy bombardment, and that we need to relearn it. Heavy bombing was used to cover precision strikes called in by Special Forces teams, the object being to conceal the particular target those troops had discovered. In Afghanistan, only heavy air force bombers offered mass bombing. Initially they operated from Diego Garcia; later, a few were based in Uzbekistan.

The most striking example of the use of bombing for psychological purposes was a few attacks using 15,000-pound Daisy Cutter bombs to terrify Taliban holding out in caves—and to encourage Northern Alliance attackers. These weapons were used for the same purpose during the Gulf War. As in that conflict, the big bombs had to be rolled out of the cargo bays of C-130s, hence could not be delivered particularly accurately. During the war, an attempt was made to develop a guided version.

Another important bombing issue was how to attack Taliban in their caves.[41] Although there was talk of simply dropping 500-lb bombs into cave entrances, in fact well-designed caves offered sufficient depth and sufficiently shielding tunnels to protect their inhabitants against any simple blast weapons. Such weapons produced visually satisfying effects but did not actually kill many (or, sometimes, any) Taliban, nor did they permanently disrupt the caves. During their time in Afghanistan, the Soviets had learned that fuel-air weapons, which they called thermo-baric weapons, were far more effective in such cases; in fact they developed thermo-baric warheads for many small tactical missiles.[42] The United States developed its own heavy thermo-baric cave-busting bombs on a crash basis, but the two actually used in combat were not successful. Because the failures could be ascribed to minor technical problems, such weapons will probably emerge in the future.

Bombing was by no means the only reason the Northern Alliance commanders chose to fight. U.S. forces, in the form of Special Operations Forces (SOF) and the CIA, were assigned directly to them. In theory they were mainly liaison, to guarantee that targets they wanted to hit would indeed be hit. However, the deeper meaning of such assignments was that they made U.S. commitment visible. They showed that the United States was willing to risk its own personnel in support of the Northern Alliance. The significance of the later Marine Corps occupation of Forward Operating Base Rhino was similar. Again, clearly demonstrating a U.S. commitment to the war helped convince Afghans to fight alongside the United States. No remote attack could possibly have had the same effect.

Once carpet bombing began, the Northern Alliance began to move. On 9 November, thirty-five days after the beginning of the bombing, the major northern city of Mazar-i-Sharif fell to the Northern Alliance, opening a land corridor to Uzbekistan. The city is particularly important because it blocks the road from Uzbekistan to Kabul, the capital. For some days Afghan Taliban troops in the city had wanted to surrender, to the extent that the Arab Taliban, acting as a Praetorian Guard, felt compelled to execute several of their officers. This pattern, in which the ethnic Afghan part of the Taliban army wanted to surrender but the Arabs stopped them, was repeated again and again. It testified to the way in which the Arabs were used much as the Soviets had used their secret police, to enforce order. Taliban claims that the defenders of the city had withdrawn in good order to regroup for a counterattack was almost certainly false; there was no second line of resistance.

The fall of Mazar-i-Sharif was also important because coalition partners, particularly in Europe, were becoming restive after thirty-four days of apparently pointless bombing. Suddenly it seemed that the Taliban really might be defeated. News reports indicated that the fall of the city, before winter came, was taken (at least in Europe) as remarkably good news. Few imagined that all Taliban resistance would end within a few weeks. For the moment, Mazar-i-Sharif offered the coalition force a major airfield inside Afghanistan, on which tactical aircraft could be based. At about the same time the U.S. Air Force finally received permission to use an airfield in Tajikistan.

Once it seemed that the Northern Alliance was winning, Afghan warlords who could do so began to defect from Taliban ranks. They saw no point in being on the losing side, and, as has been noted, ideology was at best of secondary importance to them. That was one reason Taliban resistance in the north collapsed remarkably quickly (the other was a string of battlefield victories by Northern Alliance forces backed by U.S. air support). Within two days Northern Alliance troops were within striking distance of Kabul.

The speed of the Northern Alliance advance surprised the U.S. government. It was painfully aware that the alliance did not represent all Afghans. The Pashtuns in particular might well resist a government of Uzbeks, Tajiks, and Hazaras. The U.S. solution had been to form a provisional government acceptable to all the main factions before Kabul fell. To that end meetings had been convened in Bonn. Also to that end, the U.S. government tried to slow down the advance of the Northern Alliance armies. They had other ideas. Within the Northern Alliance, the Hazaras were particularly insistent on seizing Kabul as quickly as possible. They feared that the Taliban, knowing the end was in sight, would engage in an orgy of murdering Hazara women and children living in the city. They had already massacred Hazaras in Mazar-i-Sharif.

The Taliban were aware that the fall of Kabul could have devastating consequences. They tried to defend it. U.S. warplanes repeatedly struck the city, and the accuracy of the attacks convinced the Taliban leadership that this was a new kind of threat. Many of their troops fled the city on the theory that the front-line trenches would be far safer. Often their vehicles were destroyed en route, and the trenches themselves suffered badly. According to a Haji Mullah Khaksar, the Taliban deputy interior minister who defected as Kabul fell, after a night emergency meeting on 12 November, the Taliban leadership decided to abandon the city to avoid a bloodbath and to preserve its allies there.[43] Americans said that this was by no means a foregone conclusion; the Taliban might well have decided to stand and fight.

Instead, Northern Alliance troops entered Kabul on 13 November against little or no Taliban opposition; the Taliban expected to make their stand further south, near Kandahar. The Taliban had never been particularly popular in Kabul, by Afghan standards a cosmopolitan city with little taste for their ultra-ascetic brand of Islam. Thus the world news media were treated to accounts of citizens unearthing their previously forbidden radios and television sets, of suddenly being able to hear music again, of women suddenly released from a kind of imprisonment. The Iranian official news agency reported that hundreds of people had taken to the streets to celebrate their liberation—and to curse the Taliban and their Pakistani masters. One explanation for the quick Taliban collapse was that Afghans in the Taliban forces had never been particularly enthusiastic supporters. They had been kept in line only by the Arabs. They stiffened the same mass army in combat—in this case, meaning that they could kill anyone trying to desert—as they later did in places like Kandahar.

Once the Taliban army came under heavy fire, then, the Afghans saw their chance to surrender or even to desert, the Arabs being held down by enemy fire. It is likely that most battle casualties were Arabs, because only the Arabs could not afford to surrender.

Decades of war in Afghanistan had produced some peculiar relationships. For example, many Taliban commanders personally knew the Northern Alliance commanders opposing them and communicated with them by radio. After some air strikes, alliance commanders would ask how they were; the Taliban commanders sometimes boasted that they were fine, because bombs had missed in a direction they specified. The next strikes tended to be on target. Presumably the Taliban commanders had no idea that bombs could be directed as precisely as they often were.

The last Taliban stronghold in Northern Alliance country was the city of Konduz. So many other places had fallen by negotiation that there was speculation that some agreement could be reached there as well. The key to any such surrender would have been a deal allowing hard-core Taliban fighters to flee, most likely to a third country. Those in Konduz included Chechens and Pakistanis as well as Arabs. The local Northern Alliance commander, Gen. Mohammed Dawood Khan, was perfectly willing to allow them to leave as refugees. The U.S. government managed to veto any such concession by the Northern Alliance. Even if they did not return to Afghanistan, hard-core Taliban supporters would be a potent force anywhere else in the Muslim world.[44]

In reality policy was less strict. Before Konduz surrendered, a Pakistani military airlift took many of its Pakistani defenders to Pakistan; it was too far from the border for them to escape overland. Many Pakistanis had backed the Taliban, and during the run-up to the war many of them entered Afghanistan. Apparently the U.S. government repaid the Pakistan government for its support by helping it rescue citizens who would have been caught in the fall of Konduz. This act could be read in several ways. One would be to identify the Pakistanis with the Taliban and with Al Qaeda; sparing them was merely to buy later trouble. On the other hand, by saving them, the Pakistan government was showing that it, rather than the Taliban, was their salvation. It might also be said that the Pakistan government was likely to suffer if its citizens felt that they had been betrayed in Afghanistan; after all, Pakistan had created and supported the Taliban in the first place. General Musharraf was going to have a difficult enough time explaining why his government had turned on the Taliban, without having to tell many of his people that he had left them to die at American hands in Konduz.[45]

Too, many of those who had barely escaped from Konduz were likely to feel more defeated than defiant. They would bring back to their villages the word that the mullahs who had inspired them in the first place had lured them to death and privation, that jihad had been less than inspiring. There was talk that after the disaster the fiery mullahs were finding it far more difficult to recruit jihadis.[46]

The War in the South

The southeast, around Kandahar, was more Taliban country, and it proved much more difficult to assemble a local anti-Taliban force. The Taliban, moreover, had an excellent security force there. For example, late in October a popular general, Abdul Haq, entered southern Afghanistan to meet with generals who might be willing to defect from the Taliban. Instead, on 25 October he was cornered and captured; the next day he was executed. Later it emerged that he had probably been lured into a trap by the Taliban. It did not help that reports spread that Haq had called desperately for help in his final firefight, and that U.S. forces had proved unable to save him. Followers of the ousted king, Zahir Shah, who hoped to rally Pashtuns to their cause, were arrested on 30 October despite attempted U.S. aerial intervention. It seemed that there was little hope of overthrowing the Taliban government in favor of a "moderate Taliban" movement which Pakistan might be expected to support. Alternatively, it might be said that the potential moderates would not rise unless they saw serious proof of U.S. engagement. Thus a U.S.-educated businessman and senior anti-Taliban leader, Hamid Karzai, failed to arouse interest (and barely escaped with his life when the Taliban attacked the village he was visiting).[47] Karzai soon became head of the interim government established after Kabul fell, and at this writing he is chief of state. Committing a substantial U.S. Marine force, then, was crucial to forming the Southern Alliance, which would carry the war through the Taliban country of southern Afghanistan.

The war in the south seems to have been entrusted largely to the Fifth Fleet, based in Bahrain. It was the maritime component of Central Command, and its commander, Vice Adm. Charles W. Moore, was the command's naval and maritime component commander (NAVCENT/MARCENT). Fifth Fleet in turn formed several Task Forces, of which Task Force 58 was built around a pair of Marine Expeditionary Units (MEUs) aboard Amphibious Ready Groups.[48] They were the essential heavy ground force for the south. An MEU is designed to launch an amphibious assault in which part of the landing unit is delivered inland to cut enemy access to a beachhead; the rest of the unit lands over the beach, taking with it the necessary heavy materiel. However, if the heavy equipment was not needed, the same Marines could reach a considerable distance inland using their organic helicopters. The fleet also had its own attack aircraft on board several carrier battle groups, as well as fleet support aircraft (P-3s of various types) constituting Task Force 57. There was also an Army Special Forces (Ranger and Delta Force) unit based, most likely, on board the carrier *Kitty Hawk*. Designated TF Sword, it was commanded by Maj. Gen. Dell L. Dailey. Sword did not include, but worked with, the British Special Air Service contingent. Task Force Sword began operations in southern Afghanistan very early in the war. TF 57 provided air support. In addition, there was a Joint Special Operations Task Force South (JSOTF-South), later designated TF K-BAR. This organization included Army Special Forces, SEALs, and Canadian, Dutch, German, and New Zealand Special Forces.

When the crisis broke in September, the 1st Marine Expeditionary Brigade (MEB), commanded by Brig. Gen. James N. Mattis, was participating in a multinational military exercise in Egypt, Bright Star 1/2. The MEB would normally equate to three MEUs plus additional forces. Mattis was soon designated commander of Marine forces for CENTCOM, and his staff went to Kuwait to arrange for the arrival of a U.S. force. Mattis himself arrived in Naval Support Activity Bahrain, the headquarters of Fifth Fleet, on 27 October. By this time one amphibious ready group, carrying the 15th MEU(SOC), was already in the area, having arrived on 27 September. It was built around USS *Peleliu*. Beginning on 7 October, it had set up a combat search and rescue operation at Jacobabad, Pakistan, in support of fleet attack aircraft. A second amphibious ready group, carrying the 26th MEU(SOC), had participated in Bright Star and was visiting Souda Bay, Crete, prior to a planned exercise in Albania. Built around the amphibious carrier *Bataan,* it was assigned to CENTCOM.

By this time it was clear to CENTCOM that some U.S. ground presence was needed in southern Afghanistan, and the Marines in the Arabian Sea were the only available force. About 30 October CENTCOM ordered planning for amphibious raids into Afghanistan. The Marines held their initial planning conference in Kuwait on 30 October. Vice Admiral Moore now designated General Mattis commander of a new Task Force 58, initially comprising one amphibious ready group (ARG). He immediately asked that the second ARG be added. This decision, to place the Marine commander in overall command of a mixed naval and marine force, foreshadowed the later idea of an expeditionary strike group (ESG), a Navy-Marine formation which would probably be commanded by a marine.

General Mattis's initial planning guidance called for identifying potential raid targets, pulling the 15th MEU out of Jacobabad, establishing intermediate support bases (ISBs) in Pakistan, establishing rehearsal sites, and incorporating British Special Forces in his organization. On 1 November NAVCENT called for a minimum of three to five raids into Afghanistan over a thirty-day period. At this point General Mattis planned to begin with small raids near the southern border, using his limited force of CH-53E helicopters. He hoped that raids against relatively easy targets would develop the MEU's fighting skills in operating at very long range. The enemy would probably try to counterattack, and the Marine and fleet air power available would destroy them. Mattis's intent was simply to "create chaos, denying the enemy their sense of security." Initially Mattis asked for plans for a variety of raids, from company to battalion size, to last up to seventy-two hours. On 3 November he offered Admiral Moore three alternatives: a company-sized raid operating about 40 nautical miles inside Afghanistan (350 nautical miles from the sea) for six to twelve hours; two companies attacking two objectives nearly simultaneously for twenty-four to thirty-six hours; or a battalion landing team (BLT) raid lasting forty-eight to seventy-two hours. The first proposed raid, on a drug processing facility, was abandoned because the objective had already been allocated to a coalition special forces unit. Raids would be conducted on a one-MEU basis, the second MEU planning a raid while the first executed one.[49]

Vice Admiral Moore generally approved Mattis's concept, but he emphasized the need for bold action. The Marine operation would not merely be a show of force; its raids were to defeat Taliban and Al Qaeda forces quickly and decisively. According to the admiral, "Marines don't give themselves enough credit. A squad of Marines running through Kandahar would turn the tide." Thus he asked about the ability to establish and sustain a forward operating base in southern Afghanistan for up to thirty days. The FOB became Camp Rhino. Because the Marines would arrive by air, and because they could be supported by air, the base did not need any land link to coalition-held areas. The immediate objective of seizing and holding the FOB was to disrupt Taliban lines of communication near Kandahar, though in fact the operation had a much wider significance.

General Dailey, the Special Forces commander, provided invaluable advice. By 7 November, when the two generals met, his force had been operating in southern Afghanistan for over a month, and he was well aware of the difficult conditions the Marines would encounter. General Dailey heartily approved the Rhino operation, which he felt would help destroy Taliban strategic power in the spiritual center of Kandahar. He added that "if you establish a FOB at Rhino the enemy may not even come, because you are Marines." On the other hand, some Taliban were not at all afraid to fight, and they might use ingenious ways of attacking aircraft, such as firing rocket-propelled grenades (antitank weapons) at helicopters. He also felt that Rhino would be a useful Special Forces base. TF 58 and TF Sword would work together, but the TF 58 staff encountered some problems because Special Forces operations were specially classified. On the other hand, it was Sword's good experience of P-3 support (TF 57) which led Mattis to include TF 57 in all TF 58 operations.

The first force to enter combat in the south was a special forces group which attacked the compound formerly occupied by Mullah Omar outside Kandahar, on the night of 19 October. About one hundred Army Rangers parachuted in from C-130s and secured the airstrip, killing about twenty Taliban militia. They diverted attention from a Delta Force attack, delivered by helicopter, on the compound itself. The helicopters probably came from the Pakistani base at Dalbandin, the MC-130s from Oman via Dalbandin. The operation was supported by AC-130 gunships. The Rangers were extracted by C-130, the Delta Force commandos by helicopter. An Army officer characterized the attack as one on a "confidence target," to demonstrate to the Taliban that they could be struck anywhere, even in their leader's house. The raid was the first U.S. opportunity to judge the fighting strength of the Taliban army. U.S. troops met serious resistance—the Taliban were capable of fighting, particularly for ground they valued—but none was killed.

The fight itself seems to have been confused, and some of those involved blamed incompetence at higher levels for the way in which their attack was overmanaged. There was some hope that valuable intelligence material would be recovered, but when the papers captured were examined, they turned out to be nothing more than religious material. That should have been expected; Omar was much more holy man than governor. Osama was the real governor of Afghanistan.

The most important lesson of the operation was probably that the heavily advertised Afghan fighters had very definite limits. U.S. troops respected them as fighting men, and several accounts emphasized their combat skills. However, the U.S. troops proved themselves, and they found that their body armor often saved them. Throughout the war, U.S. casualties would be extremely light.

Probably mainly in the south, U.S. and foreign special forces teams hunted enemy troops as well as they could, killing hundreds without suffering casualties. Such ambush teams would have encouraged the enemy to remain within his cities and bases and thus would have limited any timely enemy response to the quick coalition offensive. The main command and control issue was assigning each Special Forces (in the U.S. case, Delta Force) team its own operating area to avoid friendly fire casualties.

Special forces could seize an airfield or a compound, but they could not hold their ground. That would require a much more substantial force: the Marines. With no established opposition to the Taliban in southeastern Afghanistan, the Marine force, which by Afghan standards was powerful, played a crucial role. It demonstrated U.S. commitment in a way that no collection of small Special Forces teams could, because it was overt and impressive. Its mere presence thus encouraged many local leaders to abandon the Taliban for what was obviously going to be the winning side in the war. A massed Marine force presented the Taliban with a devastating problem. If they attacked, they would have to concentrate in a way which would create lucrative air targets, and most likely the key Arab troops would be destroyed. If they refused to fight, they would be demonstrating to many Afghans that they were losing the war, thus that they no longer deserved armed support.

Task Force 58 chose the airstrip the Special Forces had already raided as the place for FOB Rhino.[50] Plans initially called for the 15th MEU(SOC) to seize and defend Rhino, while 26th MEU(SOC) conducted raids from it. The leap from the sea to places deep within Afghanistan was, to put in mildly, audacious. FOB Rhino was 400 nautical miles from the amphibious ready group offshore in the Arabian Sea. Because so little could be brought quickly to Rhino, the ready group would be, in effect, the Marines' base, their source of any additional firepower in an emergency. Even distances within Afghanistan were vast. It was, for example, 95 nautical miles between Rhino and the immediate tactical objective, Kandahar. From there the Marines later had to move 180 nautical miles more to Band-e-Sardeh, and somewhat further to Khowst. A Marine report referred to the "tyranny of distance," which limited the rate at which Rhino could be built up.

The Marines, however, had one enormous advantage. They were used to operating in small formations. Thus, instead of being crippled by being limited in numbers (not least by the tyranny of distance), they could still create viable units with worthwhile firepower.[51] Commanders used this capability to limit the amount of lift required to maintain a viable Marine force. The Marines also had a considerable advantage in that they controlled their own transport aircraft, CH-53 helicopters and KC-130 refueler/transports, and thus could gain the support they needed as and when they needed it. Later Air Force C-17s were vital to sustaining Rhino.

Even so, it was very fortunate that the Taliban were unable to attack the fragile air line of supply keeping Rhino alive. That in turn was largely a consequence of the initial phase of the air war, which destroyed both the small Taliban air arm and most Taliban antiaircraft sites.

One reason the Marines could limit what they sent ashore was that so much of their crucial support came from, and remained on, the sea. For example, the amphibious group offshore normally provides much of the command/control support for a deployed Marine force ashore, particularly for a small one. In this case the sheer distance between Rhino and the sea badly strained available naval command and control systems. The Marines withdrew before sea-based support became impractical. Their replacements, conventional army forces, needed much more in the way of a logistical tail, but by that time they had the advantage of ground lines of support stretching back into the countries bordering Afghanistan on the north.

In the event, CENTCOM chose to cap Marine forces at Rhino at less than a full battalion landing team, and very little raiding could be done. No explanation of the capping was given, but probably CENTCOM wanted to avoid giving the Afghans the impression of excessive American presence in their country.[52] That in turn limited possible operations, because so much of the force was needed simply to protect the base. It also caused some problems, as some of those already landed had to be returned to ship so that others, with necessary skills, could be brought in.

General Mattis established close relations with the Pakistanis, who allowed him to establish intermediate support bases. To avoid trouble with Pakistani civilians, aircraft operated only at night. No forces went overland. Equipment was landed at night at the coastal Pakistani city of Pasni, then trucked to the airfield. The Pakistanis limited the amount of equipment at Pasni at any one time. From Pasni, all personnel and equipment were all flown to Rhino by MEU aircraft (CH-53Es and KC-130s).[53] The initial operation demanded all the aircraft of both MEUs, and later more CH-53Es and KC-130s had to be brought in. Shamshi became a forward helicopter refueling point and staging point. Jacobabad was the forward refueling and staging point for KC-130s and also a prestaging point for assault troops. The entire operation was remarkable, the longest-range amphibious operation in Marine Corps history, over a distance of 371.5 nautical miles from the ships offshore.

The Marines seized FOB Rhino on 25 November. There they met SEALs who had arrived on 21 November for target surveillance and reconnaissance. The first six assault helicopters (three from each MEU) were launched on a 350-nautical-mile flight from the USS *Pelelieu*. Three refueled at night from KC-130s; the other three encountered difficulties.

Air Force Special Tactics Squadron (STS) personnel declared the airfield KC-130-capable, so additional Marines were landed by KC-130s. The MEUs' attack helicopters (AH-1Ws and UH-1Ns) and Harriers (AV-8Bs) provided close air support. The force was supplied first by Marine Corps KC-130s and then, once the airfield had been certified, by Air Force C-17s. Much effort, by Seabees, was required to keep the dirt airstrip operational.

Once the Marines were ashore, they came under the jurisdiction of the combined force land component commander (CFLCC), designated by CENTCOM as the sole commander of ground forces in Afghanistan. CFLCC occupied a headquarters in Kuwait, staffed mainly by personnel from the U.S. Third Army. This large staff operated in a style very different from that of TF 58 and NAVCENT. For example, ultimately it demanded briefings before even small-scale operations.[54]

Task Force 58's first raid was to interdict Route 1, which connected Lashkar Gah and Kandahar. To carry it out, TF 58 needed more forces, and it asked to have the personnel cap raised to 1,400.[55] The operation itself, which began on 4 December, entailed a 120-kilometer nineteen-hour motor march across open desert. The operation netted a Taliban convoy, initially detected by a P-3; about 120 enemy personnel were reported killed. There was some hope that Taliban forces retreating from Kabul toward Kandahar would be blocked by the Marines, but it appears that no great capture of moving Taliban forces occurred. Later the 26th MEU screened Rhino from the west.

Beside the Marines, the Australian Special Operations Force (designated TF 64) was based at FOB Rhino beginning on 3 December. It was integrated with the Marine force operating out of Rhino.

By this time the situation throughout Afghanistan was shifting in favor of the coalition. Airlifted Marines provided security when the U.S. Embassy in Kabul was reopened. In the south, Marines from Rhino were assigned to seize the Kandahar airport in conjunction with local (Southern Alliance) forces. Plans called for the 15th MEU to lead, using its light armored vehicles (LAVs), then interdicting Route 1 west of Kandahar to isolate the battlefield. The 26th MEU would contribute a company of heliborne infantry, additional LAVs, and helicopter support.

Southern Alliance forces were already in place around Kandahar. As early as 18 November they had tried to negotiate the surrender of that city. The Taliban rejected their pleas. Kandahar was too valuable to surrender lightly. Not only was it the last major Taliban city, it was the center of Taliban power. The Taliban themselves may have imagined that a stiff resistance would have inspired those groups which had shifted to the coalition side to return to them. Negotiations for the surrender of Kandahar were delayed when the Al Qaeda troops began killing Afghans trying to give up. Kandahar held out until 6 December. After it fell, its inhabitants did not seem nearly so enthusiastic in greeting the coalition troops as had those in Kabul. When the Marines were assigned to seize the airport, a key question was whether they could pass safely through the city to get there.[56]

Since the 26th MEU was to the west of Rhino, its supporting element (TF Sledgehammer) had to move east to link up with the 15th MEU for the march to the Kandahar airport.[57] The two linked up on 13 December, forty miles west of Kandahar, and then the combined force linked up with a Southern Alliance and its U.S. Army Special Forces liaison team. The force encountered no resistance, and by 14 December TF 58 had established its second FOB at the airport. Close air support was provided by aircraft from the USS *Bataan* (AV-8Bs and AH-1Ws) and by other coalition aircraft. The runway was quickly repaired, and the next day the first Marine KC-130 landed. By 18 December the airport was declared safe for C-17s. An unusual feature of the operation was that the land forces commander (CFLCC) in Kuwait and his staff observed it via a live feed from a Predator UAV.

Meanwhile, TF 58 began to plan to explore villages west of Rhino which were thought to contain valuable intelligence materials. They also investigated some sites near Kandahar. It conducted these sensitive site exploitation (SSE) operations with TF K-BAR, the Special Forces unit, providing the bulk of their helicopter assault support and acting as a quick reaction force during site exploitation.

By this time it seemed likely that many of the Al Qaeda troops, and possibly their key leaders, had fled to the Tora Bora area near the Pakistani border, over two hundred miles east of Kandahar. TF 58 was called upon to plan an attack. It was never conducted; the plan was canceled on 9 January 2002. Later it emerged that CENTCOM had proposed the use of Marines to "encourage" Southern Alliance forces to attack. That seemed to work, but later there was some question as to whether a more aggressive U.S. force (such as the Marines) would have been more effective.

Task Force 58 was also ordered to prepare a mission in the Khowst-Gardez area. The local Southern Alliance commander had not fought the Taliban; he had merely raised the alliance flag. Many enemy forces remained in pockets in the area; later it would be the subject of Operation Anaconda. Cold-weather gear, which had originally been required for the Tora Bora operation, would be needed in the mountains of Khowst-Gardez. To get to the new operating area, 250 nautical miles from Kandahar, Marine LAVs would have to drive for about forty hours. In the operation, TF 58 (26th MEU) would be supported by special forces (TF 64 and TF K-BAR). Plans called for the Special Forces to identify targets which the Marines would then hammer. Given the long distance from Kandahar, a local airfield would be needed for close air support. After two sites were assessed, Band-e-Sardeh was chosen; it was an hour from the battle zone, rather than the two and a half hours from Kandahar. Ultimately the Khowst operation changed into a series of independent operations by several different organizations, with a limited Marine contribution.

Through January 2002, TF 58 was relieved in place by troops of the Army's 101st Airborne Division (TF Rakkasan, supplemented by a Canadian Light Infantry Battle Group). They did not stop fighting. For example, on 10 January Taliban forces attacked Kabul airport, and the defending Marines beat them off.[58] Handover to the 101st Airborne was not complete until the end of the month, and the TF 58 staff did not leave Afghanistan until 5 February. Even so, on 11 February CENTCOM called back TF 58 to help TF K-BAR with some SSE missions. They were finally released on 20 February. TF 58 itself was disestablished at the end of the month.

By late November hundreds of Taliban troops were in coalition hands. Coalition policy was generally to release the Afghans, but to keep foreign (i.e., Al Qaeda) troops in prison, pending return to their countries of origin—which could be expected to imprison or execute them as dangerous radicals. Thus the prisoners had very little to lose by revolting. They were concentrated in a prison at Mazar-i-Sharif, a building which the Taliban themselves had previously used as an arms dump. Unfortunately, the prisoners knew just where the arms were, and they rebelled and armed themselves. It took several days to suppress the revolt; the Taliban and their sympathizers claimed that many unarmed prisoners were killed in the process. The prisoner revolt apparently began when a team of U.S. CIA officers were interrogating the prisoners; soon the prisoners killed one of the CIA men, Johnny "Mike" Spann, who became the first U.S. war casualty. In the wake of the prison revolt, the U.S. government began moving some prisoners, including senior Al Qaeda, into U.S. custody at Guantánamo Bay, at what was called Camp X-Ray. There they could be interrogated at leisure. Many of the later warnings of possible future terrorist action can apparently be attributed to these prisoners.

This was not a conventional war against an enemy unified by ideology or nationalism. The Taliban had come to power largely by paying off the leaders of various tribes with Pakistani and, to a lesser extent, Saudi, money. In a tribal society like that of Afghanistan, tribesmen follow their leaders, not an abstract ideology. When the Pakistan government decided to join the war on terrorism, the Taliban lost their main source of continued funding. In effect many tribal leaders decided that the coalition would be the winning—and far more profitable—side. Once they switched sides, the Taliban could rely only on the limited numbers of committed Arabs. To the extent that the tribal leaders disliked the Taliban for their posturing and their arrogance, they could be relied upon to exact revenge. However, that was hardly the same as the usual Western concept of single-minded opposition. Moreover, since loyalty to the Taliban was not considered a matter of ideology, any Afghan Taliban who surrendered would be accepted with open arms. Westerners found this sort of easy acceptance puzzling in a country which had been ruled so cruelly by the Taliban.

Afghanistan is like many other tribal societies, most of them now gone, in which war is the accepted manly pursuit. Under such circumstances it is important for an individual to show heroism, but it would be fatal for society for any armed conflict to be pursued to the death, as is the case in western warfare. Afghan forces would not be pressed beyond a point. That is why so much of the Afghan civil war seemed so inconclusive, before the Taliban could bring their hard-line Arabs into combat. Westerners were not the only ones unpleasantly surprised; the Taliban manifestly found it difficult to convince their Afghan troops to fight to the death and had to execute many of them in order to keep up any sort of resistance. Such executions in turn generated the sort of resentment which helped carry many Afghan units into battle.

These factors made U.S. cash an important factor in the war. The most-publicized example was the $25 million price put on Osama bin Laden's head. Somewhat less publicized were subsidies paid to factional leaders who changed sides, for example, in southeastern Afghanistan. It is important to keep in mind, however, that they would not have changed sides unless they thought they were on the winning side. Cash alone, like bombs alone, could not have won the war. For that matter, had most of the population strongly supported the Taliban, anyone benefiting from U.S. cash would have risked his neck. Fear of reprisal may explain why the enormous reward did not snare either Osama or Mullah Omar. On the other hand, without any strong allegiance, Afghan troops would be relatively easy to bribe. Reportedly both Mullah Omar and Osama managed to slip away with the crucial aid of judiciously distributed one-hundred-dollar bills.[59]

Once Kabul had fallen, the U.S. government wanted to promote a legitimate Afghan government. In the absence of any credible Afghan army, any such government would need military support. It was essential that the United States avoid the reality—or the appearance—of occupation. Indeed, for a time Secretary of Defense Rumsfeld asserted that the United States had no intention at all of trying to rebuild the country. Eventually he reversed himself, with the realization that a failed Afghanistan would almost inevitably support either bin Laden or some equivalent. The United States therefore called an international conference to arrange financial aid for the new government, while arranging for a multinational United Nations stabilization force. It was particularly important that Muslim countries supply many of the troops, and Turkey and Jordan obliged. Other peacekeeping troops were supplied by Britain (Royal Marines) and by Germany.

Mop-up: Tora Bora and Anaconda

At the very least, by keeping its troops out of the international peacekeeping or security force, the United States could retain them as a mobile fighting force to deal with surviving Taliban and Al Qaeda. Although the major cities had fallen, none of the major Taliban or Al Qaeda leaders had been captured. Many, perhaps most, of the Arabs remained at large. Some of the Al Qaeda camps had indeed been searched, but it was not possible to make them uninhabitable. How would Al Qaeda try to regroup? A web site purporting to report news from inside the Taliban claimed that the cities had been abandoned according to plan, that the Taliban would dig into caves well stocked with arms. There they would await coalition troops, who would be destroyed in traditional Afghan guerrilla fashion. Mullah Omar said as much in his last interview. U.S. aircraft were already bombing his positions, and he had to admit that he could not put up any effective air defense. However, he said, the war was only entering its decisive phase. The Americans would ultimately have to engage in hand-to-hand combat—at which they would lose. The mullah may have been slightly naive, in that Northern Alliance forces were already on the move and important cities were falling. However, his theme, that in the end the Taliban would be able to draw coalition forces into contests in which their technology would not count, undoubtedly reflected real hopes.

There were two distinct possibilities. One was that individuals would slip away through Pakistan to escape aboard small craft crossing the Arabian Sea. Al Qaeda, it was said, was already well entrenched in Somalia and the Sudan. Late in 2001, for example, it was reported that arms were flowing into southern Somalia. It seemed an ideal refuge because there was no effective central government there; tribal leaders or warlords, any one of whom might become allied with Al Qaeda, held all the power. Some Somalis, however, claimed that no coherent Al Qaeda organization was likely to take root, and that warlords were likely to use reports of Al Qaeda presence as a way of convincing the United States to destroy their local rivals. Some survivors of the Afghan debacle might go farther afield. One press report had it that Osama had sent his youngest son to an Al Qaeda refuge in the Philippines, and that he planned to go there to resume the fight.

Against this threat, U.S. and allied warships set up a shipping interception zone in the Arabian Sea. Apparently only a few had been caught as of the spring of 2002, but that may only be because most of the Arabs had not yet left Afghanistan.[60] However, by January 2002 there were reports that some Al Qaeda had managed to escape in specially equipped shipping containers.[61] Special containers were found by U.S. sailors inspecting a merchant ship in the Arabian Sea. In another case, Italian police found an elaborately equipped container, intended to bring an operative into the United States. Its inhabitant escaped when he was released on bail. The use of containers helps explain recent U.S. efforts to examine inbound shipping containers by x-ray. Osama bin Laden is said to control about twenty merchant ships, and probably has the sort of business contacts which would arrange appropriate container routings. Aside from intercepting Al Qaeda refugees, the coalition operation in the Arabian Sea greatly strengthened the ongoing embargo of Iraq, catching numerous craft attempting to smuggle Iraqi oil to market.

The second possibility was that many of the Arabs would go to earth in systems of caves in eastern Afghanistan, near the Pakistani border. Some of the caves had been enlarged and outfitted during the war against the Soviets, often by bin Laden's own construction company. Initially it was reported that a large Taliban concentration, including Osama himself, had fled to a complex in the Tora Bora mountains. The assault was conducted, like much of the war, by Afghan troops stiffened by U.S. firepower. Apart from about forty Special Forces providing liaison, U.S. troops were not directly involved. The Afghans took the cave complex, but later it became clear that they had let many of the key figures escape. From their point of view, the war had been won, and there was no point in seeking an impossible total victory. From a U.S. point of view, they had thrown away a priceless opportunity. One reading of this operation was that without U.S. troops accompanying them the Afghans themselves would have little enthusiasm for cave attacks. Osama had a great deal of money, and he might simply buy his way out (some reports set the bribe to individual Afghan soldiers at five thousand dollars, an enormous sum in Afghanistan). For that matter, although the Pakistani government was serious about closing its border with Afghanistan, the border was inherently very porous, and the tribes along it were quite sympathetic to the Taliban.

There is, however, little question but that Tora Bora was expensive for the enemy. The bodies of at least 300 bin Laden fighters were seen, and other bodies were probably to be found in collapsed caves and bunkers which were not searched. The Pakistanis caught 150 more men trying to slip across the border. If, as was suggested, the enemy started the battle with about a thousand combatants, he lost at least half of them.[62]

Later it was suggested that General Franks's remote command explained why he had relied entirely on Afghans for so important an operation—that a commander who had never been on this particular ground could not fully appreciate the subtleties of the situation. Franks argued that he had no business imposing U.S. command and U.S. troops on local commanders, and that the potential benefits of a better operation were far less than the problems that such arrogance would have caused. Critics suggested that he was unduly afraid of U.S. casualties—that he still typified the risk aversion so crippling during the Clinton Administration.

Apparently Tora Bora taught Al Qaeda that U.S. systems such as the RC-135 Rivet Joint could intercept their battlefield radios, including their cell phones. In the next battle, Anaconda, they tried to avoid using radios altogether by massing their troops, so that runners would suffice. That in turn created a potentially lucrative target for U.S. strikes, if the concentration could be detected (for example, by infrared sensors). Remote sensing, however, was by no means sufficient. When the Al Qaeda force regrouped in Shah-e-Kot during the battle, they needed supplies, for which they sent runners into nearby villages. CIA and special forces collected key information from the villagers. No UAV or airplane or satellite would have done as well, particularly since Al Qaeda troops were not uniformed or otherwise physically distinguishable.

Operation Anaconda (Gardez and the Shah-e-Kot Valley) was conducted mainly by U.S. forces rather than by Afghans with U.S. Special Forces advisers. The British (forty-five Commandos), the Canadians (Princess Patricia's Canadian Light Infantry), and the Australians (Special Air Service) also fought in the battle. The largest ground battle of the war, Anaconda was intended to destroy what the Defense Department claimed was the last intact pocket of Al Qaeda troops, and thus to preclude their planned spring offensive. There was also evidence that Al Qaeda leaders imagined that they were safe in their mountain for the winter, that U.S. forces would not pursue them there. A winter attack would presumably benefit enormously from surprise. The hope was that the enemy troops would have either to stand and fight (and be destroyed) or flee—into the arms of a blocking force. Reportedly the U.S. command deliberately allowed enemy troops to regroup in hopes of creating a worthwhile target.[63] A substantial Pakistan Army force tried to close the border, in theory forcing the enemy to stand and fight. Conversely, there was speculation that Al Qaeda troops were concentrated deliberately to lure large numbers of Americans into the kind of close-in combat at which the Arabs and their allies supposedly excelled. Their spokesmen had often claimed that the Americans would be destroyed under just such conditions.

There was also speculation that the U.S. Army leadership badly wanted to demonstrate its relevance to the Afghan War. Until Anaconda, the only large U.S. units on the ground had been Marine Expeditionary Units. To critics, the grandiose name of the operation reflected the Army's need for credit. There was talk that some U.S. Army units had to be withdrawn because they had proven unsuited to guerrilla warfare. That an equally large British Royal Marine force appeared just after Anaconda suggested to some that the Army had been less than successful, and that some other force might do much better. Certainly the British press indicated that the Royal Marines expected to fight a large battle similar to Anaconda. That they did not suggests that Anaconda was successful overall. By this time the old Bagram Air Base had been reopened, and a command center for Anaconda was set up there.

The timing of the attack may also have been set by the completion of resupply of JDAM bomb kits; a lack of such kits may have precluded a quick follow-up to the Tora Bora attack. U.S. F-14 fighter-bombers and A-10 attack aircraft were supplemented by a six French Mirage 2000Ds flying from Kyrgyzstan and sixteen Super Etendards flying from the carrier *Charles de Gaulle,* the latter on the ship's first combat mission. The attackers also had attack helicopters (Army AH-64 Apaches, replaced during the battle by five Marine AH-1W Cobras after suffering severe battle damage) and MH-47 Chinooks to lift blockers into position on mountain tops. Also available were AC-130 gunships.

At the outset it was estimated that five hundred to one thousand Al Qaeda were in the area. The coalition force was one thousand Afghans, one thousand Americans (from the Army's 10th Mountain and 101st Airborne Divisions), and some coalition (including Australian, British, Canadian, Danish, German, and Norwegian) Special Forces troops. Both sides apparently added forces during the battle. Hundreds of Al Qaeda reinforcements were apparently killed when they were caught in the open by coalition aircraft. Tactics called for attacking just enough to force Al Qaeda to react, thus revealing positions to be attacked from the air. However, there was considerable close combat, body armor saving U.S. lives. It seemed that the enemy troops felt compelled to attack whenever they saw Americans, even if that meant attacking uphill and into fire. There was also evidence that Al Qaeda troops, though motivated, lacked sophistication and did not realize what sorts of sensors and weapons they faced. For example, they did not realize that their own mortars left a thermal signature on which American weapons could easily be directed. One postbattle evaluation was that enemy rifle fire was spirited but ineffective. Initially Al Qaeda warriors simply waited in their caves for bombers to leave, and even waved at the bombers as they flew off. They soon found that U.S. observers could hit them at just that point.

Overall, Anaconda was a disappointment, and after the battle there was much debate as to just what had failed. It was after Anaconda that army officers wrote home that the enemy should not be discounted, that he was capable of learning how to fight and could be quite effective. Troops found themselves pinned down. That only eight Americans and three coalition Afghans were killed (and seventy Americans and eighteen Afghans were wounded) seems to have been due to the quality of their body armor and the effectiveness of air support beating off the enemy in emergency situations. According to an Australian account, the key problem was that, unknown to American planners, most or all of the Al Qaeda fighters had anticipated the attack on the Shah-i-Kot Valley and had fled up into the surrounding mountains. They were, then, firing down at the advancing troops. In one case they came to control positions overlooking a landing zone selected for an American infantry company.[64] U.S. commentators observed that the U.S. Army commander, Maj. Gen. Franklin C. Hagenbeck of the Tenth Mountain Division, seems to have wanted to conduct the operation with little or no assistance from the air force. He had fifteen hundred troops and four to six Apache attack helicopters.

One problem was a wide divergence between Army and Air Force concepts of operation. The Army thinks in terms of combined arms operating tactically, that is, as a force moves into contact with the enemy. Army aircraft (helicopters) operate in close support, under control of a ground commander. The favored Air Force operating technique is preparation of the battle space by pre-battle bombardment. In this case, General Hagenbeck apparently rejected any such bombardment on the grounds that it would sacrifice the element of surprise. As it was, there was no surprise at all.[65]

Worse, an intense reconnaissance effort concentrated on a tiny battlefield (seventy square miles or less) missed at least half the enemy positions, including some from which devastating fire was inflicted. Other indicators of poor intelligence were that the operation lasted far longer than expected (twelve rather than two days) and that the expected number of Al Qaeda was increased from one hundred to five hundred on the eve of the assault (probably the correct figure was one thousand). The lack of pre-assault bombardment left the Al Qaeda troops too capable of firing at the advancing coalition force. This situation is eerily reminiscent of that at Omaha Beach at Normandy, when an attempt to achieve tactical surprise led to refusal to mount sufficient pre-landing bombardment. One consequence of the enemy retreat into the mountains was that much of the fighting was done under extreme conditions at altitudes as great as fourteen thousand feet. Helicopter operations proved difficult.

Given the failure of reconnaissance, the army planners seem initially to have expected that their advancing force could easily push the few hundred Al Qaeda troops into blocks they had set up. Resistance proved unexpectedly strong, and the initial plan apparently collapsed. The plan had called for separate assaults by seven different units, and some of them had to fall back when they encountered strong Al Qaeda units. According to the Australian account of the battle, the operation nearly collapsed altogether at this stage. For example, two Australian Special Forces veterans said that during an "ill-informed" American airmobile company assault on the first day, they experienced some of the most intense fighting since Vietnam. Trapped in the open under enemy fire, two Australian liaison officers found themselves digging foxholes with their bare hands and their combat knives.[66]

The Tenth Mountain Division had taken its antiaircraft weapons but not its air liaison officers with it to Afghanistan, possibly because it had been told that its main task would be force protection rather than offensive action. In Anaconda, it lacked organic artillery, because such weapons were too heavy to move forward in such rough terrain. As long as it was assumed that enemy opposition would be light, the Apaches seemed sufficient for support. As it was, they had difficulties operating at the very high altitudes to which Al Qaeda troops had withdrawn, and they proved vulnerable to Al Qaeda antitank weapons such as rocket-propelled grenades. None continued to operate after the first day. Air support had to be improvised.

There were other problems as well. For example, on the first day most of the radios failed, and runners had to be employed to coordinate the coalition force. On the other hand, although individual Al Qaeda troops apparently fought well, coordination was limited. For example, wounded soldiers found themselves packed into a dug-out creek bed, but Al Qaeda troops never realized that they would have been a lucrative mortar target and did not fire into them. Major enemy assaults were beaten off without many losses. Once AC-130 gunships arrived, the enemy found it far more difficult to operate at all. Troops who might otherwise have been trapped were successfully extracted by Blackhawk helicopters under gunship cover.

An army after-action report claimed that the most glaring failure in the battle was the Air Force's lateness in attacking hot (i.e., enemy-covered) helicopter landing zones before helicopters arrived. In some cases commanders sent in helicopters anyway, to keep Al Qaeda and Taliban troops from massing in even greater strength. A Navy SEAL was killed when Al Qaeda troops captured him after he fell from a Chinook transport helicopter pulling away from a planned landing due to enemy fire; the helicopter had been trying to set up a blocking position against enemy troops trying to escape. When another Chinook arrived to try to save the SEAL, it lacked vital close air support, which would have been provided by an AC-130. Six of the commandos on board were killed. This report would support Army arguments in favor of organic artillery, which the ground commander could indeed call in as needed.

For its part, the Air Force argued that the Army should never have planned to fight without Air Force support. That should have included both preparation of the battlefield and the usual close air support and time-critical operations. Where the Army claimed that air support often lagged, the Air Force could point to very quick responses, particularly when the AC-130 gunships were involved. Much of the Air Force argument was that the Army should have included it in planning, so that the daily air tasking order would have provided tactical aircraft in place to be available for close support. Once such aircraft were in place, they could execute attacks extremely quickly. If, however, they were orbiting elsewhere when called, they could not attack for quite some time. There seems to have been some dispute as to whether tactical aircraft were able to engage suddenly appearing targets such as SUVs carrying fleeing Al Qaeda troops.

At least one Predator UAV was available. Unfortunately, it could cover only a limited area at any one time, and its video tended to rivet attention. Thus a photo exists of the entire 10th Mountain Division staff staring at a Predator's footage of a fleeing truck, which might have been carrying Osama bin Laden—and not thinking at all about the wider battle they were supposed to be directing. This experience repeated that of Bosnia and Kosovo; UAVs are valuable but their output can be seductive. On the other hand, to the extent that Osama was the focus of the operation, one might argue that the divisional staff was right to concentrate much of its attention on that one truck.

Initially it seemed that few if any of the enemy had escaped. Gradually, however, it became clear that many of the Arabs and their Afghan partners had managed to slip through terrain U.S. commanders thought impassable. For example, few bodies were found, but then again, the bombs used may have destroyed many of them. There was evidence that Al Qaeda had been badly damaged. Through June 2002, later cave operations often uncovered materiel, but generally did not encounter much armed resistance. The Taliban had vanished into Pakistan or into Afghan villages. Whether they could regroup, particularly after the Americans and their coalition partners left the scene, was open to question. Since neither Osama nor Mullah Omar had been caught, and since both were considered key figures within the Taliban, it was not clear whether some resurgence was possible. Reportedly Internet traffic among Al Qaeda operatives and leaders showed that the organization was trying to regroup in Afghanistan, perhaps in hopes of overthrowing the new government.

Small groups of Taliban did continue to harass both coalition forces and the new government. There were, for example, minor raids on bases and minor ambushes. As of late 2002 such attacks had achieved very little. Presumably those involved are not highly enough motivated to risk the kinds of losses that Afghan resistance fighters had to accept when inflicting heavy casualties on the Soviet occupiers two decades earlier. The most important question may be whether the coalition can back the new central government effectively enough to marginalize potential opponents. There was, in mid-2002, a real danger that attempts to winkle out remaining Taliban would kill enough innocent civilians to inspire a new civil war. Taliban propagandists understood this possibility.[67]

Overall, cave-busting operations were well worthwhile. Masses of documents, even computers, were recovered, offering not only clues to future operations but also personnel lists and indications of Al Qaeda financial structure. These were exactly the sort of documents that no Al Qaeda mole living in the West was likely to have, but they were commonplace in the Al Qaeda sanctuary, Taliban-ruled Afghanistan.

Similar documents captured in Kabul and in Kandahar gave indications of how far Al Qaeda had managed to get in its quest for weapons of mass destruction, both chemical/biological and nuclear. The initial estimate was that the organization had pursued both, but that in neither case had it achieved much. There was, however, a report that some chemical weapons had been found in a dump near Jalalabad.[68] One irony was that Al Qaeda had pursued chemical/biological weapons only after realizing that Westerners made so much of them.

Aftermath

The main-force war ended with the United States and its coalition partners in nominal control of Afghanistan but with many unreconstructed supporters of the Taliban still in place. Just what would happen would depend on whether the new interim government and its successors managed to earn public support and trust, so that those yearning for a return to Taliban rule would gradually lose interest. Meanwhile, it was important to protect the interim government. To that end, in December 2001 the United States convinced the United Nations to assemble the International Security Force (ISAF) to stabilize Kabul. Ultimately it amounted to about forty-nine hundred troops. The core of ISAF consisted of Muslim troops from Turkey and Jordan, but there were also troops from Australia, Britain, Canada, Denmark, Germany, New Zealand, Norway, and Spain. For the Germans, the occasion was significant because it was the first overseas operation by armed German troops since 1945.[69]

By early 2002 Britain had contributed 1700 Royal Marines, who expected to be used in further sweeps of regions in which Al Qaeda operatives had taken refuge. They represented the largest deployment of British combat troops since the Gulf War a decade earlier. It seems that the Marines had been brought into Afghanistan to fight a second Anaconda, but by mid-2002 they had seen very little combat. That in turn suggested either that Al Qaeda had gone to ground and had decided not to fight, or that its operatives had all fled, for example to northern Pakistan. The Marines did find some very large arms caches, which they destroyed, and it did seem unlikely that Al Qaeda and Taliban troops would willingly abandon such reserves.

Even if Al Qaeda was merely avoiding armed contact, that was a sort of victory, because it would show many Afghans that Al Qaeda power had been broken. This sort of success can, of course, be grossly exaggerated. For example, a long lull in Vietnam, which was interpreted as evidence of American success, seems in retrospect to have been breathing time for recuperation by the enemy. Some reports, unpleasantly reminiscent of those in Vietnam, claimed that the coalition forces owned the day but the Taliban often owned the night in Afghan villages.

By March 2002, moreover, it was clear that Al Qaeda was trying to regroup. Some camps attacked in October had been reoccupied, at least temporarily. Intercepted communications, including Internet traffic, suggested that Al Qaeda was trying to regroup in Pakistan, perhaps particularly in Baluchistan, a remote area over which the Pakistan government had only limited control. Some of the e-mails involved seemed to be attempts by Al Qaeda leaders to reestablish contact with cells abroad. The organization was seeking sanctuary, and its cells had been reported active in Indonesia, the Philippines, Malaysia, Spain, and Yemen. Perhaps the most interesting implication of such reports is that U.S. intelligence was able to monitor Internet traffic. However, it is difficult to use such monitoring to intercept the individuals involved, as messages are generally sent from anonymous places, such as Internet cafés or public libraries. From a terrorist's point of view, one great advantage of the Internet is that it is effectively a mail box the recipient can empty from almost anywhere, again quite anonymously. Reports of the 11 September plot emphasized the use of the Internet by the terrorists, and some commentators at the time pointed out that, had the government been eavesdropping on the Internet, the attackers might have been thwarted. By the spring of 2002 the U.S. government was asking for just the authority which would have been required.

In the wake of Operation Anaconda it was claimed that many Al Qaeda had escaped across the border into Pakistan. As during the war itself, the Pakistan government proved cooperative; clearly President Musharraf regarded Al Qaeda as a danger to his own government. On 29 March 2002 the Pakistani police raided fundamentalist safe houses in Faisalabad and Lahore, arresting twenty-nine Al Qaeda and thirty Pakistanis (one account raised the total to sixty-five). The Pakistanis belonged to various banned fundamentalist groups, including the Harkat-ul-Mujahideen which operated in Kashmir. The others included Abu Zubaida, described at the time as the number two member of the organization, responsible for attempts to regroup abroad. He was said to be aware of all current operations. Handed over to Americans after having been injured, he boasted of the many attacks Al Qaeda planned. These boasts in turn were the basis of many of the warnings of specific terrorist threats issued by the U.S. government over the next few months. Correlated with other information, including that from prisoner interrogations, the boasts may well have resulted in the June 2002 disruption of the "dirty bomb" plot. The reported nationalities of the twenty-four foreigners arrested in Faisalabad give some idea of the extent of Al Qaeda activity: two Moroccans, seven Palestinians, six Sudanese, nine Saudis. Two others were killed. Besides prisoners, the raiders took computers and disks, which presumably provided further information not only about Al Qaeda but about its communications, including techniques. Computers, for example, would have included e-mail address books and encryption programs. This operation seems to have been the first in a series of collaborative ones.

The Pakistanis were understandably sensitive about supporting U.S. attacks on groups, such as the Kashmiris, they themselves had fostered. Thus they quickly denied reports that at least one U.S. FBI agent had accompanied the Faisalabad raiders, collecting evidence.

However, Pakistan continued to support the war against Al Qaeda. Late in April U.S. newspapers reported a covert operation straddling the Afghan-Pakistani border, in which U.S. Special Forces fought several cross-border fire fights. These attacks may have marked a new phase of the war, the assumption now being that Al Qaeda would no longer concentrate to offer massive American forces any lucrative target. Instead, small groups of its fighters would go underground or would try to blend into the population. The appropriate U.S. attackers were Army Special Forces and the covert-action Delta Force. These troops deliberately showed themselves in hopes of drawing Al Qaeda and Taliban fire. British Marines deployed behind the Americans, cutting off some western approaches to the border area. The Pakistan government apparently allowed American Special Forces to cross the border, despite the risks such action implied. Late in April Pakistan was about to vote on a referendum extending President Musharraf's administration by five years, and there was considerable opposition to the president's support for the United States. It was essential, therefore, that any cross-border activity be kept as quiet as possible; a U.S. Central Command spokesman referred only to a liaison arrangement with the Pakistan military. The U.S. view was that the operation was absolutely essential in order to keep Al Qaeda on the run, thereby precluding further attacks. Conversely, there was U.S. fear that Pakistanis who still supported the Taliban might enter Afghanistan to help overthrow the interim government. With spring snow was melting, opening up many passes through the Hindu Kush.

By early May, there were reports of small numbers of U.S. and British troops operating with Pakistani special forces on the Pakistani side of the border, in hope of flushing Al Qaeda refugees and driving them into the arms of U.S. and British troops on the Afghan side. The Afghans were about to meet in a national assembly, the loya jirga, which it was hoped would choose a government to succeed the interim government imposed by the

Northern Alliance and its backers. The hope was that Afghans would support their chosen government rather than Al Qaeda–supported rebels. Once the government was in place, the process of rebuilding Afghanistan into a peaceful country could begin. Conversely, it was very much in the interest of Al Qaeda and the Taliban to disrupt the loya jirga. Keeping them on the run, even if they were not caught, would be well worth while. Moreover, with summer ground cover would begin to blossom, blocking the view of the aerial sensors on which U.S. forces depend. It might thus be essential for coalition forces to do as much damage as possible to Al Qaeda beforehand.

There was some hope of breaking the relatively complex Taliban–Al Qaeda communications system, which made possible coordinated attacks. Destroying that net would make small groups of Al Qaeda fighters a much less potent threat.

There was certainly no feeling that the war was altogether over. At the end of May the United States set up a headquarters for Joint Task Force Afghanistan headed by Lt. Gen. Dan McNeill, who commands the Army's 18th Airborne Corps. It was expected to remain in place for about a year, presumably until the new Afghan Army can take over. Forces had previously been more directly under the command of Gen. Tommy Franks of Central Command, and it was claimed that the new headquarters would free Franks for other Central Command concerns, such as a possible attack on Iraq.

Al Qaeda fighters found escape routes other than into Pakistan. The Iranian government detested the Taliban, but it did not support the war. It seems to have permitted many of them a route out of Afghanistan. It is not clear whether Al Qaeda fighters were allowed to remain in Iran, or were simply booted from the country.

There was also some evidence that Al Qaeda fighters had found refuge in Iraq. According to one report, Saddam Hussein welcomed them into Kurdish areas because they would put down potentially pro-Western Kurds, who might later join a U.S. attack. In the United States such reports were adduced as evidence that Iraq and Al Qaeda were closely linked. Skeptics wondered whether the point of the reports was to justify a decision already made to attack Iraq.

One other feature of the war deserves comment here. In several cases U.S. strike aircraft destroyed either convoys or buildings said to be filled with Al Qaeda fighters or Taliban, only to be told later that those killed had been either innocents or even supporters of the new central government.

These unfortunate incidents only highlight the intelligence problem. Afghans of different stripes did not wear distinctive uniforms. Observers on the ground, many of them Afghan, could certainly tell who was who. However, given the endless local conflicts within the country, U.S. air power must have been an irresistible attraction, as a means of settling local scores. Without an encyclopedic knowledge of local Afghan feuds and politics, American decision-makers could have little hope of distinguishing real from bogus targets; they had to trust their coalition partners. This situation is likely to recur elsewhere in the Third World. That is not to mention accidents.

Attempts to limit attacks on civilians were sometimes criticized because they allowed Taliban or Al Qaeda forces to escape. For example, the U.S. Air Force seems to have been furious that a wartime heavy bombing mission against a group of Taliban troops was aborted for fear of killing nearby civilians.[70] It was also reported that tight rules of engagement precluded attacks on bands of Taliban or Al Qaeda fleeing caves at night.[71]

Lessons

 In 1991 the Gulf War was widely advertised as the first space war. The U.S. Air Force in particular was quick to claim that it had been an air power victory; a similar claim was made for success in Kosovo. How, in fact, should the Afghan War be characterized?

The Afghan War was both a test and a demonstration of an emerging new style of warfare, called network-centric or described as the outcome of a Revolution in Military Affairs. This type of war is characterized by the use of remote sensors, such as those aboard specialized aircraft, satellites, and UAVs, to allow both a headquarters and subordinate commanders to attack targets which the attackers often cannot see directly. The new style of warfare emphasizes quick operations to upset an enemy's timetable and, ideally, to drive him to a collective nervous breakdown. One hope is that a relatively few weapons, intelligently employed, can collapse an enemy. Clearly the older-style alternative, to bring mass forces and mass weaponry to bear, was impossible in Afghanistan, at least on the timetable the U.S. government adopted.

In effect, the initial air campaign, which concentrated on vital targets deep in Afghanistan, was a test of the pure form of network-centric theory, the idea that attacking a few key targets (the "center of gravity") could and would be decisive. It failed. The Taliban did not collapse instantly. However, when a second element, a substantial force on the ground, was added, the strategy proved brilliantly successful. Thus the Northern Alliance coalition troops made victory in much of Afghanistan possible—when they were combined with a network-centric strike campaign. The glue holding together the Northern Alliance force and the U.S. strike force was small A-Teams of Special Operations Forces. For Northern Alliance commanders, these teams were the visible face of U.S. commitment to the war. Without them, the bombers would have been blind to the most important targets. In past wars, such as the Gulf War, SOF teams have performed the vital liaison role, but in those cases it has not been obvious that coalition forces were essential to victory.[1]

The precision with which the air campaign was executed was important. From a purely military point of view, it limited the number of weapons required to achieve any particular end, and thus limited the logistical burden which otherwise would have been crippling. From a political point of view, it made possible concentration on Al Qaeda and Taliban forces, and thus demonstrated to Afghans that the war was not being fought against all of them, a point the Taliban tried hard to deny, with spurious claims of civilian casualties. Possibly quite as important as precision was air presence, in the form of both surveillance and attack aircraft. Those on the ground did not always need air support, but they did have to be sure that it would be available whenever it was needed. Thus, often aircraft did return to their bases or carriers with weapons still on board.[2] Logistical limits made it important that they did not have to jettison those weapons before landing. Particularly for carrier-based aircraft, "bring back" capacity turned out to be a more realistic measure of what could be carried on a mission than simple weight-carrying capacity.

The air war was closer to the network-centric model than past ones (e.g., Kosovo), but it did not quite get there. There were never enough sensor platforms to cover all of Afghanistan. The split in objectives, between the hunt for bin Laden and the attempt to defeat the Taliban, exacerbated this problem. That was why the manned P-3C was so important to the Marines fighting in the south; Predators, which were apparently devoted first to the hunt for bin Laden, often were not available. Another way to describe the problem would be to say that although much of the infrastructure for network-centric war had been put in place, the shift in priorities from attack platforms to sensor platforms was only beginning.

Network-centric war required precision munitions, but numbers were limited. One reason the U.S. government did not mount an attack against Iraq immediately after Afghanistan was that it knew that it would take about six months to rebuild weapon stocks.[3]

As for the Special Forces on the ground, aside from their coalition role, SOF teams were probably instrumental in paralyzing the Taliban by ambushing them when they tried to move about. Clearly they were not the only means to that end—UAVs played a very important role, for example— but also clearly they were absolutely essential.

The war in Taliban country, in southeast Afghanistan, was very different from the war in support of the Northern Alliance, because at the outset there was no determined opposition to the Taliban. The United States could offer to bribe local tribal leaders, many of whom were probably disgusted with the Taliban rulers, but they would not join a fighting coalition—they would not risk disaster—without a visible U.S. ground presence. That meant more than a few Special Forces soldiers. It took the Marines at FOB Rhino to do that. Without the Marines and the local forces, operations in southeast Afghanistan would have had to be the province of Northern Alliance forces, which represent ethnic groups that the Pashtuns of southeast Afghanistan traditionally detest. As it was, support in the southeast was far softer than in the northwest of the country (Northern Alliance country), and without a substantial U.S. troop presence on the ground the Taliban might well have prevailed.

Since the most important part of the country was the Taliban homeland, it seems fair to say that the U.S. Marine Corps combat presence near Kandahar was absolutely crucial.

Despite the dominant role of U.S. air power, the war in Afghanistan was very much a coalition affair. As such, it reflected some important features and limitations of current U.S. command and control practice. For example, over the past few years the U.S. government has erected parallel classified (SIPRNET) and unclassified intranets. During the war, the SIPRNET became an invaluable means of transferring and discussing operational plans, yet coalition governments were not necessarily granted anything like full access to it. Much key intelligence could not, by its nature, be given out to foreign governments. Moreover, standards of release to different governments necessarily vary. During the war U.S. forces found themselves producing seven quite different versions of the daily intelligence summary.

As an example of the dominance of computers, during the fight at Tora Bora the U.S. Army distributed laptop computers to Afghan coalition forces; their hard disks contained operational information. Reportedly the Afghans who could read that information got considerable amusement out of its misidentifications of important Afghans as either Taliban or friendly.

From a U.S. perspective, the war was largely maritime, in that so much of the force engaged came from the sea. A French account of the war, for example, was titled "the sea attacks the land."[4] Maritime forces were the only way to guarantee access in a hostile world. Carrier aircraft delivered the bulk of the air strikes. A carrier delivered many of the SOF teams into southeast Afghanistan. The Marines, who came from the sea, were an absolutely essential element in the victory in southeastern Afghanistan. Conversely, without maritime access, the war probably could not have been fought, because governments would likely have felt compelled to exercise their potential vetoes against U.S. operations. As it was, many of them probably did not realize just how much potential veto power they enjoyed, given the vital roles played by land-based tankers and by land-based electronic support aircraft, such as JSTARS, AWACS (often operating as a control relay), and the electronic intercept platforms.

Obviously Afghanistan is an unusual case. It is about as far from the sea as a potential battlefield can get, yet our ability to reach it from the sea was probably decisive. Anyone who read the newspapers at the time could see that our coalition partners around Afghanistan were uncomfortable. Many in their populations saw us, not the Taliban or bin Laden, as the great problem, and anything which humbled us could not help but be popular.

No government faced with a population thinking that way can lightly provide us with crucial air base support. Conversely, if we can say that much or all of the air campaign is being supported by the fleet, then governments can more easily provide subtler but vital forms of support, such as intelligence.

It is easy to imagine that a war fought in a remote place like Afghanistan is somehow peripheral; that the important wars are the ones we have been preparing for, in Korea and in the Persian Gulf. However, even if our forces had been defeated in both the Korean War and Gulf War, we would not likely have suffered the sort of casualties at home that Osama bin Laden, operating out of that remote place, inflicted on us—and is likely to try to inflict before he is destroyed. The first purpose of our forces is to protect our country, by destroying or deterring potential enemies. This war, then, turns out to be just a bit more important than the scenarios for which our forces have been built.

We may want to rethink just how special the Afghan case is. During the previous administration, the United States found itself guaranteeing the independence of many states carved out of the former Soviet Union, at least partly to convince them to surrender their nuclear weapons to the Russian government. That was a matter of U.S. national security. It left us, however, with agreements to fight, if necessary, quite far from the sea, in places like Ukraine and Kazakhstan. The first response in any such fight would have to be from the air, either by aircraft or by missile (or, more likely, by a combination). Given the logistical issues, we could not expect to insert large U.S. ground forces. Instead, we would be providing air power and, probably, intelligence support to bolster local forces—as we are trying to do in Afghanistan. Much, then, would depend on just how impressed our friends were with the air power we provided.

Afghanistan may be more typical of the future than we imagine. It is entirely possible that we will usually find ourselves fighting wars like this, in which territory is *not* the object, and it may be that in such wars the concepts of network-centric warfare (in effect, of strike warfare on a large scale) will prove particularly apt. One implication of network-centric concepts is that small units gain enormously in firepower. For example, it is said that an army battalion, properly supported—a vital caveat—can now do the work of a brigade. A subtler implication may be that such units have to be widely dispersed to preclude their attacking each other; errors in identification can be very destructive. Another feature of network-centric warfare, less widely discussed, is that network-centric really means that the concentration in investment shifts from platforms or mass units (in the case of an army or air force) to remote sensing and coordination (the net). If that is so, then as long as overall funding cannot rise substantially, the effect of adopting network-centric concepts will be to cut force structure—which will be acceptable, at least in theory, given the greater efficacy of small units. These cuts are more likely to affect ground and air than naval forces, as naval forces are already heavily netted, and are already widely dispersed.

In the case of ground forces, something is lost as force structure is cut, the main loss being the ability to occupy ground as opposed to destroying an enemy. Hence the significance of Afghanistan: if controlling ground is not the point of the war, the cuts become acceptable. If control of the ground is the point, then the ongoing revolution in military affairs may be unaffordable without coalition partners like the Northern Alliance.

The most important lesson of Afghanistan is probably that we cannot predict where serious national crises may arise in future. Even if we focus only on Wahhabi-led cults like bin Laden's, there are several places they can make their future bases. Southeast Asia is often mentioned as the next likely front in the war against terrorism. Several of its states, such as the Philippines and Indonesia, can be described as having failed their populations, though not on anything like the scale to be found in Afghanistan or, for that matter, in Somalia and the Sudan. There are large Muslim populations—Indonesia is the largest Muslim nation in the world—and there are fundamentalist parties, some of them sharing Osama's fantasies of pan-Islamic statehood. There is, to be sure, some question as to just how effective any of the Islamic terrorist groups is at present. A heavy infusion of Al

Qaeda money might make a considerable difference.[5] That these possibilities were real was demonstrated in October 2002, when Islamic militants destroyed a nightclub in Bali filled with Westerners.[6]

That Islamic jihad groups outside Al Qaeda have parallel hopes makes them rivals, but it also means that they can attack the United States independently and simultaneously. Thus it is easy to imagine parallel U.S. operations necessary in both Southwest and in Southeast Asia. Several Muslim states, such as Egypt, are unstable, so one can also imagine fundamentalist takeovers in them. Others without effective government, such as Somalia, may also end up as fundamentalist bases. Of course, there are national fundamentalists and Osama-like universal ones; by no means are all fundamentalist states inherently our mortal enemies.

More generally, the venues of future U.S. military action are now far less predictable than in the past, and, moreover, we are likely to have to fight multiple small wars more or less simultaneously. That requirement, often predicted before 11 September but rendered much more credible by the attack and its aftermath, is reshaping American national strategy. Past U.S. strategy was shaped by the need to deal with two simultaneous or near-simultaneous crises, in Europe and in Asia. Hence the "two-war" requirement which shaped cold war forces. With rapprochement with China, the Asian war was downgraded to a half-war (Korea). With the end of the cold war the European scenario was replaced by a second half-war, a new Iraq war. As resources declined in the 1990s, the demand to be able to fight two half-wars simultaneously was again reduced, the objective being to fight two in close succession (deter one while fighting the other). Plans for any such wars entailed lengthy buildups such as the one preceding Desert Storm in 1991. Naval forces were the only truly mobile U.S. assets, and it seemed that at best they could deter or slow down an enemy advance. Without major associated ground formations, they could not win decisively—or so it seemed.

An important aspect of the national strategy was that smaller wars, such as Afghanistan, were viewed as lesser included cases; it was assumed that the sort of force which could deal with, say, a North Korean invasion of South Korea could easily handle a lesser power. In fact that was not true, because the ground forces involved in a new Korean War would be relatively heavy and immobile. At the other end of the scale, naval forces were generally used to deter conflict by their presence, but that mission was not directly connected with war fighting, and generally could not be used to deduce the proper strength of naval forces.

If, however, Afghanistan is more likely typical of the future than is a new Korean War, and if several Afghanistans may have to be fought in parallel in widely separated places, then the strategy is likely to change dramatically. Naval formations performing presence may often have to fight as they are; the Afghan War was closer to a "come as you are" war than its predecessors. Instead of being lesser included cases, the small wars become the basis for force construction. If the country faces a larger war, the force employed will be built up out of those forces. That was certainly the case, at least from a naval point of view, in Afghanistan. Two and then three carrier battle groups and two ARGs provided most of the tactical firepower and most of the ground force. Another carrier was devoted to Special Forces. The Army provided follow-on forces, because it could not have deployed instantly.

By mid-2002 U.S. national strategy was often described as "4-2-1," the new element, the "4," meaning the ability to deal with four small wars simultaneously, at least to the extent of keeping crises from escalating into full-blown war. Afghanistan would have qualified as one of the "4," as nothing short of the Gulf War or a renewed war in Korea is counted as a full-blown war. It is easy enough to imagine four simultaneous Afghan-level crises in the near future, particularly since Muslim fundamentalists are hardly the only threat the United States now faces. For example, would the North Koreans see something like Afghanistan as an invitation to attack the South?

Given natural restrictions on forward basing of ground forces and land-based aircraft, the new emphasis on presence/combat implies changes in the naval force structure, which can be deployed independently of local governments.

In Afghanistan, carrier forces were not altogether independent of land-based aircraft. It took land-based tankers to support carrier strikes deep inland. The key intelligence-gathering aircraft, the Air Force/Army JSTARS (E-8), the Air Force RC-135 Rivet Joint, even the Navy's P-3C and EP-3E, all flew from air bases ashore. Some of their capabilities can be duplicated or approximated aboard carriers; for example, once it has its electronically scanned radar, the F/A-18E/F will have a limited ability to detect moving targets on the ground, as the E-8 does now. It may also be that some requirements can be filled by ground sensors strewn by carrier attack aircraft. However, one capability is gone: there are no longer carrier-based electronic intelligence collecting aircraft. Even if the EP-3E and P-3C are partly replaced by long-endurance UAVs, the latter will need ground bases. It may be that ultimately many sensing roles should be moved onto spacecraft, simply to ensure that they can be conducted whether or not the United States enjoys ground access to a theater of operations.

The Afghan air strikes demonstrated the value of a large general-purpose strike aircraft. In the absence of the retired A-6 Intruder, the next best thing was the F-14 Tomcat. Its endurance limited (but hardly eliminated) the need for tanking. Its second-seater proved ideal for tasks such as tactical air control and even to coordinate rescue. As equipped during the war, the F-14 also had the best laser targeting pod as well as a considerable bring-back capacity.[7]

The new approach to presence demands larger numbers of independent naval formations, each with substantial independent combat capability, to be used in the event that deterrence fails. In the past, the ideal presence/combat combination was a carrier battle group working with an amphibious ready group. That made a total of eleven or twelve combinations, and rules limiting overseas deployment reduced the number of forward-deployed combinations to two or three. That is probably insufficient. The new strategy would therefore imply that carrier battle groups and amphibious ready groups be independently combat-capable. A carrier battle group is already independently capable, but the implication would be that the amphibious group would need organic surface combatants, and also that it probably needs more strike aircraft. This requirement is reflected in the decision to form expeditionary strike groups around ARGs. Given limits on the number of carrier battle groups and amphibious groups, surface action groups (SAGs) become another means of assuring presence. None of this is really new. During the cold war, the Reagan administration created battleship-centered SAGs because the carrier battle force could not cover the full presence requirement. It also studied the use of amphibious ready groups as substitute carrier groups, again because available numbers were insufficient, and sufficient numbers were unaffordable.

The Afghan War demonstrated the value of naval forces which could operate free of bases. That independence in turn encouraged neighboring countries to offer basing facilities, which in turn made it possible to operate aircraft far more efficiently. Conversely, without the naval forces, the governments would have had veto power over U.S. operations, and many would have had to face intense pressure to exercise the vetoes.

As in recent wars, space and remote sensing assets were extremely important. Space sensors provided U.S. planners with precise information about Afghanistan before any agreements could be negotiated to place other sensor platforms, such as UAVs, in position. Space communications made it possible for small forward units to reach back to exploit expertise in the United States, both for planning and to interpret and exploit the tactical intelligence they collected. On the other hand, it is not yet clear that placing high-level command in Florida, so far from the battle zone, was successful. Much depends on how the Tora Bora experience is read.

It seems clear that electronic surveillance was crucial in Afghanistan; it was commonly used to cue narrower-vision sensors. This is the one type of surveillance, however, that our enemies seem to understand. Enormous publicity has been given to the exploitation of satellite and cell phones, for example. The operation at Tora Bora was justified in part by detection of Osama's voice in enemy communications. We still do not know, in mid-2002, whether that was clever deception or whether Osama was really present.[8] If it was deception, we may want to rethink just how much electronic intercept information is to be trusted.

On a tactical level, experience in Afghanistan suggests that aircraft are more important than ever, simply because they can deliver loads of ordnance and then return for more. Long-range missiles cannot possibly offer the same sort of sustained pressure, because so much more is expended each time a missile is fired. By extension, the burden is likely to fall most heavily on tactical aircraft near the battle zone, simply because their turn-around time is short. Long-range bombers can carry much greater loads, but unless (until) they are based close to the combat area they cannot sustain operations; they cannot keep up a continuous presence over a battlefield. It follows, one might think, that carriers are increasingly important and that any supplemental money released to fight the war might well go into building back the numbers of strike aircraft (and tankers) per carrier.

Human pilots may become much more important because they can spot and attack fleeting targets. No matter how good the information grid, the sheer time required to make decisions remote from the battlefield will be crippling. Moreover, the ruling fact of the military world is surely Murphy's Law. Satellite communications, on which any kind of remote control depend, work only most of the time. Some atmospheric and space conditions really do interrupt them. Murphy's Law surely implies that such interruption would usually occur just as an unmanned vehicle picked up a really important target quite close to something absolutely not to be attacked, wouldn't it?

On the other hand, often precision-guided missiles, targeted before they are launched, are quite effective. Perhaps we should rethink the role of future uninhabited combat air vehicles (UCAVs). Perhaps they ought usually to be considered reusable first stages for precision missiles—dump trucks for ordnance, just as manned aircraft are. Their advantages may include much lower maintenance overhead (the UCAVs need not fly except in combat, hence need not be maintained for proficiency flying), and even reduced fuel requirements (for the same reason). They may also operate as elements of a sensor grid, suitable to fly over otherwise forbidding defended areas.

The Marines were the only U.S. troops who could get to Afghanistan quickly enough in any strength. To the extent that their presence encouraged the southern warlords to desert the Taliban and rise in rebellion, they were crucial to the success of the war. Their presence in turn was possible because the Marine leadership had been so insistent about ensuring that an airlifted force was viable because the Marines maintain all-arms integration down to the level of the battalion landing team. The air support crucial to FOB Rhino had to be provided by the Marines' AV-8B Harriers, because the air strip they initially set up could not accommodate larger tactical aircraft. The Marines think of such aircraft as part of their organic artillery. One possible lesson would be that the Marines absolutely need STOVL (short take off/vertical landing) capability in their version of the new Joint Strike Fighter (JSF), not to accommodate the aircraft on their large-deck amphibious ships so much as to accommodate it near a battle area.

In this particular case many of the Marines were airlifted to Rhino aboard KC-130 aircraft flying from Pakistan, the initial party coming by helicopter from ships offshore. In future there may be no land base available and Marines and their equipment will have to come from ship-capable aircraft. That may mean V-22s, or some other vertical-lift aircraft, or it may be that the replacement for the current C-2 carrier delivery aircraft should be adapted to Marine requirements, as a heavier-lift transport. Such a choice would have implications for the next-generation large amphibious ship. Incidentally, the idea of using C-2s or their equivalent as tactical transports is not new; it was proposed in the early 1960s as a way of giving naval forces a long amphibious reach inland. At that time it seemed that the wars of the future would be sudden but relatively small insurgencies ("brushfire wars"), widely distributed. It may be worthwhile to look back at the ideas developed at the time, just before the Vietnam War escalated.

Special Operations Forces were essential to the war's success. Junior officers and enlisted men managed to forge individual relationships with coalition officers, and in that process learned enough to overcome U.S.

official ignorance of Afghanistan. However, tours of duty are relatively short (partly because these forces are relatively thin and must be deployed globally), and when they are up, the expertise generated during them evaporates. Postcombat comments by some SOF officers suggest that the regular army does not really understand what to do with them, and that it often assigns them to trivial duties which dull their capabilities, such as teaching ROTC courses. To the extent that SOF is a vital capability for future wars, such comments confirm the logic of uniting the various services' Special Forces under a single unified command, and suggest that such unification should be strengthened.

It is important to understand just what coalition means. As the Taliban collapsed, there were references in the U.S. press to proxy troops, and to resentment at the unwillingness of coalition forces to accept U.S. leadership or a decisive U.S. role in a post-Taliban Afghanistan. Such views betray a dangerous misunderstanding. Coalitions are, by definition, weaker than alliances. Those who join coalitions do so out of self-interest, not some abstract sense of loyalty or gratitude. They leave at will; that is why the combinations are called coalitions, not alliances. Incidentally, these considerations apply as much to the United States as to the Northern Alliance. We found the Afghan troops very useful partners in a war we could not win by ourselves. They similarly found us useful. It is foolish to act as though one or the other won—both won together, and neither could have won separately. Once the mutually agreed object, the elimination of Taliban power, was achieved, there was no particular reason for the Northern Alliance to accept U.S. dictation.

Coalitions are difficult to manage because the partners generally have diverging interests. Our coalition partners in Afghanistan wanted to liberate the country from the Taliban, who were oppressing the population. Once the war began, the U.S. government very properly pointed out just how evil the Taliban were. Critics asked why we had helped them in the past; for example, as President Bush pointed out, before 11 September the United States was the main donor of food aid to Afghanistan (albeit on a multilateral basis). There is actually no contradiction here. In foreign policy it is best not to interfere with any country's internal regime, no matter how repugnant, unless that regime becomes a threat to us. The reason is simple: if governments decide that they have the right of intervention, they may choose to attack us. We feel virtuous, but others probably feel otherwise, and, sincere or hypocritical, we would rather that the rules of international life kept them out of our business. Obviously the rules are often bent, but keep in mind that throughout the cold war we found the Soviets particularly threatening precisely because they refused to disavow subversion—meddling in other countries' internal politics—as standard behavior.

Thus until the Afghans made themselves our business we could properly avoid intervention in theirs, no matter how hair-raising the stories emanating from Kabul. We might not be very happy about that, but foreign policy is often a choice between very unpleasant alternatives. Once we found ourselves at war, however, it felt far better to be destroying an evil regime (as was and is the case) than to be attacking a virtuous one. Americans, by and large, prefer a reasonably ethical foreign policy.

The one great question about Afghanistan is, why did the Taliban collapse so quickly? The answer may well shape U.S. tactics in future warfare. There are several possibilities. One is that the effective part of the Taliban army really was limited to the Arabs, and that air attacks killed or terrified so many of the Arabs that their Afghan allies were able to surrender to oncoming forces. In this case the relatively small U.S. Marine force in the southeast really was comparable to (or greatly superior to) the effective part of the Taliban force not only in real fighting power but even in numbers. Another is that what seemed a futile air campaign, at the outset, hollowed out Taliban resources to the extent that the Taliban were unable to retreat in good order, so that the initial defeat at Mazar-i-Sharif quickly became a rout. Air attacks also made it very difficult for the Taliban to move around within Afghanistan, thus preventing them from concentrating to meet attacks. Another is that the speed of the advance, once it got going, made it impossible for Taliban leaders to react in time. This would be the OODA-loop theory of victory for a network-centric war.[9] Yet another is that, having experienced war at great length while fighting the Soviets, the Afghan Taliban troops had little interest in protracted combat and thus collapsed relatively quickly. It is also likely that U.S. strategists had learned a central lesson of the Gulf War, that in many dictatorships the important military target is not so much the opposing army as the Praetorian Guard (Republican Guard in that war, 055 Brigade in this one) which stands between the rulers and their own mass army. Much of the U.S. air effort may well have been focused on the Taliban Arabs, rather than on Taliban troops as a whole.

If the strategy applied in Afghanistan shows the way ahead, what would it look like applied to a more difficult situation, say in Iraq? The geography of Iraq is obviously radically different from that of Afghanistan, and the Iraqi military is far more powerful than the Taliban's. On the other hand, one might draw a parallel between the two situations. In this view, the Kurdish area of Iraq is something like northern Afghanistan. An opposition force—the Kurds—controls territory, in this case under Western protection. Its position is somewhat better than that of the pre-September Northern Alliance, but on the other hand it is not in combat. Indeed, Kurds interviewed in mid-2002 were quite reluctant to fight, for fear that U.S. forces would not protect them from Saddam Hussein's inevitable revenge. They had reason to be afraid, since during the 1990s the Iraqi army invaded the sanctuary, discovering no Western resistance at all.

Southern Iraq is different. The main ethnic group in that region, the Shi'ites, rose in rebellion (with strong U.S. encouragement) after Iraq was defeated in the Gulf War, only to find the Americans unwilling to protect them from Iraqi reprisals.[10] Thus Shi'ites were unlikely to chance a rebellion, and indeed their society was probably heavily infiltrated by Saddam's agents. On the other hand, the Shi'ites would not support Saddam were he in extremis. Disorganized opposition in the Shi'ite south might be analogized to the sort of unrest the United States exploited after the Marines set up FOB Rhino.

Saddam's main supporters are Sunni Arabs living between the Kurds and the Shi'ites in central Iraq, which includes Baghdad. They have probably profited most from recent relaxation of the embargo, and they associate this improvement with Saddam. Moreover, Saddam's supporters are well aware that any winning anti-Saddam coalition would want to settle scores, as the Kurds and Shi'ites did in 1991, when Saddam seemed to be on the run. That may actually offer the United States an opportunity. Once Saddam's authority in the north and south has been broken, U.S. troops on the ground may be the main potential protectors available to the Sunnis. Indeed, some observers have argued that the United States would have to deploy mass forces mainly to maintain some kind of order in a post-Saddam Iraq.

A strategy analogous to that of the Afghan War would have the Kurds form a Northern-Alliance style army supported by U.S. air power, presumably operating largely from Turkey. A U.S. ground force would have to push into Sunni country. Presumably its presence would encourage the Kurds to fight, and it might also convince the Shi'ites to rebel, or at least to be hostile to Saddam's regime.

Those advocating this kind of war claimed that the combination of economic sanctions and limited resources has precluded modernization of the Iraqi army. Given the startling success of U.S. forces in 1991, it would seem that a relatively small army could cut through Iraqi defenders and probably reach Baghdad. The effectiveness of this army would be amplified greatly by its access to air-delivered precision weapons. The necessary aircraft could come from the sea and from Kuwait, which would presumably act as a U.S. ally. However, the main point would be that, like the Marines near Kandahar, the mere presence of a substantial U.S. force would be convincing evidence of a real U.S. commitment. That in turn would negate the widespread fear that the United States would leave any local coalition partners to their fates at Saddam's hands.

Press leaks during the spring of 2002 indicated that U.S. military opinion rejected any such ideas as far too risky. Reportedly, Gen. Tommy Franks, who as commander of Central Command would be responsible for the war, said that he would need five divisions and two hundred thousand troops. Without Saudi cooperation (which was not forthcoming), it was presumably difficult or impossible to place that many troops in position to advance into Iraq. Thus Franks's statement, if correctly reported, might be a way of rejecting any idea of attacking Iraq. Those in the administration who wanted to attack regarded Franks and his planners as far too pessimistic—and far too unaware of the lessons of the war he had just fought, in which he had also wanted larger forces than proved necessary.

The argument was that U.S. strategy in 1991 had been profoundly wrong, because it identified Saddam with the Iraq he ruled. Thus U.S. forces opposed the Iraqi army, rather than concentrate on the force—secret police and Republican Guard—keeping Saddam in power. Had these forces, rather than the Iraqi Army, been the target, the way would have been opened for those Iraqis opposed to Saddam's rule, and he would have been overthrown. A satisfactory post-Saddam government could have been installed.

In Afghanistan force was concentrated on the army keeping the enemy government in power, and even more on its Arab Al Qaeda core. That was not quite enough; it took force on the ground to capitalize on the destruction or neutralization of Al Qaeda troops. On the other hand, it was impressive that much of the Afghan part of the Taliban army simply disintegrated and defected. Troops showed little interest in fighting for their oppressors. Translated into Iraqi terms, if it seemed that the United States and her allies were winning, and that Saddam's organs of control were being destroyed, would the Iraqi regular army not revolt so as to gain power for itself? How much armed force would be needed?

Iraqi emigres claimed that, given limited American support, large numbers of Iraqis stood ready to revolt, to form something equivalent to the Northern Alliance. Others said that a decade of American-sponsored embargoes, which sapped civil life in Iraq, left the average Iraqi far more angry at the United States than at Saddam; revolt is grossly unlikely. Too, whatever the capability of his army, Saddam always maintained effective secret police, who would probably destroy any potential successor the United States might plan to impose. The implication of such factors was that an Afghan-style operation would fail; to overthrow Saddam, the United States would have to insert a large ground force.

For his part, Saddam is well aware that disaffected groups, particularly the Kurds in the north, are potential coalition partners. To sap the Kurds, he allowed Al Qaeda to set up a regime of its own in the Kurdish area nominally protected by the UN. This step in turn was taken by U.S. advocates of an attack on Iraq as proof that Saddam was actually part of the Al Qaeda terror network and hence a legitimate target.

Saddam has spent well over a decade building an arsenal of weapons of mass destruction, mainly chemical and biological. From his point of view, the war the United States began is total, since his own death or removal is the object. It was widely suggested that, desperate, he would use his weapons, either against oncoming U.S. forces or against Israel. The logic of the latter kind of attack would be to demonstrate to the Arab world that he was really fighting the universal enemy, Israel, that any Arab government not supporting him would in effect be backing the Israelis. That was the logic of Iraqi Scud missile attacks against Israel in 1991. At the time, the United States managed to limit the problem by convincing the Israelis not to retaliate directly, the fear being that any Israeli involvement would break the coalition fighting Iraq. If the attacks this time were really destructive (as opposed to Scud-style pinpricks), the Israelis would probably feel compelled to retaliate, quite possibly using nuclear weapons. Saddam might die, but the Middle East would have been radicalized in favor of someone like Osama. That would not be much of a victory.

It is unlikely that the United States has good intelligence of all Iraqi chemical and biological and missile storage sites; certainly that was the case during the Gulf War. On the other hand, Saddam does not pull the trigger on these weapons; his subordinates do. They may fear postwar punishment. If it is obvious that Saddam is losing, would they be so loyal as to risk their own necks? One new factor here is the international war crimes court. Many of those in position to pull triggers can probably be charged as war criminals for acts in places like Kurdistan. Can (or should) the United States offer them sanctuary in return for not firing?

Another question is whether U.S. and coalition forces could keep fighting if Iraq did use chemical and biological weapons. It now seems that the Iraqis did not use such weapons during the Gulf War, that deterrence worked in that case. Was it deterrence applied to Saddam or was it the more personal deterrence felt by individual Iraqi officers? The answer matters now. So does the answer to whether "Gulf syndrome" had anything to do with Iraqi weapons.

It may well be argued that the best U.S. counter to the threat of Iraqi weapons of mass destruction would be a very sudden surprise attack, since to be used the weapons must be brought into place from secure storage.

War broke out in Iraq in mid-March 2003, on much the lines suggested above. War plans called for fronts both in northern and in southern Iraq, but ultimately the Turkish government refused to allow major U.S. forces to jump off from its territory. That left the Kurdish forces in the north, supported by airborne troops and by strike aircraft. Unlike the Northern Alliance, the Kurds lack heavy equipment, but air strikes may make up for that. By the second week of the war, Iraqi troops were falling back towards key regional centers such as Kirkuk and Mosul.

In the south, progress initially seemed disappointing. Shi'ites did not revolt in any numbers, and even regular Iraqi units failed to surrender as forecast. Advancing coalition troops encountered Iraqi irregulars, most likely members of the Ba'ath Party and of the Iraqi security services—all of whom had been directly involved in major crimes against the Shi'ite majority in the south, and all of whom could be expected to suffer at Shi'ite hands in the event of a coalition victory. Expectations of a very short war had been premised on the 1991 experience, when the Iraqi regular army effectively collapsed. It seems at least arguable that the 1991 Iraqi army had been much affected by the crushing experience of the 1980–88 war against Iran, much as Taliban troops had been affected by the experience of war against the Soviets. Neither army wanted a repeat experience however effectively it had fought the first time. This time most Iraqi troops had to relearn just how unpleasant war could be. Too, Saddam would have learned from 1991 that his army was unreliable, and he presumably inserted enough security personnel to make sure that units found it difficult to surrender en masse. Minimal resistance by the regular Iraqi army (as reflected in very limited coalition casualties during the first week of combat) suggests that although Saddam's enforcers could keep troops from surrendering, they could not induce them to fight. As of the first ten days of the war, it remained to be seen whether Republican Guard units (equivalent, perhaps, to the Al Qaeda Arabs of Afghanistan) would put up a stiffer fight closer to Baghdad.

There was a very important difference. Ultimately the Taliban could choose to escape into the mountainous region bordering Pakistan. They certainly did not want to lose power in Kabul and in Kandahar, but defeat did not necessarily mean death or even permanent impotence. They could choose to run to fight another day, however futile that might ultimately be. Saddam had no similar choice. It seemed likely that he would be killed if he tried to run, because merely trying to escape would be to admit to his closest associates that he had lost his power—and that he was leaving them to their fate. His regime has committed sufficient crimes that many of its minions likely face death at the hands of victim populations, most notably (but not only) Kurds and Shi'ites. It is probably impossible for the United States to guarantee safe passage or even safety to most members of the Ba'ath Party and the security services; hence many of them are likely to fight to the death. Because they are not too numerous that may not be a very serious problem, but it does preclude the quick surrender of military units in which they have been embedded.

Is Afghanistan the future of U.S. warfare? Iraq is not entirely compatible, not least because so much of the air preparation occurred prior to the formal outbreak of hostilities (in the form of attacks in the no-fly zones); because a large coalition army, rather than a small Marine force, was engaged; and because there was no real attempt to raise a partner force (comparable to the Southern Alliance) in the area friendliest to the regime, the Sunni slice of central Iraq. On the other hand, the idea of very quick, simultaneous operations in many parts of Iraq certainly exemplifies the Boyd concept of war, the hope that an enemy can be driven toward a breakdown. The big initial "shock and awe" attack on Bagdad was intended, at least partly, to cripple Iraqi communications so that their own decision cycle would be slowed badly compared to that of the coalition. Of course it was also intended to convince many Iraqis of their inevitable defeat, and thus to encourage defections. There was no comparable operation in Afghanistan.

Yet overall the strategy demonstrated at the outset of the Iraq War seems to have been quite consistent with that executed in Afghanistan.

Now What?

Where does the global war on terrorism go beyond Afghanistan? Three approaches suggest themselves. One would be to continue the attack on Al Qaeda, both to cripple it and as a deterrent to future would-be Osama bin Ladens. A second would be to deal with other terrorist or semiterrorist threats, perhaps most important among them Iraq, a key member of the "axis of evil." A third would be to attack the root causes of terrorism. Probably U.S. policy will combine the three approaches.

Attacking Al Qaeda

Al Qaeda has probably already been severely damaged. Its leaders may be dead or dying. Bin Laden, for example, looked quite ill in a video he apparently made in December 2001. Six months later there was speculation that he was dead, particularly after he failed to appear, as advertised, on television about 4 July. In November 2002, however, an audio tape purportedly made by Osama bin Laden did appear. Initially U.S. intelligence pronounced it authentic, apparently on the ground that it showed no splices, hence could not have been made by someone piecing together previous tapes. However, a Swiss audio testing institute claimed that voice prints taken from the tape did not match known bin Laden speeches and the tape, therefore, was fraudulent.[1] It may even be that bin Laden's associates have refused to admit that he is dead in hopes of retaining control of his money and his organization. If he survives, he may feel compelled to demonstrate within the Muslim world that he can still strike. If he does nothing for very long, potential backers and recruits may desert to groups they find more effective.

Through 2002 Al Qaeda and associated groups continued to operate, although not on the same scale as 11 September. Attacks, some of them clearly by other Muslim groups, included the bombing of a church (attended by Americans) in Islamabad on 17 March, an attack against German tourists at a Tunisian synagogue on 11 April, a bomb in Karachi on 8 May which killed fourteen French naval constructors helping the Pakistan Navy, a truck bombing of the U.S. consulate in Karachi on 14 June (which killed at least twelve Pakistanis), a small boat explosive attack against the French tanker *Limburg* off Yemen on 6 October, the murder of an American marine in Kuwait (by a Kuwaiti policeman) on 8 October, a horrific nightclub bombing in Bali on 12 October, the seizure of a Moscow theater on 23 October, and the suicide bombing of an Israeli-owned hotel in Kenya on 28 November (with a concurrent failed missile attack against an Israeli airliner). Some other plots, such as one to attack shipping in the Straits of Gibraltar and one against the Israeli national soccer team, were foiled. At the end of 2002, rising "chatter" among Al Qaeda supporters seemed to indicate that some larger but unspecified attack was imminent.

At least some of bin Laden's cells surely survived the Afghan disaster, and some of them may be working on preexisting plans. However, only by limiting each cell's capabilities can they be kept small and largely invisible. Each cell must, then, depend on the central organization for some vital services, such as security. Cells cut off from central authority are more likely to be vulnerable to attack. Moreover, cells are secure partly because they do not communicate directly, only through the central authority (which alone is aware of the identifications of all the leaders and members). Without the central authority, the cells must find each other, opening themselves to penetration. Without resources arranged by the center, they may often resort to crime, which in turn may lead investigators to them. Similarly, without centralized resources, cells may find themselves accumulating documentation, which itself may be incriminating.[2]

Certainly it appears that the 11 September hijackers were on a short financial string. Again and again, ATM videotapes showed them waiting nervously for money, wired from the Mideast, to arrive. Moreover, as knowledge of Al Qaeda financial operations accumulates, money transfers themselves may be used to identify cells.

Probably the Taliban disaster drastically reduced any probability that Pakistan and Saudi Arabia would collapse into Osama's hands. As the ground war accelerated, public support for Al Qaeda and bin Laden among Muslims seemed to decline dramatically, where only a few weeks before there had been noisy riots. Perhaps the many who hate the United States had been encouraged by the long line of terrorist successes, at least from

1983 onward, and by American restraint. Now that it was clear that the United States was no paper tiger, it was no longer wise to support our enemies. That did not mean that the United States had suddenly acquired hundreds of millions of friends. Those sobered by the Afghan experience were hardly about to hand over bin Laden and his lieutenants, or to become Republicans. However, those who are somewhat predisposed to betray the terrorists may now realize that they are on the winning side, that betrayal may bring them honor rather than an unpleasant death. That shift in perceptions may well be vital if, as seems likely, the war shifts toward a police or intelligence phase.

Governments have generally harbored Al Qaeda not out of strong affection for its goals but more out of fear that its operatives can destroy them if provoked. The quick U.S. success in Afghanistan, and the silence of the "Arab street" in opposition, have demonstrated to many governments that Al Qaeda is not nearly so fearsome as they had imagined. Not only are such governments likely to assist U.S. efforts to root out Al Qaeda, but they are likely to attack its known cells for their own sake. Many of the governments involved have poor human rights records—behavior which has probably made them riper for Al Qaeda penetration. Over the past decade, U.S. policy has been to cut military ties with such regimes. Now that policy is being reversed, because the destruction of terrorist cells seems more important than fostering better government behavior. This change mirrors U.S. policy during the cold war, when it seemed necessary to back many regimes because of their countries' strategic significance. The question, of course, is whether such support ultimately leads to more satisfactory regimes or to regimes violently opposed to the United States, hence supportive of some future version of Al Qaeda. On that issue the record is by no means clear. For example, after the Korean War, South Korea had a very repressive regime, but it evolved into a democratic (and prosperous) one.

As for refuges for Al Qaeda, Somalia is potentially attractive as a base because it has no effective central government to oppose the terrorist organization. As in pre-Taliban Afghanistan, Al Qaeda and a fundamentalist organization can promise an end to factional disorder in return for a safe base. Al Qaeda operated freely in Somalia in the early 1990s, and presumably it retains local assets. Local warlords are apparently alive to its threat, particularly after watching what happened to local leaders in Afghanistan. For example, about September 2001 Hussein Mohammed Aidid, one of the Somalian factional leaders, requested U.S. help against Al Qaeda personnel and training camps. There is some question as to whether such leaders see U.S. power as a useful form of leverage against their local rivals, just as some in Afghanistan did. In the fall of 2001, the U.S. official assessment was that U.S. air and ground combat power would be required to deal with Al Qaeda in Somalia, simply because there is no national government capable of doing so, however much individual leaders may want to eject or destroy Al Qaeda.

The Sudan is another possibility, and another former haven for bin Laden and Al Qaeda. For decades its Muslim government has been engaged in a war against non-Muslims, mostly Christians, in the south. In the past, the Sudanese government has been fundamentalist Muslim. As if to return favors already granted, in the past Al Qaeda has threatened Americans attacking the Sudanese for enslaving non-Muslims. In recent years, however, the Sudanese government has been conciliatory toward the United States, possibly because it fears that Al Qaeda plans to supplant it.

Yemen is another possibility. The bin Laden family comes from Yemen, and in various videos Osama has sported a Yemeni dagger as if to remind Yemenis of his origins. After U.S. forces began striking Afghan targets, the Yemeni government struck at some supposed Al Qaeda bases on its territory and became more cooperative in dealing with those who had attacked the USS *Cole* the previous year. The Al Qaeda presence in Yemen was dramatized when a CIA Predator UAV flying over Yemen fired a Hellfire missile into a car carrying a senior Al Qaeda officer, killing him.[3]

There is also a real possibility that Al Qaeda will find refuge with one of several fundamentalist movements seeking to take over the old Muslim lands of Southeast Asia: Malaysia, Indonesia, and the southern Philippines. U.S. special forces are now working with the Filipinos, and the United States has reopened the relationship with the Indonesian military which it severed due to human rights abuses in places like East Timor. In all three countries official corruption may offer an opening to fundamentalists. Indonesia in particular has seen anti-Christian (and anti-Chinese) pogroms conducted by Muslims furious at, among other things, economic disaster. The gruesome attack on the nightclub in Bali seems to demonstrate that the Indonesian Jemaah Islamiah group either has ties to, or follows, Al Qaeda.[4]

For that matter, there are ongoing fundamentalist insurgencies in places like Algeria and Egypt. Al Qaeda is already more or less closely allied to these movements. Should they become more successful, it might see these countries as superior replacements for Afghanistan. In this sense the war against Al Qaeda becomes the war against fundamentalist revolution, and it can be argued that political reform may be a precondition for the victory of the more acceptable secular government, which in turn would resist penetration by Al Qaeda or its equivalents.

Al Qaeda and its allies apparently pursue a policy of exacerbating local conflicts in order to sharpen divisions between Muslims and others. For example, after a very destructive 1994–96 war, Chechnya gained a considerable degree of self-determination. War erupted again in 1999, however, largely because the Russians blamed Chechens for some very destructive explosions in Moscow apartment buildings. Wahhabi rebels from Chechnya crossed the border into Dagestan to proclaim a fundamentalist republic there. In both cases the objective seems to have been to start a new war which would radicalize Chechens and Dagestanis, and thus push them toward the Wahhabis. The consequent Russian offensives drove many Chechens to despair and thereby encouraged a horrific suicide attack on a major Moscow theater in October 2002.

Thus, although in theory bin Laden and other Al Qaeda leaders make a variety of demands in the tapes and faxes they release, in fact, they are not interested in acquiescence. The demands are made entirely to attract Muslims to their cause. If any of them can be met by the West, they must be coupled with demands so outrageous that they cannot possibly be met. The objective is to force Muslims into a stance of constant warfare against the West, which in turn places them in opposition to moderate or even to secular Middle Eastern governments. For example, in the tape Osama bin Laden purportedly released in November 2002, he (or his Al Qaeda replacements) say that there can be no end to terrorism until the West converts to Islam (and also abandons the Israelis to their fate). Inclusion of the first condition in effect makes any peace impossible, but it also reflects the doctrine, reflected in many Wahhabist and fundamentalist writings, that any zone outside that controlled by Islam is by definition the "house of war," and that friendship between Muslims and non-Muslims is impossible. That the declaration might also be read as a prescription for the West to kill all Muslims may not be obvious to those who imagine that the West is already at war with them.

The Wider Terrorist Issue

Because Al Qaeda perpetrated the 11 September outrages, there is a widespread feeling that at present the West is faced only with Islamic terrorist threats. However, any reading of Middle Eastern history (or of current events in Israel) will show that there are also active secular terrorists; indeed, at times they have been far more destructive than the Islamic ones. For example, in the suicide bombings of Israel, the PLO's secular attack arm, the Al-Aqsa Brigade, operates in competition with the Sunni Hamas and with the Shi'ite Hezbollah movements. The Palestinian revolutionary movements of the 1970s, which continually hijacked airliners and often murdered Western civilians, were overwhelmingly secular. Indeed, as their lineal descendant, the PLO is a secular organization promoting a secular state.

There is, moreover, an important reason to avoid associating terrorism with religion, particularly with Islam. Many Muslims already believe that the West plans ultimately to destroy their religion, perhaps because they also believe that ultimately there must be a struggle for superiority between the Western religions and Islam. Many Muslims apparently already imagine that the U.S.-led war on terror is only cover for a new phase of the war against Islam which their clerics tell them has been proceeding for many centuries. This sense, that in fact the terrorists are defending Islam, is a powerful source of strength and support for them. There is little point in reinforcing such beliefs, because reinforcement will only gain adherents for Al Qaeda and its brethren—and undermine secular or even nonfanatical governments in Muslim countries. That does not mean ignoring the Islamic flavor of Al Qaeda, only recognizing that Islamic terrorism is one among several enemies of the West.

If it is accepted that the United States and the West face a wide variety of terrorist threats, mainly originating in the Middle East but not entirely Islamic, then one conclusion we can draw is that U.S. and Western restraint over the past decades has suggested that we are soft targets. We are an attractive target because we are at the same time impressive and, apparently, impotent. Attacking an impressive target demonstrates just how daring and powerful the attacker is. Whatever he says, he is not particularly interested in what the target (us) will do, but in publicizing his goals to a largely inert Muslim or Arab mass. Our willing impotence makes such a ploy reasonably safe. For example, when the Iranian radicals raided the U.S. embassy in Teheran in 1979, they were not particularly interested in changing U.S. policy. On the other hand, by publicly humiliating the United States, they could boost their own status, both within Iran and within the Muslim world. That is different only in scale from bin Laden's perception that mass murder of Americans on 11 September would gain him supporters throughout the Muslim world. Our deaths, then, are means to an overseas end. Bin Laden is not interested in peace because attacks on the United

States—and on the wider West—are his most powerful tools in his war against various Muslim governments.

Obviously there is a logical contradiction between bin Laden's two views: the United States as the most powerful (and evil) country in the world, constantly smashing the Arab populations, and the United States as so cowardly that it cannot and will not react to attacks. Bin Laden's manifestoes illustrate both perceptions, and both ideas have been repeated so often in official propaganda in the Muslim world that few probably realize that they are mutually contradictory.

The contradiction offers a direction to U.S. policy. It would be pointless and extremely unwise to reverse the sense of U.S. power, since terrorists might be even more willing to attack a badly weakened enemy. On the other hand, perhaps the image of U.S. acquiescence to attacks can be reversed. That seems to have been the central strategic choice made by the Bush administration after 11 September. It explains the interest in dealing with Iraq. It also explains why Iran was included in the "axis of evil": until the Iranian regime changes (as seems likely), to deal with it on friendly terms would be to accept the humiliation of the embassy seizure in 1979.

It is very difficult to reverse widely held perceptions. Where quite limited use of force might have been sufficient in the past to stave off defeat or to keep U.S. forces in place (as in Somalia), reversal seems to require spectacular shows of force and absolute unwillingness to brook resistance by other governments. Not surprisingly, such a policy, which is very much a response to a U.S. problem, is unlikely to be particularly popular among other governments. In trying to gain support for an attack against Iraq, for example, the administration apparently has never cited Saddam Hussein's sheer survival as an inspiration to those who dislike the United States.

Changing perceptions offers a degree of deterrence, particularly to governments which may tend to harbor anti-American terrorists. Those governments may imagine that the terrorists are a worse threat than the United States; better to harbor them than to risk their wrath. That is, after all, much of the explanation for Al Qaeda's success in infiltrating many Muslim countries. A U.S. policy of attacking governments harboring terrorists, demonstrated in Afghanistan, is indicated.

Once harbors have been denied, the antiterrorist campaign is largely a police and intelligence operation. "Stings" of the type described in chapter 5 may become very effective, and they seem to be the best available countermeasure. Note that the two are related: stings are most useful when the terrorists have no safe havens in which to meet and be recognized. They are least useful when, as in Taliban Afghanistan, the terrorists can set up what amounts to a state of their own, a safe haven in which they know exactly who is and who is not one of them.

Overall, a policy of reversing perceptions and denying harbors for terrorists is uncomfortably like old-fashioned power politics, the sort of thing the United Nations was conceived to end. In effect, 11 September told Americans that they had to rely on their own government, not the UN or international law, for their safety in a very dangerous world. Many in the military would have said the same thing the day or the year or the decade earlier, but the widespread understanding that events far away could kill thousands at home was new to the public. The Romans are supposed to have said that it is better to be feared than loved. Many Americans, including those in government, hoped that they could reverse the adage, but 11 September threw that hope into question. An aggressive assault on our enemies and potential enemies is likely to make few real friends, because it will send a message of American power. That is not a comfortable choice to make, and the ongoing debate in the United States about war with Iraq proves as much.

Iraq and the Axis of Evil

The logic of the connection between the "axis of evil" and the war on terrorism is twofold. First, by dealing with the leading Third World states openly hostile to the United States, the U.S. government can hope to reverse the longstanding perception that it is impotent. Saddam Hussein's Iraq seems to exemplify U.S. inability or unwillingness to pursue enemies to the end. Saddam Hussein himself transmuted his survival after the 1991 Gulf War into a perception in the Muslim world that he, not the United States or the coalition it led, won the war. After all, twice he proved that American pressure could be defied with few or no consequences. Once was in Kurdistan, in 1996, where his army had crushed political opposition despite a declared American policy of protection. A second was in 1998, when he ejected the UN weapons inspectors who were thwarting his program of developing weapons of mass destruction and the missiles to deliver them. True, he had to suffer some air attacks, but they were a transitory irritation. Saddam could (and presumably does) reasonably believe that once his weapons program has reached maturity, he can easily break any remaining UN-sponsored bonds restraining him.

True, the destruction of the Taliban regime in Afghanistan has demonstrated U.S. resolve. However, the Bush administration can reasonably believe that Saddam's survival and clear defiance present many enemies, particularly in the Arab world, with a larger object lesson, that the United States lacks the will to risk serious casualties in a fight against an enemy better equipped than the Taliban. It seems to follow that unseating Saddam is a necessary way of demonstrating American resolve and thus of deterring many other governments from supporting anti-American terrorists. Conversely, to many foreign governments, destroying the Iraqi government would be a terrifying demonstration of American resolve and power.

It may well be that the only antidote to anti-American fundamentalism is battlefield defeat. Those who fear our raw power may not like us, but they will find other targets for their anger. If that is true, unless Iraq is struck and destroyed, those who cheered for Al Qaeda will continue to do so. The strongest evidence for the connection between fear and our own safety is the remarkable collapse of the "Arab street" fervor for Al Qaeda after the U.S.-led coalition began to win in Afghanistan. This argument gains force because there is so little evidence that propaganda on our part can undermine the widespread anti-Americanism of the Arab and Muslim world. People really seem to be conditioned to respect power. Battlefield disaster strongly suggests that Allah is not really with those opposing us. Conversely, an apparently timid U.S. policy can be read as a policy adopted out of fear of the inevitably victorious army of Islam. In this view, restraint practiced by the United States is never appreciated as mercy; it is entirely counterproductive.

The counterargument is that decades of Israeli military success seem not to have quashed virulent anti-Israeli sentiment throughout the Arab world, although they have taught Arab governments to be cautious about starting wars. It may be that governments just find it far too attractive to make Israel the focus of their peoples' anger, but have the good sense to avoid risking destruction to do what their populations seem to demand. Will they do the same with the United States?

The other aspect of the "axis of evil" is that the governments involved, those of Iran, Iraq, and North Korea, really do present threats to their neighbors. They are developing both weapons of mass destruction (chemical, biological, and nuclear) and missiles which can deliver them to considerable ranges. It may be argued that the assault on such states is little more than an American ploy to retain freedom of action by wiping out these governments' deterrents, but it seems more reasonable to focus on their drive to be able to threaten not only immediate neighbors but also more distant countries. The North Koreans in particular seem to be a driving force in exporting ballistic missile technology to aggressive states such as Libya and Syria. In recent months there have been reports that Iraq is hiding its own weapons program by placing parts of them in other countries, such as Libya, incidentally giving them important assistance in becoming threats to the West. The U.S. government has used this wider-threat argument to convince foreign governments to join a new coalition, particularly directed at Iraq.

Of the three "axis of evil" states, Iraq is probably by far the most urgently threatening. It may also the most vulnerable to U.S. military forces. If indeed all three represent real threats to the United States, then the argument for attacking the most vulnerable of the three is partly that such a victory will deeply affect the others, not to mention other prospective American enemies. Victory over the Taliban may not have anything like the desired sobering effect, because they had only a ragtag army and, it seemed, little modern technology. Enemies who believe in technology rather than in raw religiosity may, therefore, not take the American victory too seriously. Iraq, on the other hand, is a cutting-edge Third World power. Moreover, it can be argued that Saddam Hussein has been and is a major problem in the Middle East. Iran may well change due to strong internal pressures, and North Korea is largely marginalized in northern Asia. That leaves Iraq as a very attractive target.

In March and April 2002 Vice President Cheney and Secretary of State Powell toured the Middle East, reportedly in hopes of assembling an anti-Iraq coalition. It appears they were unsuccessful, largely because no Muslim government could join while a hot war continued between Israel and the Palestinians. This truth was perceived both in Bagdad and in Washington. From Bagdad, Saddam announced large payments to the families of suicide bombers, clearly in hopes of keeping the Palestinian attack on Israel alive and thus of staving off the formation of a coalition which would ultimately lead to an attack on Iraq. In Washington, a resolution of the current conflict was widely seen as a precondition for an attack on Iraq.

Through the summer and fall of 2002, the United States continued to seek partners for war as it built up forces in the Persian Gulf. Despite failure to reach even a temporary settlement of the Israeli-Palestinian fight, various gulf states, such as Kuwait and Qatar, were clearly willing to accept U.S. forces. The Turkish position was more complicated. Turkey's government has always feared that any attack on Iraq would result in the formation of a Kurdish state in what had been northern Iraq. Such a state might attract Kurds from Turkey (not to mention those in Syria and Iran).

Given the enormous Turkish effort that has gone into suppressing Kurdish nationalism in Turkey, any such outcome would be extremely unattractive. Matters were further complicated when an Islamic party won the fall 2002 Turkish elections. Ultimately, it denied the United States the desired base for a northern offensive into Iraq.

Several governments decided that they would offer base or overflight rights in the event the United Nations backed U.S. action. Some time during 2002 the Bush administration decided that it could not, or would not, attack Iraq alone; it needed the overflight rights and the bases and the diplomatic cover of a coalition. That decision in effect offered other UN members a veto over a U.S. attack. The veto was not complete, because the U.S. government still maintained that it could and would act unilaterally if need be. From a UN perspective, the only legitimate cause of action was Iraqi refusal to comply with Gulf War demands that it abandon its program to build weapons of mass destruction. Thus official U.S. and British statements about the prospect of war all emphasized Saddam Hussein's determination to obtain illicit weaponry. As a measure of its leverage, the U.S. government was able to obtain a Security Council resolution demanding that Iraq declare its weapons program (which it did a day before the deadline, on 7 December 2002, with a twelve-thousand-page report) and threatening serious consequences if inspections are blocked in any way. The resolution was so worded that it seemed to take another resolution to trigger a UN-sanctioned war. Moreover, the very bulk of the Iraqi declaration seemed calculated to stretch out the inspection and political processes.

Through early March 2003, the Bush Administration sought the second resolution. Balked, it argued in the end that war was justified by the first resolution.

To a limited degree, the United States has been fighting Iraq since 1991, but in an indecisive way which has been terribly costly. Part of that continued war is the enforcement of southern and northern no-fly zones. Of greater consequence in the Muslim world, at the end of the Gulf War the UN set up an embargo which was intended to prevent Saddam from importing replacements for the military hardware he had lost during the Gulf War. It turned out to be a double-edged sword. Saddam managed to evade the embargo to some extent, but the Iraqi economy was brutally damaged. Throughout the Arab world, the images of Iraqi children starving due to the embargo tended to raise Saddam's prestige and to lower that of the United States, the sternest advocate of the embargo. Worse, like strategic bombing, the embargo probably helped cement the target government's power.

Iraqis who suffered badly were unlikely to blame Saddam for their plight, since it was the United Nations, urged on by the United States, which was cutting off their economy. In a weak economy, moreover, Saddam could still supply some important goods to his friends. Thus the embargo actually increased his political power, since it severely disrupted any other path to even limited prosperity. As the embargo has weakened, supplies of goods have improved, and Iraqis apparently credit Saddam for the improvement. There is also evidence, incidentally, that Saddam's claims that the embargo has killed or maimed hundreds of thousands of Iraqi children—claims very useful within the Arab world—have been grossly exaggerated or are entirely spurious. It is clearly very much in our interest to end the embargo, but not in such a way that the ending seems to be a defeat for us. Defeating Saddam Hussein altogether would certainly solve the problem.

Through early 2003 the United States and Britain sought a United Nations resolution sanctioning war. They were joined as sponsors by Bulgaria and by Spain. Inspection reports were ambiguous: Iraq was not cooperating fully, but no weapons of mass destruction were found. France, Germany, Russia, and China all opposed war, arguing that inspection was working and that it should be given more time. The U.S. and British governments in particular argued that voluminous intelligence information showed that the Iraqis were systematically evading the inspectors, even that the inspection team had been compromised by the Iraqis. It seemed self-evident that in a very tight dictatorship much could escape detection. At one juncture the Iraqis literally snatched away a crucial report an inspector had found.

It was, however, evident that at least to the U.S. government the only viable objective was to remove Saddam Hussein and his regime, an objective entirely unacceptable to many governments. The logic was simple. Whatever weapons were eliminated by inspection, the end of the inspection process would give Saddam freedom to restart his programs—this time with considerably greater resources. He certainly would not have abandoned his ambitions, which had led him into two regional wars. Given weapons of mass destruction, he might either start another invasion or simply destroy the oil reserves of the other countries of the area. In either case, his motive would be to gain power over the industrial countries, like the United States, dependent on oil. The Bush Administration could have pointed out that in 1979 President Jimmy Carter had declared the Gulf a vital U.S. national interest (in connection with the Soviet invasion of Afghanistan, which many saw as a thrust towards the Gulf). This time it was Saddam, not the Soviet leader, who threatened that national interest.

The French argued that any attack on Iraq would badly destabilize the Middle East and might well cause terrorism in Europe. They had the largest Muslim population in Europe and had already suffered from the effects of the fundamentalist war in Algeria. Many Western Europeans agreed. Their position was not really too different from that which they had adopted during the Cold War: better to preserve stability than to take chances offered by the aggressive Americans. Americans who thought the Reagan Administration won the Cold War precisely by taking the offensive disagreed strongly.

The 11 September attacks were also significant in U.S. official opinion. They seemed to demonstrate that the Middle East had already become dangerously unstable. For example, a major argument against action in Iraq was that Saudi Arabia might explode as a consequence, particularly if it were coerced into helping U.S. forces. Some in or close to the U.S. government argued that the Saudis wee already de facto enemies, in that they were sponsoring Wahhabi Islam violently hostile to the West, which inspired fanatics like Osama. Others argued that Saudi Arabia was likely to explode within the next few years no matter what the United States did, so that it was foolish to predicate action on attempts to keep Saudi Arabia stable.

By mid-March 2003 it was clear that the United States could not extract a war resolution from the United Nations Security Council. For a time the U.S. position was that it could get a majority vote; if the French or the Russians vetoed the resolution, as they threatened to do, passage would still be a moral victory. Then it became clear that even nine votes could not be secured. President Bush had always considered Iraq a vital issue. He already had the earlier resolution, demanding Iraqi compliance, in hand. He simply issued a forty-eight-hour ultimatum: Saddam could leave or face the consequences. A coalition headed by U.S., British, and Australian forces struck.

That is another story for another book, but it did define the next step in the war against terrorism. It was argued that Iraq had nothing to do with Al Qaeda. That is not entirely clear, but the larger argument is that large-scale success demands that governments be deterred from using terrorism as a means of coercing the United States. Iraq certainly has been involved in that type of state-sponsored terrorism. Breaking the Iraqi government would certainly send the message the U.S. government wants to transmit:

do not support anti-American terrorists of whatever stripe, because the United States can and will strike you down. How well the message is understood depends on how quickly the war can be concluded.

What will happen after the war? Iraq is often described as an artificial state, ripe for disintegration into areas dominated by the main ethnic groups. Yet actual disintegration might have unacceptable consequences. If the Kurds provided much of the coalition force on the ground, would their price be an independent Kurdistan? Creating such a state would alienate not only the Turks but also the Iranians. The Kurds have said that they want, instead, some sort of federal democratic state. Will Shi'ites in the south demand their own state? Presumably the hope, as in Afghanistan, would be to form some kind of acceptable national government, perhaps on a federal model. Whether that government would be acceptable to Americans depends in large part on the war aim. If the aim is simply to prove that American will is implacable, as a way of precluding Arab-backed mass terror, then it may not matter who succeeds Saddam; the fact of Saddam's removal would be enough. If the object is to turn Iraq into a less aggressive state, that will require far more.

The end state includes the status of other Muslim regimes in the region. Would collaboration in the destruction of a fellow Muslim regime cause the collapse of any government even remotely allied to the United States? After each Arab defeat at the hands of the Israelis, Westward-leaning regimes collapsed. In retrospect it is remarkable that the collaboration of so many Arab regimes in the 1991 war against Iraq *did not* cause regimes to collapse.

Finally, to what extent is Saddam Hussein directly implicated in terrorism? As head of a secular state, he cannot welcome Osama bin Laden's vision of a new caliphate. On the other hand, he and bin Laden may each feel that the other can be useful on a temporary basis. When bin Laden ranted against Western troops on Saudi soil, in effect he was offering to denude Saudi Arabia of protection against an Iraqi invasion. When Saddam offers to destroy Israel or the West, bin Laden may see him opening enemy territory to invasion by Wahhabist fanatics. After the Taliban collapsed, Saddam offered refuge to some Al Qaeda fighters—who helped attack his Kurdish enemies. It is also intriguing that Saddam put his forces on alert just before 11 September, as though expecting a Western attack.[5] Overall, attempts to link Saddam directly with 11 September have all apparently failed.

In 2002–3 world terrorism was hardly the only concern of the U.S. government, and its strategy was predicated at least in part on the need to face many problems more or less simultaneously. For example, as the standoff with Saddam Hussein escalated, North Korea announced that it was restarting its program to make plutonium for atomic bombs (it also admitted that, contrary to its 1994 agreement, it had never abandoned attempts to refine uranium for the same purpose—a program U.S. intelligence had never detected). It seemed entirely possible that the North Koreans would see U.S. preoccupation with Iraq as an opportunity to seize South Korea. The United States moved heavy bombers to Guam as a deterrent, but their value was clearly limited.

There were also other commitments. At various times U.S. forces were or were not assigned to antiterrorist support duty in the Philippines. Other U.S. forces were engaged with narcoterrorists in support of the Colombian government. The United States was trying to help avert a Pakistan-India War. And U.S. forces were still engaged in Afghanistan, in support of the new government there. The situation was complicated by the break with France and Germany over Iraq. Both countries have been quite helpful in both the global war against terrorists (who, after all, often made their bases in Germany) and in the reconstruction of Afghanistan. The United States government would not lightly abandon their assistance in either place, yet it was not at all willing to accept their attempt to veto the war in Iraq—which it, but not they, saw as integral to the new antiterrorist policy.

Attacking Root Causes

After 11 September, many urged the United States to spend more time dealing with the root causes of terrorism—whatever they might be. It was suggested, for example, that the Muslim (or Arab) rage which had inspired the attacks was caused by U.S. support of Israel. Perhaps a U.S.-brokered settlement of the Israeli-Palestinian confrontation would solve the problem. Alternatively, it can be argued that terrorism throughout the Middle East is a consequence of the failure of the governments there, that the rage is really due to the absence of democracy.

In fact, 11 September was mounted by a very small number of people. Bin Laden gained his resources from Muslims animated by rage, but he also acquired them from conservative Muslims afraid that he could mobilize their populations against them. He attracted to himself the small number of Muslims not only furious but willing to die to kill their supposed enemies. Such people always exist in the requisite numbers. In many cases they happen to take up one terrorist cause or another, but basically they are nihilists, wedded to what they see as the romance of killing. That is probably the best description of Ramzi Yousef, who was responsible for the

1993 World Trade Center bombing. It might be argued that there should be some way to convince the nihilists and their leaders to focus elsewhere, but as the world's sole superpower, the United States is the natural focus for malcontents.

Moreover, it can be argued that bin Laden adopted terrorist tactics precisely because he could not build a mass movement—that Muslim rage was not powerful enough to fuel his rise. Bin Laden may use terrorism as a way of mobilizing large numbers of otherwise politically inert Muslims. His targets were already furious at the United States. They were perfectly willing to riot but not to do much more. Bin Laden's initial attacks failed to inspire enough supporters, and on 11 September he was probably trying to start a war in which they would be forced to choose sides. That did not work, at least not immediately. It may follow that whatever is needed to assuage the fury of the Muslim masses will not have much impact on terrorists, who will still retain their fantasies and their expectation that they can somehow mobilize mass support.

An argument about root causes of terrorism may be much like that about root causes of crime. Do particular social conditions breed criminals, or are there individuals likely to become criminals whatever conditions they experience? For example, does poverty breed crime, or does it determine the kind of crimes committed by those who may be inclined to become criminals in the first place? In a wealthier society, for instance, it may be that those who would be criminal anyway will gravitate to white-collar crimes, which fall outside the usual perception of criminal activity. Probably there are some who would become criminals no matter what the conditions were, and there would be others impelled by circumstances. In the case of the terrorists, if conditions create terrorists, it is very important that we attack those conditions. If most of the terrorists would be antisocial whatever conditions they encountered, then concentrating on root causes may be pointless or even counterproductive.

Two root causes of terrorism have been advanced. One is the ongoing wound of the Israeli-Palestinian conflict. Ultimately it seems unsolvable, since the Palestinians want what they cannot have, to supplant the state of Israel with their own state stretching from the Jordan to the Mediterranean. Muslim terrorists, proponents of this view target the United States as the single great barrier to that dream. The Europeans enjoy Muslim friendship by encouraging the idea that they support the Palestinian program, without incurring any potential responsibility for its failure. The trouble with this view is that so many fundamentalist supporters of terror say that the

problem would be solved if the West would only do the right thing and convert to Islam (presumably of the Wahhabi variety). Mass conversion would
supposedly solve the Israeli problem, but the demand for it makes it clear
that Israel is a very minor part of a very large grievance which is unlikely to
be removed.

An alternative U.S. view is that the root cause of terrorism is the corruption and dictatorship common in Muslim states. To contain public rage,
governments support the Palestinian fantasy. It is to their considerable advantage that it cannot be achieved, since if it ever were, they would be held
to account for their other sins. The antidotes to this root cause would
be democracy and free enterprise. Free enterprise would promote the sort
of prosperity which, in other places, has tended to damp down sectarian
violence.

This argument speaks to the basic ideology of the United States. We favor the individual over the mass, on the grounds that no government can
be legitimate if it does not protect the rights of its citizens. It follows that we
strongly favor democratic government and free enterprise economics—
and that we identify the lack of democracy and human rights as the root
cause of problems in the world. Because most governments in the world
abuse their citizens, our ideology leads us to think of them as illegitimate.
On the other hand, no country, not even the world's sole superpower, can
possibly impose its ideology by force. We therefore subscribe to diplomatic
norms of behavior, in which we limit our attempts to intervene and accept
the domestic behavior of repugnant governments as long as that behavior
does not seem to touch us directly. The terrorist crisis makes the contradiction stark, because we can argue that the security problem we face is
rooted in those domestic practices of foreign governments we most abhor.

Those who argue that democracy helps prevent war (and its cousin, terrorism) claim that politicians and, by extension, populations in a democratic state learn the art of compromise. It is not clear that this is true; national culture may also determine just how successful a democracy can be.
However, promoting democracy and good governance is probably the best
antidote to the current wave of violence in the Arab world. Democracy
might offer us little advantage at first. Surely, at least at the outset, in many
places demagogues pursuing anti-American policies would prosper.[6] However, over time elected governments might begin to behave responsibly,
and, as a result, they would be stronger than dictatorial ones, and thus
more able to make agreements they would keep.

Democratic governments may well disagree with our policies, but they are less likely to breed the sort of desperation which creates suicidal terrorists. In the past, the U.S. government has been satisfied to back dictatorships, as long as those dictatorships supported our foreign policy. The view seems to be growing that such support does us little good, particularly when the same dictatorships encourage anti-American sentiments among their populations as a way of reducing internal tensions (which otherwise would be directed against them). At least some observers have remarked that this new U.S. approach mirrors the successful U.S. policy directed against the Soviets: for years, U.S. administrations had sought detente at a governmental level without demanding internal political reform as a condition. When the Reagan administration demanded that the Soviet government relax controls as a condition for the detente it wanted, it helped destroy the Soviet threat permanently.[7] This view of the terrorist and Third World problem may be natural for an administration staffed by many of those who helped defeat the Soviet Union.

Hence the demands that the Palestinian Authority reform itself, that it use foreign aid to develop economically rather than simply as a source of bribes to keep its chief in power (and as a source of wealth for its chief, Yassir Arafat). Above all, the demand is that Arafat stop suppressing his political rivals. The Bush administration realizes that polls show that the great majority of Palestinians support the current terrorist attacks against Israel. Clearly it believes that only democracy can lead to the sort of settled life which will give Palestinians a stake in a peaceful Middle East. That may or may not be true; many students of the Middle East argue that irrationality is at the core of most of its inhabitants. However, most of those inhabitants have never tasted democratic power. Moreover, Palestine is uniquely open to U.S. leverage. The United States can withhold money from the Palestinian Authority, and it can press the Europeans to withhold some of theirs. It can also press the Israelis to make more or fewer concessions.

Elsewhere in the region the United States has far less leverage. It cannot simply demand that its allies change their politics. They may consider it enough to adopt unpopular foreign policies in order to enjoy U.S. support. Many of them probably remember how, in 1979, U.S. president Jimmy Carter contributed to the victory of Iranian fundamentalists by sending an envoy to demand that the Iranian government refrain from attacking rioters in the streets of Teheran. That forced display of weakness may, in many eyes, have been fatal to the Shah's regime.

In this view, Iraq became an interesting opportunity.[8] It was the one major Arab state in the region to which the United States owed nothing. Ultimately, the U.S. war aim in Iraq became regime change—the end of the corrupt and vicious Ba'ath dictatorship. The lack of Arab coalition partners actually made this aim much easier to demand. Moreover, Iraq is already a fairly sophisticated secular state, presumably much riper for democracy than, say, Saudi Arabia. If a democratic state could be erected, its example might affect others in the region. Of course, these were many ifs. The post-Saddam regime might have to be—temporarily, of course—autocratic, either to satisfy other U.S. allies in the region or because the post-Saddam parties might be unable to agree on anything. Iraqis furious at the effects of a decade of U.S.-sponsored embargoes might resist our imposition of a post-Saddam regime.

If a post-Saddam regime succeeded, it could have enormous repercussions. At present the only democracy in the region is Israel, and few in the Muslim world can use it as a positive example. A secular Arab democracy would be an entirely different proposition. Its example might accelerate positive change in, for example, Saudi Arabia.

Aside from hopes of attacking root causes, the rise of a friendly democratic Iraq might solve a major U.S. security problem. Saudi Arabia, the main source of oil in the region, may be inherently unstable. If an explosion comes, oil supplies may be cut off. But Iraq is a major oil producer, and in the event of a Saudi explosion, it would probably keep pumping oil. That would buy the industrialized world the time it would take for the Saudi situation to heal. Russian and Central Asian suppliers may already have solved this problem. If they have not, in the event of a Saudi disaster the United States might feel compelled to seize some of the oil fields. That in turn would guarantee a larger anti-American explosion in the Muslim world. On the other hand, this potential to solve an oil problem also guarantees that those opposing any American attack on Iraq will claim that it is about access to oil, hence about corporate greed.

A parallel idea is a "Marshall Plan" for the Middle East. Usually that is taken to mean a massive infusion of American aid, in expectations of starting up the local economy. The reference may be misleading. The original Marshall Plan was indeed a way of restarting the post–World War II European economy with large cash infusions. However, with the cash went a degree of control. Much of the emphasis was on reducing regulations and tariffs which throttled intra-European trade. For example, the American Marshall Planners actively advanced what eventually became the European Union. The Europeans accepted American advice mainly because World War II had so badly damaged their countries. No one in the Middle

East would likely accept control on a similar scale. Nor is it clear that the commercial infrastructure exists to absorb massive amounts of cash in a productive way. Many Middle Eastern (and other Third World) governments deliberately limit trade (by regulation, for example) as a means of controlling their populations. It seems unlikely that they would reverse such important policies merely in order to make those same populations wealthier and less subject to political control. Nor should it be forgotten that excessive regulation is often a way of channeling bribes to minor bureaucrats, and that this kind of patronage is often a pillar of the regime.

On the other hand, it makes excellent sense for the United States to help our friends. Pakistan in particular was badly damaged by U.S. economic sanctions imposed when she decided to build a nuclear bomb to match what the Indians already had, across the border. In Pakistan, economic success may be the single strongest factor in restraining fundamentalists who help Al Qaeda. And, although the Indians would not say as much, that same restraint might bring some semblance of peace to Kashmir, which in turn would reduce the attractiveness of Al Qaeda style terrorists there. Pakistan was extremely helpful in the fight for Afghanistan; the country deserves our help.

The War

Can the United States win the war against terrorism? In the sense used by President Bush, of limiting terrorist power by what amounts to deterrence, the answer would seem to be yes. The U.S. attack on the Taliban demonstrated that the United States is no longer a soft target. It can and will wreak terrible vengeance on any government which stages attacks on the scale of 11 September. That may go much of the way toward ensuring against further ones. For example, in July 2002 a Saudi newspaper suggested that perhaps the sort of xenophobia promoted by Wahhabi clerics had been discredited because it had killed so many good Muslims.[9] Perhaps it was time to change. Other voices in the Muslim world had already said as much, but it was striking to see any such comment in a country so dominated by fundamentalist views. The Saudi government itself was taking steps to liberalize. Too, time may well be on our side. The intelligence effort now being put into place is likely to become more and more effective over time.

There is, of course, an important caveat. Military victory in Afghanistan itself is not victory over Al Qaeda. In mid-2002 the chief of German intelligence claimed that Osama bin Laden was probably still alive in some sort of refuge on the Afghan-Pakistani border, and that many of his fighters had survived. In his view, they had melted back into their homelands, determined to keep up the fight. That may or may not be true; they may also have realized that the fight is not going particularly well. Nevertheless, it is premature to declare victory with the apparent end of organized resistance in Afghanistan.

Success in the war against terrorism is unlikely to be complete, just as there can be no final victory in the war against crime or, almost certainly, against drugs. In each case, success is defined as holding the problem below some acceptable level, and that is not a bad definition. There will always be some terrorists. They may or may not be foreigners. They cannot always be detected or deterred, just as not all crime can be prevented. However, there is a level of threat which people can tolerate. For example, no one would say that in the 1970s the United States faced a serious terrorist threat. Yet anyone living in New York or in Chicago at that time will remember bombings (and deaths) caused by Croat nationalists; one reminder of that problem is the disappearance of lockers (which held bombs) from airports and railroad stations. The goal of the war against terror is to eliminate powerful terrorist organizations, reducing the threat to the sort of moderate and incoherent one which we faced in the past. That goal we are very likely to attain.

And Osama bin Laden? Obviously it would be preferable to bring him down, if only for symbolic reasons. However, he is not so charismatic and so inherently powerful that, whatever happens to his followers, he will always be a mortal threat to us. Bin Laden's hold on those who hate us will last as long as he can successfully run operations—spectacular ones—against the United States, as long as our proclamation that he is the Number One Terrorist bears some relation to reality. If we can frustrate him for long enough, he will lose that power. Victory in the war against him is likely to lie in that frustration.

Notes

Chapter 1. The Attacks

1. Although the reported target was the White House, detailed analysis of the flight path convinced some that it was the Capitol, which is easier to identify from the air (the White House tends to blend into the surrounding buildings, whereas the Capitol stands out visually due to its location at the end of the Mall).

2. Details were given in David Bond, "Crisis at Herndon: 11 Airplanes Astray," *Aviation Week & Space Technology*, 17 December 2001. A few minutes after the second airliner hit the World Trade Center, the FAA command center at Herndon, Virginia, asked its field centers to indicate whether any other aircraft were off course. Eleven were reported, one of which soon crashed into the Pentagon. Four minutes after that crash, the FAA ordered all aircraft grounded. Some centers had already shut down. American Flight 11, from Boston, was the first to crash into the World Trade Center, at 8:46 A.M.; at 9:04 Boston shut down all departures under its control. Two minutes later the New York center stopped all departures from airports within New York, Washington, Cleveland, and Boston center control that would pass through New York airspace, and four minutes later all U.S. aircraft headed for New York were held on the ground. At 9:41, the Pentagon having been hit at 9:41, Herndon ordered all aircraft to land as soon as possible. At 10:39 all airports were ordered shut down, but as late as 11:06 there were still 1,305 aircraft in the air over the United States (compared to 4,873 at 9:06 A.M.).

3. From Dan Balz and Bob Woodward, "The First Ten Days" (first article of a series) in the 27 January 2002 *Washington Post*. The quote is from an interview with President Bush.

4. Full asbestos fireproofing ran only part of the way up the buildings. The combination of more massive structure toward the lower part of the buildings and better fireproofing might well have given firefighters a better chance of controlling the fires. That is, it really did matter just where along the full height of each building the airliner hit. This, in turn, led some to believe that the attacks had been made with full understanding of the structures of the buildings.

5. Reagan National Airport was closed for weeks, and some security experts urged that it never be permitted to reopen. Closure made travel into and out of

Washington much more difficult and had a real impact on the local economy. Flights were resumed only after new flight paths (faster, steeper, straighter, and farther from possible targets, but over more residential areas) were introduced and sky marshals were placed on all flights into and out of the airport. It took months for airline activity to reach what it had been before the attacks, and a year later all private and business aircraft were still banned from this airport.

6. Reestablishment of a 4th Brigade was announced in September 2001, as an immediate reaction to the terrorist attacks. At a strength of forty-eight hundred, this unit was far smaller than the three conventional MEBs. Even so, it was impressive that separate Marine units could so quickly be integrated together. The 4th Brigade is intended to provide concentrated defense, for example, of ports, in the event of a terrorist attack. Like other Marine units, the 4th Brigade is designed to be deployable; its commander said in November 2001 that he expected that only a third of its missions would be conducted inside the United States.

7. This mission formally ended on 16 May 2002. NATO aircraft flew 367 operational sorties (more than 4,300 flight hours) in this Operation Eagle Assist; about 800 NATO personnel (about 200 in the United States at any one time) were involved.

8. The attack made clear the split within Muslim communities, between a mainstream which condemned the attacks and a fringe group which praised them as justified. For example, in Britain the spokesman for the Muslim Council said his community was in shock. However, Sheik Abu Hamza, heading the Supporters of Shariah, based at Finsbury Park Mosque in north London, justified the attack. Finsbury Park was later described as a jihadist mosque at which Al Qaeda had successfully recruited. "UK 'Hardline' Muslims Slow to Condemn U.S. Attackers," *Daily Telegraph*, 13 September 2001.

9. Later, when the United States successfully attacked the Taliban, many voices were raised in the Muslim world condemning those who, by raising the banner of jihad, had led so many Muslims to their deaths.

10. According to a 12 September 2001 *Seattle Times* story, "Bin Laden May Have Tricked Spies: Officials," intelligence already pointed to bin Laden, who told associates that two targets had just been hit. The title of the story refers to a belief among intelligence analysts that the imminent attacks (to which increased Al Qaeda message traffic pointed) would, like earlier ones, be overseas.

11. According to the Balz and Woodward 27 January 2002 article, at the 11 September 2001 National Security Council meeting "intelligence was by now almost conclusive" that Osama bin Laden and Al Qaeda had carried out the attacks. At a National Security Council meeting the next day CIA director George Tenet pointed out that three known Al Qaeda operatives had been on the passenger manifest of one of the hijacked airliners, and that Al Qaeda was the only terrorist organization in the world capable of the required planning and coordination. Moreover, U.S. intelligence had monitored several known bin Laden operatives congratulating each other after the attacks. On 12 September President Bush wrote in his diary, "We think it's

Osama bin Laden." According to the follow-up 28 January article in this series, a report from Kandahar claimed that the attacks had been the result of a two-year effort; another said they were "the beginning of the wrath." At 9:53 A.M., shortly after the Pentagon was hit, Al Qaeda members in Afghanistan were told that the attackers were "following through with the doctor's program," presumably referring to Dr. Ayman Zawahiri, bin Laden's closest deputy.

12. Later it would be reported that the World Trade Center had been hit in 1993 in preference to Jewish neighborhoods in Brooklyn, on the declared—and grossly mistaken—theory that more Jews would be concentrated there. Apparently many in the Muslim world also believed, or said, that the 11 September operation had to have involved a vast conspiracy, for example to keep fighters grounded long enough to allow the airliners to hit their targets. The favored author was Ariel Sharon; his motive, to unleash a vast anti-Muslim war. However, many of those who pushed this theory also seem to have seen Osama bin Laden as a hero for having attacked the United States.

13. To further confuse matters, in June 2002 it was announced that unspecified scientific tests had shown that the anthrax employed in 2001 was no more than two years old, hence could not have been old ex-Army stocks kept, presumably, in dry storage for years. On the other hand, the targets chosen (the U.S. Post Office, for example, rather than Federal Express or AOL), suggested someone thinking in 1970s rather than 1990s terms.

14. Some writers on terrorism describe this man, Sheik Omar Abdel-Rahman, as a major inspiration to the fundamentalist terrorists. During the Soviet-Afghan War he was responsible for recruiting many Arabs to fight in Afghanistan. Although on a U.S. watch list, he received a visa to enter the United States from Sudan. At the time of his trial in connection with the 1993 bombing, it was suggested that the CIA had countermanded the watch order on the ground that he had been particularly helpful during the Afghan War. The sheikh received a visa in 1987 and a multiple-entry visa in 1990. This claim in turn was the basis for many charges that fundamentalist attacks on the United States amounted to "blowback" from the successful war against the Soviets in Afghanistan. According to Simon Reeve, *The New Jackals*, new ed. (Boston: Northeastern University Press, 2001), 60, the CIA feared that the fundamentalists would overthrown the Egyptian government, just as others had overthrown that of Iran. In that case they wanted contacts among the fundamentalists, and they hoped that Sheikh Omar would be useful.

15. The second plot was exposed by an FBI informant reactivated after the twin towers bombing in 1993. He penetrated the group, led by a Sudanese, Siddig Ibrahim Siddig Ali, and employing congregants of Sheikh Omar's mosque, which was to have carried out the attack. Targets included the Statue of Liberty, the United Nations Building (the Sudanese mission was to have placed explosives in the basement), the main federal building, and the diamond district. The plotters were caught mixing their explosives. Reeve, *New Jackals*, 61–62.

16. According to Lawrence Wright, "The Counter-Terrorist" in the 14 January 2002 *New Yorker*, a profile of FBI agent John O'Neill (who was killed in the World Trade Center attack), strikes on as many as three other embassies were averted thanks to better intelligence and good fortune. Wright also reports, however, that a member of Al Qaeda walked into the Nairobi embassy a year before the attacks, told the CIA about the plot—and was dismissed as unreliable.

17. As details of the strike plan emerged, they became more and more embarrassing. Four of the five members of the Joint Chiefs of Staff, as well as FBI director Louis Freeh, were excluded from decision making (the service chiefs were told about the attacks only the day before they were carried out). Attorney General Janet Reno apparently pleaded for the raids to be delayed because the FBI had not yet assembled enough evidence to prove that Al Qaeda had attacked the embassies. Even in October 1998 it was reported that the CIA Directorate of Science and Technology was by no means satisfied that the pharmaceutical plant was producing precursors for nerve gas. When the four service chiefs were told about the operation, they managed to eliminate a planned attack on a storage facility in Khartoum, the contents of which were entirely unknown. They also pointed out that the Tomahawks were unlikely to have much impact against caves and bunkers in Afghanistan. To make matters worse, two Pakistani training camps in Afghanistan were hit, killing five ISI officers and twenty trainees. The attack badly damaged a valuable cooperative relationship with Pakistani intelligence. The Pakistanis were particularly furious that they were told about the attacks only well after they were under way, solely to keep them from worrying that the missiles were Indian weapons attacking them. These points are made in a preliminary account; see Seymour M. Hersh, "The Missiles of August," *New Yorker*, 12 October 1998. Two years later the picture was far worse. In May 2000 the Clinton administration in effect admitted that the pharmaceutical plant had not been an appropriate target when it refused to answer a lawsuit and thus released the frozen assets of the plant's owner. Later it was reported that two targets were hit simply because President Clinton wanted to retaliate for two embassy attacks. It also became clear that bin Laden and his advisors were about a hundred miles from the camps which were hit, and that the meeting to which Clinton referred had occurred a month earlier in Jalalabad—which was not hit. See Mary Anne Weaver, "The Real bin Laden," *New Yorker*, 24 January 2000. According to Peter L. Bergen, *Holy War, Inc.* (New York: Free Press, 2001), 121, Mohammed Odeh, an Al Qaeda defector, told an FBI agent that the organization had evacuated all its Afghan camps the day before the embassy bombings. For the chemical plant, see also Bergen, *Holy War*, 123–25.

18. The alternative plan is described in Bob Woodward and Thomas E. Ricks, "U.S. Was Foiled Multiple Times in Efforts to Capture Bin Laden or Have Him Killed," *Washington Post*, 3 October 2001. Options reportedly offered to President Clinton included a large missile and bomber raid on bin Laden camps, a clandestine night helicopter assault, and a massive bombing raid against Kandahar, the Taliban center

(on the ground that the Taliban were considered bin Laden's main backers). Concerns at the time were that intelligence placing bin Laden at the conference at the terrorist camp was inconclusive; that innocent people would be killed in Kandahar, which had suffered badly at Soviet hands (excessive loss of life would, it was thought, cost the United States the moral high ground); that a long-range helicopter attack might fail (as in the 1980 Iran hostage rescue fiasco); and that necessary air and staging rights would not be forthcoming. One might observe that, to the extent that Al Qaeda and not merely bin Laden was the problem, merely destroying its operatives and seizing its documents might have justified the Special Forces attack. The intelligence that bin Laden would be attending the Afghan meeting arrived in Washington two weeks after the destruction of the embassies in Africa. There was some suspicion among Clinton administration officials that bin Laden escaped the missile strike because he had been warned. The Pakistan government was warned about the attack, but only at the moment of launch, and then largely to avoid the possibility that upon detecting the missiles, they would feel under attack by India. In any case, that cannot have been more than about an hour before the weapons struck, and bin Laden apparently left the target area between two and twelve hours before the attack. The source may have been a State Department public warning of an imminent "very serious threat" to Americans in Pakistan (due to expected anti-American rage after the attack), issued four days before the attack. There was also suspicion that Pakistani intelligence detected preparations for the attack, and warned bin Laden. None of the warning theories has much evidence behind it.

19. See Joe Klein, "Department of National Security: Closework," *New Yorker,* 1 October 2001. According to Klein, both Treasury Secretary Robert Rubin and Treasury Secretary Lawrence Summers were strongly opposed. Some on the National Security Council staff argued that bin Laden probably had "sleepers" in the U.S. financial system who would unleash their own computer attacks in the event bin Laden's assets were frozen or destroyed. National Security Advisor Samuel Berger apparently pushed strongly for the computer attack.

20. According to Karen DeYoung and Douglas Farah, "Infighting Slows Hunt for Hidden Al Qaeda Assets: Funds Put in Untraceable Commodities," *Washington Post,* 18 June 2002, $254 million in Al Qaeda assets was frozen in 1998. However, this success was not mentioned in the wake of 11 September, when the call for the Treasury to seize bin Laden money was reported.

21. See, for example, Alan Cullison and Andrew Higgins, "Strained Alliance: Inside al Qaeda's Afghan Turmoil," *Wall Street Journal,* 2 August 2002. They quote a London Islamist, Hani al-Sebai: before the U.S. strike "there was no Al Qaeda."

22. See, for example, Mark Bowden, "U.S. Had Chances to Kill Bin Laden, Officials Say," *Philadelphia Inquirer,* 16 September 2001. The article claims that intelligence officials and Special Forces personnel said that for years the United States had intermittent intelligence as to bin Laden's whereabouts, to accuracies, at times, of a few feet. According to this and similar articles, Special Forces troops and CIA per-

sonnel actually conducted reconnaissance in Afghanistan on occasion, but they were always barred from attacking bin Laden, for fear of Arab reactions and also for fear of U.S. casualties. To·Clinton administration denials that any chance to kill bin Laden had been missed, the rejoinder was that they had deliberately set requirements so stringently that nothing could be done. Others blamed a culture of risk aversion at midlevel in the military—which it could be said the Clinton administration had fostered. Bowden reported that through the 1990s the Army's Delta Force had planned and trained to conduct missions in Afghanistan, even though the nearest staging place was a thousand miles away. Supposedly that referred to the same plans revealed later in connection with the U.S. 1998 attacks. Bowden reported the 1998 presidential "finding" authorizing plans to deal with bin Laden. For a similar report, describing the plan to use sixty Pakistanis of the Pakistani intelligence agency (presumably ISI) to kill bin Laden, see Woodward and Ricks, "U.S. Was Foiled Multiple Times." According to Woodward and Hicks, this latter operation was arranged by then Prime Minister Nawaz Sharif, in turn for an agreement to lift U.S. military sanctions and to provide economic aid. The plan was set up some time in 1999, and was running by October of that year, but it ended when Sharif was overthrown in the 12 October coup which brought current president Pervez Musharraf to power.

23. According to Bob Woodward and Dan Balz, "Bush and His Advisers Set Objectives, but Struggled with How to Achieve Them," in the 28 January 2002 *Washington Post,* the CIA's covert relationships in Afghanistan had been authorized in 1998, and the agency was giving the Northern Alliance several million dollars each year.

24. Bergen, *Holy War,* 197. The Indians arrested the two would-be bombers in New Dehli in July 2001; they in turn said they were acting for Abdul Rahman al-Safani, who turned out to be Mohammed Omar al-Hazari, leader of the *Cole* operation. Planning for the Indian attack had begun in 1999.

25. It is, then, interesting that it was considered newsworthy when President Bush was presented with intelligence showing that, having given them $100 million, bin Laden in effect owned the Taliban. The figure represented estimated cash and military assistance over the previous five years. Having made this estimate, the CIA concluded that bin Laden "owned and operated" the Taliban. The contribution made by his Arab troops, acting as a Praetorian Guard, must have been even greater. See Bob Woodward, "Bin Laden Said to 'Own' the Taliban, Bush Is Told He Gave Regime $100 Million," *Washington Post,* 11 October 2001.

26. This argument is developed by Cullison and Higgins in "Strained Alliance," which is based at least partly on documents found in a laptop computer the *Wall Street Journal* acquired in Kabul after the fall of the Taliban. Some were apparently letters home from various Afghan Arabs, complaining bitterly about primitive conditions (as in "This place is worse than a tomb") in Afghanistan. The article also quotes Mullah Omar as being furious when bin Laden held a showy and entirely unauthorized press conference soon after coming to Afghanistan; this particular com-

plaint also appeared in contemporary news media. The article quotes former Taliban intelligence chief Mullah Mohammed Khaksar (now a supporter of the Karzai government) to the effect that Mullah Omar was on the point of ejecting bin Laden in the summer of 1998, just before the missile strike. Khaksar claimed that moderates among the Taliban favored an opening to the world over support of continued world revolution.

27. The two alternative routes would have been through Russia or through Iran (to Bandar Abbas). The Russian route would have passed through the mountainous Caucasus and through Chechnya, which was at war. The Iranian route was blocked by the U.S. embargo. That left a route through Afghanistan and Pakistan, in which several U.S. companies were interested. All of these routes were blocked as long as Afghanistan lacked a stable government, as it did during the post-Soviet civil war. Companies and governments interested in building the pipelines naturally welcomed any force for stability, hence initially backed the Taliban. The origin of the first series of such attempts seems to have been a 15 March 1995 agreement between the governments of Turkmenistan and Pakistan for a pipeline crossing Afghanistan, a venture soon involving the U.S. oil company Unocal and the Saudi company Delta Oil. The project collapsed in 1997, when it became clear that the civil war was still very much alive. See Richard Mackenzie, "The United States and the Taliban," in *Fundamentalism Reborn? Afghanistan and the Taliban*, ed. William Maley (London: Hurst, 2001). He points out that the main attraction of the Afghan route for the pipeline was to isolate Iran—an irony, since Taliban victories had led to greater rather than lesser Iranian support for anti-Taliban forces, hence involvement in Afghan affairs.

28. According to *Foreign Report*, 28 March 2002, at that time Russia was producing 7.28 million barrels per day, compared to Saudi Arabia's 7.19, and Russian producers were adding capacity to match the Saudi maximum of 10 million barrels per day.

29. Michael Elliott, "They Had a Plan," *Time Magazine*, 12 August 2002, describes the concepts handed over to the incoming Bush administration by the departing Clinton administration. The briefing was given by Richard Clarke, who had headed the interagency Counter-Terror Group. It seems not to have been very detailed (slide 14 of the brief reportedly said simply "Response to Al Qaeda: Roll Back") and it repeated the steps the Clinton administration had taken. For example, calling for the breakup of Al Qaeda cells meant nothing without explaining how those cells were to be uncovered. Similarly, it was pointless to talk about killing bin Laden when resources sufficient to find him were never made available. Clarke did press for much-increased assistance to those fighting the Taliban, in hopes that Afghan Arabs would be forced to fight (and die) for the cause rather than allowed simply to leave their Afghan training camps in peace to spread their war elsewhere. Clarke's proposals percolated through the incoming administration. According to Elliott, it was President Bush himself who demanded an integrated plan of attack against Al Qaeda, af-

ter a briefing on the hunt for Osama's deputy, Abu Zubayda. It was in place by 4 September, before the terrorist strikes. The Bush administration had approved a plan not merely to roll Al Qaeda back, but to destroy it. Probably the best interpretation of the Clarke story is that Clarke, who was a very strong advocate of antiterrorist measures, hoped that the incoming administration would be more willing to act than its predecessor. The Clinton administration had talked about action, but it had never been willing to follow through. For example, Elliott claims that throughout the year 2000 the Clinton administration kept two attack submarines on station in the Arabian Sea specifically to fire Tomahawks in the event bin Laden's whereabouts were conclusively established—but that was never done. He also reports that the Clinton administration quashed a Delta Force plan to seize bin Laden after the *Cole* incident.

30. In November 2001 the *Observer* of London reported that according to sources in Peshawar, Pakistan, CIA operatives were trying "to exploit tribal and political differences between various Taliban commanders in the north-eastern province of Kunar, the eastern province of Paktia and among the Murzai tribe around Kandahar" but that they were hampered by a shortage of money. Of course, it is also possible that such rumors resulted from stings the Taliban themselves were known to have been running in hopes of rooting out potential rebels. CIA operations to destabilize Taliban rule would be inconsistent with a more general U.S. government perception that the problem was Osama, not his Taliban hosts.

31. Several left-wing sources, such as the British *Guardian* newspaper ("Threat of U.S. Air Strikes Passed to Taliban Weeks before NY Attack," 22 September 2001), claimed that at an unsuccessful Berlin meeting in July 2001 a U.S. representative told a Taliban representative, "Either you accept our offer of a carpet of gold or we bury you under a carpet of bombs." The quoted source was former Pakistani foreign minister Naiz Naik. However, U.S. delegate Tom Simons recalled only that he had told the Pakistanis that there might be retaliation for the *Cole* attack; another American recalled that the U.S. government was so disgusted with the Taliban that it was contemplating military action. However, the accounts of the formulation of the Afghan War plan seem to demonstrate that no such plan had been worked out in any detail. American delegates did point out that Afghanistan badly needed economic revival. Whatever was said at the Berlin meeting may have led to a minor war scare in Islamabad. Naik's overstatement may have been intended to pressure the Taliban to eject bin Laden so as to avoid destruction.

32. Probably because his sources were sensitive, President Bush did not reveal him. Apologists for bin Laden, mainly in the Middle East, made much of this hesitancy. By late September British prime minister Tony Blair was announcing that he had seen the evidence, and that he was fully convinced (see, e.g., "Blair Reveals 'Powerful Evidence' Against Bin Laden," *Independent*, 30 September 2001). Blair made his announcement in conjunction with the annual Labour Party conference. Eventually a fully incriminating videotape was captured in Jalalabad, Afghanistan. It

apparently captured a private dinner meeting; unlike other bin Laden tapes, it was not intended for distribution. In the tape, bin Laden expressed surprise and satisfaction that the destruction of the World Trade Center towers had been greater than he had expected. Proof of bin Laden's detailed knowledge of the plot was that, when he received word of the attack on the first tower, he said that more was coming—which he could not have known otherwise. Apparently bin Laden expected that the towers would collapse only down to the level at which the airliners struck. Prime Minister Blair had already quoted a 20 October bin Laden video in which, asked about the 11 September attacks, he replied, "It is what we instigated, for a while, in self-defense. And it was revenge for our people killed in Palestine and Iraq." On 4 October Blair had said that a senior Al Qaeda official, not otherwise identified, had admitted responsibility for the attacks, and in November the British said that another Al Qaeda officer, also unidentified, had admitted training some of the hijackers. Bin Laden himself had publicly denied any role in the attacks, claiming that his oath of allegiance to Mullah Omar precluded staging any such attacks from Afghanistan. See Walter Pincus and Karen DeYoung, "U.S.: New Tape Points to Bin Laden, Words Suggest Sept. 11 Planning Role," *Washington Post*, 9 December 2001.

33. The situation was particularly tense because a plot to crash a similar light plane to disrupt the G8 summit the previous year had been thwarted.

Chapter 2. Warning and Decision

1. See, for example, Bill Gertz, "For Years, Signs Suggested 'That Something Was Up,'" *Washington Times*, 17 May 2002.

2. Attribution from Woodward and Balz, "Bush and His Advisors."

3. When the two messages were leaked during the investigation of the failure to predict the 11 September attacks, Vice President Dick Cheney excoriated news organizations for having printed them. Newspapers replied that there had already been reports of vague warnings; surely the administration's real fear was that it would be taken to task for negligence. Cheney, however, may well have had a point. Presumably there were numerous messages of this kind, but repeating particular ones might indicate which communications channels, perhaps still in use, had been identified and intercepted.

4. In her testimony before the congressional committee investigating the 11 September surprise, Colleen Rowley described a "climate of fear" of failure within the FBI headquarters which made it too conservative, hence which left the bureau ill-equipped to handle new kinds of threats.

5. After Williams's memo was approved by the Phoenix office, he made three copies: one went to the FBI's Radical Fundamentalist Unit (RFU), one to its Osama bin Laden unit, and one to the New York office, the one most concerned with terrorism. It was marked routine rather than urgent, because it did not refer to any immediate crime. The RFU lacked the manpower to examine the approximately two hundred thousand U.S. flight students. It could not restrict the search to Arabs because

internal FBI guidelines prohibited any kind of ethnic profiling. Williams was aware of the problem, and suggested that the State Department be asked about immigrants who had received visas to learn to fly. In mid-August the idea was rejected and the file closed. Apparently the memo was shown to both FBI director Robert S. Mueller III and Attorney General John Ashcroft, his superior, soon after 11 September, but not to the White House, which was inquiring into security problems. See, for example, Judith Miller and Don van Natta Jr., "Ashcroft Kept President in Dark on Post–Sept 11 FBI Memo," *New York Times*, 22 May 2002, and Judith Miller and Don van Natta Jr., "Bush Aides Asked FBI About Unreported Threats," *New York Times*, 24 May 2002. According to a 26 May 2002 *London Sunday Telegraph* account, "FBI Bureaucracy Stifled Agent's Terror Alert," had they seen the Williams memo, Minnesota FBI agents would have been able to obtain a search warrant for Zacarias Moussaoui's computer, and that in turn would have given details of the aircraft used in the 11 September attacks, if not details of what was planned.

6. Moussaoui had paid eight thousand dollars to enroll in the Pan Am International Flying Academy in Eagan, Minnesota. Investigators at the time were limited by FBI rules. Moussaoui's notebook and correspondence link him to the key Malaysia meeting early in 2000.

7. The French provided an interview with a family which blamed Moussaoui for inciting their son to fight (and die) in Chechnya. To Rowley, such information proved Moussaoui's association with radical groups connected to Osama bin Laden. The FBI headquarters responded that information about Chechnya had no American relevance, hence did not justify seeking a Foreign Intelligence Surveillance Authorization (FISA) warrant, which would have given the FBI the contents of Moussaoui's computer. No such warrant was sought, and in the end Moussaoui's belongings were searched under a conventional criminal warrant. Evidence obtained at that time reportedly included correspondence identifying Moussaoui as a "marketing consultant" for a Malaysian computer firm run by Yazid Sufaat, who provided the condominium in Kuala Lumpur used for the January 2000 Al Qaeda meeting. The consultancy job, which paid twenty-five hundred dollars per month, was probably a typical no-show position used to finance Al Qaeda agents. Moussaoui also had telephone numbers in Germany for Ramzi Binalshibh, who allegedly helped finance the plot, flight deck videos (like those bought by Mohammed Atta and Nawaf Alhazmi, two 11 September pilots), and a disk containing information about crop-dusters. Binalshibh apparently wired fourteen thousand dollars to Moussaoui. See "Hill Probers Upgrade Evidence Gathered from Moussaoui" in the *Washington Post* for 6 June 2002. According to the article, Sufaat in turn was asked to host the conference (and later to accommodate Moussaoui) by an Indonesian, Riduan Isamuddin, described as the Al Qaeda chief for Southeast Asia.

8. Rowley wrote that "when, in a desperate 11th-hour measure to bypass the FBI HQ roadblock, the Minneapolis division undertook to directly notify the CIA's counter-terrorist center, FBI HQ personnel chastised the Minneapolis agents for

making the direct notification without their approval." Later it was said that agents in Minneapolis joked that the FBI headquarters had been infiltrated by bin Laden.

9. It is not clear whether these attacks were disrupted due to good intelligence or to good luck. An Algerian, Ahmed Ressam, bolted from his car when it was stopped by a border guard at Port Angeles, Washington, on 14 December 1999. It is not clear whether the border guard had been tipped off by still-classified intelligence. What is clear is that Ressam was planning to attack Los Angeles International Airport. The FBI followed up on telephone numbers Ressam had been carrying, which led them to another Algerian, Abdel Ghani Meskini, who had gone to Seattle to meet Ressam. As a result of this intelligence, Seattle canceled its planned millennium celebration for fear of terrorist attack. Meskini was arrested; ultimately he and Ressam decided to cooperate with the FBI. The main implication was that there were already Al Qaeda cells active in the United States. According to Wright, "Counter-Terrorist," the FBI leadership did not accept this view and, prior to 11 September, did not shift resources to the job of rooting out the cells. The millennium attacks in the United States were reportedly intended to coincide roughly with some in Jordan; the day after Ressam was arrested the Jordanians arrested thirteen Al Qaeda members planning to blow up tourist sites in their country and the Radisson Hotel. Later it emerged that Al Qaeda had hoped to bomb a U.S. warship, probably the destroyer *The Sullivans,* in Aden at the same time that the Jordanian sites were to have been attacked. The Aden plot failed when the boat involved sank due to the weight of its explosive cargo.

10. The visa applications of the hijackers proved embarrassing; apparently almost all of them should have been rejected because elementary questions, such as where the applicants planned to stay in the United States, were not filled out even approximately correctly. Those criticizing the INS for such lapses appear not to have checked other Saudi applications to see whether such lapses were the norm.

11. Dr. Laurie Mylroie is the main public proponent of the theory that Iraq was responsible for the 1993 bombing (as part of a war of revenge after the 1991 humiliation). She in turn bases her argument on a close examination of the voluminous evidence revealed in the trial of the bombers, which can be read to suggest that the architect of the plot, Ramzi Yousef, was an Iraqi intelligence agent. Mylroie's decisive evidence was the false identity Yousef used to escape the United States immediately after the bombing, a passport in the name of Abdul Basit Karim, who was actually a Kuwaiti official. When the Iraqis invaded Kuwait, they tampered with Karim's file, to the extent of inserting Yousef's fingerprints. People who knew Basit made it clear that he was not Yousef; the two men were physically quite different. Mylroie finds it most unlikely that Iraqi intelligence would have gone to such a length to create a false identity for anyone who was not an important agent. Too, one of Yousef's conspirators, Abdul Rahman Yasin, fled to refuge in Iraq. The explosion, moreover, came on the second anniversary of the Gulf War cease-fire, a date of distinct Iraqi humiliation. For an extensive account of Yousef's exploits, including attempted assassina-

tions of Benazir Bhutto, see Reeve, *New Jackals*. He points out that, having been brought up in Baluchistan, on the Pakistan-Iran border, Yousef formed close ties to the MKO, an anti-Iranian terrorist group run by the Iraqis (p. 247). In this account, while working in an Al Qaeda camp in 1992, Yousef met a senior MKO officer, who told him to go to the United States to prepare a spectacular attack. Some of this information came from Pakistani officers investigating Yousef. Reeve's account suggests that Ramzi Yousef was in effect a freelance terrorist, always on the lookout for those who would sponsor his operations. He apparently particularly sought Osama bin Laden's favor, and Reeve claims that Al Qaeda sent him to the Philippines specifically to work with the Abu Sayyaf group. In the case of the 1993 bombing, Yousef's "foot soldiers" were members of a mosque led by Sheikh Omar Abdel-Rahman, an Egyptian well connected in the world of Islamic fundamentalism, hence likely to be operating at the behest of Osama bin Laden. One interpretation of the Iraqi connection would be that the Iraqis saw Ramzi Yousef as an unguided missile likely to attack American targets, much as the Germans saw Lenin as a weapon to use against the Russians in 1917. In neither case would the user expect complete control.

12. See Walter Pincus, "Mueller Outlines Origin, Funding of Sept. 11 Plot," *Washington Post*, 6 June 2002.

13. Don van Natta Jr. and Kate Zernike, "Hijackers' Meticulous Strategy of Brains, Muscle and Practice," in the 4 November 2001 *New York Times*. See also Judith Miller and Dan van Natta Jr., "In Years of Plots and Clues, Scope of Qaeda Eluded U.S.," in the 9 June 2002 *New York Times*.

14. Moussaoui was initially charged as the "twentieth hijacker." However, by mid-2002 the case against him reportedly looked weak, and some within the government thought that he had been part of another parallel conspiracy, to hijack and crash other aircraft into other targets. That would fit with the anecdotal evidence of Arabic-looking passengers fleeing after aircraft were grounded on 11 September. As of early 2003, none of those passengers had, apparently, been caught.

15. There are several possible explanations. One would be that the supply of would-be martyrs is limited. Some, such as the Saudi government, have suggested that Al Qaeda deliberately used numerous Saudi nationals in hopes of poisoning the relationship between Saudi Arabia and the United States, thus weakening the Saudi government. It is also possible that the "soldiers" were regarded as too weak to be trusted with full knowledge of the operation, that they might have boasted of their coming martyrdom. An Al Qaeda manual warns against disclosing an operation completely to those involved for fear of leaks. Compartmentalization would also protect the operation against the capture of lower-level personnel. Presumably higher-level men, such as the pilots, were trusted not to talk.

Chapter 3. The Sword of the Dispossessed

1. For a summary, see Tariq Ali, *The Clash of Fundamentalisms: Crusades, Jihads, and Modernity* (London: Verso, 2002), 49–59. In the first half of the ninth cen-

tury three successive caliphs supported the view that the Koran was a human creation rather than a revealed text, and actually ordered orthodox theologians flogged. "The imams who teach by rote in hole-in-the-wall mosque schools in the cities of Western Europe and North America would probably find it too difficult even to acknowledge the existence" of the officially sanctioned sect involved.

2. The German attempt is described in Peter Hopkirk, *On Secret Service East of Constantinople: The Plot to Bring Down the British Empire* (London: Murray, 1994).

3. In one of his manifestoes, bin Laden referred explicitly to the Turkish defeat as a major recent Muslim humiliation, presumably the beginning of the disasters he swore to reverse. Apparently the reference is a familiar one throughout the Muslim world, though to Westerners it may seem arcane.

4. For a summary of modern Middle Eastern conspiracy theories, see Daniel Pipes, *The Hidden Hand: Middle East Fears of Conspiracy* (New York: St. Martin's Griffin, 1998). Such theories, as well as rumors which cause sudden panics and riots, spread in part because so many Middle Eastern news outlets are heavily censored. The independent Al-Jazeera television station may ultimately be an effective antidote.

5. The Islamist-fundamentalist distinction is clearly drawn by a French scholar, Olivier Roy, author of *The Failure of Political Islam* (London: I. B. Tauris, 1994). According to Roy, supporters of a more moderate or more traditional form of Islam often call fundamentalism Wahhabi, but its own supporters prefer the term Salafi to indicate their desire to return to the most primitive form of Islam, before the religion was complicated by various interpretations. In effect they seek the ideal society as envisaged by Mohammed and his companions. Anything outside the Koran itself, including art and culture and national tradition, is rejected. Salafis are also violently opposed to other religions (including Shi'ist Islam) and consider it justified to kill their advocates as part of a wider war to impose Islam on the world. Because the Salafi do not advocate a return to some earlier state but "a reappropriation of society and modern technology based on politics," Roy calls them neofundamentalists. One hallmark of non-Salafi Islamists has been their willingness to tolerate non-Muslims, including Christians, whereas the Salafi do not. For example, churches are prohibited in Wahhabi Saudi Arabia, but not in Islamist Iran. Similarly, the Salafi reject all religious compromise, and, according to Roy, are obsessed with the distinction between the true religion and impiety (*kufr*) within the Muslim community. This obsession reduces Islam to more and more precise rules, such as those imposed by the Taliban in Afghanistan. It requires large numbers of self-appointed preachers who spend most of their time issuing fatwas on the lawfulness of everyday acts. In Roy's view, the Salafi approach has been particularly effective because it turns a problem, cultural alienation, into a justification to reestablish universal Islam (which is universal because it is stripped of all local customs and traditions). Roy also argues that fundamentalism is attractive because individuals can claim religious authority without formal education. Roy points out that Salafism has arisen before, for example

among the Berbers of North Africa in the eleventh and twelfth centuries. Other historians have suggested that the destruction of the rich Islamic kingdom of Andalusia in southern Spain can be blamed directly on the attacks by Berbers who rejected its culture and its toleration of non-Muslims. Ali, *Clash of Fundamentalisms,* 37–38, points out the parallel with the current Wahhabis. Finally, Roy draws a parallel between Salafi fundamentalism and born-again Christianity. Others have drawn parallels with early Protestants, who demanded that the Catholic Church discard its historical structure and return to the structure of primitive Christianity.

6. Algeria exploded in rioting in 1988, apparently due indirectly to drastic reductions in government aid to the poor. The direct cause is unknown, but the poor in Algeria were ripe for revolt. The Algerian clergy initially tried to stop the rioting. Over time, younger and more radical clerics became involved, and they were politicized. The Islamists or fundamentalists formed a political party. The ruling socialist party regarded it as a dangerous rival, and in 1992 it canceled elections in which the fundamentalists were expected to make a good showing. The civil war which then erupted is still killing thousands of people each year.

7. Ali, *Clash of Fundamentalisms,* 72, likens the Wahhabis to Trotskyites, who revered Lenin but rejected developments after his death, and who claimed they were returning to the original Communist faith. The founder of the sect, Mohammed Ibn Abdul Wahhab, was the son of a cleric who preached reversion to pristine (eighth-century) values. Wahhab opposed worshiping Mohammed and condemned Muslims who prayed at the graves of holy men. Such puritanism was not new in Islam, but Wahhab began to practice the sort of literal Koranic punishments he advocated, and he was expelled by the local Ottoman potentate as a potential rebel. He began to preach against what he saw as the laxity of the Ottomans, and he was sheltered by a bandit-sultan, Mohammed Ibn Saud. Disgust with existing Muslim practice inspired Wahhab to preach permanent jihad, which comported with Saud's ambitions. Saud's forces managed to conquer central Arabia, including the holy cities of Mecca and Medina, before the Ottomans routed them. This defeat in turn was reversed, with considerable British help, by the Arab revolt against the Turks during World War I. Although the Wahhabi idea was not related to any particular humiliation, the defeat of the Wahhabis was due to the rise of a more or less independent ruler of Egypt, Mohammed Ali, after the first major Ottoman humiliation, the conquest of Egypt by the French in 1798. It took the British, not the Ottomans who nominally controlled Egypt, to expel them, and Mohammed Ali gained his position through a coup fomented in part by mullahs who had collaborated with the French. Part of the story was popular support for French tax policy, which was far less extortionate than the Ottoman.

8. For the Saudi story, see Eric Rouleau, "Trouble in the Kingdom," *Foreign Affairs,* July/August 2002. Qutb himself was executed by the Egyptian government in 1966. While imprisoned from 1954 to 1964 for the attempt to kill Nasser, he wrote *Signposts on the Road,* the book describing the fundamentalist/jihadist ideology. In

Qutb's view, by the 1950s Islamic society in places like Egypt had degenerated into a state of decadence comparable with that of the pre-Islamic world; it had to be cleansed (returned to fundamental values). Qutb visited the United States in 1949 as a student and was repelled by what he saw as a decadent society which would only tempt Muslims away from their true faith. Thus the West, too, had to be attacked as a way of defending Islam. According to Roy, *Failure of Political Islam,* the Saudi Wahhabis avoided disseminating their creed as such, but instead infiltrated other schools, such as the madrassahs of Pakistan. They emphasized that school of Islam, the Hanbal, which interpreted the Koran most literally, and they also pressed for a much shorter curriculum (three to five rather than fifteen years), which would eliminate the usual emphasis on interpretation. This movement competes with traditional centers such as Al-Azhar University in Cairo, and Saudi financing makes conditions of study more attractive in Saudi Arabia than in Egypt.

9. For the story of the fatwa as part of an ongoing Iranian-Saudi struggle, see Julian Barnes, "Five Years of the Fatwa," in his *Letters from London, 1990–1995* (London: Picador, 1995). This chapter originally appeared as a "Letter from London" in the *New Yorker.*

10. As quoted in Bergen, *Holy War,* 53. In Afghanistan, Azzam reportedly often associated with the blind Egyptian cleric, Sheikh Omar Abdel-Rahman, who would later be credited with having inspired the plotters who bombed the World Trade Center in 1993. Azzam listed the countries which, in his view, had to be conquered: Palestine, Bokhara (ex–Soviet Central Asia, including Tajikistan and Uzbekistan), Lebanon, Chad, Eritrea, Somalia, the Philippines, Burma, Southern Yemen, Tashkent (ex–Soviet Central Asia), and Andalusia, in that order. Azzam died in a 24 November 1989 mosque bombing in Peshawar. Some writers have speculated that Osama was responsible, that he regarded the charismatic Azzam as an unacceptable rival in the organization he was creating.

11. Bergen, *Holy War,* 56–57. Abu Ubaidah, Al Qaeda's ranking military commander until his death in 1996, fought alongside Osama at Jaji. Bergen dates Osama's meeting with al-Zawahiri to 1987 rather than 1985.

12. According to a biographical sketch published in the 12 November 2001 issue of *Time,* al-Zawahiri provided Osama with his political outlook; before meeting him, Osama was simply a rich young man who wanted to help the Afghans. Ayman al-Zawahiri met Osama when he was serving as a doctor, treating Afghan resistance troops in a hospital in Saudi Arabia. At that time he was also head of Al Jihad, an Egyptian fundamentalist group trying to overthrow the Egyptian government. In that capacity, he had probably helped plan the assassination of Egyptian president Anwar Sadat. Arrested as part of that plot, he had been convicted only on a lesser charge because evidence was lacking; he was released in 1984. Reportedly al-Zawahiri is now chief ideologue of Takfir wal Hijra (Anathema and Exile), which attacks Muslims it regards as unclean; for example, in December 2000 a Takfir adherent killed twenty worshipers at a Khartoum mosque. Al-Zawahiri's background is

the classic revolutionary one of power and privilege: he comes from a wealthy Cairo suburb, and his grandfather was sheikh of the principal Islamic university in Egypt, Al Ahzar. The other grandfather was president of Cairo University, and his father was dean of the pharmacy school. An uncle was first secretary general of the Arab League. According to the article, al-Zawahiri turned to fundamentalism in the wake of the 1967 Arab-Israeli War, which demonstrated (to him and to others) that the secular approach had failed. By 1979, when Egypt signed the Camp David peace accord with Israel (and thus, in his view, cemented the 1967 humiliation), he had joined Al Jihad, which pressed for a fundamentalist government throughout the Arab world. Al-Zawahiri made several attempts to kill members of the current Mubarak government of Egypt, all of which failed, and it has been suggested that these failures led him to focus on the United States. Another reading would be that after direct attacks against an Arab government failed, al-Zawahiri decided that a spectacular attack against the United States would ignite a war in which Muslims throughout the Arab world would find themselves forced to take sides. One consequence would be popular risings against pro-Western Arab governments. The numerous street demonstrations which greeted the beginning of the bombings could be seen as the initial stage of such a rising, which proved abortive.

13. According to Bergen, *Holy War,* 59, Al Qaeda was originally formed to protect Afghan Arab fighters from their home governments, who were aware of those visiting Osama under the umbrella of the MaK organization, and who feared that they would cause trouble when they returned home. It also provided documentation for the families of those who had fought in Afghanistan. Such services bound the Afghan Arabs personally to Osama. By 1989, according to Jamal al-Fadl, a member turned U.S. informant, Al Qaeda was definitely intended to fight holy wars beyond Afghanistan.

14. According to the 18 November 2001 issue of *Al-Sharq al-Awsat,* a Saudi-owned London newspaper, reporting a telephone interview with Muntasir al-Zayyat, the defense counsel for fundamentalist groups in Egypt. Sayf al-Adl (Muhammad Ibrahim al-Makkawi), a veteran of Egyptian Al Jihad, was already accused of involvement in both the African embassy bombings and in the 11 September attacks on the United States.

15. This point is made by Bergen, *Holy War,* 199. Bergen emphasizes Egypt's traditional role as the center of Sunni Muslim thought, which made Qutb's ideas particularly powerful.

16. Bergen, *Holy War,* 60–61. He quotes Bhutto, now in exile, to the effect that the recently fired head of ISI, Lt. Gen. Hamid Gul, used bin Laden's Saudi money in an attempt to bribe Pakistani legislators to eject her in a narrow 1 November 1989 vote of confidence. It failed.

17. According to Prince Turki, former head of Saudi intelligence, in a 4 November 2001 interview with Jedda Arab News and MBC television, bin Laden returned to Saudi Arabia only in 1990, shortly before the invasion of Kuwait. "Some of his activi-

ties did not strictly comply with the regulations. He started making public speeches without prior approval of the concerned government agencies. . . . He spoke at schools without the knowledge of the school authorities." He claimed to be discussing jihad and to be campaigning for the Afghans, and the prince denied that he acted subversively. He denied hearing complaints at this time by Pakistani Prime Minister Benazir Bhutto that bin Laden was stirring up the Pakistani public against her, and pointed out that attacks by Pakistani religious scholars would have been of greater concern to her. According to the prince, Osama was not banned from traveling, only told that he had to get permission to do so. That was apparently in connection with his activities in what was then South Yemen, where he had been trying to launch a jihad since 1989, "attempting to lure Yemeni youths into training camps in Afghanistan" and campaigning with tribal leaders. The prince strongly denied that the Saudi government had backed these efforts and claimed that the government had warned him against continuing them. The prince associated Osama's 1992 departure with the imminent victory of the Mujeheddin (the Afghan resistance) at that time. Overall, the prince's statement emphasizes how difficult it is to determine Osama's precise history. The accounts of Saudi backing for the Yemeni operation and of the raid on Osama's compound come from less official sources.

18. According to Jane Mayer, "The House of Bin Laden," *New Yorker,* 12 November 2001, Prince Bandar, the Saudi ambassador to the United States, said that when he first met bin Laden in the 1980s, he "thought he couldn't lead eight ducks across the street." Similarly, the story is often told of how, in Afghanistan during the war against the Soviets, bin Laden was unable to convince some companions to kill a Western reporter, not because they had some qualms, but because they saw no point in following him. In desperation he offered them five hundred dollars, but they took that as nothing more than a joke.

19. Bergen, *Holy War,* 58, quotes Essam Derez, a journalist, who told bin Laden in 1987 that "one day you Afghan Arabs are all going to prison" because "our governments hate any popular movement." According to Derez, bin Laden thought that he and his Afghan Arabs would be welcomed as heroes. Bin Laden later claimed that recognition was irrelevant, compared to the spiritual effect of fighting for Allah in Afghanistan, but he would have to say that, given his attempt to become a major Muslim leader.

20. Bergen, *Holy War,* 102, describes a cash crisis late in 1994. By that time bin Laden was subsidizing wars in Bosnia and Chechnya. According to Bergen, *Holy War,* 86, he was already contemplating an attack on the U.S. Embassy in Nairobi. He may, moreover, have been unable to extract profits from businesses in the Sudan; a Saudi he tried to convince to invest there demurred on the ground that Sudan was far too regulated a country (which probably meant that the government demanded too large a cut).

21. Gunmen who attacked worshipers in a Khartoum mosque apparently also attacked bin Laden's house. However, according to former Saudi intelligence chief

Prince Turki, in a 4 November 2001 interview with Jedda Arab News, the assassination attempt "was not real. Rather, it was an attempt by some Sudanese agencies to convince the man that he should look to them for protection. . . . The group involved was more like a competitor than an opponent. There were no fundamental differences between them."

22. Bergen, *Holy War,* 83.

23. See, for example, "U.S. Missed Three Chances to Seize Bin Laden," *London Sunday Times,* 6 January 2001. One example was the Sudanese ejection of bin Laden. Apparently the Sudanese sent a former intelligence officer with CIA connections to Washington to offer to hand over bin Laden, as the Sudanese had handed Carlos, the "Jackal," to the French in 1994. Then the Sudanese expelled bin Laden, who took off from Khartoum on 18 May in a chartered C-130, which stopped in Qatar, a gulf state friendly to the United States, on its way to Afghanistan. No attempt was made to seize him. The *Times* article also recounts an unofficial offer conveyed on 6 July 2000 by Mansor Ijaz, a Pakistani American who had been a major donor to the 1996 Clinton campaign. Ijaz wanted an Islamic relief fund for Afghan veterans set up in return for the Taliban handing bin Laden over to an unnamed gulf state—from which he could be extracted. The deal was apparently destroyed when the White House sent an official representative to the UAE, which could not formally acknowledge that it was involved. There was also apparently an official Saudi offer to place a tracking device in the luggage of bin Laden's mother, who was about to visit her son in Afghanistan. The CIA reportedly declined the offer.

24. Reeve, *New Jackals,* 207, claims that bin Laden lost up to $150 million when fleeing the Sudan, and he quotes U.S. intelligence sources to the effect that by 1998 he had no more than about $50 million and probably much less. By that time, however, according to Reeve, he could tap wealthy supporters for funds, and many of his cells were virtually self-supporting.

25. This point is made by both Bergen, *Holy War,* 92–93, and by Cullison and Higgins, "Strained Alliance." The account of the news conference is from Cullison and Higgins, quoting Pakistani journalist Rahimullah Yusufzai.

26. Bin Laden would seem to correspond to the Christian image of the Antichrist, an apparently very pious leader who attracts millions and then leads his followers to destruction. Presumably there is a Muslim equivalent, perhaps the "false imam."

27. In the late 1930s, members of the Comintern, the international Communist organization formed to spread the revolution, were told that a new world war, which then seemed imminent, might not be a bad thing. Assuming that the French and the Germans would ground each other down as in World War I, the result would be ripe for revolution on both sides. It is generally assumed that the Russo-German non-aggression pact which in effect touched off the war was a fatal miscalculation on Stalin's part, a blunder leading to a war he did not want. However, the Comintern files imply exactly the opposite. Stalin wanted a war (not involving himself, of course) that would bring about the widespread revolution he sought. He imagined that Hit-

ler would be too busy dealing with the French and the British to attack him and, indeed, that by providing vital raw materials he could buy Hitler off until Germany had ground itself up. We now know that he miscalculated, almost fatally, but that was not obvious in 1939–41. Even after the war, Stalin sometimes treated World War II as a welcome means of spreading revolution and, incidentally, of making his Soviet Union a superpower. Note that this interpretation puts Stalin's offer of an anti-Hitler alliance (with France and Britain) into a new light. In Stalin's view, the war he wanted would not be ignited unless both sides felt strong enough to fight. He would have seen the alliance with the British and French not as a deterrent against Hitler but as a way of encouraging the outbreak of war. When the British and French demurred, on the ground that Soviet assistance would buy very little, he chose the alternative, which would encourage Hitler to start the war. Again, clearly Stalin did not realize that the Germans would overrun France so quickly, giving them the opportunity to attack him before he could profit from a general Western European collapse. An August 1939 speech by Stalin, recently discovered in Russian archives, makes exactly this point. On the eve of signing the Russo-German pact, he explains to his followers that it would have been pointless to join the British and French in a security system, since that would only have convinced them to stand up to the Germans and force upon them some sort of agreement. The desired war would have been put off. However, making a treaty with the Germans would impel them into the desired war against the Western powers, a war the results of which the Soviets could later exploit. These comments run exactly counter to the usual view of the outbreak of World War II, that Stalin desperately sought some sort of security guarantee to stave off war.

28. In a 4 November 2001 interview with Jedda Arab News and MBC television, Prince Turki, former head of Saudi intelligence, recalled a June 1998 Saudi request to Mullah Omar to extradite bin Laden. It was accepted that July, but Mullah Omar changed his mind three months later, after the attacks on the U.S. embassies in Africa. Prince Turki visited Kandahar in June and September 1998 in connection with the extradition. Presumably the reality was that the Taliban did not want to enrage a major supporter, the Saudi government, but also could not afford to lose their vital internal prop, the Al Qaeda Arab army. Later in the same interview, Prince Turki said that in 1996 the Sudanese government had offered to turn bin Laden over to the Saudis, but only on condition—which the Saudis rejected—that he not be prosecuted in any way.

29. According to DeYoung and Farah, "Infighting Slows Hunt," bin Laden inherited far less than the $300 million usually reported, possibly as little as $30 million, and most of that was probably spent forming Al Qaeda in the first place. As of mid-2002 the official U.S. estimate for the annual cost of running Al Qaeda and supporting the Taliban and fighters in Chechnya and Bosnia was $100 million, but that was freely described as a gross estimate. Attempts to starve Al Qaeda after 11 September met limited success, partly because it was difficult to distinguish entirely legitimate Islamic charities from ones which performed legitimate services but also functioned

as Al Qaeda fronts. Many governments did not provide information, and others resented what they saw as arbitrary U.S. demands based on incomplete or incorrect information. The initial U.S. goal was to block bank accounts linked to individuals and organizations on a set list; by February 2002, more than $100 million had been frozen. At least some had to be unblocked when evidence of terrorist links was not forthcoming. Another $10 million had reportedly been added by June 2002. Even so, there was a sense that Al Qaeda was being squeezed, not least because it was increasingly difficult for charities to raise new money for it.

30. For an account, see Paul Harris and Martin Bright, "How the Fleet of Death Menaces Britain," *London Observer*, 23 December 2001. Harris and Bright call bin Laden's ships the "phantom fleet" and claim that intelligence organizations had been searching for them since September 2001.

31. See, for example, Douglas Farah, "Al Qaeda Cash Tied to Diamond Trade: Sale of Gems from Sierra Leone Rebels Raised Millions, Sources Say," *Washington Post*, 2 November 2001. Farah reports that Al Qaeda had been profiting from diamonds mined by rebels in Sierra Leone since a September 1998 visit by a senior Al Qaeda advisor, Abdullah Ahmed Abdullah. The shift from cash to commodities, which are untraceable, was apparently motivated by the loss of considerable funds frozen by the United States after the 1998 attacks on embassies in Africa. Al Qaeda bought below market prices and then sold the diamonds in Europe; probably millions of dollars were involved. The diamonds were sold in Monrovia, Liberia, in government-protected safe houses. It had widely been reported that diamonds were the prize in the Sierra Leone civil war, and that the Liberian government had backed the RUF rebels (who committed horrific crimes against the population) in return for diamond profits; but this was the first report tying Al Qaeda to the war. In July 2001 Al Qaeda began buying much larger quantities at premium prices, converting accounts (which likely would be frozen) into portable assets. Farah reported further that only recently had U.S. and European intelligence officials come to realize just how important the diamonds were, not only to Al Qaeda but to other terrorist organizations. They were at least as important as conventional money-laundering. Hezbollah is apparently also involved in the Sierra Leone diamond trade. The estimated market value of RUF "blood diamonds" sold in 1999 was $75 million; mining accelerated in later years. According to Douglas Farah, "Digging Up Congo's Dirty Gems: Officials Say Diamond Trade Funds Radical Islamic Groups," *Washington Post*, 30 December 2001, the Congo and possibly Tanzania had earlier begun to serve as a similar source of diamonds, mainly for Hezbollah. Their operations had become really significant since about 1998, when a rebellion destroyed the remnants of the national government. Johan Peleman, who monitors the illegal weapons and diamond trades in West Africa for the United Nations, characterized "failed or collapsed states" such as Congo, Liberia, and Sierra Leone as "free-trade zones for the underworld." He did not distinguish between terrorists and international crime networks as exploiters.

32. See Douglas Farah, "Al Qaeda's Road Paved with Gold: Secret Shipments Traced Through a Lax System in United Arab Emirates," *Washington Post,* 17 February 2002. According to Farah, when the Taliban regime in Afghanistan was about to collapse, it sent couriers with gold bars (representing the Afghan gold reserve) and dollars across the border to Pakistan. U.S. officials estimated that about $10 million was involved. Gold smuggling has long been endemic in this part of the world, where it is seen as a hedge against drastic political uncertainty. A system therefore exists to buy and sell gold, and to transfer cash to places where it can again be converted into gold. According to Farah, Al Qaeda in effect systematically used the existing system, which includes hawala money transfer shops—a shop at one end of the circuit accepts money, and it maintains credit with another, which can transfer an equivalent amount. The system is widely considered untraceable, and has not been much affected by international attempts to seize or freeze terrorist assets. Hawala brokers often use gold to balance their books. Compared to diamonds, gold is much bulkier for unit value, but it is also much easier to use as cash; in effect, it is an international currency, and it is untraceable because it can be melted down and then recast into new ingots. Dubai has long been one of the world's largest and least regulated gold markets. It is also a major open banking center; reportedly, it was the source of much of the $500,000 which funded the 11 September hijackings. Reportedly there were unusually large gold shipments from Dubai to the United States after 11 September.

33. Farah, "Al Qaeda's Road," quotes a French intelligence report to this effect. It claims that many of the same people who ran BCCI are now running the Al Qaeda financial network. Few of them ever went to jail in the aftermath of the BCCI collapse. The sister of Saudi banker Khalid bin Mahfouz, a former BCCI director, is married to bin Laden. He paid a $225 million fine in 1995 for his involvement with BCCI and then became director of the Saudi National Commercial Bank. However, he was arrested in April 1999 when Saudi officials audited the bank and found that he was passing millions of dollars of its funds to charities controlled by bin Laden.

Chapter 4. The Afghan Base

1. Each region is centered on a regional bazaar: Herat, Kandahar, Mazar-i-Sharif, Jalalabad, Khost. Kandahar is the center of the Pashtuns. The east (Jalalabad and Khost) is most fragmented tribally. The northwest, around Herat, is populated mainly by Persian speakers (but includes some Pashtuns). Mazar-i-Sharif is the center of the most multiethnic area. Kabul is in effect ethnically neutral and thus could remain the capital.

2. The 1919 war could be described as a fight to regain full nationhood, the Afghans having in effect surrendered to the British after the 1878–80 war (which led to losing much territory when the Durand Line was accepted in 1893).

3. The main factions were the Khalq and Parcham, the latter largely Pashtun. When Daoud seized power, the Parchamis worked with him. The Khalq argued that

it was time for revolution, to establish a Communist state. Ejected from Daoud's government in 1977, they reunited with the Khalq (probably under Soviet pressure), and together they took power in a 1978 coup under Nur Mohammed Taraki, a Pashtun. In September 1979 Taraki was smothered in his bed on the orders of Hafizullah Amin. Amin in turn was killed during the Soviet invasion that December, to be replaced by Babrak Kamil, his contemporary as an Afghan Communist leader. He in turn was dropped in 1986 in favor of Najibullah, the last head of the Soviet-sponsored Afghan state. Under Soviet occupation, the Khalq and Parcham fought each other. According to Barnett R. Rubin, *The Fragmentation of Afghanistan*, 2d ed. (New Haven: Yale University Press, 2002), 126, the KGB and the International Department of the Soviet Communist Party favored the Parcham, whereas the Soviet military and their intelligence branch (GRU) favored the Khalq.

4. After Sir Mortimer Durand, the foreign secretary of the British Indian government. After the attempt to absorb the Pashtuns on the British side of the frontier failed, the British left their area largely ungoverned as the Northwest Frontier Province, which they saw as a buffer zone against Pashtuns across the frontier. As an indication of just how the Durand Line divided pre-Durand Afghanistan, until 1893 Peshawar was the winter capital of Afghanistan. Now it is a northern Pakistani city, in fact the base for much of the resistance movement against the Soviets in 1979–89.

5. The Pashtuns had (and have) their own nationalist movement, beginning at least as far back as the 1920s. Its leaders resisted the new Pakistani government in 1947, as they had resisted the British. The key leader of this movement, Badsha Khan, died only in 1988. In the mid-1980s his son, Wali Khan, founded the Awami National Party, which pressed for a secular democracy in Pashtunistan. The Pakistan government has periodically tried to suppress the party. See Isabel Hilton, "Letter from Pakistan: The Pashtun Code," *New Yorker*, 3 December 2001. After the partition of India in 1947, Afghan refusal to accept the Durand Line led the Pakistanis to block oil shipments through Karachi; the Afghans turned more toward the Soviets. According to Rubin, *Fragmentation*, 20, the Soviets were the dominant source of assistance between 1955 and 1978, providing $1.27 billion in economic aid and $1.25 billion in military aid, compared to $533 million in U.S. economic aid. The Soviets were entirely responsible for equipping the Afghan military. As prime minister in 1953–56, Mohammed Daoud became more aggressive, and the Pakistanis helped cause his ouster. King Zahir Shah tried to reduce tensions, but he could not officially recognize the Durand Line. Daoud returned to power in the 1973 coup and revived his pressure against the Pakistanis.

6. Isabel Hilton, "Letter from Pakistan," reports that according to Asfundiyar Khan, grandson of a Pashtun secular political leader, it was Pakistani dictator Zia ul-Haq who had his security service (ISI) back only fundamentalist groups, so that any refugee from the Russians had to go to them for support, including weapons. According to Khan, ISI chose the main resistance leaders, who owed everything to it. None had any political organization inside Afghanistan. Khan's examples include

Gulbuddin Hekmatyar. Khan claims that pre-Soviet Afghanistan was effectively secular—at least moderately Islamic—because there were so many Islamic sects that no politician could rely on any one of them. In fact Hekmatyar had been a minor pre-coup Afghan politician.

7. There is no strong sense of Tajik ethnic identify; to many Afghans a "Tajik" is simply a detribalized Afghan living in northern Afghanistan.

8. See, for example, Dexter Filkins, "Mass Graves Reportedly Tied to Last Days of Taliban Rule," in the 7 April 2002 *New York Times*, referring to Bamiyan and the Hazaras. Amnesty International charged that the Taliban killed thousands of Hazaras when they took Mazar-i-Sharif in August 1998.

9. Aside from the ruler in Kabul, the Pashtuns never developed a consistent or accepted leadership on a regional or tribal basis. In contrast, the four northern (non-Pashtun) regions did produce consistent national-level leadership: Ismail Khan, Abdul Rashid Dostum (Uzbek), Massoud's heirs, and the Hizb-i-Wahdat of Khalili (Shia). The consequence is that Pashtuns may both feel themselves entitled to rule the country and may have no natural way of contesting that leadership.

10. Visiting Saudi Arabia in 1977, Daoud said that he would use the Communists and then discard them: he would "have them for lunch before they had him for dinner." Prince Turki, the Saudi intelligence chief of the time, commented that instead the Communists "had him for breakfast."

11. Nur Mohammed Taraki became president. The Khalq and Parcham wings of the Communist Party found it difficult to coexist, and in July 1978 the Parchams were purged; their leader, Babrak Karmal, was sent abroad as an ambassador. In March 1979 Hafizullah Amin, a Khalq, gained most power as prime minister. The rebellion had begun after the 1978 harvest, in July, and there was a general uprising in Herat in mid-March, followed by an army mutiny in Jalalabad in April. Amin was killed by the Soviets during the December 1979 invasion. That spring they had already tried to convince Amin to step down in favor of Taraki, who they thought would be more effective. This time they installed Amin's competitor, Karmal.

12. In 1973 he had been placed in charge of political activities by a new revolutionary Muslim organization formed at Kabul University. An engineering student, Hekmatyar was then in prison on charges of having murdered a Maoist student. He and other activists fled to Peshawar in Pakistan after the Daoud coup that year. The movement was soon named Jamiat-e-Islami (Islamic Society). Its chief was Burhanuddin Rabbani, later president of post-Soviet Afghanistan. Rabbani sought foreign help and spent six months in Saudi Arabia in 1974. However, the Saudis cut their support when the Daoud government turned toward them and toward Iran in 1975. Meanwhile the Daoud government was pressing Pakistan on Pashtunistan. The Pakistanis saw the Islamists, already in exile in Peshawar, as a way of defusing the issue. They chose Hekmatyar over Rabbani, at least partly because Hekmatyar was a Pashtun, hence a legitimate actor on Pashtunistan, whereas Rabbani was a Tajik. Hekmatyar's leadership role was formalized when he broke away from Rabbani's

movement in 1975 to form his own Hezb-e-Islami group. Both possible alternatives to Hekmatyar, Ghulam Mohammed Niyazi and Abd el-Rabb al-Rasoul Sayyaf, were in prison in Kabul. Niyazi was killed in a 1979 prison massacre; Sayyaf survived to form his own fundamentalist (Salafi) Afghan resistance party, later linked to the Taliban. See Rubin, *Fragmentation*, 84–85. Note, however, that Hekmatyar only gradually became the "chosen instrument," and that the transition to this status was not complete until after 1987.

13. Soviet military involvement actually began when the post-coup government asked for help in 1978. The 1979 invasion and military coup can be seen as a Soviet response to local reports that the Afghan government was losing its war against "counterrevolutionaries" and that some more capable leader had to be put in place. It can be likened to the U.S. government decision in 1963 to support a coup against Ngo Dinh Diem in Vietnam because he seemed to be losing the Vietnam War; several Presidents later said that this coup had locked the United States into Vietnam.

14. See Mohammed Yousaf and Mark Adkin, *The Bear Trap: The Defeat of a Superpower* (1992; reprint, Havertown, Pa.: Casemate, 2001), 25. Yousaf was head of the Afghan Bureau of ISI, 1983–87. He claims that in 1979, when the Soviets invaded, Gen. Akhtar Abdul Rehman Khan, then head of ISI, made a convincing case to General Zia that Afghanistan could be made into another Vietnam, and the Soviets defeated. As chief of the Joint Chiefs of Staff Committee, Akhtar was killed with General Zia when their C-130 was bombed in August 1988.

15. Limited revolts began in July 1978 after the initial coup. A purge of Parchams in the government left it more Pashtun than it had been for a century. That alienated non-Pashtuns, but left the Pashtuns quiescent. The Iranian revolution (February 1979) inspired revolts by Shia groups, including the Hazaras. Eastern Pashtuns joined the revolt after the 1979 harvest, and the rest followed after the Soviet invasion. Rubin, *Fragmentation*, 185–86.

16. It mixed Pashtun tribal conservatism with Wahhabi and Deobandi ideas. To motivate resistance fighters, the madrassahs stressed a political form of Islam (Islamic revolution) and the romance of jihad. Traditional Afghan Islam was relatively tolerant and recognized that there could be no compulsion. For example, Afghanistan supported the sufi or mystical Islamic tradition, part of which involves invocation to saints to intercede for man. The sterner Wahhabis absolutely rejected any such intercession, and thus the madrassah-educated Taliban persecuted Afghan sufis as, in effect, heretics.

17. It seems arguable that Zia's shift brought more Pashtuns into senior army positions and thus was intended to strengthen Pakistani ties with Pashtuns on both sides of the Afghan border, in conformity with the Pakistani policy of seeking strategic depth in Afghanistan. Previous policies favoring secular education for officers would presumably have favored the dominant Punjabis.

18. The World Bank report, a Country Assistance Strategy, is described in a 2 Au-

gust 2002 report by Nadeem Malik in the *News* of Islamabad. The bank blamed wholesale recruitment of madrassah graduates into the Pakistani civil service for growing sectarian problems in Pakistani society. The madrassahs were particularly attractive to the poor, since they provided free boarding and lodging. Those which did not provide any career-oriented education produced marginalized graduates who could earn their living only through sectarian violence; in effect, then, the madrassahs were producing an Islamic or fundamentalist army.

19. According to Rubin, *Fragmentation*, 200, in 1987 Hekmatyar's force accounted for 16 percent of resistance fighters and received 18–20 percent of support. Rabbani's force accounted for 34 percent of fighters and received 18–19 percent of support. Sayyaf's party, accounting for only about 2 percent of fighters, received 17–18 percent of support, most likely thanks to its Saudi connection. These figures do not include Mahsood's Islamic Army. Rubin claims that Rabbani's army had the best of the guerrilla commanders. It encompassed most of the non-Pashtun rebels. In social terms, Rabbani enlisted the Kabul University faculty and its Tajik students, whereas Hekmatyar had the most radical of the students, and the Pashtuns.

20. According to ibid., 198, General Zia also feared that a national government formed by a *loya jirga* would escape his control. He had been a military advisor in Jordan during Black September 1970, when the PLO nearly overthrew King Hussein. He may have seen the *loya jirga* government as a potential PLO, a dangerously unified government-in-waiting which Arab heads of state had created in 1964. By way of contrast, the Pakistanis often said that they could control Hekmatyar, their creature.

21. Ibid., 192–93.

22. At least before 1987, Hekmatyar did have some effective subordinates. Some of these remarks are based on comments by David C. Isby, who interviewed Hekmatyar in 1983. Afghans began to complain about Hekmatyar as early as 1981; in 1985 the Congressional Task Force on Afghanistan heard that Hekmatyar's was the most corrupt of the Afghan resistance parties. In 1990 the State Department particularly attacked him for killing fellow Afghans. According to Bergen, *Holy War,* 69, General Zia commented that Pakistan had made Hekmatyar and it could always choose to destroy him if he misbehaved.

23. Rubin, *Fragmentation*, 196–98. In 1980 ISI formally recognized six mutually hostile resistance movements, or parties; later it added a seventh, Sayyaf's. From then on, only the seven recognized groups got assistance, whereas initially even small bands of rebels might claim a few weapons. The Pakistanis argued that they were reducing a chaotic situation to something approaching order.

24. For its part, ISI claimed that traditionalist resistance forces had failed badly in 1979–83. Nationalist resistance was limited because many of the traditionalist/secular (tribal) leaders showed little interest in fighting; in the words of a contemporary observer, they would rather drive cabs in New York than live under terrible conditions in Pakistan. The ISI limited aid to Mahsood because he was not under its

control. It claimed that the United States agreed with its policy of supporting Hekmatyar and limiting support to Mahsood, but critics could charge that this agreement was inevitable, given the initial U.S. decision to aid the rebels via ISI.

25. Despite the alliance, the Soviets conducted large-scale intelligence operations in Pakistan, using the Kabul regime's secret service (KAD/WAD) as executive agent. There was large-scale intelligence penetration of Afghan resistance groups. In 1986, the sabotage campaign in Pakistan caused the world's highest level of state supported terrorism at that time. In August 1988 a still-unexplained bomb—with rumors of KGB-backed sabotage—destroyed an airplane carrying General Zia, the major Pakistani supporter of the resistance fighters, many of his associates, and the U.S. ambassador to Pakistan.

26. In the fall of 2001 a Russian writer attributed the fall of the Najibullah government to the end of Russian arms deliveries (due to economic trouble) rather than to the prowess of the Mujeheddin.

27. In a 4 November 2001 television interview with Jedda Arab News, Prince Turki, the former Saudi intelligence chief, remarked that the war had destroyed traditional leadership; those who passed the test of war suddenly became the leaders. One implication, which the Prince did not draw, was that the Afghanistan experience had opened the eyes of those who had worked there, including Osama bin Laden, to the possibility that traditional governments, such as that in Saudi Arabia, might be de-legitimized and destroyed. The prince said that he would never forget a comment by Ahmad Shah Ahmadzi, prime minister of the transitional government the Afghans formed in Pakistan in 1987 before the Soviets withdrew: that "the best means to achieve the interests of the people" would have been to arrest all nine Afghan leaders attending the meeting, including himself. That is, the only way to form a stable Afghan government would be by some outside force capable of suppressing individual ambitious leaders like himself. Every attempt to form a unified Afghan resistance failed for the same reason. The first attempt was symptomatic of the problem. At Mecca in 1980 the Afghan resistance leaders met, pledging before the Kaaba, the holiest place in Islam, to unite. They chose Sheikh Abdrab Al-Rasoul Sayyaf—and some dissociated themselves from him the same day—as their leader before returning to Pakistan. Prince Turki described the 1987 attempt as the "cleanest" of all, a *loya jirga* comprising those who had gained respect and loyalty (note that it was not traditional leaders, but those who had proven themselves). The attempt collapsed when a major military leader, Gulbuddin Hekmatyar, decided to withdraw. He accused some countries of trying to influence the outcome; presumably his main complaint was that he was not winning.

28. In September 1991 the United States and the Soviet Union agreed that all military assistance to both sides would end at the beginning of 1992; the Soviets were already tightening such aid. According to Larry F. Goodson, *Afghanistan's Endless War: State Failure, Regional Politics, and the Rise of the Taliban* (Seattle: University of

Washington Press, 2001), 70, after withdrawing the Soviets continued to supply $250 to $300 million in military aid per month, including long-range rockets (Scuds and FROGs). In contrast, the United States cut aid to the rebels to $40 to $50 million per month, as its main objective, a Soviet withdrawal, had apparently been met. Goodson reports that many Soviet advisers stayed on after the withdrawal, and that there were even reports of Soviet troops in Afghan uniform.

29. The ISI and elements of the Pakistani military plus their instruments, Hekmatyar and radical mujeheddin, were part of an international Islamic opposition to the U.S.-led coalition. The Pakistani government, as well as moderates and Afghan nationalists, supported the coalition. This split may explain why the Saudis had to suspend plans to transport two thousand mujeheddin to Saudi Arabia as a symbolic part of the coalition force. Rubin, *Fragmentation*, 253.

30. The northern force included Rabbani's party as well as Hezb-i-Wahdat, the umbrella Shia Party; later the Parchamis (the non-Pashtuns of the Communist Party) joined, together with Dostum's Uzbeks. Ibid., 270.

31. Mahsood and Dostum competed for control of Kunduz, in the north, and jointly controlled most of the center of Kabul. The Pashtuns under Hekmatyar occupied the high ground in the south. The Iranian-backed Hezb-i-Wahdat (Unity Party) controlled the western part of the city. Fighting it was a Saudi-based party, Ittehad-i Islami, under Abdul Rasoul Sayyaf. Kandahar was run by a council dominated by Hekmatyar and by Sayed Ahmed Gailani. Herat was controlled by Ismail Khan (Jamiat), who relied on Iranian support. Mazar-i-Sharif was Dostum's (Uzbek) de facto capital. Jalalabad, on the road from Kabul to the Khyber Pass, was held by Yunus Khalis and his Hezb-e-Islami. Of the major resistance fighters, only Nabi Mohammedi and his Harakat-i Inqilabi-i Islami had no area to dominate, which may be why he later joined the Taliban.

32. Pashtun exiles working for major media such as the BBC and the Voice of America helped publicize supposed Taliban virtues, and the much darker side of their rule was not really well publicized in the West almost until war broke out in September 2001. Even then many in the media argued for their incorruptibility compared to the supposed evils of the Northern Alliance warlords. For the U.S. position, see Mackenzie, "United States and the Taliban." Mackenzie emphasizes disgust at Taliban policy toward women as a factor in U.S. policy from 1997 on. After Madeleine Albright became secretary of state, the Afghan Desk in the State Department ceased to welcome the Taliban and began to see them as unacceptable. Its new occupant, the former U.S. consul in Peshawar, Michael Malinowski, was much less inclined to accept their claims at face value. At about the same time the Taliban were demonstrating that they could not take the north, hence could not deliver the nationwide security, the promise of which was their main virtue in Western eyes. On 22 October 1997 Undersecretary of State for South Asian Affairs Karl F. Inderfurth told the Senate Foreign Relations Subcommittee on the Near East and South Asia that

the United States sought a broad-based multiethnic Afghan government, not least on the ground that it was clear that no party in that country could win a military victory.

33. This version is given by Ahmed Rashid, *Taliban: The Story of the Afghan Warlords*, rev. ed. (London: Pan, 2001), 22–28. Rashid states that, according to senior Taliban, the founders of the movement had fought together and knew each other. With the war over, they were studying in madrassahs in Kandahar and in Quetta. They long discussed what to do. It is not entirely clear how Mullah Omar came to be their leader. For Rashid, the most credible story of the Taliban's first action was that, in the spring of 1994, neighbors told Omar that a local warlord had abducted two teenage girls, taking them to his camp where they were repeatedly raped. Omar assembled a group of thirty students who stormed the camp, rescued the girls, and hanged the commander from the barrel of a tank. A few months later Omar rescued a boy over whom two commanders were fighting. The local population began to see Omar as its protector, and he began to send emissaries to other commanders and even to President Rabbani. However, he was more closely linked to the main Pakistani Islamist party, the Jamiat-e Ulema Islam (JUI). Rashid traces Pakistani government support to Benazir Bhutto's interest in opening a direct land route to Central Asia. Ongoing fighting around Kabul blocked the shortest route, from Peshawar to Kabul to Mazar-i-Sharif to Uzbekistan. That left a route from Quetta to Kandahar to Herat to Ashkabad in Turkmenistan. The Pakistani government began to negotiate with the warlords in Kandahar and in Herat, the object being to build a modern road on which trucks would have to pay only a few tolls. However, a test convoy was stopped short of Kandahar. By this time the Pakistan government was supporting the Taliban, and the local warlords made the end of that support (as well as a share of the goods) a precondition for releasing the convoy. The Pakistan government considered a military operation to release the convoy, but instead chose the Taliban as a less dangerous option. This was in November 1994. According to Anthony Davis, "How the Taliban Became a Military Force," in Maley, *Fundamentalism Reborn?* Omar and his associates got their first support from Haji Basher, a Maiwand commander in the Hezb-e-Islami of Yunos Khan, and from the main warlord in neighboring Helmand Province. In September 1994 they visited Kabul, where Rabbani saw them as a valuable counter to Hekmatyar. Probably by this time the Pakistanis were already aware of them. In October, a substantial Taliban force (two hundred men in three groups) routed a Hezb-e-Islami garrison at Spin Boldak, just across the Pakistani border. This victory gave them access to a huge Hezb-e-Islami arms dump at Pasha. Some reports suggested that the Taliban had been supported by artillery fire from Pakistan, which would suggest that they were already considered a Pakistani asset. As for the arms dump, it may or may not have been heavily looted by this time. Davis points out that supposed Taliban possession of the dump would have been a way of deflecting attention from any arms support the Pakistan government was providing. He argues that the detention of the Pakistani convoy near Kandahar

was actually an act of political extortion, in hope of ending Pakistani support for the Taliban. The conquest of Kandahar gave the Taliban more weapons, including tanks and aircraft. Davis reports that a key commander in the city was bought for $1.5 million, a huge sum in Afghanistan. The JUI leader, Fazlur Rahman, served in the Benazir Bhutto government. His associate was Interior Minister Maj. Gen. (ret.) Naseerullah Babar, who had arranged asylum for Afghan Islamists (such as Rabbani, Hekmatyar, and Mahsood) in the 1970s. In the early 1990s he argued that direct Pakistani access to Central Asia would solve Pakistani economic problems. Babar announced the road project (through Kandahar) at a Pakistani cabinet meeting in June 1994. Part of the Taliban connection with the JUI was that the latter ran the madrassahs in Pakistani Baluchistan which provided the Taliban with free education.

34. According to Davis, "How the Taliban Became a Military Force," by January 1995 the Taliban were clearly shifting from a regional force operating around Kandahar to a potential national force which could announce that it was neutral between Rabbani and Hekmatyar, both of whom it despised. ISI shifted from Hekmatyar to the Taliban about this time, when they were "achieving a legitimacy, popularity, and a momentum of victory in the heartlands of Pashtun Afghanistan far beyond anything Hekmatyar, a Ghilzai Pashtun from northern Afghanistan, could ever have hoped to achieve."

35. See Goodson, *Afghanistan's Endless War,* 78. Ultimately more than four thousand Taliban troops were killed in Mazar-i-Sharif. Their objective had been the mouth of the Salang Tunnel leading north to former Soviet Central Asia. Mahsood's counter-offensive cut that off; according to Goodson, "After briefly holding more than 90 percent of Afghanistan and being poised for final victory, the Taliban suffered their most significant defeat of the war." Mahsood was soon on the outskirts of Kabul.

36. According to an 11 October 2001 report, Russian assistance was worth $40 to $45 million, the weapons being paid for by the United States. Transfers included fifty tanks and eighty infantry fighting vehicles, six batteries of 122-mm howitzers, two batteries of 100-mm antitank guns, ten sets of multiple rocket launchers, and numerous lesser weapons. The Russians also supplied uniforms.

37. See Goodson, *Afghanistan's Endless War,* 84.

38. See Ahmed Rashid, "Pakistan and the Taliban," in Maley, *Fundamentalism Reborn?*

39. John K. Cooley, *Unholy Wars: Afghanistan, America, and International Terrorism* (London: Pluto, 2000), 133–36, describes heavy prewar Afghan poppy production and its consequences. He cites Soviet claims that the warlords who fought the Soviets financed their operations largely by growing poppies, a trade the CIA willingly tolerated. At the least, smuggling routes used for arms were also used for drugs. Later it would be claimed that the fundamentalist militias fighting in former Soviet Central Asia were financed largely by the drug trade. See also Goodson, *Afghanistan's Endless War,* 100–103. According to Goodson, although Afghanistan had long grown poppies, cultivation increased enormously during the war against the So-

viets, and local processing of heroin began about 1980. By 1999 Afghanistan was the world's largest opium producer, its forty-six hundred tons amounting to more than 75 percent of global production. Afghanistan produced virtually all of the heroin used by an expanding Pakistani drug addict population.

40. According to Goodson, *Afghanistan's Endless War*, 41, the Afghan king of the time, Amanullah, considered himself head of a pan-Islamic movement, and thus offered the Central Asians some support. They had declared independence during the collapse of the czarist state, but by 1921 they had been occupied by Soviet troops, and in 1924 they were formally incorporated into the Soviet Union. Amanullah apparently imagined himself at the head of a Central Asian confederation, perhaps even a new caliphate.

41. The key Ferghana Valley was split among the republics of Tajikistan, Uzbekistan, and Kazakhstan. Tajikistan was cut off from its cultural and economic centers, Bukhara and Samarkand, which were incorporated in Uzbekistan.

42. See Ahmed Rashid, "They're Only Sleeping," *New Yorker*, 14 January 2002. The movement began with the creation of a Saudi-financed Wahhabi mosque in 1991. Many of those involved were members of the Islamic Renaissance Party, created in 1990 in the Soviet Union. They split from it because it was slow to demand the formation of an Islamic state.

43. The Uzbek government began to label its perceived radical Islamist opponents "Wahhabi" in 1992. By 1997 it was applying that term to anyone practicing Islam unofficially or studying it privately.

44. See Robert Rand, "Tashkent Postcard: Backhands and Bombs," *New Yorker*, 22 October 2001.

Chapter 5. The Terrorist International and Its Predecessor

1. The key NSC meeting is described in Woodward and Balz, "Bush and His Advisors."

2. Quoted in Dan Balz and Bob Woodward, "Bush Awaits History's Judgement," *Washington Post*, 3 February 2002.

3. In November 2002, an Israeli news web site, Debka, claimed that an IRA spy ring was selling information to various Arab governments and terrorist groups as a way of raising money for the IRA. The British government closed down the Stormont (Northern Ireland) legislature after the spy ring was discovered, but initially the British media generally treated it as a case of domestic espionage. However, on 8 October the *Telegraph* reported that the spies had obtained copies of transcripts of sensitive telephone conversations between President Bush and Prime Minister Blair. Since the conversations generally did not deal with Irish affairs, one likely implication was that the spies were seeking information others, such as the Iraqis, might want to buy. But another might be that the IRA wanted to know when the United States and Britain planned to attack, say, Iraq on the theory that it would be able to gain concessions as the British felt themselves badly stressed by such a war. It ap-

pears that Debka was the only news source to claim that the IRA was collecting information in order to sell it.

4. For example, immediately after World War II there was apparently a widespread view that those who had fought successfully in underground armies would reject governments trying to return to power after the fall of the Nazis.

5. The most famous case of all is that of Gavrilo Princip, who shot Archduke Francis Ferdinand in June 1914 and thus precipitated World War I. He in turn was a creature of the Serbian intelligence service, and the Serbian regime it served had been put into place by the Russians in 1903. To what extent did the Russians retain any sort of control over the Serbians and their irregulars by 1914? Were they really interested in the sort of conflagration Princip set off? Much the same might be said of the Kashmiris who attacked the Indian Parliament in 2002, coming very close to setting off a nuclear war on the subcontinent—hardly what the Pakistani ISI had in mind.

6. The 1 June meeting was described in the 14 June 2002 issue of *Al-Watan al-Arabi*, an Arabic-language pro-Saudi magazine published in Paris. According to the report, both the revolutionary (Islamic) and reformist wings of the Iranian government were represented, the message being that Iran could still export revolution and terrorism and therefore that it should continue to dominate the Palestinian terrorists. Note that there was apparently no interest in the wider sort of war being waged by bin Laden.

7. The administration's thinking may be reflected in an interview with Kenneth Adelman, included in Nicholas Lemann, "Letter from Washington: What Terrorists Want," *New Yorker*, 29 October 2001. Adelman had been President Reagan's head of the Arms Control and Disarmament Agency; under the Bush administration he is on the Defense Policy Board. Adelman distinguished two alternative approaches to the terrorist problem, what he called the "narrow" and the "wide" one. The narrow approach would simply be to hunt down bin Laden and his lieutenants and possibly his organization as a whole. The wide one would see bin Laden as no more than one part of a larger problem of weapons of mass destruction, networks, and governments supporting terrorists. In Adelman's view, the wide view was the right one, and it was typified by Iraq: "If we're going after international terrorism and weapons of mass destruction and states that support both, Iraq comes up three cherries. Two, just because we have no intelligence linking Iraq to nine-eleven doesn't mean it didn't happen. Three, we know Saddam Hussein harbored the mastermind of the bombing of the World Trade Center in '93 and that he tried to assassinate President George H. W. Bush in Kuwait the same year." Adelman said that he would have told President Bush that he had a mission, to wage a global campaign against terrorism and weapons of mass destruction; that he had been given the opportunity, by tragedy, to solve the larger problem. This interview was given *two months* before the president said much the same thing in his "axis of evil" speech.

8. The Saudis were uncomfortable because it appeared that most of the 11 Sep-

tember hijackers were Saudi subjects. On 2 October 2001 the Saudi official news agency reported that Prince Bandar Bin Sultan Bin Abdulaziz, the Saudi ambassador to the United States, had just told CNN that the hijackers had used stolen Saudi passports and identification cards; "true Muslims" would never be terrorists. The Saudi Ulema (religious council) had recently said as much. However, more than a year later it appears that most of the hijackers really were Saudis, although there is some evidence of false identities.

9. See John Arquilla and David Ronfelt, *Networks and Netwar: The Future of Terror, Crime, and Miltancy* (Santa Monica, Calif.: RAND National Defense Research Institute, 2001). Arquilla and Ronfelt define netwar as warfare conducted by small groups with limited central control; thus the destruction of the central control does not necessarily end the problem.

10. None of this is really new. During the cold war, the Soviet Navy adopted physical dispersion which made it unlikely that U.S. forces could destroy Soviet naval threats at the outbreak of war. The fleet was, however, united by a tight web of information, which it needed to carry out its own missions. By the 1980s the U.S. counter was based largely on strategic deception, that is, on the destruction of the information the Soviets needed to conduct their war. This battle can be seen as a very early stage of network-centric warfare. See, for example, Norman Friedman, "C3 War at Sea" in the May 1977 (Naval Review) issue of U.S. Naval Institute *Proceedings*.

11. For Azef's story, see Richard E. Rubenstein, *Comrade Valentine* (New York: Harcourt Brace, 1994). In Rubenstein's view, Azef saw himself as an independent operator, exploiting both the Czarists and the revolutionaries to push Russia in a direction he liked.

12. Christy Campbell, *Fenian Fire: The British Government Plot to Assassinate Queen Victoria* (London: HarperCollins, 2002). The plot was to have blown up the queen during the 1887 Golden Jubilee thanksgiving service in Westminster Abbey. Campbell argues that the plot was actually set up by the British secret service with the knowledge and approval of Prime Minister Lord Salisbury. Salisbury's object, according to Campbell, was both to smash the Fenians and to discredit Charles Stewart Parnell, the politician most successfully advocating Irish home rule. For the Guy Fawkes plot as a sting, see Hugh Ross Williamson, *Who Was the Man in the Iron Mask and Other Historical Mysteries* (London: Penguin, 2002, reprint of 1974 edition). Williamson argues that Stalinist and Nazi propaganda and show trials shed a very useful light on a wide range of false plots in the sixteenth century and beyond.

Chapter 6. A New Kind of War

1. See, for example, David S. Alberts, John J. Garstka, and Frederick P. Stein, *Network-Centric Warfare: Developing and Leveraging Information Superiority*, 2d ed. (Washington, D.C.: C4ISR Cooperative Research Program, 1999) for tenets of network-centric warfare. See also Norman Friedman, *Seapower and Space: From the Dawn of the Missile Age to Net-Centric Warfare* (Annapolis: Naval Institute Press,

2000). For the consequences of precision navigation and strike, see Michael Russell Rip and James M. Hasik, *The Precision Revolution: GPS and the Future of Aerial Warfare* (Annapolis: Naval Institute Press, 2002).

2. Tomahawks could not depend entirely on inertial navigation because inertial systems were likely to drift during their relatively lengthy flights. To achieve the required precision, they periodically checked their positions using TERCOM (terrain comparison), a system in which the missile periodically checked its height above ground while flying in a straight line. The series of heights could be checked against a digital map. Remarkably, such periodic checks offered the missile extraordinary precision. However, they could be conducted only over land with some consistent variation in height, which meant not above the sea and probably not above deserts. Moreover, any area in which Tomahawks were to operate had to be mapped first.

3. See Craig Covault, "Military Air Operations Grow Over Balkan Crisis," *Aviation Week & Space Technology*, 19 April 1993.

4. See Craig Covault, "Bosnian Air Operations Test NATO/UN," *Aviation Week & Space Technology*, 30 August 1993.

5. See "Key Role for EC-130s," *Aviation Week & Space Technology*, 30 August 1993.

6. See Craig Covault, "F-16 Data Link Sharpens Close Air Support," *Aviation Week & Space Technology*, 13 May 1996. The Aviano CAOC had recently transmitted targeting data directly to an F-16, in what must have been an early RTIC test. The "nearly 40" F-16s of the 31st Fighter Wing had just been fitted with IDMs, joining another two hundred Block-50 aircraft; IDM and the associated software were also planned for two hundred more Block-40s. At least in its initial form, IDM transmitted target coordinates directly to the airplane's mission computer, which provided the necessary cues to bring the pilot there. Only somewhat later did the need for images become obvious. On the other hand, the system could cue the airplane's IR targeting pod, which would provide the pilot with at least a target image. The link could also be used to pass data from one platform to another, for example, from an OH-58A Kiowa scout helicopter to an F-16; and it could also be used to pass GPS-derived targeting data directly to the F-16. IDM already existed, having been developed by the Naval Research Laboratory, but the effort to integrate it for targeting was apparently undertaken as a crash project specifically for Bosnia, in order to provide close air support aircraft with precise targeting at minimum risk of collateral damage. This article also describes the new close air support integrated targeting systems (CITS) ground unit, which integrated a GPS receiver and a laser rangefinder. The ground controller would use the rangefinder to measure the precise coordinates of a target, which could be transmitted to a nearby airplane via IDM. This was the unit used heavily in Afghanistan. It had a peculiarity, which on one occasion proved fatal. When its battery was changed, it reset itself to its own coordinates. When the operator did not re-lase the target, a GPS-guided bomb hit him instead of it. IDM itself was slow because it used limited bandwidth. The next best alternative was Link 16, ultimately to be installed on board all U.S. and many NATO strike aircraft. Al-

though Link 16 normally carries the coordinates of targets an airplane spots on its radar, it can also carry text and images such as those used in RTIC. An elaborate 1996 experiment employing Link 16 and an F-15E is described by William B. Scott, "Strike 2 Demonstrates Feasibility of RTIC," *Aviation Week & Space Technology,* 1 September 1997. This was a simulated attack on a mobile missile launcher located by a Special Forces team, which transmitted both coordinates and some local video via a satellite link to a distant air operations center (AOC). The AOC cued its other intelligence assets, such as a U-2 with a synthetic aperture radar and a signals intelligence aircraft, to form both a package describing the target area and sufficient information to plan a safe route in and out for the F-15E. Data sent to the F-15E even cued its onboard radar. One lesson was that the fighter needed sufficient software to reorient the images it received in the direction it was headed, so they were meaningful to the pilot.

7. See Craig Covault, "NATO Hits Missile Sites, Large Force Bombs Air Base," *Aviation Week & Space Technology,* 28 November 1994.

8. See Craig Covault, "Air Power Alters Bosnia Equation," *Aviation Week & Space Technology,* 4 September 1995.

9. See Craig Covault, "NATO Airstrikes Target Serbian Infrastructure," *Aviation Week & Space Technology,* 11 September 1995.

10. GPS guidance was already incorporated in one other U.S. missile, SLAM, which flies through GPS-defined waypoints. However, SLAM terminal guidance is based on an operator's view through the missile's optical seeker. SLAM was first used during the Gulf War.

11. In October 1999, Secretary of Defense William S. Cohen told Congress that Milosevich had proven far more effective than NATO in the propaganda war.

12. The first such raid was conducted on 15 May 1999, which was day fifty-three of the bombing campaign. It was preceded by a wave of warnings transmitted by e-mail, fax, and cell phone. The targets were a steel plant at Smederevo and a copper smelter at Bor, both identified by U.S. intelligence as being used directly to enrich the ruling clique. This campaign was reportedly developed on the basis of an "influence net" which modeled the Milosevich inner circle, the theory being that particular individuals could be pressed to demand that Milosevich respect their interests. The model was also used to identify bank accounts to freeze and to press various countries to deny entry to particular individuals who might be trying to escape the war.

13. However, according to Strobe Talbott's recent memoir, *The Russia Hand* (New York: Random House, 2002), the Russian army dash to occupy part of Kosovo seems to have been undertaken on army initiative, based in part on fury that the Russian government was abandoning Milosevich under U.S. pressure. Thus it seems unlikely that Milosevich gave up based on any Russian guarantee, as opposed to giving up based on the loss of hope of Russian support. Given the lack of any land frontier between Russia and Kosovo or Serbia, it is not clear why Milosevich expected serious

Russian military support. Presumably the Russians themselves were responding to U.S. diplomatic pressure, backed by economic pressure.

14. See Stephen Biddle's extensive review of three books about Kosovo, "The New Way of War?" *Foreign Affairs*, May/June 2002. The Serbian references to carpet bombing are from Stephen T. Hosmer, *Why Milosevich Decided to Settle When He Did* (Santa Monica, Calif.: RAND, 2001). If it is true that Milosevich abandoned Kosovo when his own power was threatened, then he could never say so. Remarks about the (nonexistent) threat of carpet bombing would have been a valuable way of justifying withdrawal to Serbians who had already suffered from the war. They are, however, entirely misleading.

Chapter 7. Coalitions

1. For example, early in October 2002 the Russians announced that they had passed the U.S. government evidence that four of the hijackers had fought in Chechnya, and claimed that the attacks on the United States reflected terrorist experience in Chechnya.

2. Saudi officials have argued that this is simplistic. Bin Laden, the head of the terrorist organization which attacked on 11 September, is a Saudi national, but he is also a sworn enemy of the Saudi state. Many of his terrorist acts were committed inside Saudi Arabia. The Saudis even experienced the assassination of one of their kings (by a dissident prince). The great question is whether a Saudi government critically dependent on the support of its clergy, yet probably not in control of that clergy, can afford to infuriate it by supporting attacks on terrorists who claim Islamic justification.

3. The Pashtuns showed their displeasure during Pakistani national elections in the fall of 2002, when they elected a pro-Taliban state government which vowed to end U.S.-sponsored antiterrorist activities in their area. The Pashtun state legislature honored a Pakistani from Baluchistan, Mir Aimal Kasi, who was executed in the United States in 2002 for murdering two CIA employees in 1993.

4. During wartime Pentagon briefings, Secretary of Defense Rumsfeld denied that there had been any problem with the use of the center. He emphasized the spirit of cooperation exhibited by the Saudis so vehemently that reporters concluded that the United States had had to pressure the Saudis to obtain access.

5. Rowan Scarborough, "Size of Force on Ground Key in Plan for Iraq War," *Washington Times*, 26 April 2002. Franks reportedly wanted four or five divisions to attack Iraq, and the comparison was made with his estimate of what would be needed for Afghanistan.

6. Of the bordering countries, Iran helped train the forces of Ismail Khan, in camps around Mashhad. Uzbekistan backed Gen. Abdul Rashid Dostum (an Uzbek); because the Uzbeks are ethnically allied to Turks, Turkey also backed the general. Tajikistan backed ethnic Tajik forces fighting in the north and east of the coun-

try. All three backers were united in their desire to limit Pashtun influence. In this they opposed the Saudi and Pakistani backers of the Taliban (and of any non-Taliban Pashtuns). However, the Turks and Uzbeks also wanted to counter Iranian influence. India helped the Northern Alliance in hopes of limiting Pakistani power in the region.

7. Reportedly the Taliban intelligence agency, the Istakhbarat, used many of the personnel and the facilities of the earlier regime's agency, KHAD, which had been created and trained by the KGB during the Soviet occupation. Reported arrests of numerous plotters in Kabul and in Khost, in the fall of 2001, suggested that the Taliban did not yet have firm control of Afghanistan. The Taliban assassinated major potential opposition leaders like General Haq, operating in Pakistan as well as in Afghanistan (Haq's wife and son died in such an operation in 1998). Thus the assassination of Mahsood was very much in character. They also lured potential dissidents with offers of discussion and compromise, then jailed them.

8. See an AP report by John Solomon, "At Least Two Attacks Said Thwarted," distributed 27 September 2001. At least some information was provided by a bin Laden associate, Djamel Begal, captured in the summer of 2001. Given his information, U.S. intelligence pressed European governments to begin rounding up suspects. In several cases no single government had sufficient evidence, but combinations of information from different governments, who were willing to cooperate after 11 September, proved decisive. The implication in the article is that the CIA provided the links by acting, in effect, as an international clearing house for terrorist data.

9. Bob Woodward, "50 Countries Detain 360 Suspects at CIA's Behest; Roundup Reflects Aggressive Efforts of an Intelligence Coalition Viewed as Key to War on Terrorism," *Washington Post*, 22 November 2001.

10. For example, according to the 22 November 2001 Woodward article, two Al Qaeda suspects arrested in Bahrain were questioned in Saudi Arabia. They in turn provided the Saudis with an Al Qaeda telephone contact number. On the basis of calls made to that number, the Saudis arrested six Al Qaeda members about to leave the country, including a senior man, "Abu Ahmed." As of November, he was described as the most senior Al Qaeda officer being questioned, with detailed knowledge of earlier attacks such as the strike against USS *Cole* and the planned attacks on the millennium celebrations; he also knew some of the 11 September hijackers. This rather sensitive information may have been leaked to demonstrate that the Saudis were indeed cooperating with the U.S.-led antiterrorist war; many writers have suggested that Saudi Arabia, with its fundamentalist ideology, actually is the problem.

Chapter 8. Objectives

1. The situation may be somewhat analogous to that of Japan in 1941. At that time, Japanese military leaders reportedly said that their soldiers were the last generation likely to be absolutely obedient; foreign influences (like baseball) were undermining their authority. Hence it was important to act at once.

Chapter 9. Striking Back

1.   Dan Balz, Bob Woodward, and Jeff Himmelman, "Afghan Campaign's Blueprint," *Washington Post,* 29 January 2002; Bob Woodward and Dan Balz, "At Camp David: Advise and Consent: Bush, Aides Grapple with War Plan," in the 30 January 2002 *Washington Post;* and Bob Woodward and Dan Balz, "Combatting Terrorism: 'It Starts Today,'" in the 1 February 2002 *Washington Post.*

2.   According to Woodward and Balz, the CIA authorization, a Memorandum of Notification, was formally a modification to President Reagan's 12 May 1986 intelligence finding. It was signed on 17 September. This document authorized the use of armed Predator UAVs against bin Laden. Other aspects included cooperation with foreign intelligence services and financial attacks on Al Qaeda.

3.   A 14 September 2001 article in *Moscow Nezavisimaya Gazeta* presumably reflected Russian military opinion; it argued that preparation for any full-scale anti-Taliban campaign would take 6 months. The assumption was that the forces required would amount to ten to fifteen divisions, fifteen hundred to two thousand tactical aircraft, up to one hundred strategic bombers, five to ten carriers (presumably including large-deck Marine amphibious ships), submarines armed with conventional and nuclear cruise missiles, and hundreds of warships. The assumption was that the massive ground force would be based in Pakistan, at that time the only country to have given permission to use its airspace.

4.   Sergey Sokut, "Five Scenarios for an American-Islamic War; None of Them Gives Washington Absolute Guarantees of Victory Given that the United States Will Inevitably Be Conducting Hostilities on Its Own" in the 14 September 2001 *Moscow Nezavisimaya Gazeta.* Sokut's unnamed sources were clearly military. The options he cited were nuclear strikes on terrorist bases; a limited non-nuclear air-sea operation; a Special Forces operation against the terrorist leadership; a full-scale invasion of Afghanistan; and a combination of all four. Sokut also made much of limited U.S. resources, recalling that during Desert Fox (December 1998) U.S. forces were reportedly up to 25 percent undermanned, and that for the Kosovo operation in 1999, forces transferred from the Indian Ocean had to be replaced by others from the Pacific, opening the possibility that the Chinese would take advantage of the resulting gap and attack Taiwan. Sokut emphasized that the only U.S. bases in the region were in Saudi Arabia and Kuwait: "If a large-scale air operation . . . is organized, there will be a requirement to find airfields . . . existing bases in the Persian Gulf region, because of their remoteness from Afghanistan, are not very suitable for basing tactical aircraft." Sokut did mention carriers, and he was aware of the need for in-flight refueling.

5.   Maksim Yusin, "Five Lessons to Be Learned from Afghan War," in the 19 September 2001 *Moscow Isvestiya.* Other lessons were to avoid a protracted war; so far as possible, to let others fight for you (i.e., to turn the Northern Alliance into an effective army); not to be afraid of decentralizing the country; and to neutralize Pakistan as a potential Taliban rear area. According to Yusin, the U.S. government had favored

the Taliban specifically to unify the country, and incidentally to make it possible to build the desired pipeline from Turkmenistan to the Persian Gulf. In fact unification had backfired. Of the five ideas advanced, the U.S. government certainly managed to avoid a protracted war, it turned the Northern Alliance into an effective army (but did have to provide crucial air power), and it did manage to get Pakistan on its side. In early 2003 it is still not clear whether the effort to centralize the post-Taliban regime will succeed.

6. On 9 November 2001 the U.S. Air Force announced that it would be using an airfield in Tajikistan to support its first sustained tactical strikes against the Taliban. The base would accommodate up to fifty aircraft; squadrons of F-15Es and F-16s were envisaged. Later they were apparently joined by A-10s.

7. No official description of basing has been released. However, the February 2002 issue of the British magazine *Air Forces Monthly* includes a base list, with descriptions of aircraft present. According to its list, tankers were based at Diego Garcia; in Bahrain (Sheikh Isa Air Base); in Oman (Thumrait Air Base); and in the UAE (Al Dhafra). The RAF tankers (two Tristars and four VC-10s) were based at Thurmrait in Oman. Special-purpose aircraft bases were Bahrain (P-3s and three EP-3Es at Muharraq), Kuwait (Special Forces aircraft at Ali Al Salem Air Base), Oman (Special Forces aircraft and AIP P-3s at Masirah, RAF Canberras, Nimrods, and E-3Ds at Seeb Air Base, U.S. E-3s at Thumrait Air Base), Pakistan (Special Forces aircraft at Dalbandin and possibly also Predators), and Uzbekistan (Predators and Special Forces aircraft at Khanabad, including gunships). CIA Predators were reportedly based in Tajikistan. The EC-130E Commando Solo psychological warfare aircraft were based at Khanabad. The airborne battle command posts of the 7th Airborne Command and Control Squadron (EC-130Es) were based at Masiran in Oman. E-8 JSTARS were at Thumrait Air Base in Oman. Global Hawk long-range UAVs were based at Al Dhafra Air Base in the UAE. Also at this base were French reconnaissance aircraft (two Mirage IVP and one C-160 Gabriel for ELINT), as well as two French KC-135 tankers. U.S. Air Force Air Expeditionary Forces (F-15s, F-16s) were based in Bahrain (Sheikh Isa Air Base), and in Kuwait (Ahmed Al Jaber and Ali Al Salem Air Bases). British-based F-15Es flew from Oman. Oman was reportedly the base from which the Rangers flew on their October raid near Kandahar. Qatar (Al Udeid Air Base) has facilities for an Air Expeditionary Force, but it seems not to have been used. Some aircraft, such as U-2s, may have operated from bases outside the Middle East, such as Cyprus.

8. Although the U.S. Air Force provided the bulk of all tanking, reportedly U.S. naval aviators particularly appreciated the relative flexibility shown by the British, who were far more willing to adjust their orbits and continue to operate in advanced locations rather than remain in established safe zones.

9. The MEU is the smallest Marine Air-Ground Task Force (MAGTF), comprising a command element (CE), a ground combat element (GCE), an air combat element (ACE), and a combat service support element. It is intended to be self-sup-

porting for up to fifteen days of combat. The GCE is the Battalion Landing Team (BLT), an infantry battalion reinforced with a reconnaissance platoon, an antitank (TOW missile) section, a tank platoon (four tanks), an amphibious assault vehicle platoon, light armored vehicles (LAV-25s), artillery (a battery of six M198 howitzers), engineers, and other combat support such as a scout sniper platoon. Typically the battalion itself is built around three infantry companies (each of three rifle platoons and a weapons platoon; each company comprises three squads, each of which can be carried by an assault amphibian. A typical MEU might employ sixteen LAVs, thirteen or fifteen amphibians, and sixty-three Humvees, the latter being considered support rather than combat vehicles. During the Afghan War, the MEUs brought only their light vehicles (LAV-25s and Humvees) ashore; they never landed their tanks or their artillery. The "SOC" in the designation means Special Operations Capable due to training and equipment. An MEU is deployed on board the three ships of an amphibious ready group: a large-deck amphibian (LHA or LHD), a transport (LPD), and a cargo carrier (LSD).

10. Reportedly after bombing the B-2s fueled on the ground and changed pilots at Diego Garcia, before starting the long run back to Missouri. Apparently B-2s were used only during the first week of the war. They had to operate out of the single base in Missouri because it had the unique maintenance facilities they needed (which are now being duplicated at other U.S. bases around the world). In December it was reported that U.S. heavy bombers had dropped most Air Force bombs. See David A. Fulghum and Robert Wall, "Heavy Bomber Attacks Dominate Afghan War," *Aviation Week & Space Technology,* 3 December 2001.

11. As of 17 December total Air Force sorties were 7,100; the U.S. Navy flew a similar number, and other countries flew about 1,420 sorties. About 12,000 weapons (8,500 tons) were dropped, of which the Air Force dropped about 6,500 tons, 72 percent of which were precision-guided. The Navy dropped about 2,100 tons. The Air Force sorties included 3,500 for airborne refueling (49 percent), 3,150 for bombers and transports, and 450 for intelligence support. B-52s accounted for 10 percent of missions but more than 70 percent (presumably by weight) of ordnance dropped. Probably the B-52 figure should have included B-1Bs and perhaps also B-2s. Data are from the 2 January 2002 *Jane's Defence Weekly* and from Andrew Brookes, "The Air War in Afghanistan," *AIR International,* August 2002, based on U.S. Air Force data.

12. For opposition to early plans to send an Aegis ship, see a 29 September 2001 report in the *Yomiuri Shimbun.* The idea had originally been to send a ship to support the deployment of the Japan-based carrier *Kitty Hawk.* However, it would not have been permitted to enter combat of any kind; the pretext suggested at the time was that the ship would study Japanese commercial shipping routes and the routes used to support U.S. forces. Later the Japanese administration sought parliamentary permission to support U.S. counterattacks logistically.

13. According to Mikhail Khodarenok, "Hard to Get Set Up on Ruins," in a Russian military newspaper, *Moscow Nezavisimoye Voyennoye Obozreniye,* 28 Sep-

tember 2001, as of that date most of the former Soviet republics had offered some facilities to the United States, the main holdout being Turkmenistan. The title of the article referred to the very limited facilities in these countries.

14. For example, in an interview published on 30 September 2001 in the Jedda newspaper, *Ukaz*, the Saudi defense minister, Prince Sultan Bin-Abd-al-Aziz, explicitly denied that any foreign soldiers were in Saudi Arabia to fight Islam and Arabs. The Prince seems to have been using the distinction between soldiers and airmen to avoid admitting that substantial U.S. air forces remained after the Gulf War. He did admit the presence of aircraft (and airmen) supporting Operation Southern Watch, the enforcement of the no-fly zones in southern Iraq.

15. See Thomas E. Ricks, "Un-Central Command Criticized: Marine Corps Report Calls Florida Headquarters Too Far from Action" in the 3 June 2002 *Washington Post*. Reportedly both the Marines and the CAOC in Saudi Arabia had problems. Much of the problem was due to the higher headquarters' "insatiable" demand for control and information. Army Special Forces seemed less distressed, but that may be because they were less subject to attempts at detailed control.

16. Bomb keep-out zones are taken from Vernon Loeb, "An Unlikely Super-Warrior Emerges in Afghan War: U.S. Combat Controllers Guide Bombers to Precision Targets," *Washington Post*, 19 May 2002.

17. Air Force EC-130Es Airborne Battle Command Communications and Control aircraft (ABCCC), which had been used in Bosnia and in Kosovo, were deployed to Afghanistan. There they seem to have had a more executive role.

18. See, for example, Rowan Scarborough, "Navy's P-3 Orion Aircraft Played Prominent Role in Afghanistan," *Washington Times*, 2 April 2002, and Frank Wolfe, "P-3s Providing Vital Support to Operation Enduring Freedom," *Defense Daily*, 20 December 2001. Wolfe quoted Rear Adm. Anthony Winns, commander of the Pacific Fleet Patrol and Reconnaissance Force, to the effect that the P-3 was the favored Operation Enduring Freedom surveillance platform, its electro-optical sensor being particularly valued. At that time one ten-plane squadron, VP-9, had just returned from the Persian Gulf, to be replaced by VP-4. The key aircraft were those which had been modified under the AIP program, of which VP-9 had five, and VP-4, four.

19. A third KH-11 imaging satellite was launched 5 October 2001, to join two others launched in 1995 and 1996. Although the launch had been planned for some time, apparently it was accelerated because it was considered particularly important as operations were about to begin in Afghanistan. Reportedly, too, the satellite and launcher together cost $1.3 billion, as much as the entire increase in the U.S. intelligence budget after 11 September. Reportedly three smaller and more secret imaging satellites were also involved in war planning. To use its assets more effectively, a new NRO (National Reconnaissance Office, which operates intelligence spacecraft) Operational Support Office (OSO) staffed by military and intelligence agency personnel, was formed. It was intended to meet criticism of NRO failures during the

Gulf War. A new NRO-developed Rapid Targeting System receiver was deployed on board ships and at ground centers.

20. One advantage enjoyed by Special Forces is that personnel of each Special Forces Group (SFG) are trained in particular geographical specialties: 5th SFG (Army) is associated with Central Command and is trained for Central and Southwest Asia. Its teams had worked, before the war, with military forces throughout the region, helping to build the relationships which proved important once war broke out. Each fourteen-hundred-strong SFG in turn fields three battalions, each of which has eighteen twelve-man A-teams. In addition to the A-teams, Special Forces Command (SOCOM) deploys the Army's Delta Force (Special Forces Operational Detachment Delta), a larger unit, the 75th Ranger Regiment (Airborne), an even larger unit, and the 160th Special Operations Aviation Regiment. The latter provides special helicopters, for example to move the A-teams. Unlike the A-teams, the Rangers and Delta Force are not geographically specialized. Delta Force itself was created in the wake of the failure of the Iran hostage rescue, as a small "can-do" military unit, larger than an A-team. The Rangers are a larger combat unit. Delta Force and the Rangers fought together in the 19 October raid on Mullah Omar's home.

21. See, for example, Ann Scott Tyson, "Elite Air Force Scouts Brave Friendly Fire, Runaway Horses" in the 27 March 2002 *Christian Science Monitor,* and Loeb, "Unlikely Super-Warrior."

22. See, for example, Lance M. Bacon, "Secret Weapons: The Airmen Who Are Winning the Ground War," *Air Force Times,* 8 April 2002.

23. See Dana Priest, "Team 555," *Washington Post,* 3 April 2002. According to Priest, ultimately there were eighteen A-teams, four company-level, and three battalion-level (fifteen-man) units in the country, a total of 316. For nearly a week only two A-teams were in Afghanistan, and for more than another week only two more. Note that the only missions listed were liaison with Northern Alliance forces, fire direction, and liaison with the Pashtuns. Presumably raiding was the province of foreign Special Forces, of SEALs, and of Army Rangers and Delta Force.

24. I. Grady, "Team 555: 'We Provided Them an Air Force,'" in the July 2002 *AUSA News.*

25. See, for example, the AP report, "Official: U.S. Forces in Afghanistan," by Christopher Newton, *Washington Post,* 28 September ▪ 2001.

26. For example, on 2 October 2001 the Russian government news agency Interfax reported that Russian defense minister Sergey Ivanov had reached agreement with Iranian Defense Minister Ali Shamkani on increasing cooperation, in part to meet the Afghan threat felt by both countries. Both, Ivanov said, were victims of international terrorism, and both had long supported the Northern Alliance for that reason. Iran was also fighting drug exporters operating across the Afghan border. A Russian web site quoted Shamkani as saying that Iran would support bombing of terrorist bases in Afghanistan only if the UN supported such attacks. Ultimately the

Iranians opposed the war, but apparently they did not help the Afghans. The main context of the Russian-Iranian agreement was a major arms deal between the two.

27. A typical account was Michael Evans, "Delta Force 'Has Killed Hundreds,'" *London Times,* 24 November 2001.

28. According to Rowan Scarborough, "Military Closes in on Bin Laden, Omar," *Washington Times,* November 2001, the raid was actually intended to seize Mullah Omar himself, who had been reported at the compound earlier in the day. The expectation was that his capture would end Taliban resistance. Scarborough cited an unnamed intelligence official and a senior administration official as his sources. The U.S. official view was that the raid was intended mainly to gather intelligence, and that Mullah Omar was not considered likely to be present. Initial AC-130 operation near Kandahar presumably refers to this raid, reportedly employing three such aircraft.

29. Robert Wall, "MH-47 Crews Detail Conflict's Exploits, Woes," *Aviation Week & Space Technology,* 15 April 2002.

30. For example, on 21 November 2001 Australian prime minister John Howard said that bin Laden was the primary objective of the Australian Special Forces (SAS) assigned to Afghanistan, amounting to 150 troops. British media made similar claims about the British SAS troops. The British media devoted considerable attention to an account of a large-scale SAS attack on a Taliban cave, which left at least 18 Afghans dead and "dozens" wounded, and 4 British troops wounded. The four-hour battle was described as one of the largest of all SAS operations, involving 90 troops (two squadrons). The SAS had not fought on this scale since operating in South Yemen in the 1960s, when about 60 raided a fort in the Radfan. See, for example, Robert Winnett, "SAS seeks Victoria Cross for Shot Soldier," in the 23 December 2001 *London Sunday Times.* This article claims that 27 enemy troops were killed, about 30 more injured, and about 30 more captured in the assault on an Al Qaeda camp near Kandahar. The odds against the British force were said to have been at least two to one. The operation was described as the only significant battle involving SAS squadrons in Afghanistan. The Victoria Cross was being sought for the NCO who led the raid, and who was wounded during it. British sources claimed that American Special Forces were involved mainly in directing strikes and in organizing the anti-Taliban forces, leaving the SAS to hunt down bin Laden and other Al Qaeda leaders.

31. This list is from Peter Slevin, "7 Nations Have Units Aiding U.S. Offensive: Gardez Battle Raises Coalition's Profile," *Washington Post,* 8 March 2002.

32. Ricks, "Un-Central Command Criticized."

33. See Neil King Jr. and David S. Cloud, "Drones Saw Bin Laden, Couldn't Fire: A Tale of Technical Delay, Indecision, Interagency Squabbles," *Wall Street Journal,* 23 November 2001. One of the squabbles described in the article was over who would take responsibility for a failed attack. Predators were grounded less than two months after they began to operate over Afghanistan, and the program was revived only after 11 September. The article claims dozens of Predator strikes since the outbreak of

war. According to the Journal, the Predator program began after U.S. officials believed they had narrowly escaped major terrorist attacks scheduled for New Year 2000. That spring the CIA and the Joint Chiefs proposed, and the Clinton administration approved, using Predators to monitor Al Qaeda operations. The Uzbek government agreed to covert basing, and the first flights were launched in September 2000. From the first, there was fear that the operation would be revealed if a Predator crashed or, worse, was shot down. However, the Predators delivered the first real-time footage of Al Qaeda camps in action, including crude experiments with chemical weapons. A short time later a Predator actually saw Osama bin Laden. In October, however, weather worsened significantly, and the operation ended. Meanwhile the CIA became interested in attacking targets, such as bin Laden, using the Predators observing them. It discovered that the Air Force was trying exactly the same thing, and in February 2001 a Predator destroyed a tank using a Hellfire missile. By early spring 2001 the CIA had brought its Predators home for upgrading, and it wanted to fit them with missiles. By August the system was working, but the Bush administration was not sure an attack was worth the risks involved. It remembered the botched unintended attack on the Chinese Embassy in Belgrade during the Kosovo war. The eleventh of September solved that problem. However, the armed Predators were awaiting transportation back to Afghanistan when the terrorists attacked. According to David C. Isby, "Predators Launch Hellfire ATGMs Over Afghanistan," *Jane's Missiles and Rockets*, 1 December 2001, armed Predators were deployed after an unarmed one located (but obviously could not attack) Mullah Omar early in the air offensive (which would counter the story about the vetoed CIA attack). According to Isby, Hellfire-armed Predators entered combat about 17 October and were successful; each could attack within five minutes of target location. One reportedly unsuccessfully came to the assistance of Hadji Abdul Haq before his capture and execution by the Taliban. Hellfires were used not only to destroy targets, but also to mark them for attack by Navy aircraft.

34. The story is told by Seymour M. Hersh in "Annals of National Security: King's Ransom: How Vulnerable Are the Saudi Royals?" *New Yorker,* 22 October 2001. The title refers to the bulk of the article, which recounts Saudi telephone messages (supposedly intercepted by the NSA) illustrating both the corruption and the instability of the regime. Other news coverage had Secretary of Defense Donald Rumsfeld supposedly so angry about the Predator incident that he was "breaking glass." The incident was never officially confirmed, however.

35. See Robert Wall, "EA-6B Crews Recast Their Infowar Role," *Aviation Week & Space Technology,* 17 November 2001. In a new approach to communications jamming, these aircraft used their ALQ-99 radar jammers rather than their dedicated USQ-113 communications jammers. That suggests that they were working against enemy signals in radar bands, presumably those from cell phones and line-of-sight radios. Wall reported that jammers had been particularly useful in jamming Taliban communications so that they could not deal with Special Forces inserted behind

their lines. EA-6B tacticians adopted the communications jamming role after their usual target, enemy air defense, was destroyed at the outset of the air war. EA-6Bs were teamed with EC-130H Compass Call communications jammers, with EC-130E Commando Solo propaganda broadcast aircraft, and with RC-135 and EP-3E communications intelligence aircraft. Frequencies to be jammed were divided between EA-6Bs and EC-130Hs and deconflicted with the intelligence-gathering aircraft to insure that frequencies they monitor are not jammed. One problem was inadvertent jamming of GPS. According to notes from an EC-130H visit to Washington after Anaconda (gathered by Kernan Chaisson of DMS/Forecast International), this communications jamming aircraft became a key asset in preventing coordinated Taliban responses to ground operations, to the point where operations were canceled when one was not available. Compass Call support was demanded for Operation Anaconda. The EC-130H carried the new SPEAR (special emitter array), which was still in the development stage. It could generate four independent jamming beams simultaneously. Compared to the EA-6B's USQ-113, SPEAR was described more discrete and selective in what it jammed. It could jam on command from an off-board source, or in response to pre-planning, or in response to its own on-board operators and processors. Thus the presence of linguists on board was important, helping to focus jamming on enemy radio links controlling troops. Typically the EC-130Hs focused on discrete targets while the EA-6Bs attacked over broad portions of a net. Two EC-130H with SPEAR were deployed to Afghanistan, flying a total of 108 missions.

For details of EC-130H operations, see Kernan Chaisson, "Till Their Ears Bleed," *Journal of Electronic Defense*, July 2002. Besides a flight crew of four, an EC-130H carries a mission commander (EW officer), a cryptologic linguist/mission crew supervisor, and one high-band operator for its Rivet Fire countermeasures suite. There are also a special signals analyst, four linguists, and an airborne maintenance technician. Each of the two electronic combat squadrons (ECS) has its own linguistic specialties: Spanish, Arabic, and Farsi for the 41st; Chinese, Russian, and Serbo-Croat for the 42d. Other linguists, such as Creole speakers for operations in Haiti, can be borrowed as needed. Begun in January 2000, Project Suter provides a direct link between EC-130H aircraft and RC-135 Rivet Joint electronic intelligence aircraft, the airborne information transfer (AIT) data link. Procurement began in fiscal year 2002 (September 2001) and accelerated using emergency funds (Defense Emergency Relief Fund).

36. See, for example, a sidebar, "From the Experience of the Russian Special Services" to the article "How We Called Bin Laden" (actually, his abandoned Iridium phone), by Viktor Baranets, Viktor Zozulya, Aleksandr Kots, Nikita Mityayev, Aleksandr Sinelnikov, Mikhail Falaleyev, and Maksim Chizhikov in the 13 March 2002 Moscow *Komsomolskaya Pravda*. The Russian security services had been hunting the victim, Dzhokhar Dudayev, for almost a year and half. Then a huge bribe convinced a Chechen to tell them that he often used a particular cell phone. An attempt

to home an airplane on the phone itself failed, but the Russians managed to develop a means of locking onto the signal from the telephone to the satellite. On 21 April 1996 an A-50 (Il-76 airborne early warning version) flying at high altitude picked up the signal and located Dudayev's telephone, passing that location to a pair of Su-25 fighter-bombers, one of which hit and destroyed the target. This was very much the technique used by U.S. forces in Afghanistan.

37. It is not clear to what extent such tactics saved Taliban units. Fear of killing civilians may have contributed to the death of Abdul Haq, the opposition leader caught and then killed by the Taliban in southeast Afghanistan. According to Bill Gertz, "U.S. Refused Executed Afghan Rebel's Call for Air Strikes," *Washington Times*, 27 October 2001, Central Command told Haq that it would not provide him with air cover for fear of injuring civilians. It would strike pursuing Taliban only if they were in armored vehicles, that is, in clearly military vehicles. As it happened, the Taliban were in cars, and Haq's reported pleas for air support went unanswered (however, according to a report in the *Observer*, a British newspaper, there was one attempt to attack Haq's pursuers using a missile-armed Predator). In another incident, a planned attack on massed Taliban troops, using a "Daisy Cutter" bomb, was aborted because analysts at headquarters level feared killing numerous nearby civilians, infuriating forward commanders who did not look forward to facing those same troops on another occasion.

38. This tabulation of demonstrations is taken largely from an extensive chronology of the Afghan War in the French naval magazine *Navires & Histoire* (issues 9, 10, and 11).

39. On 3 November 2001 the pro-government Arabic newspaper *Abha Al-Watan*, published in Saudi Arabia, reported secret U.S. contacts with Pakistani officials and with Afghan leaders in hope of fomenting a coup against the Taliban regime.

40. For example, on 21 October 2001 Agence France-Presse reported that the Taliban had hanged two opposition commanders and three soldiers in Mazar-i-Sharif, which was then under attack and about to fall. The opposition commanders were probably disaffected Taliban, since no one from outside would have been able to get into the city while it was under attack.

41. See David C. Isby, "U.S. PGMs Target Afghan Caves and Bunkers," *Jane's Missiles and Rockets*, 1 December 2001. The main hard-target bombs available at the outset were the 5,000-pound laser-guided GBU-28 used in the Gulf War and the GPS-guided GBU-37. Reportedly a single B-2 dropped two GBU-37s on the first night of the air war. Several GBU-28s were later delivered by F-15Es. In at least some cases large secondary explosions demonstrated the success of the heavy bombs in penetrating cave and bunker systems. The heaviest penetrators carried by naval aircraft were laser-guided 2,000-pound BLU-109s delivered by F-14s.

42. Thermo-baric bombs create a strong pressure wave over a large area. By way of contrast, a conventional explosive creates a localized shock wave, more intense at short range, but falling off within a short distance. The first such bombs were fuel-air

explosives (with liquid filling) used in Vietnam. Those used in Afghanistan used powdered metal as the reactant. For reasons not clear to the present author, much was made of the distinction between two-stage weapons like the earliest fuel-air explosives and single-stage thermo-baric weapons, on the ostensible ground that a two-stage weapon could be classified as a weapon of mass destruction.

43. Quoted in Scott Peterson, "A View from Behind the Lines in the U.S. Air War: Special Operatives Are Key to the Success of American Airstrikes in Afghanistan," *Christian Science Monitor,* 4 December 2001.

44. This policy was sometimes described as bloodthirsty. For example, on 20 November 2001 the *London Times* reported that "America Will Take No Prisoners" (story by Ian Cobain in Konduz Province and Damian Whitworth in Washington).

45. For the airlift as betrayal, see Seymour M. Hersh, "The Getaway," *New Yorker,* 28 January 2002. Hersh claims that among those trapped in Konduz were Pakistani Army officers, intelligence advisors, and volunteers. Although both Pakistani and U.S. spokesmen denied that any airlift had occurred, Hersh quotes unnamed American intelligence officials and senior officers as saying that it had; that a limited evacuation had "slipped out of control," allowing the escape of Taliban and Al Qaeda fighters. Pakistani president Musharraf is quoted as arguing that the humiliation of losing hundreds or thousands of Pakistanis in a Northern Alliance massacre in Konduz might destroy him. Hersh claims that Indian intelligence (RAW, the Research and Analysis Wing) monitored the evacuation and claimed that about five thousand Pakistanis and Taliban had been brought out. The Indians claimed that Pakistanis accounted for about half of the eight thousand fighters trapped in Konduz, and that about 3,500 surrendered to the Northern Alliance. Given Indian intransigence and fury that the United States was befriending Pakistan, these figures are probably grossly exaggerated. Another, credible, source suggests that there were no more than dozens of Pakistani officers in Konduz.

46. This was much the logic of releasing Iraqi prisoners en masse at the end of the Gulf War: they would return to their villages with the clear message that Saddam's power had been broken. It is not of course clear whether that was effective.

47. Karzai's escape is described, for example, in "The New 'Great Game'; Torture, Treachery and Spies—Covert War in Afghanistan; America May Be Carpet-Bombing Afghanistan. But the Real Battle for Power Is Being Waged with Bundles of Cash and More Sinister Means" in the 4 November 2001 *London Observer.* Karzai was a leader of a key Pashtun tribe. He entered Afghanistan early in October, and the newspaper claimed that he was rallying Pashtuns to fight to restore the exiled king. The Taliban attacked during a tribal council meeting (a jirga) in the village of Dehrawut. This time U.S. fighters drove them back.

48. This account of the Marine campaign is largely drawn from the unclassified version of the Task Force 58 Command Chronology for 27 October 2001 to 26 February 2002. In addition, I used a copy of the Marines' "Initial Observations Report:

Enduring Freedom Combat Assessment" produced by the Marine Corps Combat Development Command, dated 6 May 2002. The latter includes many specific recommendations.

49. Vice Admiral Moore specifically directed that no higher-level (MEB, Marine Expeditionary Brigade) command structure be set up, partly because no suitable command ship was available. Operating the two MEUs together would have required a MEB command structure. Tandem operation required no more than an MEU structure at any one time.

50. During planning, the objective shifted to Kandahar airport, Herat, Shindahand, and then back to Rhino.

51. In technical terms, they could task-organize down to the smallest unit level. The one great gap the Marines felt was the lack of organic UAVs, for example to provide low-altitude images of proposed landing zones and airports. Predators, which could provide such images, were not under MEU control. In February 2002 a Marine Corps UAV plan was approved by the Marine Requirements Oversight Council (MROC) to provide three UAVs: an improved Pioneer for extended range, Dragon Warrior for medium range, and Dragon Eye for short range. The Marines had been experimenting with such devices for some years.

52. Probably for similar reasons, Tampa ordered General Mattis to take down the American flag he had raised at FOB Rhino. The cap, imposed on 29 November, was initially set at 1,000, then at 1,078, and ultimately at 1,400 personnel. The ships could not act as a floating reserve because they were too far away to provide forces quickly in an emergency.

53. All the Marines could have flown directly from the ships to Rhino by CH-53E helicopters, fueling en route. Using CH-53Es alone would also have limited the range of equipment which could be brought into Rhino. In either case, intermediate support bases would be needed. Early in October the Pakistan government offered three primary sites, Jacobabad, Shamsi, and Pasni. Shamsi had originally been offered to support Special Forces operations in southern Afghanistan, and some Special Forces facilities and equipment were turned over to the Marines. Pasni was valuable because it was close to the sea; it became the site of an administrative landing. The force offshore used nine air-cushion landing craft (LCACs) and four conventional landing craft (LCUs) to bring equipment ashore, initially at night to avoid offending the Pakistani public. The airport was about an hour from the beach via a dirt road. According to Capt. Jay M. Holtermann, "The 15th Marine Expeditionary Unit's Seizure of Camp Rhino," *Marine Corps Gazette,* June 2002, the total mission package for the seizure of Rhino was six CH-53Es, four AH-1Ws (attack helicopters, for close air support), three UH-1Hs, six KC-130 (two tanker, four cargo), a P-3 (with a Marine SOC aviator on board), four AV-8Bs, and a command/control platform (not specified). The six CH-53Es (three each from the *Bataan* and *Peleliu*) would lift the first wave of Marines. The short-range Cobra and Iroquois (UH-1H) helicopters had to fly

to a forward arming and refueling point (FARP) in Pakistan before proceeding to Rhino. The CH-53Es could fuel in the air from a KC-130. As it happened, two of the three CH-53Es in the second group could not fuel in the air. That left them with enough fuel to get to Rhino, but not to get back to the ships offshore. They had to land at the FARP in Western Pakistan to fuel. That left them in Pakistan after sunrise, and they did not return to USS *Pelelieu* until thirteen hours after launching.

54. The CFLCC seems to have been grossly oversized for the force actually engaged. Perhaps it was sized for General Franks's initially planned multidivision force, which might have entered Afghanistan after the initial U.S. attacks. One consequence of the sheer size of the CFLCC bureaucracy was a slow decision cycle. The Marines were proud that an MEU could be expected to act on a six-hour cycle, from receiving an order to executing it. As an example of CFLCC standards, in one case 26th MEU radio reconnaissance elements and TF 64 (Australian Special Forces) Squadron A cooperated in locating a potential target using radio direction-finding. 26th MEU isolated the target area using its helicopters, one of which was damaged in a rough landing. TF 58 had been working on this mission for over a week and had reported it to CENTCOM, yet CENTCOM expressed surprise that the mission had occurred as quickly as it had.

55. The cap was raised only after personal intervention by CFLCC deputy Maj. Gen. Edwards. Despite the operations order which had caused the cap to be raised, CENTCOM then stated that the only TF 58 mission was to seize an FOB; but the same day TF 58 was told to interdict Route 1 to isolate Kandahar.

56. The key meeting was held on 12 December, with the two Afghan commanders who had forces around Kandahar: Shirzai, who later became governor of Kandahar Province, and Hamid Karzai, already head of the Afghan Interim Authority (AIA). Shirzai had the forces to the south, Karzai those to the north. Karzai felt certain that the Marines could pass through Kandahar in daylight. Special Forces were also involved in the meeting and in the subsequent operation.

57. Sledgehammer consisted of LAVs and the 26th MEU's Combined Anti-Armor Team (CAAT) Humvees. To link up with 15th MEU, Sledgehammer had to march along Route 1, a favorite site for ambushes during the Soviet-Afghan War.

58. Some soldiers of the 101st Airborne had just arrived. According to the Marine history, they could not participate in the defense of the airfield because they had no ammunition; the U.S. Air Force insisted that ammunition not be carried on board its airlift aircraft.

59. Those opposing the war on the left, for example in Britain, tended to use the role of money as proof that the war was illegitimate. The Russians noted that cash payments had been very useful in their own war. In December 2001 the Japanese *Yomiuri Weekly* (associated with largest Japanese newspaper, the *Yomiuri Shimbun*) reported that the Northern Alliance was being subsidized at the rate of $3,000 per soldier per month, or $45 million per month; Afghan gross domestic product per

capita is about $200. In 1993, before the Taliban entered the country, the national budget was about $200 million. According to the Japanese reporter, representatives of the Northern Alliance presented their demand as a starting point for bargaining, and were shocked when the U.S. accepted without demur.

60. The 16 July 2002 edition of the *Toronto Globe and Mail* reported that the capture of two Al Qaeda suspects by the Canadian destroyer HMCS *Algonquin* was the first capture of suspected terrorists since the beginning of the war in Afghanistan by a coalition warship. Three boats suspected of smuggling migrants in the Gulf of Oman were spotted by a Canadian maritime patrol aircraft, which vectored the French frigate *Guepratte* to intercept them. One of the boats contained ten Afghans. Names and pictures were sent electronically to intelligence agencies. Two were verified as terrorists. The boats fled into thickening fog and haze, but *Algonquin*, cued by a Dutch maritime patrol airplane, reintercepted the boat. In Canada, the incident raised questions about whether the United States, to whom the prisoners were passed, was in violation of the Geneva Convention for its treatment of Al Qaeda prisoners at Guantánamo Bay. The same question had already been asked about prisoners handed over by Canadian Special Forces in January 2002. Despite the limited number of refugees actually caught, there is good reason to believe that a much larger number were deterred from leaving Pakistani ports. That avoided an expansion of the war into, say, Somalia. It may also have kept some prominent Al Qaeda officers, such as Khalid Sheikh Mohammed or even Osama (if he is still alive), in Pakistan, where they are subject to capture by U.S. and Pakistani forces.

61. See, for example, Bill Gertz and Rowan Scarborough, "Inside the Ring: Container Flight," *Washington Times*, 4 January 2002. They report the discovery of an Al Qaeda container on board a freighter searched by the U.S. Navy; the terrorists themselves were not in it.

62. Figures are from Susan B. Glaser, "The Battle of Tora Bora: Secrets, Money, Mistrust," in the 10 February 2002 *Washington Post*. A few Al Qaeda fighters, perhaps fifty-seven, were captured in the battle. The figures are credible because they were presented as disappointing rather than triumphal, Afghans reportedly saying that American reluctance to penetrate caves and bunkers showed a lack of willpower.

63. Rowan Scarborough, "Enemy Forces Allowed to Regroup," *Washington Times*, 5 March 2002.

64. Alone of the Special Forces involved, the Australians posted detailed accounts of their operations on a web site, www.efreedomnews.com. Their August 2002 account, "The Australian SASR at War in Afghanistan," was written by Benjamin James Morgan of Brisbane.

65. One might speculate that at least some of the Afghan units had been infiltrated by Al Qaeda. That would be a typical situation in a civil war such as that Al Qaeda and the Northern and Southern Alliances were fighting in Afghanistan, and it was reminiscent of the situation in Vietnam. Surprise was further compromised

when the operation had to be postponed for forty-eight hours due to bad weather.

66. Interview with the *Brisbane Courier Mail*, 17 June 2002, cited in Morgan, "Australian SASR at War."

67. For example, at the end of June 2002 a U.S. force hunting Taliban accidentally attacked a wedding party. Those on board an AC-130 gunship apparently took celebratory gunfire as antiaircraft fire and fired back, with tragic results. A few Afghans, possibly fewer than ten, were killed. Any deaths would have been unacceptable, but Taliban supporters quickly inflated the total to 300. The incident was so serious that new Afghan President Hamid Karzai asked that U.S. air operations be curtailed to prevent recurrences. To the extent that he was still threatened by Taliban and Al Qaeda fighters, any such ban might prove fatal in the future. However, if Afghans came to associate U.S. aircraft with their own destruction, Karzai's government had a more serious problem. In the aftermath of the AC-130 affair Karzai demanded pre-approval of air attacks, to avoid just such problems.

68. According to the 19 November 2001 issue of the major Milan newspaper *Corriere della Sera*, at Farm Hada, a former Taliban base abandoned hastily in the retreat from Jalalabad, Italian and Spanish reporters saw boxes labeled "Sarin" in Cyrillic script, each containing twenty glass phials.

69. By February 2002, Germany had both a Special Forces unit (one hundred personnel) and a battalion-sized Infantry Task Force, the latter part of ISAF. Chancellor Gerhard Schroeder won a crucial vote in November, to despatch the force at U.S. request. Opponents included members of his own Social Democratic Party and the Greens who participated in Schroeder's coalition. Up to thirty-nine hundred troops could be sent, as well as ships for the Arabian Sea. None of the troops would be permitted to participate in air strikes or in offensive ground combat. Schroeder considered the issue so important that he was willing to risk a vote of confidence; he managed to get 336 votes, against a required majority of 334. Reportedly the French government, which had avoided participation, felt compelled to match the Germans and send ground troops (up to four hundred personnel). The French also committed eight Mirage 2000D fighter-bombers, which were based in Kyrgyzstan, and which participated in Operation Anaconda. They also sent electronic warfare aircraft and a Mirage IVP reconnaissance aircraft. For one account of ISAF, see Charles Clover, "Attack on Terrorism: Military Strategy: 'Try and Speak Slower,'" in the 25 March 2002 *Financial Times*. At that time British and French units were responsible for securing Kabul International Airport. Besides maintaining security in Kabul, ISAF was responsible for training a future Afghan police force.

70. According to Rowan Scarborough, "Change of Target Saved Hundreds of Taliban Soldiers" in the 21 November 2001 *Washington Times*, the chance to kill hundreds of Taliban troops was lost when the target of one of two 15,000-pound bombs used in Afghanistan was changed in mid-mission for fear of killing Afghan civilians. The troops were in civilian buildings. While the C-130 was in the air, the pilot was given new target coordinates in a barren area devoid of confirmed Taliban. Accord-

ing to Scarborough, the story was leaked in protest against what seemed to be undue interference from Washington, which changed the target even after the original site had been studied by Central Command targeters for days.

71. See Rowan Scarborough, "U.S. Rules Let Al Qaeda Flee," *Washington Times,* 21 December 2001. Scarborough's informant, described as a senior military official, said that the rules of engagement allowed immediate attacks only in self-defense or in the course of raids. Otherwise Special Forces had to obtain specific approval before attacking. They had to indicate how many people they saw, which way they were headed, and why they were identified as Al Qaeda. The official argued that anyone fleeing across the border at night had to be either Al Qaeda or drug runners, hence deserved to be attacked. For example, a Special Forces team spotted 22 Al Qaeda moving along a trail, but had to wait for approval from Central Command in Tampa before attacking. That delay forced them to reposition twice. As it happened, they were not spotted, and once they got approval they attacked and killed the Al Qaeda band.

Chapter 10. Lessons

1. At the end of the war the Army Special Forces (Green Berets) reportedly complained that, although they had been effective (they claimed to have killed over six hundred of the enemy), they had not been well enough equipped, partly because the peacetime Army made little effort to keep them ready. According to Bill Gertz and Rowan Scarborough, "Notes from the Pentagon: Green Beret Lessons," in the 28 December 2001 *Washington Times,* one Green Beret complained of insufficient weapons training due to assignments like "cutting grass and teaching ROTC cadets how to use a compass." He wanted more specialized equipment, such as specialized UAVs which A-teams could operate, special vehicles, and organic aircraft (beyond the very expensive special helicopters and C-130s assigned to Special Forces). The prewar standard of two or four radios per team had proven grossly insufficient; every man needed his own radio. He also reported that language skills were not nearly good enough. Such demands did not, of course, take into account the need for logistic and maintenance back-up for vehicles and aircraft, which might transform lean A-teams into unwieldy battalions.

2. During the pre-briefed phase of the war, aircraft never returned with their weapons. Once the advance began, and aircraft were switched to close support, they often had to do so. Not only were targets not always assigned, but in some cases it was impossible to drop weapons for fear of hitting friendly forces too closely engaged with the enemy. For example, all F-14s despatched to Kabul soon after the fall of Mazar-i-Sharif returned to USS *Carl Vinson* with their loads. See Robert Wall, "Navy Adapts Operations for Afghan War Hurdles," *Aviation Week & Space Technology,* 19 November 2001.

3. Worldwide levels of JDAMs reportedly fell to 5 percent of war-reserve requirements. Levels of the two chief laser-guided bombs, GBU-12 and -16, fell to 20 and 25

percent, respectively. Tomahawks were still available in large numbers, because there had been few opportunities to use them after the first attacks.

4. "Enduring Freedom: La mer frappe la terre," *Navires & Histoire* 9 (December 2001).

5. John Gershman, "Is Southeast Asia the Second Front?" gives a somewhat skeptical account of Muslim insurgents in the July/August 2002 issue of *Foreign Affairs*. The main groups in question are Abu Sayyaf, Jemaah Islamiah (JI), and the Kumpulan Mujeheddin Malaysia (KMM). Abu Sayyaf, operating in Mindanao in the Philippines, is sometimes described as comparable in concept to the Taliban, but it has been far less successful, operating in a limited area without a major organized base. Originally its leader and Osama bin Laden were close, bin Laden having helped set the group up; now they are more or less estranged, possibly because both leaders have similar, competing, goals. The JI advocates establishing by force an Islamic state extending from southern Thailand through the southern Philippines. It seems to have been founded in the mid-1970s, but perhaps to have been revitalized by Al Qaeda representatives in the 1990s. Gershman claims that only it and the KMM, which have a largely middle-class membership, are capable of large-scale attacks. The membership would seem to parallel that of Al Qaeda. To Gershman, Abu Sayyaf and some other groups, such as Laskar Jihad in Indonesia, are paramilitaries with a large criminal component. Laskar Jihad has announced sympathy with the Taliban, but probably has had no direct link with Al Qaeda. Such groups are sometimes used by local governments to attack their enemies—as in East Timor. The government-sponsored irregulars are typified by the Indonesian FPI (Islamic Defenders Front), formed in 1998 to fight in East Timor; it was responsible for many of the anti-American demonstrations after 11 September. Gershman points out that fundamentalists (i.e., those advocating an Islamic state of some kind) have had little success in Indonesian elections, despite the serious problems that country is now encountering. In the most recent election they received only 16 percent of the vote, compared to 40 percent in the last free Indonesian election, in 1955. The pan-Malaysian Islamic Party managed to win 27 out of 193 parliamentary seats in 1999; Gershman attributes even that to anger over official repression of reform. Note, however, that it may have been exactly such anger which energized fundamentalist movements in the Arab world. Moreover, it is by no means certain that in 1994–96 the Afghan populace as a whole was particularly enthusiastic about the Taliban and their fundamentalism; what counted was firepower and bribes.

Apparently, JI was responsible for the Bali attack in October 2002. Its leader, Hambali (Riduan Isamuddin), was widely regarded as the Osama bin Laden of the Far East. A veteran of the anti-Soviet war in Afghanistan, he is said to be in touch with Al Qaeda through Muhammad Khalifa, bin Laden's brother-in-law. One report describes him as the chief Southeast Asian representative and travel coordinator for Al Qaeda. He is said to have provided accommodation in Malaysia for two of the 11 September hijackers, for Moussaoui, and for one of the participants in the *Cole* attack. He was wanted by four countries for earlier terrorist activities. Hambali is wanted in the Philippines for ordering an attack on commuter trains in Manila (twenty-two dead) and for plotting to smuggle explosives from the Philippines to Singapore in 2000 to attack U.S. and Israeli targets. Indonesia wants him for a bombing attack on Christian churches and schools in ten cities on Christmas Eve 2000 (twenty-two people were killed and ninety-six wounded in a total of thirty attacks). Malaysia wants him for bank robberies (to fund militant activities) and a political assassination, and he has been linked to Yazid Sufaat, in whose Kuala Lumpur flat the 11 September attacks were planned. Hambali has also been connected to the 1995 plot to destroy twelve U.S. airliners over the Pacific and to a plan to explode seven large car bombs in Singapore; Singapore also wants him. See Anton La Guardia, "Hambali, the Steely Terrorist, Linked to Bombs," *Telegraph*, 16 October 2002. According to an account in the Asian edition of *Time*, Hambali was particularly attracted to the idea of an Islamic pan-Southeast Asian state because he had been forced to flee Indonesia. He and other exiles were, it was said, afraid that if an Islamic state were ever established in Indonesia, they would be left out, whereas a pan-Asian state would necessarily include them.

6. Initially the Indonesian government was loath to accept that homegrown Islamic terrorists, rather than foreigners, had carried out the bombing. For example, senior intelligence officials told the *Jakarta Post* that their investigation was focusing on telephone calls made just before the explosion between Solo City and the Middle East. The foreigners involved had entered the country through Semarang in central Indonesia. There was much talk of how, despite polls and elections showing little popular support for fundamentalists, the Indonesian government refused to attack militants for fear of losing popular support. However, after a time it certainly mobilized its forces. President Megawati Sukarnoputri signed tough new antiterrorism decrees. One major difference between the Bali attackers and those who executed the 11 September attack was that they were associated with militant fundamentalists living openly in their own country. Thus in October 2002 the Indonesians arrested a charismatic fundamentalist preacher, Abu Bakar Bashir, at his school. He was suing *Time* for having linked him to Al Qaeda, then staged a physical collapse when called for questioning by the Indonesian police. He had been implicated in terror plots by Omar al Faruq, an Al Qaeda operative captured in June in Java (in Indonesia) and handed over to the CIA for questioning. Apparently Bashir tended to preach the merits of jihad and the honor of martyrdom in pursuit of an Islamic caliphate across Southeast Asia, the goal of the Jemaah Islamiah organization. His classroom sported a poster announcing that "Americans are the terrorists" and Bashir reportedly claimed repeatedly that the United States had carried out the Bali bombing specifically to discredit Islam and Indonesia—a view many Indonesians are said to share. Bashir's school was apparently a center for a variety of Islamic militant groups which form the "Ngruki network." Jailed for four years by the Suharto regime in 1978, Bashir fled to Malaysia in 1985 and returned to Indonesia in 1998,

Suharto having been ejected. In 2000 he was named "commander" of the Indonesian Mujahiddin Council, which espouses the creation of an international Islamic state, nominally by peaceful means. He had served as a recruiter for various Muslim militias, such as Laskar Jihad (Soldiers of the Holy War), which fought Christians in the Moluccas. Reportedly, Bashir had been protected by his friends, including Indonesian vice president Hamzah Haz, but they deserted him after the Bali bombing.

7. Obviously the F-14 was not designed with such missions in mind, but it gained from its sheer size and carrying capacity, the latter due in part to its design fleet air defense mission using a heavy Phoenix missile, which had to be brought back aboard the carrier after almost every mission. By way of contrast, the F/A-18, at least through the C/D version, was a point design with limited growth margin. LANTIRN incorporates a GPS, so using the laser ranger the airplane can determine target position accurately enough to pass target coordinates to another attacker. In one such case, an F-14 guided a B-52 into an attack. In this case coordinates were passed through an AWACS (E-3) aircraft acting as controller for Air Force strike aircraft, but ideally Link 16 would be used instead, without any such intermediary. LANTIRN could be used either to designate a target for another aircraft or to support a direct attack by the F-14. F-14s also carried the TARPS camera reconnaissance pod (which they had used so successfully during the Gulf War). See Robert Wall, "F-14s Add Missions in Anti-Taliban Effort," *Aviation Week & Space Technology*, 19 November 2001.

8. By mid-2002 there was considerable debate as to whether bin Laden had been wounded at Tora Bora or in some other attack, and indeed as to whether he was still alive. Rahimullah Yusufazi, a *Time Magazine* correspondent in Peshawar, Pakistan, reported that ISI believed that bin Laden had escaped, leaving dummy voice recordings to lure his pursuers.

9. According to an interview with Rep. Mark Steven Kirk (R-Ill.) in *Sea Power*, June 2002, in Afghanistan the U.S. "Boyd Loop" time was 19 minutes, compared to a two-day cycle for the Taliban. Kirk gave previous figures: six weeks in Napoleonic times, a week in World War II, a day and a half in Vietnam, and 111 minutes in Kosovo. Presumably the more recent figures referred to close air support in the U.S. case, and to moving troops in the case of the Taliban. Kirk is a lieutenant commander in the Reserves and has served as an air intelligence officer for an EA-6B squadron.

10. Apparently the U.S. expectation was that imposing a no-fly zone over parts of Iraq would preclude any suppression of local rebellions. Unfortunately the U.S. negotiators botched the terms of the agreement, leaving the Iraqis free to use helicopters—with devastating results in 1991.

Chapter 11. Now What?

1. The tape, released in early November, was clearly current, because the speaker in it praised recent terrorist attacks such as those on the theater in Moscow and on the nightclub in Bali. He also warned U.S. allies that they would pay for sup-

porting the United States. The speaker equated President Bush to pharaoh, an evocative phrase in Islam because in the Koran the story of the fall of the ancient Egyptian pharaoh is said to exemplify the fate of men who think their power is God's. An earlier bin Laden tape calling for attacks on U.S. economic interests was judged authentic, but it could not be dated because it did not include any references to recent events. It was suggested that bin Laden had released an audiotape rather than the usual video tape because he feared that any video would reveal either his location or his deteriorating physical condition (or his current disguise). However, anyone wishing to represent the tape as real would surely benefit from not having to show bin Laden at all. There is no question but that the speaker on the tape sounded like bin Laden, but actors can mimic voices well enough to fool listeners familiar with the supposed speaker. Initially the U.S. view was that the tape was authentic, but that may have meant merely that it showed no visible splices; it had not been assembled from bits of previous tapes. On 29 November 2002, however, the Lausanne-based Dalle Molle Institute for Perceptual Artificial Intelligence (IDIAP) claimed that, based on a study of 20 earlier accepted tapes, it was 95 percent certain that the speaker on the tape was not bin Laden. IDIAP's study was commissioned by the France-2 television channel. When the tape surfaced, in conjunction with a tape said to have been recorded by al-Zawahiri, suggested refuges for bin Laden were the Pashtun area of Pakistan, Yemen, and the city of Karachi in Pakistan. The presence of an armed Predator, which was used to kill a senior Al Qaeda operative in Yemen, suggests that the CIA believed Al Qaeda was transferring operations there.

2. Operating as a freelancer in the Philippines in 1995, Ramzi Yousef apparently felt compelled to enter many details of his plans into a laptop computer, which he imagined was secure. When it was seized, it revealed, among other things, his plot to bomb airliners over the Pacific.

3. The missile killed Qaed Salim Sinan al-Harethi and five lower-level operatives. Al-Harethi was associated with the October 2000 attack on USS *Cole*. The U.S. government described the operation as the most successful since the capture of Abu Zubaydah in Pakistan in mid-2002. Other Predator attacks accounted for Muhammad Atef in Afghanistan in 2001 and for an unnamed senior Al Qaeda officer in February in eastern Afghanistan. According to an account in the 5 November 2002 *Washington Times*, CIA Predators are typically controlled directly from a control room at U.S. Central Command in Tampa, Florida, via satellite links rather than from some forward control station. The Yemeni government reaction to the attack on al-Harethi was that it would have preferred much less publicity, as many Yemenis did not entirely support its cooperation with the Americans.

4. The speaker in the supposed November bin Laden tape, presumably associated with Al Qaeda, specifically praised the Bali attack, observing that it was special punishment against Australians for supporting the United States. The official Australian reaction, announced early in December 2002, was to adopt a policy of preemption against any plotters who might be found to be planning to kill Austral-

ians. The governments of Indonesia and Malaysia, which would most likely be host-ing such plotters, were less than supportive, arguing that the Australians should trust their police forces to deal with any such subversives. In effect, the Australians were saying that the Indonesians and Malaysians could not be trusted to do so.

5. Con Coughlin, *Saddam: King of Terror* (New York: Ecco, 2002), xxv. No expla-nation for the high alert ordered has been forthcoming.

6. This is not a new idea. For an entertaining account of an American attempt to promote democracy in Syria in the early 1950s, see Miles Copeland, *The Games Player: Confessions of the CIA's Original Political Operative* (London: Aurum, 1989), 85–87. Copeland discusses in detail the machinations of the Egyptian Moslem Brotherhood and its involvement in Nasser's 1954 coup.

7. This point was made by Natan Scharansky, the former Soviet dissident.

8. These arguments were reportedly made in particularly provocative form by Laurent Murawiec, a RAND analyst and former adviser to the French Ministry of De-fense, in a 10 July 2002 briefing for the Defense Policy Board. He saw removing Sad-dam Hussein as a valuable spur to change in Saudi Arabia, which he described as the larger problem due to its role in financing and supporting radical Islamic move-ments. Reportedly Murawiec recommended that the United States demand that the Saudis stop backing terrorists or face seizure of their oil fields and their financial as-sets. Saudi compliance should include ceasing to fund fundamentalists around the world, stopping all anti-U.S. and anti-Israeli propaganda in Saudi Arabia, and "pros-ecute or isolate those involved in the terror chain, including in the Saudi intelligence services." Given the intimate connection between the Saudi state and its Islamic (Wahhabi) clergy, these steps would amount to Saudi political suicide, hence cannot be undertaken. The last of Murawiec's twenty-four slides reportedly described Saudi Arabia as "the kernel of evil, the prime mover, the most dangerous opponent" in the Middle East. The briefing generated intense embarrassment, the U.S. government assuring the Saudis that it did not represent official policy. See Thomas E. Ricks, "Briefing Depicted Saudis as Enemies: Ultimatum Urged to Pentagon Board," *Wash-ington Post*, 6 August 2002. According to Ricks, the briefing really did reflect a grow-ing trend within the Bush administration to consider Saudi Arabia a serious prob-lem and to stop rationalizing Saudi behavior. On the other hand, Murawiec's briefing could be read as support for a larger administration view that, in the words of one of its officials, "the road to the entire Middle East goes through Baghdad." In this view, having defeated Saddam Hussein, the United States could and would im-pose a democratic regime, as it did in Germany and Japan after World War II.

9. See Neil MacFarquhar, "A Few Saudis Defy a Rigid Islam to Debate Their Own Intolerance," *New York Times*, 12 July 2002. In spring 2002, 160 Saudi scholars and intellectuals signed a manifesto urging greater dialogue with the West, implicitly at-tacking Wahhabi xenophobia. They were subject to considerable attack by Saudi clerics, but MacFarquhar suggests that this outcry was particularly fierce because

the clerics were already under attack in fields they expected to dominate, such as education. Saudi education is considered poor because of the emphasis on religious study. There was also a scandal: fifteen girls died in a fire at their school because religious police blocked men from rescuing them and themselves from leaving (they did not have their all-enveloping cloaks). That the scandal was aired in Saudi media was considered remarkable.

Bibliography

Books

Alberts, David S., John J. Garstka, and Frederick P. Stein. *Network-Centric Warfare: Developing and Leveraging Information Superiority.* 2d ed. Washington, D.C.: C4ISR Cooperative Research Program, 1999.

Ali, Tariq. *The Clash of Fundamentalisms: Crusades, Jihads, and Modernity.* London: Verso, 2002.

Arquilla, John, and David Ronfelt. *Networks and Netwar: The Future of Terror, Crime, and Militancy.* Santa Monica, Calif.: RAND National Defense Research Institute, 2001.

Barnes, Julian. "Five Years of the Fatwa." In *Letters from London, 1990–1995,* by Julian Barnes. London: Picador, 1995.

Bergen, Peter L. *Holy War, Inc.* New York: Free Press, 2001.

Campbell, Christy. *Fenian Fire: The British Government Plot to Assassinate Queen Victoria.* London: HarperCollins, 2002.

Cooley, John K. *Unholy Wars: Afghanistan, America, and International Terrorism.* London: Pluto, 2000.

Copeland, Miles. *The Games Player: Confessions of the CIA's Original Political Operative.* London: Aurum, 1989.

Friedman, Norman. *The Fifty-Year War: Conflict and Strategy in the Cold War.* Annapolis: Naval Institute Press, 2000.

———. *Seapower and Space: From the Dawn of the Missile Age to Net-Centric Warfare.* Annapolis: Naval Institute Press, 2000.

Goodson, Larry P. *Afghanistan's Endless War: State Failure, Regional Politics, and the Rise of the Taliban.* Seattle: University of Washington Press, 2001.

Hosmer, Stephen T. *Why Milosevich Decided to Settle When He Did.* Santa Monica, Calif.: RAND, 2001.

Maley, William, ed. *Fundamentalism Reborn? Afghanistan and the Taliban.* London: Hurst, 2001.

Pipes, Daniel. *The Hidden Hand: Middle East Fears of Conspiracy.* New York: St. Martin's Griffin, 1998.

Rashid, Ahmed. *Taliban: The Story of the Afghan Warlords.* Rev. ed. London: Pan, 2001.

Reeve, Simon. *The New Jackals.* New ed. Boston: Northeastern University Press, 2001.

Rip, Michael Russell, and James M. Hasik. *The Precision Revolution: GPS and the Future of Aerial Warfare.* Annapolis: Naval Institute Press, 2002.

Roy, Olivier. *The Failure of Political Islam.* London: I. B. Tauris, 1994.

Rubenstein, Richard E. *Comrade Valentine.* New York: Harcourt Brace, 1994.

Rubin, Barnett R. *The Fragmentation of Afghanistan.* 2d ed. New Haven: Yale University Press, 2002.

Talbott, Strobe. *The Russia Hand.* New York: Random House, 2002.

Williamson, Hugh Ross. *Who Was the Man in the Iron Mask and Other Historical Mysteries.* London: Penguin, 2002.

Chapters and Articles

Bacon, Lance M. "Secret Weapons: The Airmen Who Are Winning the Ground War." *Air Force Times,* 8 April 2002.

Balz, Dan, and Bob Woodward. "Bush Awaits History's Judgement." *Washington Post,* 3 February 2002.

———. "The First Ten Days." *Washington Post,* 27 January 2002.

Balz, Dan, Bob Woodward, and Jeff Himmelman. "Afghan Campaign's Blueprint." *Washington Post,* 29 January 2002.

Baranets, Viktor, Viktor Zozulya, Aleksandr Kots, Nikita Mityayev, Aleksandr Sinelnikov, Mikhail Falaleyev, and Maksim Chizhikov. "How We Called Bin Laden." *Komsomolskaya Pravda,* 13 March 2002.

Biddle, Stephen. "The New Way of War?" *Foreign Affairs,* May/June 2002.

"Bin Laden May Have Tricked Spies: Officials." *Seattle Times,* 12 September 2001.

"Blair Reveals 'Powerful Evidence' Against Bin Laden." *Independent,* 30 September 2001.

Bond, David. "Crisis at Herndon: 11 Airplanes Astray." *Aviation Week & Space Technology,* 17 December 2001.

Bowden, Mark. "U.S. Had Chances to Kill Bin Laden, Officials Say," *Philadelphia Inquirer,* 16 September 2001.

Brookes, Andrew. "The Air War in Afghanistan." *AIR International,* August 2002.

Clover, Charles. "Attack on Terrorism: Military Strategy: 'Try and Speak Slower.'" *Financial Times,* 25 March 2002.

Cobain, Ian, and Damian Whitworth. "America Will Take No Prisoners." *London Times,* 20 November 2001.

Covault, Craig. "Air Power Alters Bosnia Equation." *Aviation Week & Space Technology,* 4 September 1995.

———. "Bosnian Air Operations Test NATO/UN." *Aviation Week & Space Technology,* 30 August 1993.

————. "F-16 Data Link Sharpens Close Air Support." *Aviation Week & Space Technology,* 13 May 1996.

————. "Military Air Operations Grow over Balkan Crisis." *Aviation Week & Space Technology,* 19 April 1993.

————. "NATO Airstrikes Target Serbian Infrastructure." *Aviation Week & Space Technology,* 11 September 1995.

————. "NATO Hits Missile Sites, Large Force Bombs Air Base." *Aviation Week & Space Technology,* 28 November 1994.

Cullison, Alan, and Andrew Higgins. "Strained Alliance: Inside al Qaeda's Afghan Turmoil." *Wall Street Journal,* 2 August 2002.

DeYoung, Karen, and Douglas Farah. "Infighting Slows Hunt for Hidden Al Qaeda Assets: Funds Put in Untraceable Commodities." *Washington Post,* 18 June 2002.

Elliott, Michael. "They Had a Plan." *Time Magazine,* 12 August 2002.

"Enduring Freedom: La mer frappe la terre." *Navires & Histoire* 9 (December 2001).

Evans, Michael. "Delta Force 'Has Killed Hundreds.'" *London Times,* 24 November 2001.

Farah, Douglas. "Al Qaeda Cash Tied to Diamond Trade: Sale of Gems from Sierra Leone Rebels Raised Millions, Sources Say." *Washington Post,* 2 November 2001.

————. "Al Qaeda's Road Paved with Gold: Secret Shipments Traced Through a Lax System in United Arab Emirates." *Washington Post,* 17 February 2002.

————. "Digging Up Congo's Dirty Gems: Officials Say Diamond Trade Funds Radical Islamic Groups." *Washington Post,* 30 December 2001.

Filkins, Dexter. "Mass Graves Reportedly Tied to Last Days of Taliban Rule." *New York Times,* 7 April 2002.

Friedman, Norman. "C3 War at Sea." U.S. Naval Institute *Proceedings,* May 1977.

Fulghum, David A., and Robert Wall. "Heavy Bomber Attacks Dominate Afghan War." *Aviation Week & Space Technology,* 3 December 2001.

Gershman, John. "Is Southeast Asia the Second Front?" *Foreign Affairs,* July/August 2002.

Gertz, Bill. "For Years, Signs Suggested 'That Something Was Up.'" *Washington Times,* 17 May 2002.

————. "U.S. Refused Executed Afghan Rebel's Call for Air Strikes." *Washington Times,* 27 October 2001.

Gertz, Bill, and Rowan Scarborough. "Inside the Ring: Container Flight." *Washington Times,* 4 January 2002.

Glaser, Susan B. "The Battle of Tora Bora: Secrets, Money, Mistrust." *Washington Post,* 10 February 2002.

Grady, I. "Team 555: 'We Provided Them an Air Force.'" *AUSA News,* July 2002.

Harris, Paul, and Martin Bright. "How the Fleet of Death Menaces Britain." *London Observer,* 23 December 2001.

Hersh, Seymour M. "Annals of National Security: King's Ransom: How Vulnerable Are the Saudi Royals?" *New Yorker,* 22 October 2001.

———. "The Getaway." *New Yorker,* 28 January 2002.

———. "The Missiles of August." *New Yorker,* 12 October 1998.

"Hill Probers Upgrade Evidence Gathered from Moussaoui." *Washington Post,* 6 June 2002.

Hilton, Isabel. "Letter from Pakistan: The Pashtun Code." *New Yorker,* 3 December 2001.

Holtermann, Capt. Jay M. "The 15th Marine Expeditionary Unit's Seizure of Camp Rhino." *Marine Corps Gazette,* June 2002.

Isby, David C. "Predators Launch Hellfire ATGMs Over Afghanistan." *Jane's Missiles and Rockets,* 1 December 2001.

———. "U.S. PGMs Target Afghan Caves and Bunkers." *Jane's Missiles and Rockets,* 1 December 2001.

"Key Role for EC-130s." *Aviation Week & Space Technology,* 30 August 1993.

Khodarenok, Mikhail. "Hard to Get Set Up on Ruins." *Moscow Nezavisimoye Voyennoye Obozreniye,* 28 September 2001.

King, Neil, Jr., and David S. Cloud. "Drones Saw Bin Laden, Couldn't Fire: A Tale of Technical Delay, Indecision, Interagency Squabbles." *Wall Street Journal,* 23 November 2001.

Klein, Joe. "Department of National Security: Closework." *New Yorker,* 1 October 2001.

Lemann, Nicholas. "Letter from Washington: What Terrorists Want." *New Yorker,* 29 October 2001.

Loeb, Vernon. "An Unlikely Super-Warrior Emerges in Afghan War: U.S. Combat Controllers Guide Bombers to Precision Targets." *Washington Post,* 19 May 2002.

MacFarquhar, Neil. "A Few Saudis Defy a Rigid Islam to Debate Their Own Intolerance." *New York Times,* 12 July 2002.

Mackenzie, Richard. "The United States and the Taliban." In *Fundamentalism Reborn? Afghanistan and the Taliban,* edited by William Maley. London: Hurst, 2001.

Mayer, Jane. "The House of Bin Laden." *New Yorker,* 12 November 2001.

Miller, Judith, and Don van Natta Jr. "Ashcroft Kept President in Dark on Post–Sept 11 FBI Memo." *New York Times,* 22 May 2002.

———. "In Years of Plots and Clues, Scope of Qaeda Eluded U.S." *New York Times,* 9 June 2002.

"The New 'Great Game': Torture, Treachery and Spies—Covert War in Afghanistan; America May Be Carpet-Bombing Afghanistan. But the Real Battle for Power Is Being Waged with Bundles of Cash and More Sinister Means." *London Observer,* 4 November 2001.

Newton, Christopher. "Official: U.S. Forces in Afghanistan." AP report. *Washington Post,* 28 September 2001.

Peterson, Scott. "A View from Behind the Lines in the U.S. Air War: Special Operatives

Are Key to the Success of American Airstrikes in Afghanistan." *Christian Science Monitor,* 4 December 2001.

Pincus, Walter. "Mueller Outlines Origin, Funding of Sept. 11 Plot." *Washington Post,* 6 June 2002.

Pincus, Walter, and Karen DeYoung. "U.S.: New Tape Points to Bin Laden, Words Suggest Sept. 11 Planning Role." *Washington Post,* 9 December 2001.

Priest, Dana. "Team 555." *Washington Post,* 3 April 2002.

Rand, Robert. "Tashkent Postcard: Backhands and Bombs." *New Yorker,* 22 October 2001.

Rashid, Ahmed. "They're Only Sleeping." *New Yorker,* 14 January 2002.

Ricks, Thomas E. "Briefing Depicted Saudis as Enemies: Ultimatum Urged to Pentagon Board." *Washington Post,* 6 August 2002.

———. "Un-Central Command Criticized: Marine Corps Report Calls Florida Headquarters Too Far from Action." *Washington Post,* 3 June 2002.

Rouleau, Eric. "Trouble in the Kingdom." *Foreign Affairs,* July/August 2002.

Scarborough, Rowan. "Change of Target Saved Hundreds of Taliban Soldiers." *Washington Times,* 21 November 2001.

———. "Enemy Forces Allowed to Regroup." *Washington Times,* 5 March 2002.

———. "Military Closes in on Bin Laden, Omar." *Washington Times,* November 2001.

———. "Navy's P-3 Orion Aircraft Played Prominent Role in Afghanistan." *Washington Times,* 2 April 2002.

———. "Size of Force on Ground Key in Plan for Iraq War." *Washington Times,* 26 April 2002.

———. "U.S. Rules Let Al Qaeda Flee." *Washington Times,* 21 December 2001.

Scott, William B. "Strike 2 Demonstrates Feasibility of RTIC." *Aviation Week & Space Technology,* 1 September 1997.

Slevin, Peter. "7 Nations Have Units Aiding U.S. Offensive: Gardez Battle Raises Coalition's Profile." *Washington Post,* 8 March 2002.

Sokut, Sergey. "Five Scenarios for an American-Islamic War; None of Them Gives Washington Absolute Guarantees of Victory Given that the United States Will Inevitably Be Conducting Hostilities on Its Own." *Moscow Nezavisimaya Gazeta,* 14 September 2001.

"Threat of U.S. Air Strikes Passed to Taliban Weeks before NY Attack." *Guardian,* 22 September 2001.

Tyson, Ann Scott. "Elite Air Force Scouts Brave Friendly Fire, Runaway Horses." *Christian Science Monitor,* 27 March 2002.

"UK 'Hardline' Muslims Slow to Condemn U.S. Attackers." *Daily Telegraph,* 13 September 2001.

"U.S. Missed Three Chances To Seize Bin Laden." *London Sunday Times,* 6 January 2001.

Van Natta, Don, Jr., and Kate Zernike. "Hijackers' Meticulous Strategy of Brains, Muscle and Practice." *New York Times,* 4 November 2001.

Wall, Robert. "EA-6B Crews Recast Their Infowar Role." *Aviation Week & Space Technology,* 17 November 2001.

——. "F-14s Add Missions In Anti-Taliban Effort." *Aviation Week & Space Technology,* 19 November 2001.

——. "MH-47 Crews Detail Conflict's Exploits, Woes." *Aviation Week & Space Technology,* 15 April 2002.

——. "Navy Adapts Operations for Afghan War Hurdles." *Aviation Week & Space Technology,* 19 November 2001.

Weaver, Mary Anne. "The Real bin Laden." *New Yorker,* 24 January 2000.

Winnett, Robert. "SAS Seeks Victoria Cross for Shot Soldier." *London Sunday Times,* 23 December 2001.

Wolfe, Frank. "P-3s Providing Vital Support to Operation Enduring Freedom." *Defense Daily,* 20 December 2001.

Woodward, Bob. "Bin Laden Said to 'Own' the Taliban, Bush Is Told He Gave Regime $100 Million." *Washington Post,* 11 October 2001.

——. "50 Countries Detain 360 Suspects at CIA's Behest; Roundup Reflects Aggressive Efforts of an Intelligence Coalition Viewed as Key to War on Terrorism." *Washington Post,* 22 November 2001.

Woodward, Bob, and Dan Balz. "At Camp David: Advise and Consent: Bush, Aides Grapple with War Plan." *Washington Post,* 30 January 2002.

——. "Bush and His Advisers Set Objectives, but Struggled with How to Achieve Them." *Washington Post,* 28 January 2002.

——. "Combatting Terrorism: 'It Starts Today.'" *Washington Post,* 1 February 2002.

Woodward, Bob, and Thomas E. Ricks. "U.S. Was Foiled Multiple Times in Efforts to Capture Bin Laden or Have Him Killed." *Washington Post,* 3 October 2001.

Wright, Lawrence. "The Counter-Terrorist." *New Yorker,* 14 January 2002.

Yousaf, Mohammed, and Mark Adkin. *The Bear Trap: The Defeat of a Superpower.* 1992. Reprint, Havertown, Pa.: Casemate, 2001.

Yusin, Maksim. "Five Lessons to Be Learned from Afghan War." *Moscow Isvestiya,* 19 September 2001.

Index

About the Author

Norman Friedman is an internationally known strategist and naval historian who throughout his career has been concerned with the way in which policy and technology intersect. He spent more than a decade at a major U.S. think tank, ultimately as its deputy director for national security affairs, and another decade as consultant to the secretary of the navy. He has written design histories of U.S. Navy carriers, battleships, cruisers, destroyers, submarines, and small attack craft. Dr. Friedman also writes articles on a variety of defense subjects for journals worldwide and contributes a monthly column on world naval developments to the Naval Institute's *Proceedings* magazine.

Dr. Friedman holds a Ph.D. from Columbia University in New York City, where he resides. A regular guest commentator on television, he lectures widely on defense issues in forums such as the National Defense University, the Naval War College, and the Royal United Services Institute.

The Naval Institute Press is the book-publishing arm of the U.S. Naval Institute, a private, nonprofit, membership society for sea service professionals and others who share an interest in naval and maritime affairs. Established in 1873 at the U.S. Naval Academy in Annapolis, Maryland, where its offices remain today, the Naval Institute has members worldwide.

Members of the Naval Institute support the education programs of the society and receive the influential monthly magazine *Proceedings* and discounts on fine nautical prints and on ship and aircraft photos. They also have access to the transcripts of the Institute's Oral History Program and get discounted admission to any of the Institute-sponsored seminars offered around the country.

The Naval Institute also publishes *Naval History* magazine. This colorful bimonthly is filled with entertaining and thought-provoking articles, first-person reminiscences, and dramatic art and photography. Members receive a discount on *Naval History* subscriptions.

The Naval Institute's book-publishing program, begun in 1898 with basic guides to naval practices, has broadened its scope to include books of more general interest. Now the Naval Institute Press publishes about one hundred titles each year, ranging from how-to books on boating and navigation to battle histories, biographies, ship and aircraft guides, and novels. Institute members receive significant discounts on the Press's more than eight hundred books in print.

Full-time students are eligible for special half-price membership rates. Life memberships are also available.

For a free catalog describing Naval Institute Press books currently available, and for further information about subscribing to *Naval History* magazine or about joining the U.S. Naval Institute, please write to:

Membership Department
U.S. Naval Institute
291 Wood Road
Annapolis, MD 21402-5034
Telephone: (800) 233-8764
Fax: (410) 269-7940
Web address: www.navalinstitute.org